W9-AUS-590

Prayer & Community

Prayer & Community

The Havurah in American Judaism

Riv-Ellen Prell

WAYNE STATE UNIVERSITY PRESS DETROIT 1989

93 92 91 90 89 5 4 3 2 1

Library of Congress Cataloging-in-Publication Data

Prell, Riv-Ellen, 1947–
Prayer and community : the havurah in American Judaism / Riv-Ellen Prell.
p. cm.
Bibliography: p.
Includes index.
ISBN 0–8143–1934–3 (alk. paper). ISBN 0–8143–1935–1 (pbk. : alk. paper)
1. Fellowship—Religious aspects—Judaism. 2. Prayer groups—Judaism. 3. Prayer—Judaism. 4. Judaism—United States—Liturgy.
I. Title. II. Title: Title: Havurah in American Judaism.
BM720.F4P74 1989
296.4'0973—dc19 88–25107
CIP

ISBN 0-8143-1934-3
ISBN 0-8143-1935-1 (pbk.)

To Barbara G. Myerhoff
1935–85

"When she speaks there is wisdom; and the Torah of Lovingkindness is on her lips."
Proverbs 31:17

Contents

Acknowledgments

From the time I began this research to the completion of this book has been more than a decade of my life. In this period I have enjoyed sharing this work with many people in many ways. My understanding of anthropology, religion, gender, and Judaism has been enriched by these contacts.

I am grateful above all to members of the Kelton Minyan who invited me to join them in order to learn more about religion in modern society. This was no colonial encounter. They interviewed me, thoroughly discussed my intentions, and voted on my conducting research with them. Yet they took a great risk in allowing me to observe and understand them. The group no longer exists, though I have enjoyed the privilege of keeping up with many members' lives through letters, visits, and second-hand reports. My interpretation of them is unlikely to be the same as theirs, not simply because I was an observer and they were participants, but because our perspectives on their experiences are inevitably different. I hope that those members who read this book will see in it the deep respect I held for them as people and for the community they created.

I began this research when I was a graduate student in the Department of Anthropology at the University of Chicago. I am indebted to the department for its initial financial support of my training and to the members of my dissertation committee: Professors David Schneider, Terence Turner, the late Victor W. Turner, and Rabbi Daniel Leifer. Each was an outstanding teacher of ritual and symbolism and a thoughtful respondent to my work.

The Danforth Foundation through its Kent fellowship supported my dissertation research and subsequent graduate education. The University of Minnesota, where I am currently a member of the faculty, provided support for further research and writing. I am indebted to these institutions for their financial assistance.

Several people read many drafts of this manuscript with generosity and insight. While none of them can be held responsible for the final product, I believe I benefitted immeasurably from their collegial assistance. They are Isa Aron, Harry Boyte, Michael Fischer, Frida Furman, Steven Foldes, Don Handelman, Lawrence Hoffman, John Ingham, M. J. Maynes, Louis Newman, Paul Rosenblatt, and Earl Schwartz. The members of my long-standing weekly research and writing group read not only the manuscript but the notes for it as well. I am deeply indebted to Sara Evans, Amy Kaminsky, Elaine May, and Cheri Register for their continuing interest and our shared pleasure in our work.

I have also had conversations with colleagues who have been essential to my ability to further develop a number of arguments in this book. They are Barry Cytron, Lary May, the late Barbara Myerhoff, Louis Newman, Mischa Penn, and Naomi Scheman. Marcia Eaton and David Noble provided helpful bibliographic references.

All photographs, with the exception of the Minyan mizrach in Chapter 3, are the work of Bill Aron. They record the activities of other Jews, not Minyan events or members whose anonymity I agreed to maintain. Aron's work on Jewish communities is a striking record of Jewish life. I am honored to include them and believe that a group committed to new images should be seen as well as described. Some of these photographs are included in Bill Aron's collection, *From the Corners of the Earth: Contemporary Photographs of the Jewish World,* (Schocken, 1985) which includes a section on the New York Havurah.

At Wayne State University Press, I appreciated Robert Mandel's persistent interest in this project. Anne Adamus helped in many ways, kindly and efficiently, to bring this project to its final form.

I also wish to express my appreciation to those people who provided moral and emotional support for the labor involved in producing a book. My parents, Mary and Samuel Prell, helped in every way they could. My friend Marge Goldwater was unflagging in support and nudging during the final revision of the book. My friends and colleagues Sara Evans and Elaine May never waivered in their belief in me and my work. Their friendship is one of the great gifts of my life. My children,

Lila Sima and Livia Sara Foldes, have lived with this book all of their young lives. It took me away from them when we wanted to be together. Their love as well as complaints always helped, at least to put things in perspective. Of the many things I learned in the course of writing this book none was as important as the meaning of my partnership with Steven Foldes. There is no aspect of this book we have not shared, from the research as young graduate students, to the ideas and writing style. Steven gave his love, patience, respect, and critical mind to me unsparingly. I cannot adequately express my debt to him, but can only place it in the context of our shared lives.

The two teachers who were most influential in my training as an anthropologist died prematurely before the completion of this book. Victor Turner was an extraordinary model as man, scholar, humanist, and religious person. His ability to grasp the multiple meanings of any religious encounter—ontological, political, aesthetic, and poetic—set a standard that is impossible to imitate but essential to remember.

Barbara G. Myerhoff, my teacher, mentor, and friend, shared all of the stages of this work with me until her death in 1985. Her counsel was always wise. Her insights were always unique and profound. Her understanding of religion and ritual was virtually unmatched. I dedicate this book to her and her memory with gratitude and love.

Introduction

In the fall of 1973 forty Jewish men and women gathered, as they did every Saturday morning, for Sabbath prayer. They were members of the Kelton Free Minyan, praying together in the neighborhood of Kelton University, a large California state university in Los Angeles. Strictly speaking, a *minyan* is the quorum of ten people—traditionally male—required for the recitation of Jewish blessings. In general usage, however, a minyan refers to a group that meets for common prayer. Their community was not Orthodox, Conservative, or Reform.[1] They were affiliated with no denomination, considering their group first and foremost an alternative to the American synagogue. They chose, in their embrace of Judaism, neither to be fundamentalist nor minimally observant. Rather, they remained committed to a Judaism that allowed them to struggle with the Jewish issues that they believed their parents ignored or dismissed, in an alternative form to any available in American Judaism.

On this particular Sabbath, during the Torah service at the midpoint of their prayers, Joseph, one of the members, requested the honor of blessing the Torah (*aliyah*).[2] As he approached the scroll he asked another member, Jay, a rabbi but not the leader of this formally leaderless group, to recite a prayer following Joseph's blessing. Though this is a ritually acceptable act, it was relatively unusual and was precipitated by the Yom Kippur War in Israel that was occurring at the time. Joseph, a little uncomfortable with his ability to read Hebrew, asked Jay to recite a prayer that called on the "God of healing" to bring a full recovery to Israeli soldiers. Joseph had lived in Israel during the previous year and was considering returning there, perhaps permanently. The members of the group said "Amen" to the prayer, joining Joseph and Jay in their support for Israel, where many had lived or visited, and to which all felt deeply attached. This war coincided with the holidays of the Jewish new year that brought members together more frequently than their usual weekly observance of the Sabbath. All of the members followed the war closely, reading the newspaper, listening to the news, and calling friends or relatives in Israel for any information. Unlike the Six Day War of 1967, this war did not have a quick and decisive resolution. The future of the state, and the kind of future it would have, were all in question. The combination of the war and ritual cycle, therefore, made it a tense and emotional time.

Later that morning, Joseph, a relatively new member to the group, again wanted to offer a prayer, but this time for Israel's victory. He asked Minyan members to pray together for that victory as they were about to recite the grace after the lunch they shared following their service. This precipitated a long, serious, and sometimes angry discussion. Many said flatly that they could not pray for the bloodshed of Arab men and women. Others questioned what victory was if it did not ensure peace, so why pray for victory rather than peace. Joseph claimed that if they were unwilling to pray for victory, nothing was worth praying for at all. Many members asserted that Judaism had always taken account of the concerns of all people in war.

Minyan members rarely, if ever, created prayers; normally they prayed the traditional liturgy from a Sabbath prayer book. However, out of concern for Joseph and the issue he raised, they discussed the matter until they were able to agree upon the language to be used. Together they recited a simple sentence expressing their hope for the peace and safety of all. Jacob, a founder of the Minyan and one of the rabbis in the community, concluded the discussion by commenting, "You see how important prayer is to us. We are willing to fight over it."

That these men and women in their twenties and thirties, mostly students and some professionals, should turn to community prayer to express their greatest concerns, and also negotiate what they were willing to pray, is only comprehensible in light of that final remark. Jacob's comment on the event was calculated to remind them all that prayer was not something to be repeated routinely, but was so significant that its words were worthy of detailed discussion and negotiation. They prayed a traditional liturgy with which they did not always agree, but that did not render them unwilling to carefully weigh the words they prayed. Prayer articulated their values and perspectives as much because it was "traditional" as because they were willing to examine it. Prayer evoked both their cognitive concerns and emotional reactions.

This brief, though unusually dramatic, event in the Minyan summarizes how prayer and praying expressed personal relations within the community, as well as articulated identity and a place for each Minyan member among the Jewish people. Prayer was simultaneously self-conscious, as their discussion of prayer language revealed, and frequently unself-conscious, as their praying of traditional Jewish liturgy revealed. They did not discuss the war as an abstract problem. On two occasions they prayed about it, moving from an emotional discussion to a ritual performance, valuing both equally.

This book is about why these men and women prayed, why prayer was a language and ritual with which they formulated identity, history, and values, though it required constant discussion and negotiation. To understand their use of prayer I address a problem introduced to the social-scientific study of religion by Max Weber ([1904] 1958). Why does a religion take the form it does within a particular historical period and within a specific culture? What are the forces that shape religious forms and meanings for a particular era and generation? In addition, I look at religious activities, in this case all aspects of prayer, to understand not only how they reflect these social forces, but how these ritual forms in turn affect the experience of the worshiper. I suggest that the analysis of religion in any society—traditional or complex—requires this dual understanding of the broad social/historical context and of the performance of its ritual activities. The connection between these phenomena is less apparent in a complex and pluralist society where mainstream religion has a less direct and encompassing affect on its adherents than in traditional societies. Nevertheless, without understanding both, as few studies of contemporary religion do, one cannot understand either what ideas are communicated by religion, or how they are made effective and authoritative for the worshiper. Nor can one address why they may not be effective, leaving worshipers with doubts and uncertainties.

The fact that Minyan members are Jews places some of these questions in a particular context. Their "religion" is the product of the meeting between Jewish culture, a way of life, and modern European and American society, which cast religion as a denominational preference to be kept separate from work and daily life. The grandparents and great-grandparents of these men and women came to America from Europe and most participated in shaping Judaism into a religion by building synagogues, creating institutions, and maintaining a persistent attachment to Judaism, even though they dismantled most of its obligations, requirements, and theology. Nothing has preoccupied American Jews and American Judaism more than the maintenance of identity that is neither exclusively religious nor exclusively ethnic, but both. This book, then, pays special attention to features of religion that create identity and focuses on how social relations and sacred concerns meet in prayer.

Only a tiny fraction of American Jews pray weekly, as Minyan members did, though approximately 40 percent belong to synagogues. Even fewer would think to address their near unanimous concern for the safety of the State of Israel through prayer. What set Minyan members apart from the great majority of Jews in the United States cannot be explained by the religious observances of their parents, their educations—secular and religious—or their degree of belief in Jewish theology. Rather, they shared a generation and commitment to joining their Judaism to American countercultural attitudes so that protesting American policy, formulating alternatives to American society, and reconceptualizing gender relations were expressed within Jewish rituals, symbols, and observances. Similarly, Jewish texts, requirements, and prayer had to express many of the values and aesthetics of the American counterculture, particularly equality and expressive individualism. Indeed, the discussion of Joseph's prayer caught up the themes of nationalism and peace and their relationship to prayer, because the Minyan often discussed these topics as they read their own sacred texts. After the service when Joseph angrily dismissed Minyan members' opposition to his prayer as "liberal American idealism," he understood that everything that occurred in the Minyan was an attempt to synthesize a generational outlook (American liberalism and idealism) with traditional Judaism. They believed that this synthesis was unique to their generation and they rejected all previous generational formulations of American Judaism and American society.

The Minyan was not a unique community. It was one of many such groups called *havurot* (fellowships; the singular form is *havurah*) that developed from the late 1960s to the mid-1970s, and continued to flourish in all the major Jewish population centers of the United States. They had high visibility in the Jewish press and in subsequent scholarly and popular assessments of American Judaism of that period (Dawidowicz 1982b; Waxman 1983; Cohen 1983; Silberman 1985; Elazar 1987; Silverman 1987). Those who commented on the havurah looked for comparable groups that predated the 1960s. Some noted that Reconstructionist Judaism used the havurah concept decades before as alternatives to synagogues (Neusner 1972a). One early work on havurot traced their true origins to the Jewish Commonwealth in the centuries preceding the Christian era. Wilderness communities and "fellowships of the faithful," were organized in this period. (Neusner 1972b, 1–2).

The havurah movement however, was the first movement in American Judaism to criticize the suburban and monumental urban synagogue as a viable expression of Jewish life. Its members rejected denominations, impressive buildings, and other imitations of American society and Protestantism. They did not however, reject Judaism, only their parents' version of it. Instead they created small, homogeneous groups that prayed, usually weekly rather than daily, studied, and provided a community to share personal events and the holidays of the Jewish year. The members of the groups were usually close friends. They were committed to maintaining their small size and their complete independence from large institutions.

The most accessible expression of havurot is the volumes of *The Jewish Catalogue* (Siegel, Strassfeld, and Strassfeld 1973; Strassfeld and Strassfeld 1976; 1980), which describe a Jewish life that is compatible with the attitudes and activities of the counterculture. The many contributors to the volumes, virtually all havurah members, meant their own lives as models. The books closely resemble the popular counterculture handbook, *The Whole Earth Catalogue*. The success of these books is legendary in Jewish publishing circles. By the early 1980s, they had sold more than 200,000 copies. The books are reputed to have outsold every publication of the Jewish Publication Society, their publisher, other than the Bible. Hence, the havurah approach to Judaism—personal, independent and activist—spread to many people who may have had no affiliation with any other Jewish organization.

In the late 1970s synagogues began forming their own havurot. Soon many American Jews associated with Conservative, Reform, and Reconstructionist synagogues also thought of themselves as belonging to havurot. In fact, many synagogue members found themselves preferring the small face-to-face groups because they too found synagogues large and alienating (Reisman 1980; Bubis, Wasserman and Lert 1983). Some wanted a different kind of praying where liturgy was interspersed with Torah reading and discussion. Some sought to explore spirituality, and some wanted a traditional framework for prayer where women were accepted as equals. Some synagogue goers simply wanted a more intimate sense of community. Whatever the motivation of individual members, what began as an alternative organization in American Judaism quickly became standard fare for American Jews. In 1984 Abba Eban, Israel's former ambassador to the United Nations, narrated an eleven part series on Jewish history, *Heritage: Civilization and the Jews*. In the segment about American Judaism, he described havurot as a widespread but uniquely American adaptation of Judaism.

The project of the havurah movement—to integrate Judaism with a generational outlook and thereby create a more authentic Judaism—caught up powerful contradictions. At the core of normative Judaism is *halaha,* a set of prescriptions for every aspect of life. Halaha structures activity and provides the basis for community through prayer, study, and responsibilities to others. Minyan members, like the vast majority of American Jews, did not feel bound by all the requirements of halaha. Their ability to adapt some of the requirements to their own lives did not mean that they did not, in turn, feel obligated by other rules. The choices made by most havurah members, sometimes apparently inconsistently, led members of a havurah in Philadelphia to refer to themselves as "pick and choose Jews" (Weissler 1982). Nevertheless, they understood themselves to be "observant" and "traditional" Jews and differentiated themselves from Reform Jews who more willingly reject halaha. Though some havurot thought of themselves as religiously "liberal," in the seventies havurot were more likely to be traditional than liberal.

Even a modified halaha was not the only system structuring the activities and outlooks of Minyan and havurah members. They adhered strongly to democracy and expressive individualism, which committed them to equality in all activities and the right of the person to stamp something of him or herself on Judaism, hence altering it. The type of discussion about prayer that members had with Joseph, involving cognitive reflection and asserting a wide range of values, expressed just this outlook and was an intrinsic aspect of all Minyan worship.

The obligatory nature of halaha is inevitably at odds with an American democratic individualism based on choice and the needs of the self. I argue that the Minyan's solution to this contradiction was to create a prayer community that synthesized the poles of normative community and expressive individualism through what I call *aesthetics* and *performance.* Members shared a similar definition of what made prayer desirable, obligatory, effective, and beautiful within a homogeneous community. They believed that there were no others anywhere in Los Angeles who shared these definitions. In their view their differences from synagogues—their informality, lack of formal leadership, discussion of disagreements with text, and a style of praying that involved everyone's active participation—defined their uniqueness. They did not change the prayers; they altered the aesthetics of prayer by praying differently than mainstream American Jews. Their aesthetics were put into practice and made believable and real through the performance of prayer. Ritual activity formulated through a generational aesthetic generated their conviction of the authenticity and effectiveness of their prayer and their Judaism.

This aesthetic solution engaged the same issue that has been relevant to all generations of immigrant Jews and their children: how to formulate a relationship between community, tradition, and the self within America. Minyan members formulated those relations in the way they organized the social relations of their community, their liturgical services, and in the ways they addressed conflicts that arose between halaha and other values. None of these conflicts were "resolved" for the Minyan's generation any more than they were for other generations. However, what was unique about the Minyan and havurot was how they juxtaposed the self and tradition so that aesthetic activities and prayer performances could constitute solutions to these inevitable contradictions. Minyan members lived their lives as Jews successfully when they prayed the words of the tradition and at the same time challenged it through their discussions and debates. Rejecting the synagogue in favor of a countercultural alternative constituted for them a Judaism they found far more authentic than any Jewish movements or denominations that preceded them in the United States.

Religion in Complex Society

This community, though particular, was an ideal setting in which to examine how contemporary Jews modified their traditional religious formulation to accommodate their sense of self, which was caught between the counterculture and that tradition. The significance of the self within Western culture makes it crucial to understand how the autonomous person is bound into a system of religious obligation and how, ultimately, the tensions between tradition and self were minimized. In the group, these issues were focused on problems of how ritual expressed and transformed experience, how tradition was affected by changing social relations and changing conceptions of gender, and how religion was made authoritative in the absence of a homogeneous institutional structure obligating participation.

Though Minyan members were particular, they were not unique. They were representative not just of their generation but of Americans, who, despite their doubts and even grave reservations, have a deep sense of attachment to their religion or church. What these people have in common is a desire to create identity and personal meaning within a historical tradition that defines community. Although the traditional forms require rationalizing both beliefs and doubts within a given system, they also provide a rich resource for addressing contemporary problems. Though an issue in the study of religion in modern society is how precisely to define it, it is these traditional forms that separate denominational religion from joggers, anarchists, and other "life styles" that may well be embedded in complete world views, but lack a history and traditional system of transcendent authority.

It is a curiosity that the study of American Judaism and American religion has paid little attention to how religious experience is constituted. Rather, the overriding concern of this field is with how religion has changed as a result of losing its all encompassing hold over the lives of adherents. Secularization theorists have argued effectively that a changing society has altered the institutions, authority, and ideas in which religion is embedded. Therefore, what is worth knowing about Jews is, for example, how minimal is their observance of law. For Christians, on the other hand, studies feature church attendance and changing theological beliefs. These studies frequently demonstrate that Christians continue to go to church while believing few of their doctrines.

The most important body of scholarship about American Jews is sociological, largely written by American Jews. Recently these studies have been increasingly statistical and social structural in character. Typically such studies focus on ritual observance and synagogue attendance, usually cross generationally. The results have been striking and consistent. Undoubtedly the overt signs of religious life have radically diminished. Jews practice fewer rituals, attend synagogue less often, and rarely observe unique Jewish requirements. Cohen notes, as have others, that a few ritual observances have increased, but these are compatible with mainstream Christian observance (1983, 49; Goldscheider 1986). Hanukah rituals, such as lighting the *menorah,* have gained popularity because of their family focus and apparent compatibility with the celebration of Christmas. Yet Jews continue to join synagogues and educate their children to be Jews, albeit with some decrease by generational distance from immigration. Judaism does not appear to be nearing a demise in American culture.

This apparent paradox is consistently explained in light of what social scientists call "ethnic cohesion." In short, this explanation holds that Jews remain religious in order to remain Jews. Religious articulation of life passages, family events, and history seems to be the way Jews have found to continue a sense of their uniqueness without jeopardizing their successful acculturation to American society. In its most extreme form, those who look exclusively at the statistical nature of Jewish religious practice are driven to see such behavior as markers of identity. For them, ethnicity is an empty category that stands for nothing other than Jewishness, reinforced by shared social class. It does not possess a unique value system, an outlook or consciousness, or require specific behavior. Religious life is minimal and it merely establishes the social category "Jewish" (Goldscheider and Zuckerman 1984; Goldscheider 1986).

Charles Liebman, a political scientist who has written extensively and insightfully about modern Jewish life, formulated another answer to this dilemma in an influential book, *The Ambivalent American Jew* (1973). His solution was classically anthropological in that he posited the development of two kinds of Judaism which he called "folk" and "elite." The elite formulation is the normative one associated with Jewish law (halaha) and practiced by Orthodox Jews. It is clearly on the wane in modern life; only a minority of American Jews are Orthodox observers of Judaism. The folk formulation is unselfconscious and emotional. Liebman argued it is more adaptive because it is more flexible. The majority of American Jews who attend synagogue irregularly and occasionally practice certain rituals have combined nostalgia, ethnicity, and a selection of Jewish rituals to create a folk Judaism, accepted by them as authentic. Liebman's claim, while innovative, suffers the limitations of all such dichotomies. In overlooking the continuities and tensions between folk and elite models, made conscious in the lives and communities in which men and women are Jews, Liebman and others fail to see how a religious life is created, omitting a critical part of normative religious life. For the relationship between elite and folk formulations, well illustrated by the Minyan, is articulated by both halaha and modern life. In sharply differentiating normative and nonnormative expressions of a religion, they ignore their impact on one another. They also fail to examine the particularities of historical periods that create certain relations between the folk and elite formulations. The pervasive force of the normative tradition is overlooked in the analysis; Minyan members were in no sense free from normative Judaism despite their willingness to transform it.

My analysis of this community of American Jews reasserts the religious character of Judaism, even when it is practiced by non-Orthodox Jews. Acknowledging the fundamental transformation of modern society from a "closed" and "tradition bound" world into a plural one has led scholars of religion to abandon the project of understanding both the sources of religious continuity and the possibilities for religious change. The social structuralists have discerned accurately a difference in behavior. They have failed, however, by the limitations of their method, to explain the significance of that behavior. Although we may know the occasions on which Jews enact their Judaism, we do not know what is enacted or what it means. We do not know how Judaism is created in religious settings as opposed to nonreligious settings, such as secular philanthropic groups. In short, until recently social scientists concerned with American Judaism have not asked how Jews are made Jews and why Jews remain Jews. Explaining religious behavior as the pursuit of cohesion, apart from understanding the meaning of that cohesion, is a partial exercise that has often overlooked the most important question one asks of any religious system: How is it constituted? What is the historical context that leads to the organization of religious community and the structure of ritual action within it? That is, what is the impact of the larger social system on how any system of beliefs and actions communicates meaning in the form that it does? In turn, how do religious and ritual activity structure and orient the experience of the worshiper? What are the sources of authority and the premises of belief? Only in ethnographic studies of Jews creating a shared religious life may such questions be addressed.[3]

I contend that these questions can only be answered by studying religious behavior, like all human behavior, as meaningful in action. How religion is lived must be understood as well as its normative rules. It is the relationship of religious rules and action that must be sought, but within behavior itself, rather than simply measuring behavior against a single norm. For the patchwork that is created and recreated as a religion by adherents provides them both the critical continuity and the possibility for change within a traditional religion. For Minyan members, as for most American Jews, this constantly innovated religion expressed their American Jewish lives, constraining them by transmitting elements of an authoritative history and observance while allowing them to place their individual stamp upon it.

In the last decade, many anthropologists have become concerned with what are called studies of "performance," the enactment of ritual and cultural events.[4] Rather than focusing on idealized versions of these events, they have asked what effect the actual performance has on the participant, the audience, and its meaning in the culture. They share an interest in "emergent meaning." How does the significance of the activity develop out of the performance itself, rather than out of a static text. Though the majority of these writers discuss traditional societies, their work is crucial to understanding religion in complex society. They point attention to how meaning is made in society, rather than assuming it is given. In the act of performing rituals that convey cultural ideas and assumptions, people come to hold and value them. There are differences among these writers about how homogeneous such ideas are. Not even the simplest societies, some anthropologists argue, share a single given set of assumptions about the world. Performance, then, is crucial in developing and expanding cultural ideas. People do not simply enact a given view, but expand and even alter that view in performance. This is even more true in complex society, where general meanings are made authoritative and believable in performance because of its capacity to evoke conviction. Therefore, an emphasis on the performance of religious ritual and its impact on worshipers is an essential focus for the study of how religion is constituted in complex society. The expressive self and the authoritative ground of tradition meet in performance rather than text. I advocate a view of American religion that emphasizes the study of performance.

Samuel Heilman's survey of the sociology of American Jews (1983) notes that scholarship on Jews in any period tends to reflect the concerns of Jews themselves. The study of anti-Semitism corresponded to a period of rising anti-Semitism in American society. Similarly, the recent trend toward ethnographic studies may reflect renewed pride in ethnicity. But more importantly, ethnographic research allows one the possibility of seeing not only what is practiced but also how and why it is practiced in the form it is. It allows one to focus on the performance of religion within normative forms, emphasizing what meanings are transmitted and how they are made convincing for participants. This ethnographic study focuses on how Minyan members constituted their religious experience. Following on more recent studies of contemporary religious communities (Stromberg 1986), I examine the fragmented and varied beliefs that were held within this community to understand how these beliefs, as well as religious participation, were made plausible, convincing, and effective for worshipers. In the Minyan I examined prayer, not only because this was their central activity, but because this was the arena where the worshiper's convictions (or doubts) were transformed into religious action in order to create his or her Judaism.

I understand their Judaism to be the product of their own beliefs and feelings of ethnicity brought to life within a particular social context and marked by a unique aesthetic. Aesthetics are of particular importance, because when religious beliefs are less firmly planted in the soil of social interaction and social relations, as is the case in a complex plural society, they take on a general and more metaphoric quality. The feelings formed by and associated with ritual activity are focused in aesthetic media rather than doctrine. Religious beliefs and attitudes are not mirrored in the world around where people are different, but in personally held cultural images, feelings, and a sense of community formed with people like themselves who are joined and differentiated by aesthetic media.

They might best be understood as engaged in what I will call a ritual rehearsal of identity. It is not that the ritual is simply a means to an end, an exercise to promote family ties and Jewish ethnicity, as a number of sociologists have argued. To the contrary, prayer in the Minyan enabled Jewishness (identity) as well as Judaism (religion) because of the association of ritual with the covenant, the sign of the continuity of the Jewish people. Ritual is ideally performed in community. At the same time, ritual creates a private, unarticulated experience. The performance of Jewish ritual is persuasive: sound, movement, and engagement are built into prayer. Minyan members acknowledged that tradition pulled them into observance, but the power of secular, American values—which pervaded and dominated their lives—undermined the tradition and allowed them to remain American. They found in Judaism an alternative to American life, yet they continued to embrace the liberal egalitarianism of Western society. Minyan prayer emphasized these various meanings, both traditional and liberal, by the way it was performed and organized. Jewish identity was made and refashioned in the community.

The Judaism thus recreated in this community was both radical and conservative. Members' performance of the tradition demanded the forms of the tradition; the forms of the tradition required the performance. They were persuaded they were Jews because in their community they did what Jews do: they prayed the Sabbath liturgy. At the same time, their community was predicated on the integration of secular values, intellectual debates, gender equality, and the acceptance of one another's Judaism, all of which tended to undermine the tradition. The result was a mutually generating process of creating, retaining, and recreating Judaism. For the members of the Minyan at least, Judaism became more meaningful precisely because it was made to assimilate contemporary political and social values. This book, then, is about how one group of modern Jews persuaded themselves that they were Jews. It is about how they took ritual into their own hands, and with those hands they grasped the tradition even as they changed it.

This was not a process controlled by halaha. Their Judaism was more voluntaristic and individualistic, making the self the ultimate integrator of various possibilities. Nevertheless, it was certainly religion, because religion, a system of beliefs and rituals, is articulated in complex society through the person, where virtually all meaning is experienced as self defining and identity conferring. This book examines not only what contribution religion makes to the formation of identity for a contemporary person, but more importantly, how that identity is authenticated through ritual. In examining people who are liberal about religion and politics, rather than fundamentalist, I suggest that their struggle to maintain ties to the past in the context of the present needs to be understood in terms of ritual and community and their relationship to generational formulations of social values. I point to the levels of analysis required for studying the integration of the social and the sacred, as well as the person and the religion, by focusing on how to define prayer as an activity rather than a text and analyzing ritual as a performed activity. In examining activity rather than institution, I hope to introduce balance to the study of religion in secular society, which has exclusively focused on what has undermined the significance of religion in the organization of society. Without understanding what continues to make religion effective for its adherents, it is impossible to understand pluralistic society. I account for the fact that the religion of contemporary people is an expression of their social class, their ethnicity, their gender, and their use of the voluntary association as a medium of identity in complex society. When the person is the locus where meaning is made, then the analysis of religion belongs in personal development, in social relations, in ritual, and in history.

Studying the Minyan

To understand how religion is constituted requires the close observation of participants' performances. This book is based on eighteen months of participant-observation fieldwork in Los Angeles from 1973–1975. In many ways this research was an odd choice for an anthropologist. In the past, the cardinal rule of the discipline was to conduct research in a non-Western setting with people as different from oneself as possible. The many recent exceptions to this rule demonstrate that anthropology is a discipline in transition. Foreign fieldwork, however, remains relatively normative for anthropology. Nevertheless, I did not seek out an exotic setting in which to conduct my research. From the University of Chicago, where I was pursuing my graduate degree, I moved to Los Angeles, where my most distressing burden was to find an affordable apartment in the expensive neighborhood where the Minyan met.

Yet my "culture shock" was just as real and just as profound, though different, as that which I experienced eighteen months later when I accompanied my husband, Steven Foldes, to a town in central Mexico, the setting for his doctoral research. The culture shock arose from assuming the odd role of anthropologist. I was always there and yet I never belonged. No matter how like me they appeared—and that counts for a good deal in one's psychological adjustment—I was not there to join their group. I was there to study it. Of course, I could "pass" as a member. I was a Jew, a student, and in my twenties. But I was also different. I was not raised as an observant Jew, and I was not one by Minyan standards. What I learned in order to enter this community (basic Hebrew, knowledge of prayer, and the festival cycle) I learned mostly as part of my doctoral degree training in preparation for the field. What proved critical in my research was to actively work at undermining my natural sense of affinity with the group's members. My position was the classically ambiguous one of the participant-observer, complicated by my unavoidable and unmistakable similarity.

A key step in participant observation has been remarked upon by other anthropologists: One is resocialized into a new culture. He or she must become a group member to fully understand the new culture. That membership implies both the ability to survive in the culture and to communicate what one learns in the categories of one's culture and the social sciences. The enterprise is one of translation, of comprehending, and communicating. I, too, underwent a resocialization despite the fact that the group immediately "made sense" to me. That resocialization demanded that I distance myself from what was easily comprehensible and relearn the sense they made to themselves. The danger was, of course, that they were not alien enough to allow me to censor my own sense making. The advantage, which for me was considerable, was working in my own language so that as their sense emerged, the subtleties of it were readily graspable.

I pursued this sense making through classical qualitative methods. I was the observer, and I observed all formal Minyan activities from August 1973 to December 1974, then intermittently from January 1975 to July 1975. The Minyan met for Sabbath and festival prayer services. In addition, they held two weekend retreats, quarterly evaluation meetings, and innumerable smaller social events. From these data I discerned the formal and informal structures of the group: how it worked. Equally important were the approximately one hundred hours of discussions during the services in which members expressed and disagreed over interpretations of prayer, the Torah, Judaism, and issues in current Jewish life. Almost none of these observations could be recorded immediately because of the Jewish prohibition on writing during the Sabbath. When I once tried to write on the Sabbath I was asked not to again. I recorded my observations of these events immediately after they occurred and those of any non-Sabbath or festival events as they transpired. Another major source of data was formal interviews conducted at least once with virtually every member of the group. In each case I used the same open-ended questions in order to attain, whenever possible, comparable data.

Although I had no key informant, no individual guide to the complexities of Minyan life, I talked with some members at greater length, particularly those who dominated the public life of the group. Initially I talked more to "founders" than "newcomers" of the group, more to men than to women. My status also affected who wanted to talk to me. I most often interacted with married rather than unmarried members, academics rather than nonacademics, and, ultimately, as much with women as with men.

It was impossible to hide my own beliefs and ideas, unless I was to stay among these people in utter anonymity, which was intolerable both for me and for Minyan members. After half a year I was enough of a participant to be expected to take roles in the Sabbath service. I most often led discussions, offering anthropological interpretations of texts, alongside the feminist, political, psychological, and normative Jewish interpretations offered by others. I was neither an observant nor religiously educated Jew. I did not hide that I was a feminist when I went to observe planning meetings for a feminist service (see Chapter 7). Despite these distinguishing features, by the end of my stay all regular members had talked to me about what they thought of the Minyan and their place in it.

How I initially saw the Minyan affected what I continued to see. I was preoccupied by the group's structure, its organization of social relations, and the competition for power. Because the members' organization and their activities and the infinite variations of who was friends with whom concerned them constantly, these issues also became central for me. My concern with organization helped me to make sense of them initially (Prell-Foldes 1978b). Committed as I was to discerning their sense, educated as I was in social structuralism, their sensitivity to one another combined with my interest in politics inclined me initially to concentrate on group dynamics.

But this initial focus drew me away from the substance of their activities: why prayer and tradition should be the medium through which they would express themselves. After completing my dissertation I began to rethink who these men and women were. As I read more about American Judaism, I came to understand the strong parallels between Minyan members and their parents' generation's constructions of Judaism. I was struck by what these parallels revealed about American religion, namely, that religion had been voluntaristic in America ever since immigrants arrived. What appeared, for example, as a countercultural rebellion had its roots deep in immigrants' attempts to maintain their Judaism within American society. Voluntarism of this magnitude required an understanding of how people managed to imbue their religion with the aura of authority and authenticity no longer held by institutions.

Finally, the results of my research and writing about this group have been shaped by the fact that I was deeply moved by my experience in the Minyan. Because my father, the strongest Jewish figure in my early life, had to work on the Sabbath and thus could not have a consistently Jewish life, he felt sullied enough to dispense with most of the religious observance of his late adolesence. The stories he told of himself as a Jew concerned a distant past when "he really had been Jewish." He wistfully longed for something he would never have again, as he worked to perfect a successful American life in business and in the secular organizations of Jewish ethnicity. I glimpsed his lost passions twice a year during new year rituals in a Reform synagogue where he was never comfortable. At the family *Seder* (ritual and meal) he led during Passover, he told me stories of his mother's devotion to Judaism. His eyes brimmed with tears—which I never comprehended—as he droned the long grace after meals while I cleared the dishes from the table. Perhaps his profound ambivalence about Judaism, his deep attraction to it, and his impatience with its laws and requirements that disrupted his business, contributed to my enthusiastic interest in the remote religions of Africa that drew me to study anthropology. But in the Minyan and havurot I saw people healing wounds like those of my father and others of his generation who could not reconcile the Judaism of their parents and the American lives they sought. Like their parents, who constituted the first American born Jewish generation following mass migration to the

United States, Minyan members also reacted to the Judaism of their parents' past and an American life of their own present. Their reaction was one of compromise and authenticity, which I grew to respect. My identification with that vision came to be as deep as the anthropology that taught me to understand it. Both are central to this book.

The argument of the book develops in the following way. In the first two chapters, I assert that during the period in the United States when an urban, professional middle class was emerging (1820–1910), Jews were immigrating in large numbers. These Jews, who immediately set their sights on entering this middle class, brought to their Jewish observance their concerns for respectability, uniformity, and democracy.

The countercultural rebellion against some of these values created the havurah movement. Though groups such as the Minyan rejected the decorum and aesthetics of their parents' generation, they maintained these commitments to autonomy and expressive individualism and their struggles to maintain Judaism within American culture. The Judaism that emerged in the havurah focused on maintaining a basically traditional liturgy, but it radically altered the way that worship was organized by using what I call organizational solutions to the problem of how to pray.

I then turn to an analysis of Jewish prayer in the Minyan (Chapters 3 through 6), the primary medium through which they have chosen to express their Judaism and to integrate their other identities—student, pacifist, feminist, and others—with it. I suggest that the only satisfactory model for understanding their prayer lives examines three fundamental constituents of prayer: community, interpretation, and halaha. Prayer is more than text, and its performance in this group relied on a community with which members mutually reflected on prayer. In so doing they interiorized prayer, making the text and self reflect one another. Understanding prayer solely as a statement requiring assent makes it impossible to understand not only why these members prayed but what they expressed when they prayed: their relationship to history, to one another and, for some but not all, to God.

In Chapters 5 and 6 I examine a crisis that developed around members' ability to pray and their attempted resolution in order to demonstrate how prayer aesthetics and performance unified and synthesized the prayer constituents, making them reflect one another and integrating them with the self. Identity was generated out of this synthesis because it located the self in the social, mythological, historical, and cosmological relationships created by Judaism.

The final ethnographic event focuses on a Sabbath service in which women members addressed their feelings of attachment to and alienation from Judaism. This chapter asserts that prayer can be constituted only when members validate and authenticate one another's participation. Both events taken together, the crises about prayer and gender, underscore that prayer can only be interiorized when the self is visible in community and halaha. Performance, I suggest, is the essential way to engage the self in the formulation of identity. I conclude by returning to the issues of religion in complex society.

Notes

1. These American denominations will be discussed and described historically in Chapters 1, 2, and 3.

2. The Torah service occurs within regular Jewish liturgical services three times a week. The *Torah* is the Hebrew word for the five books of the Bible believed to have been written by Moses. During this service, a section of the Torah is read from the sacred scroll where these books are inscribed. This service will be discussed at greater length in Chapter 3.

3. Some examples of recent works that adopt this perspective are Heilman 1983; 1976; Weissler 1982; Myerhoff 1979. This perspective on the study of American Judaism is also advocated by Charles Liebman (1982) in a paper presented to evaluate what research approaches a center for contemporary Jewish studies might take.

4. These anthropologists and their views are discussed in Chapters 4, 5, and 6.

1

Decorum in American Judaism

The Sacred in Social Interaction

> I can remember when I was a child how much Judaism appealed to me aesthetically. I thought *Adon Olam* [a hymn] was the most beautiful song I had ever heard. I loved the synagogue building. But it was never anything intellectual. I never wondered how there could be a God with so much evil in the world.
>
> Neal

The grandparents and great-grandparents of havurah members created American Judaism. As these men and women came to the United States from Germany and Eastern Europe, first steadily by the hundreds and then rapidly by the thousands and tens of thousands, they created what had not existed before the nineteenth century, a distinctive American Judaism that was to be counted as one of America's three major faiths. What Judaism became was shaped as much by the America they encountered as it was by the world the immigrants left behind.

Judaism became Americanized in the latter half of the nineteenth century as America was confronting massive urbanization. The centralized government bureaucracy of experts and professionals that dominated American society, as well as movements for social reform in the same period, affected all American religions and what the American people wanted from a religious experience. Americanization occurred in a society newly formulating middle-class manners and aspirations and the meaning of American citizenship in an industrial capitalist society. Jewish acculturation was as improvisational as were the mainstream American social and religious movements that developed in this period of dramatic change.

The synagogue was the first and most potent religious institution created to articulate this encounter between European Jews and the American life they immediately sought to emulate (see Figure 1).[1] European Jews came to America eager to stay. So many fled oppression

FIGURE 1

The Synagogue in America After 1840

	Immigrant-Producer	Americanized-Consumer	American Counter-culture
Synagogue form	Ethnic—2nd generation synagogue	Corporate suburban synagogue center	Havurah
Organization type	Lay dominated—democratic, electoral	Lay—rabbi relationship within denomination. Bureaucratized	Egalitarian
Constituency	Adult males	Families—primary focus on children ages 7–13	Individuals—young married or attached men and women ages 20–30
Decorum and aesthetics	European derived followed by unsystematic imitation of mainstream Protestantism. Emphasis on uniform social behavior.	Degrees of Protestant imitation dependent on denomination. Performancelike. Emphasis on uniform behavior and uniform prayer.	Focus on individual experience and participation within community to evoke both Europe and the American counterculture.
Relationship to God	The synagogue is a home for a God-made person cut off from the past.	The synagogue is a home for the self-made person, made by people as monuments to their changing social status and relationship to America.	The havurah is a home for people seeking self-expression through rejection of an immediate past in favor of a distant past.

that America promised to be home and haven. Immigrants imitated Americans because they wanted to be Americans. In America the synagogue was laity dominated, ultimately to the exclusion of rabbinical authority in America. The laity was primarily concerned with the form rather than the content of Judaism, particularly in the early years of immigration. Though American Judaism remained focused on continuity with the Jewish people through time and space, the synagogue was particularly committed to evolving forms of worship that resembled the dominant society. These forms were influenced by the middle-class aesthetics of mainstream Protestant worship and the values of middle-class Americans. Jews became American and Judaism became Americanized. These synagogues were later rejected by the havurah generation, but the principles on which they were founded remain powerful. In the 1970s young men and women accepted lay control of the synagogue and of Jewish worship. In the 1970s activists in havurot rejected the synagogue as inauthentic and too Americanized. They never considered returning to the hierarchic synagogues or communities of European Jewry. Rather, they remained committed to a lay organized synagogue created by their parents and grandparents. They chose a form for worship attuned to their peer group. The havurah, then, is a quintessential expression of American Judaism, despite its claim to rest on a rejection of it.

Nineteenth-Century America: Religion and the Synagogue

Jews fled Europe to escape brutal political and economic repression. When they arrived in the United States, primarily in large cities, most of them immediately sought relatives and acquaintances from their small towns and villages. Most often they joined with them for communal worship. Such gatherings constituted natural forms of community. At the outset they existed not only for the purpose of prayer but to maintain the customs and liturgical music that were unique to one or another region. These organizations that were to become synagogues, and later the foundation of denominations, took shape within a society that was dominated by mainstream Protestantism, the "arbiter of religious beliefs, values and practices in American culture." (Bednarowski 1984, 24–25).

Post Civil War Protestantism promoted activism and a simplicity emphasizing a few central ideas and a minimal ritual life. (Albanese 1981, 256) Revivalism, a personal relationship with Jesus and purification of the self and society, emphasized the democratic and inclusive quality of late nineteenth-century Protestantism. Protestants promised that all men and women could be saved and that they could work to achieve social and individual purity. The Protestantism that spread rapidly through the United States with evangelical zeal was a religion of and for the laity.

Lay control among Protestants emerged as society secularized and political power shifted away from the clergy. Jewish immigrants, then, entered a secular society dominated by a Protestant middle class. So it was that in the Jewish community the laity created a strikingly different religious and institutional framework than they had known in their European Jewish communities. Historians of nineteenth and twentieth-century American Jews have noted the continuities between European and American Jewry, but the remarkable economic and social opportunities available to Jewish immigrants led to transformations in all the basic institutions of Jewish life. Indeed, American Judaism was created out of the transformation of Judaism as a religion, in the context of social mobility. As social class aspirations developed Judaism changed, altering its forms of prayer, synagogue architecture, expectations for participation, and even synagogue membership.

New formulations of Judaism in America were controlled not by rabbis but by the rank and file membership. Theology, consistent observance of law, and, initially, religious education were not the concerns of new Americans. Their vision of Judaism was not laid out in ideological programs but within institutions. In Europe in the eighteenth and nineteenth centuries, the rabbis and knowledgeable members of the Jewish community controlled religious tradition and reform. In the Jewish communities of Europe, rabbis were not only spiritual leaders but legal arbiters as well. They set the standards for proper behavior. When Jews responded to the social changes wrought by the Enlightenment and nationalism, liberal rabbis also spoke for change, particularly concerning community organization and ritual observance.

By contrast, in America the members of immigrant synagogues formulated, even if unsystematically, their evolving Judaism. The laity was concerned with carefully orchestrated forms of interaction and decisions about ritual matters that would reflect what it meant to be an American Jew. Ideology followed, shaping these changing and volatile definitions into the Jewish version of denominations. The synagogue was and remains the domain of the laity. As such, it provides the mirror for the individual's self understanding as an American Jew within, in tension with, or at the margin of that society. Religious change in America emphasized form. Synagogues were then like many ethnic churches of the period. Robert Wiebe, a historian of the nineteenth century, noted the role of ethnic churches:

> The desire for self-determination encouraged the development of organizations that would express the spirit of community autonomy . . . They [ethnic groups] faced much deeper hostility from their neighbors. Partly for these reasons, the ethnic groups placed a much higher premium on the organization itself. Rather than using it as a platform for reform, they perfected its contents, its peculiar American Germanness or Irishness. Nothing served them as well as their churches. (1967, 55–56)

Immigrants' urgent sense of self-determination, their new-found freedoms in America, and their need to shape a new sense of community and self within America led to an emphasis on the expressive quality of the organization and its capacity to articulate identity. Organizations, no matter how instrumental their purpose, also articulated members' identities. When an immigrant used democratic procedures, he or she was making a statement about him or herself. Every organization whose purpose was to preserve or to change the past or present aided in creating a new American's sense of self.

Similarly, every generation of American Jews since the nineteenth century has brought to the synagogue its needs for continuity, acculturation, and an articulation of changing social class. The synagogue has been capable of expressing these concerns, at least in part, because Protestant churches have also articulated its members' relationships with secular society. As immigrant Jews created American Judaism they responded to their own displacement within a dramatically changing America. Nonimmigrant Protestants did not have to join American society as did all immigrants, but they did have to develop ways to live in an urbanized nation no longer dependent on face-to-face ties in the community. Those dislocating and reorienting tasks were also addressed by their churches. The Jews most likely to identify with Americanizing synagogues were the aspiring middle class, so those most drawn to the evangelical churches of cities were white-collar workers who had come from the rural areas. It was the office or store clerks and not the mill workers who involved themselves in revival and Sunday school movements that tended to be interdenominational and rooted in the local, rather than denominational, association (Hudson 1981, 297). Both those Jews and Protestants identified with an emerging middle class were most likely to use the synagogue or the church as a means of entering and conceptualizing their place in American society.[2]

Another development, the challenge to religious authority in two scientific areas, affected every aspect of nineteenth-century religion. Within a decade following the Civil War, scholars accepted Darwin's theory of biological evolution. It was the subject of public debates and editorials. These discussions clearly drew the implications for religion. Science and scientists directly challenged the authority of the Bible. Simultaneously, scholars in German universities developed new approaches to studying the Bible. They historicized sacred text arguing that it was authored by humans, over time, and edited to create a coherent narrative. This textual criticism was also the source of widespread popular interest, leading to new publications of the Bible that included scholarly discussions of its authorship. In 1881 the English Revised Version of the New Testament sold 200,000 copies in one week in New

York (Hudson 1981, 266). There were a variety of responses to these challenges to authority. The nineteenth-century developments of liberal evangelical Protestantism and fundamentalism and the rise of new and Orientally inspired religions have all been traced to this attack on traditional authority.[3] Just as Protestant Americans were in search of their identities in their churches, so too Jews sought their identities in the new American synagogue. Jews forged their acculturation on the anvil of changing formulations of religious authority and a nineteenth-century Protestant emphasis on the church shaping and reflecting individual experience.

Traditional Authority and Synagogue Development

At two different points two different groups of Jews developed immigrant synagogues. German Jews who arrived after 1820 constituted the first mass of Jewish immigrants. By the time Eastern European Jews began immigrating in 1880, German Jews were already well established in the American middle and upper classes. Their synagogues were now identified with the Reform denomination that had begun in Western Europe in the early nineteenth century. European reformers asserted that Judaism was incompatible with their new civil status as citizens. In the earliest years in Europe, the rationale for reform was often more aesthetic than doctrinal, a rationale shared later with new Americans. Reform leaders wanted Judaism to abandon what seemed alien to Europe and conform to "reason," the idea dominating the age. By the 1840s in Germany, Reform had become institutionalized, led by rabbis and committed to a theology, a new prayer book, and developing religious expressions compatible with German life. Jewish Messianism was interpreted as a human commitment to social welfare in the present. Reform Judaism ultimately flowered in the United States, where by 1880 almost all of the two hundred synagogues were affiliated with it.

Religious Eastern European Jews, as opposed to secularists, were far more pious than their German predecessors. They arrived in the United States after 1880. German and Eastern European communities, however, underwent similar processes of first establishing small lay dominated synagogues, followed by building larger synagogues as members of the family moved to better neighborhoods, found more lucrative jobs or expanded businesses, and began to climb the social ladder within American society.[4] Even the secularists, or at least their children, ultimately succumbed to American Jewish norms and joined synagogues. Though they brought secular Jewish associations, such as trade unions and mutual aid groups, to America, they did not flourish and continue to grow. Only synagogues did that (Woocher 1983, 2). Religiously liberal synagogues dominated new neighborhoods, though the liberalism was relative to how observant these men and women had been. Jewish denominations developed in the United States as communities became more acculturated. Each wave of immigrants, then, generated successive types of synagogues, each reflecting increasing acculturation, each articulating different ideas about the relationships between Judaism and American society for Jews. At later points the immigrant communities overlapped and created synagogues together, but originally their synagogues made different statements about these critical relationships. By the 1970s such distinctions broke down and both denominations consisted of offspring of Eastern European Jewry.

The synagogue developed as the domain of the laity because of the historical circumstances that kept rabbis in Europe and brought the less educated Jews to the United States. Virtually all differences between European and American Judaism for the German immigrants who arrived after 1820 may be attributed to either the absence of Jewish authority or a traditional religious structure in America. Without rabbis, access to kosher meat, or the communal enforcement of the obligations of Jewish law, no Jewish community existed as it previously had. Because such a community did not exist, its most pious members could not come to what was essentially a wilderness. Secularized German Jews were equally unwilling to come initially because of their identification with German culture and their conviction that America was far behind Europe, intellectually and culturally. Those who came in the 1820s came because little held them, and when they arrived they improvised religious lives because they had no other choice.

The life that immigrant Jews left behind posed one question for men and women: "What do I *do* to be a Jew?" The answer had been provided by Jewish law, upheld and interpreted by the community governed by religious authority responsible to a local noble or monarch.[5] Individual Jews were responsible to traditional religious authority. The majority of Eastern European Jews had lived in homogeneous, traditionally bound communities since the sixteenth century. Their indigenous authority, the *kehillah* (polity), originated in Poland in the seventeenth century and was intermittently outlawed and revitalized. It guided all civic and economic as well as religious matters through a combined executive body of the wealthy members of the community and religious experts. The organization oversaw a wide range of voluntary associations that controlled and organized the lives of many individuals. Charity committees and the burial society were some examples of such groups (Goren 1970, 5–8).

Immigrant American Judaism, by contrast, reflected the place of religion in American society. For the nineteenth-century Jewish immigrant, Judaism for the first time was a "preference," a choice. From the point of view of American society, religion was a voluntary activity, not a governmentally controlled one.[6] This was the first time many Jews had not lived in a church-dominated nation. Tradition in America was enforced communally, if at all; it was not the concern of the state. Many immigrant Jews underwent a transformation as a result. They had once lived within a Jewish culture, and now they practiced a religion called Judaism. Obviously more cosmopolitan Jews in Europe had been exposed to pluralist enclaves within society. But no immigrants had experienced the total separation of church and state enjoyed by Americans. The traditional question for Jews, "What do I do?" was replaced by the new American question, "*How* do I complete this religious requirement?" Shortly, the question also became "Why do I do it?" Judaism increasingly became the concern of the individual rather than the community and was focused on option rather than obligation, and on personal identity rather than group norms.[7] Immigrants' work lives hurtled them into economic success and aspirations for Americanization. The synagogue came to answer the newly acculturating immigrants' questions about how to be Jews in the new world.[8]

The First Wave: The German Jewish Synagogue

In the United States in 1820, there were hardly any Jews. In 1695 the one hundred Jews in New York were descendants of Portuguese Jews expelled from Portugal and Brazil. By 1795 only 350 Jews lived in a city whose population numbered 33,000. They shared a single synagogue and maintained an elite subculture identified as neo-Portuguese throughout the nineteenth century (Mitchell 1978, 23, 25). Between 1820–1850 more than 245,000 Jews arrived, mostly from Germany. They moved beyond New York, and synagogues and Jewish settlements proliferated throughout the United States. The absence of authority and hierarchy within the community did not signal the end of Jewish observance for these people. Though Judaism became a less demanding system of observance than it had been, it persisted. The synagogues were media of acculturation, but they also provided links with the past.[9]

The early nineteenth-century immigrants to America came wanting economic freedom, and their piety was then necessarily compromised.[10]

For most it was virtually impossible to avoid violating religious prohibitions because of the need to work constantly. People worked on the Sabbath and Jewish festivals, which the tradition forbade. Some laws and observances fell into disuse. The immigrants' lives required a different kind of synagogue and Judaism than they had known in the traditional communities of Germany.[11]

Synagogue leaders in America did not receive Jewish educations of any substance in Germany. They therefore lacked the ability to understand much beyond their own experiences and needs; hence, lay synagogue life focused on only those needs. Religious authority became what members remembered from their childhood homes in Germany and what was necessitated by the American life style. No one exhorted them to Sabbath observance. They could not seek out a rabbi for answers to questions about the requirements for observances. Necessity and sentimentalized religion counted for more than the authority of classical texts that guided the highly educated European rabbinate. The laity chose and discarded laws according to their new lives (Dawidowicz 1982b, 19). Domination by the laity in America began as a necessity. Synagogues were created and then chosen by people on the basis of affinity with peers. One sought a synagogue where other men from one's hometown worshipped. Synagogues were initially the domain of men. Though women attended at certain times of the year, usually for short periods, sitting behind the curtain or in the gallery mandated by Jewish law, they were literally only peripheral figures. What a man sought from hometown ties, as noted above, was not only friendship but familiar worship. In a hometown synagogue the same prayer melodies and all the minute, particular customs and local variations in the liturgy were available. Though Jewish liturgy is virtually standard, its melodies and associated gestures vary even within the same country or region. (Blau 1976, 30, 49). The familiar music, faces, and customs in worship made the past available in the present. America was a long way from that past, but through prayer immigrants could bridge the distance.

In time rabbis came to America, as did increasing numbers of the educated Jewish elite. The failed liberal 1840 revolution in Germany forced many such people to leave. Those who preceded them, however, were not anxious to cede their power to experts, and laities continued to dominate. Rabbis served rather than led (Jick 1976, 69–70). Thus, immigrants who had been at the bottom of the Jewish hierarchy in Europe came to regard themselves as the only necessary authorities on Judaism.

The laity was affected not only by its release from traditional communal structures and authority but by its attraction to democracy as well. Jewish immigrants and their children were known for creating organizations, miniscule or grand, that boasted elaborate bylaws, constitutions, and meetings conducted according to parliamentary procedures canonized in *Roberts' Rules of Order.* Slates of officers demanded extensive electoral politics. Democracy was institutionalized in synagogues as it was in subsequent family-based social clubs. "Cousin clubs" were formed by the children of these immigrants. The cousins and siblings now met formally because upward mobility made it possible for extended families to live in separate houses and neighborhoods (S. Rosenberg 1965; Mitchell 1978).[12] Lay leaders invoked American political ideology to support their control in religious matters. As a result, not only was the power of rabbis undercut, but the possibility of creating a single kehillah-like structure for American Jews was precluded in the dense population of New York.[13]

One nineteenth-century attempt to create a synod of congregations, for example, was defeated by member synagogues with voices of opposition like this one from the Congregation Beth Elohim of South Carolina:

> All conventions founded or created for the establishment of any ecclesiastical authority whatever . . . are alien to the spirit and genius of the age in which we live and are wholly inconsistent with the spirit of American liberty. (cited in Temkin 1973)[14]

Lay control of the synagogue made changes in Jewish liturgical services a relatively easy matter. Initially, the changes were rarely grounded in doctrinal disagreement. Beliefs were not the subjects of conflicts in America as they were at the same historical period in Europe. Contested issues concerned decorum or etiquette (Sklare 1972; Jick 1976, 47; Hoffman 1987). American Jews were concerned with the commonsense meaning of decorum, "good taste," in their religious lives. It preoccupied them because a changing society had altered their sense of what "good taste" meant. Lawrence Hoffman describes decorum as "prayer service choreography," contrasting it with prayer content and structure (1977, 140). Jews achieved this "good taste" through altering choreography. Decorum has been a matter of importance to sociologists, historians, and Jewish laity and rabbis because of its centrality to the development of the synagogue in both Europe and America. Decorum involves what Erving Goffman (1959) called "impression management," a presentation of the self to the self and others carefully controlled to communicate particular meanings.[15] In the prayer context, it refers quite specifically to how people behave as they pray, as they listen to others praying, and how their participation in general is orchestrated. Impression management extends from the individual to the environment for prayer he or she creates. Synagogue appearance, interior and exterior, also reflects issues of decorum because it symbolizes and regulates statements about the self in relationship to others.

The "Orientalism" of traditional European Jewish prayer, as German Reformers put it, was judged offensive. Jewish worship appeared to their increasingly American eyes and ears as chaotic, lacking harmony and Western aesthetics. Men prayed apart from women at their own pace, mumbling, shuffling their feet and swaying their bodies. Cantors used chants with Oriental origins. There were no weekly sermons to parallel ministers' lessons on the Bible. There was no singing in unison. European synagogues customarily auctioned off honors associated with the Torah reading. On certain holidays men would pay for the honor of blessing the Torah, most of them unable to read the difficult Hebrew in which the Torah scroll is written. That money, like other funds raised by appeals during services, went to support the synagogue and rabbi. The conjunction of money and the sacred was judged coarse and inappropriate by Americanized Jews and their children. Most immigrant Jews highly regarded the use of English in the service, as well as rabbis who could "preach" in English rather than Yiddish or German. They also desired an orderly service freed from private side conversations that characterized the old world *shul.*

Nineteenth-century immigrant decorum changed dramatically within the German Jewish community over time and subsequently differed in the German and Eastern European communities. Initially the hometown synagogue provided the decorum for the first gatherings for prayer of new Americans. It was derived from the traditional Jewish service of European orthodoxy and most resembled the sort of service described above. As Jews began to acculturate in the immediate decades following the first wave of immigration in 1820 much of this prayer choreography changed. Within a decade the laity of these synagogues turned its attention to matters of decorum, passing rule upon rule dictating how people were required to behave. Though head covering was still required for men, for example, the appearance of head covering was legislated. Variation in hats was considered undignified and ugly. Some synagogues required that all men put on identical paper caps provided by an usher.

The changes in decorum multiplied and became more dramatic by 1840. Jews began disregarding the tradition's laws. As Americanizing Jews began to create a more American service, they took more liberties with halaha, the content of the tradition. Men stopped covering their heads in the synagogue. Men and women sat together in "family pews" introduced by Rabbi Isaac Meyer Wise in Albany, New York, in 1851. Rabbis took pulpits and were expected to preach sermons in English, as Protestant ministers did. Organ music was introduced. New prayerbooks were written, primarily in English, excising portions of the traditional liturgy.[16] These changes did not constitute a systematic program. They were piecemeal, as were German Jews' observances of religious law, much to the chagrin of Reform rabbis from Germany who were among the first to come to America after the failed liberal revolution of 1848. When David Einhorn, one of the great proponents of classical Reform, arrived in 1855, he was horrified by the melange of ad hoc innovations he found in synagogue rituals. American Judaism presented to him a strange conjunction of total laxness in personal piety and selective conservatism in the synagogue. He explained to his first congregants that a real reform of Judaism, modeled on the movement in Germany, could not be completed in this manner, but needed to be consistently and truly radical. His own followers ignored and criticized him. Early Reform rabbis moved from synagogue to synagogue rather often over such disagreements (Jick 1976, 167; Raphael 1984, Chapters 2 and 3).

By 1870 the changes were far more dramatic. Lay boards transformed liturgy and law creating synagogues, particularly among the elite, that were replicas of churches. Once impoverished immigrants of the early 1800s were now firmly established, affluent Americans, constituting a society of their own. Their mode of worship signaled that arrival. Stephen Birmingham's description of Temple Emanu-El, one of the most famous synagogues of New York's German Jewish elite, clarifies what the synagogue symbolized.

> The attempt to bridge opposing worlds is apparent in the physical structure of Temple Emanu-El itself. Inside, with its pews and pulpit and handsome chandeliers—where hatted women worship alongside the men (unhatted), and not in a separate curtained gallery—it looks very like a church. But outside, as a kind of gentle gesture

> to the past, its Moorish facade calls to mind a synagogue. (1967, 131)

The changes that accompanied such architecture reflected acculturation on the way to assimilation.

The developments in the American synagogue reflect the common and opposed interests of the rabbinate and the laity. The Reform rabbis who came to the United States wrote the prayerbooks that carefully reflected developing theologies debated among colleagues. It was the rabbis, in fact, who created an American Reform denomination and began rabbinical training by the 1870s. Though these activities had lay support, they were not lay motivated. The laity maintained control at the local level within the synagogues. And while the denomination was interested in continuity and ideological platforms, the rank and file created synagogues and passed rules that maintained social class homogeneity and a Judaism that would reflect their growing affluence and place in American society.

Though these Jews called themselves Reform by 1840, it was decades before their Judaism resembled the movement envisioned by the nineteenth-century founders of Classical German Reform. And it was the rabbis who actively created that resemblance. The new Americans were not interested in applying Jewish messianism to contemporary society to create a liberal utopia. In the nineteenth century in Germany and Eastern Europe, a deeply ideological battle was waged among Jews. Reform Judaism developed platforms and tenets of belief that were used to differentiate it from traditional Judaism. Reformers conceptualized a Western rather than an "Oriental" religion. They wanted to return to the biblical origins of Judaism and to exclude the rabbinic laws, associated with what they called Orientalism, that gave normative Judaism its shape. These changes, they believed, would bring European Jews who had left their religion back to Judaism and would place Jews at the core of Western life (Heller 1966). But few American Reform Jews, even the most philanthropic, saw themselves as "a light to other nations," or a model for social justice and equality. Rather, the Reform the new Americans constructed was an outward form of accommodation to a society they yearned to enter without abandoning their uniqueness (Jick 1976, 140).

By 1850 German Jews were remarkably successful economically. They solidified the link between synagogue and social class by excluding new immigrants, some from Germany but most from Eastern Europe (Jick 1976, 140). They fashioned an American Judaism that was

A classical Reform synagogue in Los Angeles built in the early twentieth century. The use of human figures in the wall decorations, the absence of a women's balcony, and the grand style all communicate the members' aspiration to Americanization.

directly imitative of mainstream Protestantism. They and their leaders sought continuity with American culture, minimized their differences from Protestantism, and created a decorum that in the end was like American Protestantism: uniform, using Western aesthetics, and making the rabbi into a minister. Birmingham, in fact, notes that during the Civil War when Reform Rabbi Sarner was examined by an army board of chaplains, they listed his denomination as "Lutheran" (1967, 131). His attitudes and ideas were apparently compatible to the point of being indistinguishable from the dominant religion.

The synagogue remained the place to pray to God. How one prayed became a powerful expression of social status, of acculturation, and of Americanization. Synagogue decorum modeled and reflected American life. Every ritual gesture seemed worthy of consideration for what it communicated about the immigrant and his or her children's relationship to America. The appearance and comportment of members in prayer defined a synagogue for a prospective member, indicating the degree of acculturation and prosperity of the membership. These social indicators usually signaled that traditional Jewish practices were dramatically altered. German Jews in America generated philanthropic organizations, social clubs, and a world of socializing. But unlike the synagogue, none of these activities bore the primary burden of maintaining and transmitting Judaism. Hence, the synagogue was a volatile institution, constantly changing and reformulating its articulation of Jewish and American worlds.

The immigrants of the 1820s and 30s appeared to have little interest in maintaining the decorum of their hometowns for more than one or two decades. The more cosmopolitan Jews who came after the 1840s were acculturated and minimally observant. Over the span of fifty years, a recognizable institution emerged: the German Reform synagogues of German Jews in America. While there were variations across the country, this type of synagogue emphasized Western decorum and a dramatically altered liturgy. Reform Judaism stood for liberalism and a Judaism that was compatible with America. The synagogue was only one of the concerns of these German Jews in America. However, it was important enough to remain in the control of the laity, setting the pattern for lay domination of synagogue life.

It was in this task that they differed most dramatically from nonimmigrants who were at the comparable period seeking purity: temperance and an end to political corruption. Native-born Christians were trying to find their place in an America that had grown in scale and dimension far beyond what most knew from their small towns. Their attraction to religious movements aimed at reforming society and the self aided in giving them a sense of control in a society that was taking a new shape (see Wiebe 1967). Jewish immigrants flourished economically in this society, but they also struggled to grasp their place in it, not through movements but through the synagogue and other organizations. Few could abandon their Judaism or be singularly encompassed by it. A Judaism that was only generally, rather than particularly, tied to the tradition within a Western aesthetic was their answer. Irving Howe's description of Eastern European immigrant life is remarkably apt for German Jewish immigrants as well:

> Released from the constraints of Europe but not yet tamed by the demands of America, Jewish immigrant life took on a febrile hurry of motion and drive. After centuries of excessive discipline, life overflowed—its very shapelessness gave proof of vitality. Moral norms, while no longer beyond challenge, continued to be those implanted by Orthodox Judaism, but manners changed radically, opening into a chaos of improvisation. The fixed rituals that had bound the east European Jews broke down under the weight of American freedom. The patterns of social existence had to be remade each day. (1976, 170)

While the German Jewish, late nineteenth-century synagogue and religion minimized tradition, those who followed, the Eastern European Jews, formulated a Judaism for America far more evocative of tradition through a different vision of synagogue and decorum.

Eastern European Immigrant Synagogues

From 1840 to 1880, American Judaism appeared to have taken a decisive shape that would determine all future development. In retrospect that shape was peculiar to one period of German immigration, though the power and influence of those more established Jews remains today. What followed was to be more significant for the creation of American Judaism at large. The final mass wave of Jewish immigration began in 1880. It was the largest, ending finally in 1924, interrupted by World War I (Goldstein and Goldscheider 1968, 2). These Jews, originally from Eastern Europe, came in such large numbers that their organizations and ideas about Jewish life overwhelmed any that preceded them. In 1880 there were fewer than 250,000 Jews in America (Goldstein and Goldscheider 1968, 1–2). From 1870 to 1924, 2.5 million Jews migrated to the United States. As different as Eastern European and German Jews were, their synagogues developed in a similar fashion. Decorum emerged as the singular preoccupation for Eastern Europeans as well. They, too, were ready to take control of their religious lives, despite their far deeper commitment to traditional Judaism and Jewish authority.

East European Jews came as the poorer, coarser, and embarrassing kinspeople of the now successfully acculturated German Jews. Both their own and their children's upward mobility and acculturation were equally meteoric. By 1940 their children entered commercial occupations and professions and lived in affluent areas (Eisen 1983, 26–27). They were established in the suburbs having left behind the dense and homogenous ghettos epitomized by New York's Lower East Side where they initially lived. They also left the adjacent areas of the "second settlement" in order to move to the "third settlement"—the residential areas that ring the city. They shared their neighborhoods with more Protestants than Catholics, with more higher status Jews than lower status ones, and with fewer Jews than in the previous settlements. If they wanted to attend worship, they found either large Reform synagogues or a few small Orthodox congregations available (Sklare 1972, 68; Glazer 1956). These neighborhoods demonstrated the successful rise in status of immigrants and generated alternative synagogues as well.

In this environment, Eastern European Jews created a new synagogue and a new decorum. Again, the purpose of the decorum was to bridge old and new worlds and to make worship expressive of that bridging process. These immigrants came to America either as Orthodox Jews, like their German predecessors, or radical secularists, something unknown in Germany (see Howe 1976). Their offspring, the second generation, initially participated less in religious activities than any previous generation of Jews.[17] Most of the synagogues that flourished in the dense Jewish ghettos of the first settlement resembled their early German Jewish counterparts. They consisted of small groups of laity who had lived in the same *shtetels* (small villages) or urban ghettos of Europe. They first formed tiny storefront shuls or synagogues (Howe 1976, 191). These *landslayt* (fellow townsmen), like the earlier Jewish German immigrants, shared styles of worship, melodies for chanting the Torah, and customs in ritual observance. Even when more substantial Orthodox synagogues were built in the areas of the first settlement, their membership continued to reflect the hometowns of participants. Deborah Dash Moore's excellent work on second generation New York Jews describes such immigrant synagogues in an area of Brooklyn (1981,

124–31). All the synagogues followed Orthodox Jewish ritual and barred from membership men who violated the Sabbath. Even these institutions, however, were caught up with Americanization. Moore cites the constitution of one such synagogue. "Every member is required to conduct himself quietly, and not wander about the synagogue during services. During such services he must also refrain from conversation with others" (1981, 125). Moore also notes the lack of aesthetic attractiveness of such synagogues. Generally, smaller ones were housed in rented spaces such as basements or lofts. These small synagogues were ubiquitous in New York's Lower East Side, appearing on every street. They were religious and ethnic in nature, meeting daily for prayer and providing financial and moral support for members in times of need.

These immigrant shuls, however, were not transferred to the more affluent suburbs where immigrants and their children moved as quickly as possible. Like the German Jews a half century before, synagogue membership reflected economic homogeneity based on neighborhood and a shared decorum. By 1924, only 100,000 Jews remained in New York's Lower East Side, where more than 250,000 Jews had previously resided (Moore 1981, 19). The synagogues of the poorer suburbs were not dramatically different from storefronts. They were slightly more affluent and orderly. They continued to emphasize the European aesthetic associated with Ashkenazic Jewry. Order was maintained in behavior rather than prayer. Manners concerned the laity, but so did the maintenance of tradition as it was known in Europe.

The Reform synagogues of the new residential settlement initially held little attraction for Eastern European Jews. The radical transformation of Judaism created by the Reform denomination was unpalatable for them. Instead, they identified with the growing American movement of Conservative Judaism. The third settlement produced loyal adherents who built synagogues and offered a constituency of upwardly mobile immigrants and their offspring.[18] When religion in general revived in the United States in the 1940s and 1950s, Conservative Judaism became the most popular choice for American Jews (Glazer 1972, 122–23). In their rush to Americanize, not only did formerly Orthodox Jews join the more American synagogues, but those who were secularists and previously unaffiliated did so as well. Religion and the suburbs went hand in hand to articulate postwar middle-class American values of consumerism, progress, and generalized ties to tradition.

Conservative Judaism as it is practiced in America began with the endowment of a theological training institution for rabbis, the Jewish Theological Seminary of America. The institution was supported pri-

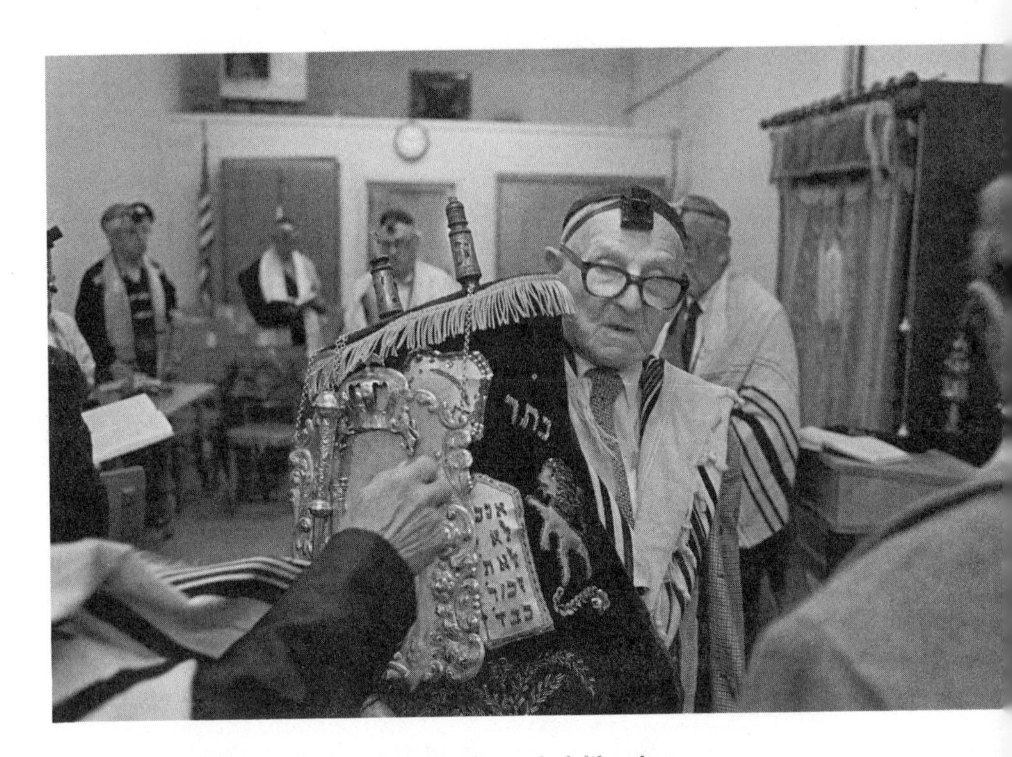

A contemporary Los Angeles storefront shul like those created by Eastern European immigrants. These men are engaged in daily morning prayer which requires the male worshiper to put on the arm and forehead leather straps and a box containing biblical phrases (tefillin). If women are present they are seated behind a curtain adjacent to this room.

marily by wealthy American Reform Jews for the purpose of providing leaders for the newly Americanized Eastern European Jews, who found Reform synagogues unacceptable. It defined itself in opposition to the Reform seminary, Hebrew Union College. Conservative Judaism was associated with a greater commitment to traditionalism, and its leaders invoked the term often.[19] The seminary was also committed to the principles of modern scientific scholarship and differentiated itself from Orthodox Judaism less in terms of religious observance than the faculty's willingness to understand sacred texts in light of the German ideas about biblical criticism. For all the prominence of the seminary, Conservative Judaism is thought of as a lay movement because the men and women who formed the first synagogues in the suburbs chose settings for worship that, in the words of one early Conservative partisan in Minnesota, "promote Modern American Judaism, the old traditional form of the Jewish ritual, [and] omitting such portion of it that would not interest the younger folks and the coming generation" (cited in Raphael 1984, 92). Conservative Judaism developed in its seminary where rabbis were trained *and* in its synagogues where members tried to preserve Jewish tradition and make it compatible with a suburban, affluent life. The seminary was always more conservative than the synagogues. The laity and the seminary often ignored each other, leaving rabbis in the middle. This dual organization within Conservative Judaism allowed these Jews to both maintain a Commitment to tradition and enter the mainstream of American life.

Over time Conservative synagogue decorum in the third settlement encompassed more than the regulation of behavior in worship. Local synagogues embodied an entire approach to Judaism, including service choreography, education, and social organizations. Uniformity pervaded worship as well as manners, not unlike in German American Reform synagogues. In both cases the primary aesthetic was shaped by mainline Protestants. Conservative synagogues differentiated themselves from Reform synagogues precisely around their commitment to religious tradition and law; however, where they relaxed religious observance they maximized an assimilating aesthetic: the use of an organ on the Sabbath or allowing men and women to sit together for worship. The larger the synagogue the more its services necessarily resembled spectacles, orchestrated events that coordinated sermons, choral and cantorial performances, and English responsive readings. Sociologist Marshall Sklare recorded the reaction of a congregation member to his new third settlement synagogue:

> I was born and bred in an orthodox shul with the accompanying multitudinous prayers, jams of people and children all joined together in a cacophonous symphony of loud and sometimes raucous appeals to the Almighty. Here it was different on Yom Kippur [the new year Day of Atonement]. A large group of Jews, men and women, sitting quietly together for hours at a stretch, subdued prayers, no mass movements, no rustling and bustling, no weeping and wailing, no crying children, just the music of the choir and cantor being the only sounds heard. . . . The Machzor (holiday prayer book) was clear, concise, and arranged in order so as to be easily followed when the rabbi announced the page numbers. . . . I listened to the sermon and understood what it was all about. After the services I sat for a few minutes and pondered. What was the score? Which of the sects of Judaism is getting to the ear of heaven first? (1972, 112)

As Eastern European Jews left the first settlement, their Conservative synagogues developed a decorum sensitive to the maintenance of tradition within America. With the increasing affluence of American Jews, the synagogue became more remote and bureaucratized than hometown based associations. It resembled the society in which Jews flourished.

American Judaism and the Third Generation

Both German and Eastern European Jews came to America in a century characterized by the classic Protestant ethic. The dominant ethos encouraged hard work, savings, and sacrifice. Success could be measured by what one amassed. It was the era of the producer (Susman 1984). The goal of the successful individual was to amass and build, not to have and consume. Productivity and sacrifice remained central values for Jewish immigrants with their eyes on success. They worked hard, expected little, saved a great deal, and rapidly created a middle-class life. They saw themselves as producers.

Subsequent generations of American Jews, the descendents of these producers, lived in a dramatically different America for which there were rather different expectations on men and women. Social historian Warren Susman suggests America moved from a producer to a consumer society after 1910, most dramatically in the 1920s and 1930s (1984). Clearly American society felt the effects of that consumer ethos beyond the Second World War and until the 1960s counterculture. As Jews Americanized fully, living in suburbs, moving up in their jobs, and getting better educations, they too felt the effects of these changing expectations, which were reflected in their synagogues. The transition to the suburban synagogue was begun by Reform Jews whose first grand synagogues directly imitated the Protestant churches of the upper classes. Conservative synagogues also reflected their neighbors. Synagogues inevitably would reflect this consumer society. They consciously marketed more activities for families with increasing leisure time. Churches and synagogues competed to capture the additional time available to their members through expanded, often secular, activities.

The third generation encompasses the children of the native born.[20] Those men and women were socialized into the Judaism of America. Most lived in the third settlement and the suburbs. They lived in the postwar affluence that characterized the increasingly consumer oriented, suburbanized society. Most identified themselves as Conservative Jews. Their Judaism was marked by several powerful experiences. They were raised during the American religious revival, a period when Jews and Christians were more involved and active in churches and synagogues. Members of the third generation belonged to the synagogues their parents joined as a result of their birth. Their parents understood their Judaism as compatible with life in America. Indeed, for the second generation being a good Jew and being a good American were virtually the same thing (Eisen 1983, 41).

Jews increasingly identified themselves with certain types of Judaism, with denominations that were either Reform or Conservative. Finally, they belonged to synagogues that aimed to meet a vast array of needs quite apart from worship. The synagogues sought to dominate many of the activities that families either did not participate in or participated in elsewhere: social activities for children, clubs for "young marrieds," and an array of educational and leisure events. In short, the suburban synagogue was increasingly directed to socializing children into a denominationally defined Judaism, keeping them within a Jewish sphere within Jewish neighborhoods. That socialization was upheld by American society and accomplished by the newly developed synagogue center, the type of synagogue that reached its apogee in the third settlement.

In 1964 about three-fifths of all American Jews were affiliated with a synagogue (Hertzberg 1975, 15).[21] The early sixties was the period of Minyan and havurah members' adolescence. They, like most Jews, belonged to synagogues. In the late fifties, sociologists Sklare and Greenblum conducted a major quantitative study of Jewish attitudes and activities in a Chicago suburb, as well as historical research on that organized Jewish community. From 1957–1958, in a generally affluent Midwestern area occupied by German and Eastern European Jewish descendants, 87 percent belonged to synagogues during the eight years of their children's religious education (1979, 181–82). Among the third generation of Eastern European descendants in that area, 96 percent affiliated with synagogues during those years. This affiliation rate is all the more remarkable because regular synagogue attendance was, and remains, very low. For example, a study of Boston Jews in 1975 revealed that only 32 percent of Jews attended synagogue on an occasion other than the new year holidays (Cohen 1983, 56). There was no question that more American Jews belonged to synagogues during the postwar years than ever had before, but the significance of that membership for their religious lives, or the significance of religion in their lives, has not been understood systematically.[22] Precisely because personal religious laxness was high and Jewish education of that generation was minimal, and because Christian suburban families were affiliated with churches, the synagogue appeared as the only stage on which to articulate and present Judaism, particularly for children. For example, one of the older members of the Minyan, raised in a New York suburb in the 1950s, belonged to a Reform synagogue that he often attended alone without his parents. At the same time, he remembered the "magical aura" of the synagogue that he loved; he also remembered his "pleasant memories" of Christmas. "We hung stockings and Christmas was a big thing. My parents kept observing some form of Christmas until my first year at Hebrew Union College when I said I wished they would give it up." This man received all of his Jewish education within the synagogue his suburban parents joined, even though they kept up their protest against their Orthodox immigrant parents by celebrating Christmas at home.

The most significant figure in defining the surburban Conservative synagogue was Rabbi Mordecai Kaplan, who sought to formulate the unique nature of the Conservative synagogue. Kaplan, a long time member of the faculty of the Conservative seminary, ultimately founded another denomination, Reconstructionism, considered the first thoroughly American Jewish denomination, which remained connected to Conservative Judaism ideologically.[23] Out of his loyalty to Conservative Judaism he stayed at the seminary until the 1970s and influenced decades of rabbinical students who were to provide the leadership for the suburban congregations.

The synagogue Kaplan envisioned was a "synagogue center," an idea he introduced in 1918 but that did not take hold fully until the 1920s and 1930s. Kaplan was convinced that Judaism must be lived as a "civilization" rather than as a "religion" (1981). He encouraged Conservative Jews to develop the nonreligious aspects of Judaism, to meet all the needs of synagogue congregants. He wanted Jewish life to focus on the synagogue. The synagogue center included—in addition to facilities for worship—gyms, libraries, youth groups, meeting rooms, clubs, and kitchens. Many observers of the period noted that one could make extensive use of the synagogue without ever participating in worship (for a vivid description, see Dawidowicz 1977). Indeed, quantitative studies of synagogue attendance demonstrate this very point. This was completely contrary to Kaplan's intent, yet the dominant nonreligious aspects of Judaism that his vision enabled created a different Jewish experience than that of other denominations. It would have been unnecessary to create such a synagogue for Orthodox Jews, for whom worship and study were not acts of choice but requirements, and the variety of secular activities would simply be a distraction. Reform Jews, having rapidly attained a higher class, would have found such a center both unnecessary, since leisure needs were well met, and inappropriate, as it might attract lower-class Jews. But the synagogue center, like Conservative Judaism, was a powerful expression of American Jewish life.

The suburbs necessitated concern with the transmission of Judaism because Jews were now a minority, as they had not been in the less affluent settlements they first occupied. In the second settlement, Jewish community centers, modeled on the Young Men's Christian Associations, were a dominant community association. They emphasized the development of the normal Jew who could do everything done by others, and their primary activities were sports and group work. (Moore 1981, 134) The synagogue was centrally concerned with uniqueness, with the maintenance of Jewish tradition, religion and culture. In the suburbs one was forced to be more conscious of Judaism and what it meant, because the surrounding world of neighbors did not reflect or enforce Judaism. In New York, synagogue building reached its pinnacle in 1929. Synagogue centers were built in the uptown portion of the city as well as in the suburbs (Moore 1981, 135). In this period of growth and building, these synagogues were independent and urged to affiliate with a denomination by a confederation of synagogues. The majority of centers, because they sought to define themselves "in the middle," joined the barely developing association of Conservative synagogues, the United Synagogues of America.

As these synagogue centers were pioneered by the second generation and flourished in the suburbs, they continued to define the Jewish religious experience beyond World War II. Sociologist Marshall Sklare asserts that the Conservative synagogue, a more modest facility than the synagogue center, emerged as the crucial institution of Jewish life in the 1950s and 1906s. It was in this period that Kaplan's vision for the synagogue center was realized far beyond New York. From the 1920s to the postwar period, Jews moved to and remained in suburbs and joined synagogues in unprecedented numbers.

Along with the synagogue center and the growth in the number of synagogues, the Reform and Conservative movements emerged as dominant forces in American Judaism. These increasingly organized denominations were attached to elaborate institutional frameworks.[24] As Marshall Sklare so ably demonstrates in his study of the Conservative movement, denominations committed considerable energy to replicating themselves. The denominations did not simply produce rabbis to lead congregations; they also provided leadership in formulating the directions for youth groups, camping movements, education systems, men's and women's divisions, and the host of activities generated by the synagogue center. Because these various divisions were increasingly "denomination specific" after the war, they necessitated an increasingly complex bureaucracy. These activities helped cultivate the loyalty of young Jewish men and women to the Conservative or Reform Judaism they would then perpetuate. One identified oneself as a Jew through these affiliations. One was, for example, a Conservative Jew now, no longer simply a Jew.

As Lavender (1977) shows in his 1971 replication of a 1949 University of Maryland student survey, only a tiny minority thought of themselves as Jews without denominational affiliation. Goldstein and Goldscheider's 1960s data on Providence, Rhode Island, revealed that 95 percent of their sample identified with a Jewish denomination (1968, 176). Respondents in various studies were likely to comment that their observance of dietary laws, or the Sabbath, indicated to themselves, as well as to others, whether they were Conservative or Reform. One Minyan member raised in a Conservative synagogue and Jewish parochial school explained that Judaism was defined for her by what she was told to do and to observe. "I had no kinship feelings with any other Jew who wasn't Jewish as I was. If you are Jewish you do certain things." The denominations defined what was to be done. Denominational identification does not necessarily indicate synagogue membership. Even the unaffiliated often identify with a denomination, though they do not choose to belong to a synagogue.

Postwar American Judaism retained the pattern of a lay-dominated decentralized community, despite the national and institutional nature of denominations. Though denominations had centralized bureaucracies, in reality they were shaped at the local level in synagogues. Denominational youth groups were particularly powerful agents for religious socialization. In the synagogue, denominational styles created loyalty to a particular vision of Judaism. Synagogues were still concerned with decorum, with appearances, with manners, with how to behave and how to pray. Denominations sanctioned what was done in synagogues, and synagogues affiliated with them because their members felt compatible with that denomination. Nathan Glazer illustrated this point in his discussion of what occurred at denominational summer camps.

> What is the good, it has been asked, of taking children away for a summer to a Hebrew-speaking camp so they can learn to say "Please pass the butter" in Hebrew? It makes one no more of a believer to know how to speak in Hebrew than in English. What is happening, however, is that the Conservative Jewish leaders . . . are trying to provide an example of a Jewish life so that it will not be necessary to argue and put out apologetic literature—it will only be necessary to say, "Be a good Jew" and give an example. (1956, 24)

Glazer here distills the very essence of suburban denominational Judaism. Judaism was transmitted by showing people how to be Jews. However, this quotidian of cultural transmission was altered thoroughly. For it was not the family showing one how to be a Jew; it was the synagogue or its denominational camp. It was not the parent or even one's own rabbi showing, but leaders trained by denominations. And it was not the showing of prayer or the traditional forms of Jewish life that taught people how to be Jews. Rather, Jewishness was defined at a peer-oriented camp setting, where Judaism was made normative through knowing the Hebrew word for *butter,* a secular concern at best. The camp Glazer describes is not even a Zionist camp committed to sending children to Israel, which would logically require knowledge of Hebrew. It was a Conservative Jewish camp teaching people to think of themselves as Jews through finite particulars and activities that are not so much religious as Jewish. Camps are not as localized as synagogues, but the camp is reinforced by the synagogue where a similar, though not identical, set of particular actions—music, discussions, prayers, and peer relations—are enacted.

Several Minyan members attended this particular camp in the East and Midwest. One woman described her experience. "There was my camp experience which tied Jewish things to beauty for me. I went every year from 1958–1969, except for the year I lived in Israel. The camp really raises to an art Judaism as an aesthetic and beautiful experience. There, beauty, creativity, even anti-war sentiments were put into a Jewish frame." She learned from the camp what Judaism could be, even if it was not realized in her own synagogue experience, and it created a positive Jewish identity for her.

As religiously lax as the homes of most of the campers may have been, the parents wanted their children to learn to be Jews and remain Jews. They agreed with their denominations that through activity and example they would learn what an American Jew is. They chose their synagogue or denomination according to their level of comfort as Jews and Americans, by the look of the synagogue and the ability of the synagogue "staff" to make them feel comfortable. The postwar family was the synagogue consumer.

Why the denominations provided, in conjunction with the local synagogue, an accessible and useful formulation for one's Judaism is a more complex process than the simple sociological truism that institutions replicate themselves. The denomination had a different effect on the second and third generations. For the second generation Jews who swelled the ranks of the suburban Conservative synagogues, Conservative Judaism, as Sklare noted, provided the best repository for their own childhood memories of Judaism. Their immigrant parents brought and immediately altered their own European Judaism. Yet they seemed to have instilled a concern for Jewish tradition in their children that their German counterparts had not. Conservative synagogues maintained more of the traditional liturgy and ritual prohibitions, alongside services that were still American and decorous. They Americanized worship without rendering it unrecognizable. The second generation of American Jews used American Jewish institutions, both for their own social and religious needs and as models, to "fashion their own moral community." These institutions were "instruments of self perpetuation" reinforcing the participants' Americaness and Judaism simultaneously (Moore 1981, 9). They perpetuated a communal Jewish life, and did so under a religious, as opposed to secular, banner. Denominations flourished in America. Orthodoxy did not die as predicted; it was shaped by the denominational model into modern orthodoxy (Liebman 1974). Reform and Conservative Judaism solidified their institutional bases.

Each had hoped to speak for all American Jews. Each came to recognize it would not, concentrating instead on developing a denomination.

Because the third generation, children of the native born, was the first generation raised predominantly as Conservative Jews, they did not expect or need a repository for memories because their childhood experiences were not tied directly to Europe. Hence, the denominations for this generation were agencies of socialization charged with ensuring continuing Jewish identification by these children. Precisely because synagogues were capable of socializing children through their schools, they came to play a new and essential role for American Jews. They took over the basic form of Jewish socialization that a century before was associated with the family (Ackerman 1969). In addition to teaching Hebrew and sacred texts, the denominations and their synagogue centers institutionalized the "child orientation" of Judaism. If, as Herbert Gans suggested, the major question facing second generation parents was "how to make them [their children] *feel* they were Jews," the answer lay in a child oriented synagogue Judaism (1956a, 426). As one synagogue official said at a 1948 convention of Conservative synagogues:

> Conservative Judaism maintains dignity in Judaism. . . . After all, why did we drift away from the so-called Orthodox point of view? Because we recognize that . . . [it] is obsolete in America. We want to create a service that should be applicable to our children and to future generations. (Sklare 1972, 96)

Conservative Judaism's orientation to children focused community resources and synagogue programs on children's needs and problems. Adults "abstained" from Jewish activities and communities because they were not drawn to the synagogue by the obligations of Jewish law or the force of community. The traditional Jewish community is and was oriented to adults, and children learned to be adults by preparing to assume adult functions (Gans 1956b, 556). Indeed, a study of the Boston Jewish community reveals that parents with school aged children are most active in Jewish life and most likely to belong to synagogues (Cohen 1983, 125). As imperfect as the suburban Jewish education might have been, it provided children the norms of Jewish life. Most families usually generated the sentiments that would attach their children to Judaism, but synagogues had to provide the rest.

One Minyan member commented on how he acquired a religious education and how his parents participated.

> My parents were not religious people, but because they had grown up in a small town they thought it was very important to be around other Jewish people. In the third or fourth grade, my father asked if I wanted to become bar mitzva. I asked what that was. I said yes and he said it was up to me, but I would have to go three afternoons a week and on Sunday. I did that for six years. By osmosis this stuff got to me, though I learned almost nothing. I became very pious. My parents never got more observant. My mother's not natural at observing things.

This institutional orientation to the child was by no means unique to Jews. It tended to characterize the entire American middle class. Beginning with the period of demand for reform early in the twentieth century, America's new middle class seemed unusually preoccupied with children and focused more of their socialization within institutions. Christopher Lasch noted that educational reformers hoped the schools would, rather than merely educate, socialize by isolating the student from other influences. In the eyes of Progressive reformers, the schools were preferable for socialization precisely because they were centralized and bureaucratized, the very conditions of American life that emerged to create an urban middle class (1979, 233, 239). The Progressives viewed the child as the hope for a new world they envisioned. If Americans in the nineteenth century viewed the process of molding youth as "like cyclically reproducing like," then the Progressives thought of that molding as "fluid progress," a process demanding constant attention (Wiebe 1967, 169).

American Jews participated centrally in the orientation to children begun early in the twentieth century. For the children molded by synagogues and families were not like their parents or grandparents and required religious educations to instill not only ritual knowledge, history, and a certainty about Judaism but a place to feel normal as a Jew among Jews. These were no longer immigrants creating an ad hoc decorum. Rather, parents looked to experts and specialized institutions to provide an important service that they felt unable to provide.

As denominations grew in numbers and expanded their activities, American Jews, as noted, became less observant. What the synagogue sought (increased commitment of all Jews) was not achieved. Stuart Rosenberg summarized the "common denominator" of American Judaism as "laxity, compromise and non-meticulous concern with the comprehensive regimen of religious conduct which the tradition requires" (1965, 206). His assertion was borne out by the major community studies that demonstrated that in the 1950s and 1960s individuals attended the synagogue four to eleven times per year. Attendance was minimal, but more widespread than home observance of rituals (Sklare and Greenblum 1979, 62–64; Cohen 1983; Kramer and Leventman 1961, 152–53, 159; Goldstein and Goldscheider 1968, 171–205). However, Jewish "identification" remained palpable. Jews continued to join synagogues, educate their children religiously, and encourage their participation in youth groups (Herberg 1950). One Minyan member who described his father's ambivalence about being Jewish, nevertheless remembered that when he was five his father bought a *menorah* (the nine-branched candelabra lit on the festival of Hanukah) saying, "You should know that you are a Jew."

The synagogue-oriented transmission of Judaism focused on "being a Jew," or what came to be called identity. Jewish identity was expressed through synagogue membership for a great majority of the Jewish community. From the perspective of individual Jews, what was sought was a continuing expression of Jewishness articulated occasionally through prayer. The needs of institutions and American Jews met in that denominational codification of Judaism, Jewishness and American middle-class suburban life. Historian Arnold Eisen noted that the second generation produced almost no Jewish theology, interested instead in ideology and loyalty. He calls the Judaism of that generation a "halfway covenant," concerned with tradition and not God (1983, 178–179). Denominational Judaism flourished in the soil of organizational loyalty.

Occupational specialization was linked to affluence, and a specialized synagogue provided identity without demanding the total commitment of orthodoxy. Middle-class identities were continually segmented between loyalty to religion, profession, family, and leisure interests. The synagogue drew in all members of the family and often drew its membership from a limited number of professional and commercial occupations. But it could not integrate the identity of its members in a society that had fragmented them. Its most important function was to keep the religious-ethnic identity alive and vital.

The children who grew up in the suburban synagogue centers, amid often unobservant families, were the recruiting ground for membership in groups like the Minyan. They focused on the contradictions of the suburbs. Deborah Dash Moore noted the effect of these contradictions.

> So successful were they [the second generation] in binding middle-class norms to visions of Jewish fulfillment, that their children often could not disentangle the two. In the children's eyes even the over-stuffed furniture of their parents home reflected a middle-class synthesis, as utterly bourgeois and Jewish as a decorous synagogue service. Though second generation Jews did not jettison their Jewishness, they rejected much of their immigrant background as "foreign," and adopted American styles instead. (1981, 11)

The Power of Synagogue Decorum

In the beginning of the twentieth century, a period in which the majority of American Jews acculturated, Conservative Judaism developed and Reform Judaism consolidated its gains as an urban American middle class emerged. Historian Robert Wiebe suggests that this social class was increasing in numbers and influence in the 1890s (1967, 111–12). The new social class was not well defined. It encompassed men and women in law, medicine, teaching, architecture, business, labor, and agriculture. Though diverse in occupation, they held in common their professional specialization, their ability to contribute to the new urban-industrial system, and their expertise certified by special training and degrees. The occupations of the middle class provided an identity (Wiebe 1967, 113, 129). Indeed, these men and women, full of confidence and drive, Wiebe asserts, had not broken cleanly from their ethnic pasts because the feelings invested in that past were "too powerful to destroy" (1967, 131). Perhaps it was in response to their own outsider identity that they sought to make achievement the basis of success in American society and to merge loyalty to their ethnic or religious ties with loyalty to America. The children of Eastern European Jews and second and third generation American German Jews aspired to and entered many of these very professions in their search for social mobility, though not until the 1930s. They were people focused on action, the hallmark of the new middle class. They committed themselves to building synagogues and creating settings for their children's religious educations. Ironically, they rarely participated in worship, but founded the synagogues as monuments to their own ideas of a Judaism consistent with America, to be used by their children. People for whom being a professional was a key element in achieving an American identity were people in flux, men and women who were creating new identities because the old ones no longer worked. Judaism was a key component in that identity, and their search is more than apparent in the development of American Judaism.

Members of the professionalized and occupationally specialized middle class were consumers. Work was in large part motivated by consumption. Work provided an identity for the professional and consumer goods for the family. Consumption, suburban living, and work all contributed to family members' identities. These self-definitions were self-made and self-expressive. They did not rest entirely in history, in place of origin or extended family, but in what came to be called the lifestyle. There were no master identities, one version of reality that encompassed all others. The professional identity was important, but in the case of Jews, it did not erase one's connection to Judaism. As Wiebe noted, ethnicity was not wiped out. Rather, this crucial time from 1890–1930 marked the period in which Jews began to occupy new professions, move to new areas of cities, and to create new kinds of synagogues. Following the Second World War Jews were fully associated with the consumer society. Their synagogues did not create Americanization, but they effectively responded to it by socializing immigrants and then their children to that society. As Harold Weissberg put it:

> American Jews reflect the general social and economic changes since the war and possess strikingly similar institutional apparatus and ideological attitudes to those of the general American-leisure-consumption status class. They manifest so many of the traits which sociologists and social critics attribute to the new American bourgeoisie (the familiar affluent society) that they may be said to epitomize it. (1972, 349)

Through a chosen decorum, those at prayer communicated to themselves and others who the people at prayer were. In a pluralistic, rapidly changing society that fostered mobility, self-presentation was the constant concern of acculturating people. The synagogue was expressive of Americanization and served as a bridge between worlds and a medium for formulating identity in part through decorum. The synagogue also constituted a community, one that represented the Jewish people themselves. Identity then was formulated and expressed within the synagogue, symbolic of the Jewish people. Because synagogue decorum articulated the relationship between Jewishness and Americanization for Jews collectively, it mirrored Jews together relating to America and to themselves. Even though Jews infrequently prayed, synagogue membership was an essential component of Jewish identity and uniqueness within America. Their synagogue had to enable that act of identification. Frequently Jewish identity took form and was reinforced in relationship to the synagogue.

Uniformity came to characterize American decorum.[25] How uniformity was articulated within decorum became one of the major divisions between synagogues. The more traditional the synagogue was, the more its participants were willing to enforce uniformity in behavior, but not in prayer. In contrast to immigrant, first settlement synagogues, both acculturating German and Eastern European Jews, at various points on the social-class ladder, were committed to keeping people in their seats quietly and forbidding private conversations. Both communities were concerned with issues of good taste and American standards of attractiveness for their buildings. However, they did not agree on extending decorum to praying. It was only Reform Jews, and the most acculturated and suburbanized Conservative Jews, who thought decorum should govern how people prayed and who legislated the tone, volume, and pace of prayer. These more acculturated communities encompassed all of religious life into an aesthetic of uniformity and order. The cacophony and responsiveness that typified Ashkenazic prayer were banished (Heilman 1983). Prayer was to resemble mainstream Protestant worship, so that Jews could assert continuity between their own worship and that of their American neighbors.

Historians of German Reform and American Judaism inevitably associate decorum with an early stage of religious change. Decorum is presented as paving the way for the more serious issues of theological developments. If ideological platforms, prayerbooks, and theology were the provinces of rabbis, decorum was the province of the laity, and an embarrassing one at that. As Temkin writes:

> Trivial as the differences in practice might seem when viewed against the philosophy of religion and the history of Judaism, they assumed great importance in the eyes of the unlearned and could lead to discord within congregations and strained relations between them. (1973, 7)

I have understood decorum, the province of the laity, as key to the formulation of Jewish identity in America. Decorum engages the individual at the juncture of the social and the sacred. It symbolizes social identity more readily than theological meaning because it emphasizes form and convention. It is enforced socially and not by religious law (Grimes 1982, 40). Precisely that juncture, however, was and remains vulnerable for persons whose ability to fit into America is itself a religious issue. How to remain a Jew and hence maintain Judaism was the bedrock issue for all Jews seeking uniqueness within their American lives. Decorum—formal and conventional synagogue action—supported claims to both Judaism and Americanization. Immigrant decorum evolved and changed as the meaning of Judaism was altered for each generation. The producer's decorum was not that of the consumer's decorum. The suburban Conservative synagogue sought to define more than etiquette; it attempted as much to create a Jewish identity within a middle-class framework as it sought to create a middle-class identity within a Jewish framework. The suburban synagogue emphasized activity, organization, and finite, concrete expressions of Judaism. It was neither a benevolent society nor exclusively a house of prayer. It was an extension of middle class suburban life that could maintain one's compatibility with America and ensure one's uniqueness as a Jew. Liturgy, education, and social clubs within the synagogue shifted Jewish forms to make a general Jewish message of continuity with tradition most palatable.

Synagogue activity and decorum are examples of what Erving Goffman called a "focused gathering," an encounter fenced off from everyday life by gates (1961, 8). Reality is to some extent held off by these artificial fences, but is nevertheless introduced through them. The world provided by the fence introduces, but controls, the larger reality (1961, 78–80). In the earliest immigrant synagogues where decorum was a fence that regulated behavior alone, the alien and desired society of America was there to be imitated. Wealth was to be produced, and America was to be claimed. The early synagogues were proving grounds for the possibility of Americanizing Judaism. The fences became more complex as Eastern Europeans wished to retain more of the Jewish tradition and to maintain their compatibility with America. Decorum then became one expression of the creation and perfection of that developing identity.

This identity carried the weight of the answer to their question, "How and why do I observe Jewish law?" To know oneself as a Jew through activity and organization sanctioned by the synagogue directly replaced traditional law as the expression of Judaism. "How do I act as a Jew?" the question which the entire synagogue addressed, overshadowed the question of tradition, "What do I do to be a Jew?" The latter question was the product of a closed culture, a culture not similarly preoccupied with identity. The traditional Jew sought to accurately perform the law of God. He or she asked "Have I done this properly and with the right intention?" The answers appeared to be free of time and space because they were offered by authorities who were eternal and immutable—divine texts.

The questions of American Jews, who seem above all concerned with the meaning of their identity, are not focused on what are the right traditional acts. They rejected the unambiguous answers of orthodoxy that provided a series of right actions that did not take account of American society. Acculturating Jews are people who live in a "leaky" rather than a "closed culture." American Jews are not so much concerned with getting it right, that is, fitting in. Judaism is viewed by these adherents as a historically based religion, no longer an unchanging or eternal one. And it must now be acceptable to one's diverse neighbors, relevant to the issues of one's secular American life and era. That acceptability was tested by the standards of one's immediate world. One can negotiate an absolute religion because the basis of negotiation is much clearer. The fragility of American Judaism rests on the fact that negotiation is difficult because the foundation for change or continuity is uncertain. The fragility of the unchanging formulation was evident in the American experience, however, because its claim was total. When a total Jewish experience was impossible, all was threatened. Tradition as a total way of life collapsed. What remained was "being Jewish," or identity. Decorum seemed the most potent medium for translating world view to identity, the timeless to the historically relative.[26] Ronald Grimes (1982) suggests that decorum is a social matter displaying roles and statuses. Among American Jews, decorum borrowed ritual authority because it was endowed with religious significance. Decorum was the medium through which Jews articulated the significant messages they wished their religion to convey. These often contradictory messages emphasized identity, continuity, and change.

The religious enterprise potentially roots its adherents by defining reality both broadly and particularly. To know who and where one is in the world is to embrace a world view. Synagogue decorum did and does this. What is both striking and predictable in American Judaism is that because a synagogue decorum evolved that broke so radically with childhood, it transformed the synagogue into an assimilating vehicle that helped "relocate" what had been dislocated.

While decorum may guide behavior, it engages an internal experience as well. In fact, the synagogue audience is a rather narrow one. One's suburban Gentile neighbors do not watch a service. They see the outside of a synagogue, not the minute matters of head covering or conversation inside. If the decorum of the new world turned old-world Jews into Americans, the audience for this transformation was other Jews and, most importantly, the self. Like all ritual, etiquette and decorum are actions that necessarily precede belief. As they acted out synagogue decorum, they became convinced of who they were, where they belonged, and what aspirations they might have. Synagogues looked American and sounded American, even those that also echoed the sounds of tradition. In performing a ritual, one rehearsed one's own identity and became convinced of it. Synagogue attendance not only renewed the old but asserted and defined the present.[27]

The synagogue, then, followed the pattern for Jewish participation in all of American life. It acculturated Jews. But, in addition, it preserved and maintained continuity with a Jewish past that was religious, communal, and appeared less likely to change. The synagogue kept alive the rich symbols of Jewish life, even while it changed them. It provided a context for individual rites of passage, making sure a Jewish setting was available. And it was there for the festivals of the Jewish year, even as participation in these events dwindled. By providing a transitional context for acculturating Jews, the synagogue continued to maintain the volatile relation between ancient tradition and secular society that would be constantly readjusted.

The synagogue has waxed and waned in popularity. Even in its most popular times, it has never been successful at attracting the majority of American Jews to attend even monthly Sabbath services. It no longer provides a transition because contemporary Jews no longer require Americanization. Yet the "empty gestures" of decorum remain full of significance. They continue to preoccupy Jews and continue to act as the basis for the acceptance or rejection of a synagogue or Judaism itself. The Minyan and groups like it attacked the decorum of Conservative Judaism because of its aesthetics, its blend of tradition and American society. And like all the generations that preceded them, Minyan and other havurah members preferred to create a new decorum rather than to challenge theology or liturgy, attack tradition, or take on the entirety of its requirements.

The year the Minyan was founded, sociologist Marshall Sklare wrote, "It is hard to find a principled opponent of the American synagogue" (1971, 124). What appeared to one generation as a bland and completely acceptable fixture of the American Jewish landscape was to be another generation's rallying point for a "new" Judaism.

Notes

1. John Bodnar's (1985) analysis of immigration in this period stresses that the ethnic church was vulnerable to strains and conflicts experienced by no other immigrant

institution (Chapter 5). My argument in this chapter suggests why religious institutions would be vulnerable to such conflicts.

2. David Martin notes that a voluntary association like a church could play this role only because the scale of society was still intimate enough so that meaning could be expressed within organizations that provided relationships. Massive industrialization destroys the relational nature of society, he argues, and focuses human beings on the mass media, where their empathy, rather than relationships, rapidly turns to apathy (1978, 91–92). I argue throughout that the voluntary association is still a viable form for expressing meaning because mass-scale society necessitates the creation of relationships between, rather than within, the institutions of complex society.

3. I found useful discussions of this period in Hudson 1981, and Marsden 1980.

4. Bodnar (1985) argues that the normative pattern for immigrants was for earlier generations to model middle-class behavior for newer ones (118). German Jews not only provided a model but actively worked to demand middle-class behavior of Eastern European Jews through their distribution of philanthropic funds.

5. For a discussion of the transformation of traditional Jewish authority in Europe, see Katz 1971; 1981.

6. Goldstein and Goldscheider describe this process as a "triple melting pot, single structure." They claim that ethnic or religious differences maintain visibility, while a single structure homogenizes and encompasses them (1968, 240). Handlin suggests this is true for all nineteenth-century European immigrants as well (1951).

7. Bellah et al. (1985) argue that since its eighteenth-century founding, America has been a society that promotes individualism and has remarkably underdeveloped ideologies of community. The rapidity with which European Jews acculturated to this individualism is noteworthy.

8. Perry Miller's essay "Errand Into the Wilderness" (1964) addressed how succeeding generations of Puritans descended from America's European settlers shaped their Christianity. He notes that subsequent generations were preoccupied with their spiritual failures, actually cataloging them in church. They turned to a preoccupation with work and success as a result of their failure both in Christian ideals and in living up to their forebearers visions. Any immigration that originally and subsequently took on religious symbolism inevitably led to a transformation of that religion.

9. See Will Herberg (1960) for a discussion of the evolution of the "immigrant church."

10. See Feingold for his discussion of the economic opportunities German Jews encountered (1982, 27–55).

11. I am indebted to Leon Jick's excellent work (1976) on the Americanization of the synagogue for much of this discussion.

12. In his study of New York family clubs, William Mitchell (1978) notes that cousin clubs had elaborate governance procedures. While there was a great propensity to form and join organizations, there was also a persistent insistence on "maintaining personal identity within a group." A disorderly democracy emerged from the contradiction, which he contends is characteristic of American-Eastern European Jewish culture.

13. Arthur Goren describes the New York Kehillah that existed in the 1920s, the one attempt to recreate the polity. The founders sought "to establish a comprehensive communal structure. [They] envisioned a democratically governed polity which would unite the city's multifarious Jewish population, harness the group's intellectual and material resources and build a model ethnic community" (1970, 3). Goren also explains why the model could not be sustained.

14. Timothy L. Smith argues that the claim that lay domination of American ethnic religious organizations was the sole result of immigrants' encounter with democracy in host societies misunderstands the importance of the laity in central or southern European religion (1971, 241). However, Smith does not discuss how a tradition of lay domination was affected by the absence of religious leaders, nor does he acknowledge the implications of the laity refusing to give up its power for the practice of religion in America. His conclusions, nevertheless, agree with my own, that new citizens focused on "their own needs" in fashioning religious communities, and that these needs were conceived in both new as well as traditional terms.

15. Lawrence Hoffman described what I define as decorum in the following way: "The very act of worship takes on the function of identifying for the worshiper what he or she stands for, what real life is like, what his or her aspirations are" (1987, 67).

16. See Hoffman (1977) for a discussion of the development of Reform prayer books.

17. The "generational hypothesis" has been a particularly popular one in the sociology of American Jews. Distance from immigration is interpreted as a major determinant of religious behavior, profession, education, and the place and type of residence. These differences are dramatically marked for the three to four generations that followed mass Eastern European Jewish migration. Homogeneous behavior between generations in the last decade has been demonstrated (Goldscheider 1986). In other words, the children of native-born Jews and their offspring will not differ as dramatically from one another as the foreign born and their children and grandchildren differed from one another (see, for example, Sklare and Greenblum 1979; Goldstein and Goldscheider 1968; Gans 1958; and Kramer and Leventman 1961).

18. See Moore (1981) for a thorough discussion of second generation Jews in New York. Lucy Dawidowicz also wrote about this generation, characterizing it, in part, by the fact that at least three-fourths of the first generation of Jewish parents neglected to educate their children as Jews. This fact obviously contributed significantly to their estrangement. (1982a, 60)

19. Hoffman (1987) argues similarly that all American Jewish denominations are created in opposition to other groups that appear on the scene. Hence, every denomination and prayer book's self-definition was necessitated by the presence of a new movement or group from whom they were differentiated (67).

20. Generational reckoning must inevitably be fluid because each decade brought masses of immigrants who differed in age. Hence, the first generation of Jews included men and women who were acculturated at different points, and who, depending on their ages, acculturated with varying ease. Moore suggests that the second generation was more "cultural" than "chronological." The transitional generation shared "experience" rather than a rigid chronology (1981, 10). One could argue a similarly homogeneous experience for the post-war generation.

21. While Hertzberg was willing to make this guess, Marshall Sklare wrote that there are no reliable statistics indicating national rates of synagogue affiliation. Smaller communities of Jews have higher affiliation rates than larger cities. He notes, for example, that Flint, Michigan, with a population of under three thousand, had an affiliation rate of 87 percent. Communities with ten thousand to twenty-five thousand Jews commonly have an affiliation rate of about 70 percent. In Boston, where there is a larger Jewish community, the rate is 50 percent. But in New York, where no reliable statistics exist, the affiliation rate, observers suggest, is measurably lower than other cities. Membership is "widely diffused" through the population (1971, 123–24). These developments are subsequent to World War II because, Glazer notes, in the 1930s membership in all forms of the syn-

agogue represented a minority of American Jews (1972, 105). The trend may be reversing itself. In the late 1970s, only one-fourth of Los Angeles Jews were affiliated with a synagogue. This percentage is the smallest of any major American city (Dart 1986, 4).

22. Both Sklare (1972) and Liebman (1973) note this paradox.

23. Kaplan's ideas are set forth in *Judaism as a Civilization* (1981).

24. While denomination is the familiar term for the divisions of North American Judaism, it is not an entirely accurate term because differences between them do not rest on theological disputes. Partisan organization might be more appropriate (see Herberg, 1950, 318).

25. J. M. Cuddihy wrote about the decorum of European Jews in his analysis of Freud, Marx, and Levi-Strauss as thinkers who resisted Western culture because of their Judaism (1974). Robert Alter's review of this book largely rejected Cuddihy's perspective on European decorum for misunderstanding the social class distinctions among Jews as well as their integration within European society (1975).

26. This discussion of "leaky" and "closed" cultures owes much to a conversation with the late Barbara Myerhoff in 1983.

27. Hoffman's claim (1987, 3) that it was choreography above all that remained faithful to the past is a view I reject. Decorum was altered from the start; otherwise the synagogue would not have been as effective an institution of acculturation.

2

Havurah Judaism

Old World Decorum and Countercultural Aesthetics

> Once I had a religious experience. I came out of a drug trip and had a tremendous feeling I was one with the universe. It was just like what I had read about in books. But it wasn't Jewish, and because of that, it wasn't religious for me.
>
> Aaron

Following the Second World War, American Judaism at last appeared to conform to a stable pattern. Upwardly mobile, suburban Jews had Americanized and settled their religious differences by forming three separate denominations. Most were Conservative Jews. Synagogues and philanthropies absorbed holocaust survivors from Europe, but these institutions were not transformed as they had been by previous waves of immigrants. Not only were Jewish children now native born Americans, but so were their parents and some of their grandparents. If the second generation longed to create a Judaism that would appeal not only to themselves but to their children, then their suburban synagogues and youth groups seemed to have succeeded. By the 1960s it appeared that the distance from one generation to another among American Jews had narrowed at last.

By the close of the volatile decade of the 1960s, however, groups of college-aged American Jews asserted once again that American Judaism required dramatic alterations in order to speak for its young adults. Again the synagogue, and alternatives to it, became the stage on which the definition of Judaism, and American Judaism in particular, was contested and redefined. The era of the consumer was under attack from the "youth culture" of the 1960s and 1970s, who rebelled against all that suburbia exemplified, particularly its fragmentation. The relationships between the individual and society, between making and consuming, between membership and community, and between instrumental-ity and authenticity were the issues that dominated the formulation of Judaism advanced by havurah founders.

The havurah generation recast Judaism partially in rebellion against its parents, but this was not their only motivation. For these men and women "created" Judaism as they emphasized their continuity with the past, their inheritance of a tradition, and their urgent desire to reassert its true meaning. Anthropologist Michael Fischer has written about the phenomenon of second generation American ethnicity in his analysis of autobiographical writing. He reads this genre insightfully and underlines the dynamic struggle required to assert ethnicity across generations. Fischer argues that each generations' ethnic identity is newly made, because, for example, being Chinese American is not the same as being Chinese. One must learn how to be an ethnic as one lives as an ethnic. Those who seek to understand their ethnicity, often in search of a unified and coherent life story, individually "invent" and "reinterpret" their history in every generation (1986, 195). This interpretive process is necessary because second and third generation ethnic Americans inevitably define themselves through "inter-reference" between the cultural traditions that surround them. Hence, Armenians, Chinese, and Mexicans, as they hyphenate their traditions to America, define that ethnicity in light of one another (1986, 201, 230). Every assertion of ethnicity in America takes account of other ethnic groups. Differentiation, then, is not necessarily an act of isolation. So, too, the Jews who founded the havurah were particularly affected by the Black Power movement and the cultural politics of the 1960s and 1970s associated with American minorities. They incorporated much of the language of these movements into their own definitions of their ethnicity.

The generational search for an American ethnic identity often leads individuals to traditional forms and relations (Fischer 1986, 231). This inevitable conjunction between what is inherited (traditional forms) and what is created (individual interpretation) allows the individual to experience transformation, the sense that one has found a past and made it one's own. The development or establishment of an ethnic identity expands the frame of possibilities for an individual to an entire historical tradition. The "cultural artifice," as Fischer calls tradition, is essential for authenticating and framing the ethnic identity. It is more like a mythological charter than a closed system of rules and provides an authenticating but open-ended framework in which the individual, often in interaction with other cultural traditions, creates his or her ethnicity. The "creation" works precisely because the person feels her-

or himself to be discovering or uncovering what was always his or her own.[1]

The entire havurah movement was an exercise in this construction of the meaning of third generation Judaism by American youth. Its participants sought their ethnicity within the cultural forms of traditional Judaism, but continually recreated those hallmarks of European Jewish life within the context of the youth-dominated America of the 1970s. Indeed, the decorum developed by havurah members acted as a counterdecorum to normative American Judaism and the America of their parents. They established a new generational rendering of Judaism built upon a new aesthetic and new organizations more suitable in their view to the creation of Jewish community.

The Judaism of the third generation provided a surprising context for a countercultural statement. This period in American history was characterized by men and women who advocated denying limits and social norms. Whether cultural and political groups longed for a new utopia or a mythological past, they imagined a world that embodied freedom. By contrast, Jewish tradition and its historical and cultural forms necessarily impose limits. Both the imposition of chosen limits and the will to abandon them represented a cultural critique, and each made the individual the ultimate authority in drawing boundaries and acceptable constraints.[2]

American Judaism in the hands of the 1960s generation revealed a new set of answers to concerns about Jewish uniqueness within American society. These young men and women sought their mythological past, one that would inform, though not control, their present and future. If they found radicalism in prayer and Torah, or saw secular political protest as a vehicle for Jewish identity, it was because they invented their ethnicity even as they inherited it. They seemed to stand for contradictory things. They yearned for continuity even as they separated themselves from their parents' and grandparents' lives.

As havurah members created new forms for prayer communities or political protest, they were inventing and inheriting social, cultural, and personal expressions of ethnicity and religion. They negotiated that process within their historical moment. This generation offered their own transformations of the key themes in American Judaism: authority, decorum, and organization. They neither transformed the voluntary structure of the American Jewish community nor abandoned organizations, chiefly the prayer community, as a source of Jewish identity. Rather, they refashioned the nature of Jewish organizations in light of the aesthetics of the American counterculture and found a new generational articulation of Judaism for themselves. Their counteraesthetic and alternative decorum constituted a means by which they differentiated themselves from their parents and from American society.[3]

Organizational Life: The Suburbs versus the Counterculture

At the turn of the century, voluntary organizations in general, and religious ones in particular, effectively allowed newly urbanized Americans to articulate their own emerging middle-class identities as well as their programs for a progressive America. Ethnic Americans tended to use their churches as places to perfect their changing status within America. They decided what language to use and what customs to include for weddings and other rites of passage within an ethnically homogeneous environment. Their cumulative decisions developed into an ethnic identity within America, maintaining some uniqueness within an acculturating process. Newly urbanized Americans, at the same time, used independent Christian organizations to change people spiritually and to alter the lives of the needy within a progressive program for America.

I return again to such voluntary religious organizations because they continued to play a central role in articulating an identity and program for "newcomers." These postwar newcomers, who were the suburbanites, and their children often used organizations to express their central values and ideas in a society that was pluralistic and segmented. As the ethnic church could be the staging ground for a developing identity, so voluntary organizations also could provide the models for the ephemeral community of the suburbs, or the social transformation for the counterculture. Precisely because such organizations in urban areas were separate from work and family, they were good settings to express issues of identity and community. Expressing identity can never be the sole responsibility of the family or workplace, which never encompass the whole person. Like other Protestant and Jewish voluntary organizations before it, the havurah played this role in the context of the sixties and seventies.

Voluntary organizations had a unique place in suburban communities following World War II. The early twentieth century "cult of personality" and self-realization was harnessed to the needs of a new type of community. Organizations placed increasing emphasis on the unique person, on being liked and expressing oneself. The *Organization Man,* William H. Whyte's incisive critique of corporate America and its domination of family, leisure, and religion, described an era where organization became associated with what Whyte called a "social ethic," which he related to the society's emphasis on self expression (1956). The organization, whether it was corporate, voluntary, leisure, or residential, required certain attitudes and values. Whyte, and many social scientists of the period, noted a shift in the basic values of American society. The individual and the Protestant Ethic, mainstays of the American experience, yielded to the demand for well roundedness, for suppression of uniqueness, and above all for an emphasis on utility. The transience and rootlessness that resulted from urbanization were then compounded by the national or international corporation that continuously moved its employees and their dutiful families. All relations outside the nuclear family were necessarily temporary, resulting in what Whyte called "pragmatism" or "utilitarianism," not simply as an expedient but also as a "moral imperative" (1956, 435). That expedience required loyalty to the group, to peers, to the organization, and to the community, all representatives of the corporation. Suburbs drew together friends without family in a flurry of activity, which created shallow but overlapping roots. Such communities required conformity to coalesce quickly and meet general needs. The ability to adjust was the individual's greatest virtue. It made it possible for everyone to get along. What social historian Warren Susman saw developing at the turn of the century, with the increasing importance of "personality" over "character," reached its culmination in the 1950s. Consumer society and corporate society met in the suburbs, where a world of "personality" and "well roundedness" made conflict unnecessary and conformity essential. Susman notes the direct and developing relationship between the feeble "rituals of the external world" and the value on an "inner self" (1984, 272). With the attacks on all the authorities noted in Chapter 1—religious tradition, the stable American town, and continuity with parents' occupations and residences—the individual's inner life and self-expression took on greater significance. But that inner life became relegated to the need for conformity to society as the organization dominated family life and work life. Emphasizing personality meant teaching people to get along, a skill that was useful to the corporate world.

Religion in the fifties followed this pattern of orienting individual needs to group ends. This was the era Will Herberg described in which religion encompassed and replaced ethnicity for most Americans. Participation in church was high, but apparently not motivated by doctrinal allegiance, according to quantitative measures of church participation. As Martin Marty argues, the scholars of religion of the period were convinced that a pervasive secularization was afoot and that religion masked and even redefined religion in the secular theologies of the period (1983, 276–77). No period in American Protestant history, for example, demonstrates more cooperation between denominations, or more predictions of the possibility of an imminent unified Protestant church. Whyte's study of a 1950s Chicago suburb supports this view. Protestant suburbanites formed a unified church and actively worked to overcome denominational differences. Churches were capable of cooperation precisely because they wanted to put doctrinal differences aside.

The underlying purpose of religious affiliation in this period seemed to be what Whyte called "social." Church became a good setting for making friends in a new community. It promoted the ties of the nuclear family. In Chapter 1, I described a similar trend for the suburban synagogue and synagogue center. Most sociological studies of Judaism point to this period for the strong overlap of ethnicity and religion in the Jewish community. Under the influence of Protestant neighbors, Jews attended synagogue more often than before, though for the most part their personal observance of Jewish rituals and laws decreased. Utility was a strong message from the synagogues. The synagogue was good for the family, good for maintaining Jewish identity, and good for helping Jewish children establish their identities.

My concern is not so much with secularization as with the middle-class penchant for joining churches in order to achieve community and find identity. Sociologist N. J. Demerath demonstrated that the Christian and Jewish middle and upper classes join churches, but that lower classes who less frequently join churches verbalize more religious sentiments and beliefs when interviewed (1984, 334–40). More than a place for believers, the church draws people in search of the like-minded or socially equal. Organization seems to be a key issue in the middle classes' understanding of their own lives and the place of religion in it.

By contrast, organization took on a radically different meaning in the sixties and seventies within the flourishing counterculture. Not only did participants criticize social utility for lacking authenticity but voluntary organizations took on new meaning within the counterculture. They became what Kenneth Keniston called models of "exemplary reform." (1968, 286–90). These organizations were the focus of cultural politics: both a protest against and transformation of society. If a free clinic, women's health collective, or alternative prayer community could exist, the mass, alienated, impersonal society itself was undermined. A Jewish counterculture developed in the early seventies that both criticized American Judaism and offered an alternative to it. Organizations carried the program and formulation for alternatives to Judaism. Though many young Jews assimilated, many of those who might ordinarily have joined synagogues and taken their places in suburban Judaism chose instead to create havurot.

The havurah, then, combined both roles played by voluntary organizations in America over the last century. It was a new form of synagogue able to communicate uniqueness and identity just as ethnic churches did. But it was also an exemplary reform organization, anti-institutional and committed to an alternative status. The change it declared by its existence provided a new view of American Judaism. Traditional and countercultural aims were combined in the havurah that intensified the organization's load as a purveyor of personal identity and cultural alteration.

The Jewish Counterculture and the Havurah

Havurot were the most tenacious and successful of several organizations of ethnically and religiously self-conscious Jewish college-aged youth in the early 1970s. Though no single or widely recognized name exists for this phenomenon, it was often referred to as the Jewish counterculture. Jack Porter and Peter Dreier characterized this uncentralized movement as a "quest for historical roots, personal identity, and intimate community amidst a mad, technocratic and antiseptic society" (1973, xii).

Three books, *The New Jews* (Sleeper and Mintz 1971), *Jewish Radicalism* (Porter and Dreier 1973), and *Contemporary Judaic Fellowship in Theory and Practice* (Neusner 1972a), contain essays criticizing American Judaism and the failure of Jewish organizations to provide "authentic religious community." Other articles discuss Israel, Zionism, the Holocaust, the New Left, feminism, and Soviet Jewry from the point of view of American radical Jews. Some writers present alternatives to mainstream American Judaism. Many of the articles are reprinted from local radical Jewish newspapers with titles such as *Up Against the Brooklyn Bridge* and *Genesis 2. Response Magazine,* originally located in New York and later in Boston, had a national circulation by 1968. It was the movement's national forum.[4]

The Jewish counterculture generated a diverse set of activities and interests under its broad title. Its activities were political, religious, cultural, and communal. No participants shared interests in all of them. Many activities were focused on campuses, but some in the general communities of major cities. All their activities and programs strove to integrate Jewish concerns with countercultural issues and forms of organizing (Glanz 1977).

A self-conscious group, activists in the Jewish counterculture and havurot wrote and spoke about themselves, produced publications, and reflected on their enterprise as five, ten, and fifteen years passed from the founding of the first havurah. Hence, for some years the links between groups were informal, and official statements, newsletters, manifestos, and official descriptions of havurot by their members were nonexistent. They remained antipathetic to extensive organizations and the trappings of bureaucracy. Bill Novak, who was involved in beginning two havurot, claimed that the ephemeral nature of the organization was crucial to maintaining a successful community. Havurah members had to guard vigilantly against the organization's "form dictating its contents" (1972a, 266). Members often spoke of the wish "to meet our own needs." They believed they would be deterred from their purpose if forced to recruit or act as models for others. In avoiding becoming too bureaucratic, they hoped to maintain the vitality of their communities.

As individuals, Jewish countercultural activists were willing spokespersons for a vision they shared. As noted, they wrote books and journal articles, published newspapers and edited journals. In 1982 several activists graciously gave me interviews about their communities.[5] Most were accustomed to interviews about their ideas. They were a vanguard.

Minyan and havurot participants identified with the youthful counterculture that emerged out of the New Left in the late sixties and early seventies.[6] Havurah members shared the counterculture's ideology that social transformation was essential and could be accomplished in part through the creation of alternative institutions.[7] They claimed that shared Jewish activities were important acts of protest. They embraced the New Left's criticism of American politics and culture. They separated themselves from the rest of the New Left, nevertheless, by their belief that through their shared past as a Jewish people they would find a future vision for themselves. As Porter and Dreier wrote in their "Introduction":

> Thus the desperation of the late 1960's led some to the senseless violence of the Weathermen. But others found new directions in their effort to build a viable radical community . . . within their own kind—women, Catholics . . . homosexuals, teachers and Jews. This development is an affirmation as well as a protest. (1973, xxviii)

A 1977 New York rally for the rights of Soviet Jews. The Jewish counterculture claims to have been responsible for making the plight of Soviet Jews a concern of the larger Jewish community. This multigenerational protest brought together mainstream Jewish groups like Hadassah, a women's Zionist organization, with countercultural Jews.

The authenticity of the changes proposed and described rested in large measure on the cultural uniqueness they promoted. In the case of the havurah in particular, what was rejected was an assimilationist's model of religion and its link with middle-class life. James Sleeper wrote in his "Introduction" to *New Jews:*

> Their [young people's] rejection of the Jewish community is less a denial of Judaism as such than it is part of a more general rejection of the deficiencies of a more general and misguided priorities inherent in the American dream their parents have pursued. (1971, 15)

Americanization, these activists argued, destroyed Judaism as a system of values and as a religious and political vision. They charged that Americanization and acculturation were accomplished through narrowing Jewish life to a successful imitation of American Protestant, middle-class values. They stood the success of American Jews on its head. What previous generations of Jews called success, they defined as "accommodation." To havurah members, rapid upward mobility marked the end of Jewish community.

Porter and Dreier articulated the Jewish Left's rejection of the success of American Jews.

> The obsequiousness of the Jewish establishment is a sign of the Jew's marginality and ultimate vulnerability. Despite popular stereotypes, studies show that few Jews are to be found among the corporate elites. Rather, where Jews are involved at all, it is as technocrats; they may oil and run the machine, but they don't own it. Jewish success was bought at a price. It destroyed Jewish culture and ethnic solidarity, forced Jews to rely on others' good will and alienated masses of young Jews. It is a price the Jewish left is unwilling to pay. (1973, xxxvi)

The language and substance of this analysis is indebted to the American New Left. Its leaders articulated a fundamental discomfort with power elites upon which technocracy, bureaucracy, and a massive society were dependent. Activists rejected that system and refused to cooperate with it. The 1965 Berkeley protests against university bureaucracy made popular the phrase "I am a student: do not fold, mutilate, or staple." They perceived every level of bureaucracy from the corporation to the university as inhuman because its size and scale made it unapproachable, and made Americans mere cogs in the machine. They refused to join the corporation, to participate in war, or to accept a place in a massive and alienated society; they planned to change society. These postwar baby-boom children rejected the security their parents, often returning soldiers and spouses, had sought in suburbs, cars, consumer items, and corporate employment (May 1988). Jews and gentiles within the New Left opposed the success produced by the affluent technocratic society. Havurah members who were identified with the New Left rejected the society that had created their affluence.

The New Left was committed to two kinds of revolutions that directly implicated Jews in reinterpreting their own place in society. The national liberation struggle of revolutionary groups outside the United States, principally the Vietnamese, was of central concern to the Left. Much closer to home was the Black Power movement and its own rhetoric of liberation (Carmichael and Hamilton 1967). The message of these movements was that only in the uniqueness of one's own people could one find power and freedom. When Robert Greenblatt wrote, "The experiences of Vietnam and Cuba have demonstrated the possibility of revolutionary nationalism, a consciousness of peoplehood which contributes to the revolutionary process while maintaining the international perspective (1971, 46)," he asserted that Jews would find in their own peoplehood a cultural and political alternative to mainstream American life. This view was echoed by the most prominent radical Jew of the seventies, Arthur Waskow:

> We have felt more and more confident about our ability to 'enter' America. But in the 1960s this confidence was shattered. When the blacks tried to enter the melting pot, the temperature inside got too high and the pot shattered. Simultaneously, the Vietnam War showed America, not as a defender against a holocaust, but as a perpetrator of one. From both events, many young Jews whose parents had proudly assimilated to the American promise . . . find they do not want to be American after all. . . . The eighty-year upward-mobility process was shattered. (1973, 15)

America and American Judaism then became a "shattered world" for the Jewish Left. Fischer's suggestion that ethnicity is defined in dialogue with other ethnic groups, as well as through the cultural forms of one's own traditions, was borne out by the Jewish counterculture. Community and cultural autonomy became their themes, articulated largely in a borrowed language, particularly from blacks, though with acknowledged debts to European Zionism. The application and revision of those issues occurred within an American Jewish context. Some voices in the movement were actively Zionist, urging American Jews to "return" to

Israel; the majority were not. Zionism would have been the most consistent with a position of national liberation. But without being anti-Zionist, these activists, like their parents, remained sympathetic to Israel but committed to creating what they believed their grandparents had abandoned, a flourishing Jewish culture within America.

Though mainstream society was identified by the Jewish Left as the problem, most of their critical writings were directed against assimilated American Jews, both the middle class and political radicals, who seemed to epitomize all that was wrong with America. They argued that both types of American Jews were indifferent to the uniqueness of the Jewish people. Both groups thought a distinctive Jewish identity was "parochial" and denied it in favor of assimilation with suburbia or political movements indifferent to Jews. However, Jewish activists, inspired by other contemporary movements, held their cultural uniqueness to be essential to activism. They argued that the current Jewish community was thoroughly unacceptable, but that it could be changed, just as the counterculture was provoking change in the larger society. The Jewish counterculture's efforts were directed toward constructing a critical analysis of its own Jewish community and tradition. The alternative that resulted would be their counterculture, one inspired by American youth but different from it.

One activist described how his generation was transformed from Jewish radicals to radical Jews, to the realization that the best alternative to America lay in what they called "authentic" Jewish community.

> The Jewish publicists spilled seas of ink bemoaning our alienation. Rarely, though, was an honest appraisal made of the source of our alienation. Perhaps it was a sign of our health that we were not attracted to a Jewish life devoid of intellectual and spiritual energy. . . . We woke up from the American dream and tried to discover who we really were. For many of us this now means turning our concerns inward into the Jewish community because we are disenchanted with the crass materialism of the larger society. Yet where can we find inspiration in the multimillion dollar Jewish presence of suburbia? (Levine 1973, 185)

Levine referred to identity, to material success, and to spiritual values in drawing his contrast between American culture and authentic Judaism. America and American Judaism represented materialism, emptiness, and mass society. Judaism should represent an alternative. Alan Mintz, active in two havurot and the first editor of *Response,* articulated this realization:

> A most startling discovery has been that Judaism does not have to be identical to the scheme of middle class values. . . . A new consciousness of the past has brought us to believe that a more fundamental and nourishing Judaism existed, was discussed and did not need a middle-class life style and its constellation of values. (1973, 32)

It was the task of the Jewish counterculture to assess how American society had ensnared and undermined a true Jewish life, so its founders might create a new one.

The voices of the Jewish counterculture emphasized the culpability of three institutions in the assimilation of American Jews. The first, if most remote, was the Federation of Jewish Agencies, the essence of the secular Jewish establishment. This agency exists at national and local levels (Elazar 1980). It disburses funds to all Jewish philanthropic agencies. The federation consists of professional staffs under the direction of affluent lay boards. In consultation with their staffs, these boards decide how money collected through the United Jewish Appeal, (a national fund-raising campaign organized by federations) will be disbursed. The boards, by the nature of their decisions, determine the priorities of the Jewish community. They decide what funds will be sent to Israel, and how much will stay in the local communities. They also decide what funds will be spent on Jewish education and Jewish culture, and how much will be spent on the aged, the facilities of the community center, and youth work.

Young Jewish activists criticized values promoted by federations. They argued that education and the arts were underfunded. They noted that the Jewish education supported by the federation was inadequate, ineffective, and incapable of teaching the radical values implied by Judaism. They were particularly critical of the lack of democracy and dissident voices in federation organizations. Although the affluent people who became board members represented themselves rather than the whole community, they made decisions for that community. For example, an article by a sociologist reprinted in the collection *Jewish Radicalism* noted:

> It is too obvious that the goals of the people and of the federation leadership are by now far apart and being a voluntary association, the leadership would not long support a program other than its own, even if the program was that of the majority of the people. The leadership, therefore, is really without a following, nor does the

> Jewish population of any locality really have an organized community. (Shapiro 1973, 204)

Young activists organized a protest against the Council of Jewish Federations and Welfare Funds. In 1969, 1500 delegates met in Boston to plan communal affairs for the upcoming year at the annual General Assembly. A Jewish Activist League planned a sit-in to protest these priorities. They published their intentions and concerns in a mimeographed sheet that they circulated to the press.

> In affirmation of our Jewishness and our concern for Jewish survival we feel we can no longer be silent. Distortions in the budget priorities of Jewish federations have long been decried . . . We demand that while maintaining the generous level of support for Israel, all local federations undertake drastic and immediate reordering of domestic priorities in the local communities, in order to improve the quality of Jewish cultural life on campus and in the community. (cited in Navara 1972)

The council of Federations blunted the protest by offering the platform to one movement representative. What followed was a reasonably typical pattern of responses to New Left protest. After a stirring address by the dissidents' representative, the federation formed a commission to study youth. It allocated funds on a one-time basis to extend youth activities, supporting an alternative Jewish press as well as other ventures. Then activists wrote articles decrying federation policies and indifference in federation-supported publications (see Navara 1972; *Newsweek* 1969).

The federation was the ultimate establishment of American Jewish life. Its problems paralleled all those of American society described and analyzed throughout the sixties. It embodied the elitism and values of mainstream American society. Jewish students used the analysis and the models of protest of the period to respond to that system. They also sought alternatives to the federation-constructed Jewish community. They realized, even in their minimal involvement in the federation, that they would engender no real change if they stayed within it.

The second institution attacked by the Jewish counterculture was the synagogue. Havurot were organized by people whose plans for an alternative community called for a new vision of the worship community. From physical space, to the organization of the service, to the types of melodies sung, the synagogue had to be reinvented.

The synagogue, according to havurah activists, exemplified the split between religion and culture that the Jewish counterculture aimed to heal. It was viewed as the institution in which "Jewish values" had been cut off from Jewish activity. Activists asserted that the only synagogue values that mattered were suburban success, wealth, and rote religious performance. They believed that the synagogue lacked spirituality, meaningful study, and real Jewish activity. Its congregants were rendered "passive." James Sleeper characterized suburban Judaism as "a spiritual Hiroshima which had been the setting for the transformation of the Hebrew spirit into an increasingly dispensable appendage of middle class culture" (1971, 7). Sleeper claimed that the "appendage" had tailored an "almost forgotten religion to the norms and aesthetics of middle class culture" (1971, 14).

Given the centrality of worship to the havurah it is surprising, in retrospect, that the critique of the synagogue was rather generally drawn. The image of the large suburban affluent synagogue appears in most of the writings of movement participants. But the synagogue simply seems one reflection of the Americanization of the Jews. It was not the source of protest, as were the federations. The havurah, an exemplary reform, was activists' most effective critique of the synagogue because of the alternative it provided.

Stephen Lerner, a mainstream Conservative rabbi, wrote one of the first assessments of the havurot for the American Jewish community. His primarily sympathetic portrayal included his analysis of why these men and women found little hope for changing synagogues:

> Few of the *haverim* (havurah members) consider this to be a realistic goal, for they seem to share a certain Puritan sense of the corruption of the existing order and the concomitant requirement for a new Zion. . . . Clearly, they think that they can't "do their thing" meaningfully with the corrupted or deadened elders. (1972, 135)

The view Lerner described was derived from the activists' analysis that the synagogue contributed to narrowing Jewish culture into a denominational religion. While counterculture participants understood that this separation originated in Europe, they believed the synagogue hastened the process because it fostered assimilation to American culture, the tragic error of immigrant Jews. Activists claimed that the synagogue could stand for no more than a reflection of the America they rejected.

Finally, the Jewish counterculture turned its analysis to the suburban Jewish family, declaring Jewish daughters and sons to be "at odds" with their parents and "the establishment," which they regarded as synonymous (Porter and Dreier 1973, xvii). Their parents and grandparents chose assimilation and suburban materialism. The Jewish family, understood by one writer as the "greenhouse of human values," taught children to assimilate rather than to hold Jewish values or to maintain Jewish practices. Second generation American Jews made even worse choices than to assimilate. They confused their children with contradictory and ambivalent messages. As their children followed the same path of assimilation, particularly when they chose gentile partners for marriage or dating, the second generation balked and blamed their children for inappropriate choices (Navara 1971, 103; Rosenfeld 1973, 224). The writings of third and fourth generation Jews, then, emphasized not just the Americanization of Jewish culture perpetrated by the second generation, but the personal cost resulting from the confusion, absence of world view, spiritual emptiness, and shattered legacy that they lived with. Their desire to hold onto Judaism—while wresting it away from their corrupting elders who polluted it—was clearly at stake in a generational conflict played out in religious, secular, and familial communities.

At the same time, many who wrote criticizing their parents also described feelings of warmth, love, and security attached to the family and Jewish events. They sympathetically acknowledged their parents' difficulties in adjusting to American society because of their own search for security. The family, then, raised a series of emotions named by participants as central to their own struggles with how to be a Jew. They bypassed their parents to find Judaism, but most were rooted to Judaism through their parents and grandparents. They were ambivalent actors rejecting and embracing tradition. Their protests and alternatives drew them toward and away from the family.

For the counterculture, Jewish values involved community, spirituality, learning for its own sake rather than achievement, and political radicalism expressed through national and personal liberation. These values also involved the rejection of achievement, success, and assimilation, all associated with America, although havurot were primarily populated with students pursuing graduate degrees. Jewish communal institutions were the havurah members' targets for protests and critical articles. The family was always the implied target in countercultural attacks on values and materialism, as it was by others in the rebellious generation of the sixties. The call for "real community" and "real intimacy" was an attack on both family and community. The family was the intimate target of the public outrage directed at community.

Jewish Youth and the New Left

One would not have predicted the rise of a university-based Jewish counterculture in the 1970s. Jewish men and women typically spend their years at a university preparing for a job or profession and usually do not participate in Jewish activities. The Jewish community has few services to offer them. The Hillel foundation, a world-wide campus organization begun in the 1920s and subsequently supported by B'nai B'rith, an ethnic and secular Jewish organization, specializes in meeting the needs of this age group. For the most part, Hillel appeals to a small percentage of Jewish students on campus. Because the majority of Jews attend college after high school, an entire age cohort virtually is disconnected from the Jewish community, except for a minority that joins peer associations such as Hillel or secular sororities and fraternities with a majority of Jewish members.[8] Yet it was this very age group that began havurot. It was predictable that they should do so as a homogeneous group of peers, but it was unusual that their concern should be for Jewish activity, which would separate them from mainstream campus life.

These Americanized and well-acculturated countercultural Jews, despite all of their dissatisfaction with the Judaism they knew, found something in their tradition that was not available in the popular and widespread counterculture. Havurah members, though close to the New Left critique of society, were made uneasy by it. The political activism of havurah founders was certainly in keeping with the New Left. These men and women identified with their generation's involvement in politics. If their own commitments were less extensive, and there was of course variation among early members, their outlook was shared. Hillel Levine, in his address to the 1969 Federation General Assembly, characterized himself and others in this way, "But perhaps you would be more interested in knowing who we are. . . . We went down to Mississippi for summers, marched against the war" (1973, 184–85). Probably only a few of these people were involved in civil-rights work in the South because many of them were young teenagers at the time. They were still aware of the Jews who were active in the South in civil disobedience, and they identified with two of the Jewish civil-rights workers murdered in 1964.[9]

Virtually all of them had participated in antiwar protests. A woman who was a member of the first havurah founded in Boston spoke during an interview with me about student protests in 1968 and how she responded to the daily reports of students closing down college campuses.

> We really learned a sense of our own power. I think nothing else, nobody telling me that, could have made me understand that power, the way living through the period helped me understand that we didn't have to be powerless.

Despite their agreement with the New Left on many issues, the founders of the havurot became alienated from radicals' criticisms of Israel and Zionism. Like other American Jews they strongly supported Israel, especially after the 1967 Six Day War.[10] American Jews on campus translated their political activism to the support of Israel. Students raised large sums of money to send to Israel; some volunteered to work in Israel to relieve those who were called up to fight. Many of the activists reported previous indifference to Israel and to Judaism. Jews throughout the United States, but especially students, intensified activites that allowed them to make statements concerning their Jewish identity. Israel's apparent vulnerability and decisive victory evoked strong feelings of responsibility, elation, and pride in Israel among Jews.

The non-Jewish New Left responded differently. Their analysis of the Middle Eastern war attributed Israel's victory to the expansion of Western imperialism. They did not see a conflict between a small vulnerable nation and powerful Arab states; they saw the Six Day War as another war similar to that in Vietnam. Westerners were occupying the land of others and were using Western forces to subdue rightful inhabitants. New Left activists became increasingly anti-Zionist just as many Jewish students began to identify themselves as Jews through the rhetoric of the Left. Bill Novak wrote about this dilemma.

> The New Left, at one point the only hope for morality in this country, sold him [the Jewish activist on campus] out by its pointless acceptance of the "good-guy-bad-guy" dualism in the Middle East. (1972b, 143)

Jews who identified with Israel were then increasingly polarized from the New Left. They found themselves choosing between assimilation, which required renouncing their attachment to Israel, or identification with American Judaism and all of the problems that came with this identification.

In 1967 at the National Conference for New Politics in Chicago, the Black Caucus demanded an anti-Zionist platform. The radical Black Power movement was increasingly identified with the third world and with the political analyses of Arab nationalist Franz Fanon. Many Jews walked out of the conference, breaking their tie to the New Left (Porter and Dreier 1973, xxv) M. J. Rosenberg, a rabbi, responded to this devastating event in a short piece for the *Village Voice* in 1969. He expressed sentiments that virtually all those who identified with the Jewish counterculture repeated:

> And thus from this point on, I will support no movement that does not accept my people's struggle. If I must choose between the Jewish cause and a "progressive" anti-Israel SDS [Students for a Democratic Society], I shall always choose the Jewish cause, not blindly, not arbitrarily, but always with full knowledge of who I am and where I must be. (1973, 10)

Young activist Jews embraced the New Left only to find themselves unable to be both Jews and radicals. They were outsiders to America and outsiders to an alternative vision of America. They wanted out of the melting pot, uncertain of what their alternatives were. They clung to one belief, which they did not share with the rest of the New Left. They believed that the past held the key to who they would be. They would not go back, but they would bring their European Jewish past, their immigrant ancestors' heritage, and their view of what Judaism could offer them into their new society. In 1968, with the formation of the first havurah, they began to weave a Jewish world view into a New Left vision. Robert Greenblat summarized the moment. "I am a Jew, an American, a Revolutionary. I am all three at once because each flows out of and merges into one life history" (1971, 47).

Alternative Organization as Politics

By 1968 the ubiquitous protests of the New Left were replaced by proliferating alternative organizations that provided new ways of living in society, and with that an alternative way to establish "personal identity" (Flacks 1971, 100). These alternatives were at once the medium and end of protest. If the family oppressed individuals and maintained inequity in society, then destroying the family through organizing communal living arrangements was both a protest and a solution. New organizations were the medium for radical protesters who set about creating a parallel society (Eisen and Steinberg 1969, 83–84).[11]

Indeed the parallel society grew directly out of self-transformation. New Left activists were committed to changing the world by changing themselves. They rejected the "Old" Left in large measure because its strategies for change did not begin with the self and therefore seemed inevitably doomed to failure. However, New Left activists' emphasis on self-transformation created unmeetable expectations. They not only held a utopian vision for the future, but for the present as well. They envisioned no steps or process to take them from a flawed present to an ideal future. Rather, every group they organized would immediately embody a new era or be judged a failure. Alternative communities inherited this identical strategy (Lerner 1988, 46).

Revolutionary activity transpired without revolutions. "Alternatives" were ubiquitous whether they were organizations or "life styles." Forms of residence, such as the commune, coexisted alongside free clinics for health care, free stores for distributing food, cooperative businesses that shared profits rather than amassed them, and free universities where knowledge was shared and not directed toward earning degrees. These innumerable alternatives demonstrated that antibureaucratic, humanistic, and antiauthoritarian organizations were possible. Kenneth Keniston summarized the form all such alternatives took.

> Indeed, within the New Left there is a certain anarchistic strain that opposed *all* large institutions in favor of small face-to-face groups. If there is a hidden utopia, it is the utopia of small groups of equals, meeting together in mutual trust and respect to work out their common destiny. (1968, 18)

Alternative organizations that flourished in the seventies were not developed by weary New Leftists. By the early seventies, many had been engaged in years of constant protest and were suffering from what was called "burnout." At the same time, ethnics and black Americans, who might not be associated with a protest movement, also created parallel institutions and life styles. They rejected a white, middle-class society committed to homogenization; cultural radicalism flourished. Minority groups developed music, art, social service agencies, and styles of appearance that reflected their uniqueness. Hence, politics, music, style, and activism became inseparable and, in the minds of some, comparable. If white society valued straight hair, then blacks made naturally kinky hair a symbol of pride, calling the hairstyle an "Afro." In cultural politics, wearing an afro became a political statement. Jews followed suit, naming their naturally kinky hair-style a "Hebrew Afro" or just a "Hebrew."

Cultural radicals turned toward their own communities through alternative organizations, which drew them away from the American norms that excluded them. Their homogeneity paralleled the New Left's commitment to alternatives created by the like-minded. Similarly, the politics of cultural groups, particularly in the 1970s, relied more on alternative institutions than direct action. Community was often the goal of such alternative organizations. If those outside the mainstream reclaimed their uniqueness and community, they had escaped the fantasy as well as the illusion of the melting pot.[12]

Activists in both the New Left and in cultural politics rarely based their alternative organizations on a well-articulated ideology, nor did they advocate massive change through a rigid ideological program. Gitlin and Kazin described the New Left as "a ragged, messy hodgepodge of movements, stronger on impulse than programatic clarity and in constant flux." (1988, 49). These alternatives amounted to a "transformation by example" (Howard 1969). Kenneth Keniston called them "exemplary social reform" (1968, 286–90). Protesters created alternative institutions to translate action into organization. The best antidote to the system was to ignore it. The new society was at hand and it coexisted with the unsatisfactory one. One could take authority in a collective organization.

Authority in America seemed bankrupt and wrong to countercultural activists. Violence and confrontation were only a means to attack that authority. Without revolutionary change they established a new authority in the collective, and when alternative authority or nonauthority was established, the aims of the Left were rerouted rather than abandoned. Alternative institutions were, therefore, both a means and an end for social change.

The authority of the New Left, however, was never ultimately vested in the group. The best known slogan of the period, "Do your own thing," only emphasized the problem. Community will was to come out of individual will. Community responsibility could not be imposed. Discussion and group interaction characterized the New Left as it did the human potential movement. As experts in the twenties in America recommended cultivating a personality that was unique yet likable and never alienating, so the sixties emphasized cooperation growing out of individual uniqueness. In the fifties Americans wanted to "get along." In the sixties and seventies, one sought groups with whom one would be in agreement. The collective, then, not only accomplished tasks but created noncoercive community for its participants.

Authority was as central an issue for the Jewish counterculture as it was for the New Left. Havurah members rejected the norms of the Jewish community, secular and sacred: rabbis, synagogues, and all the trappings of formality and authority. Unlike the New Left, however, Jewish counterculturalists found themselves paradoxically both attracted to authority and repulsed by it. They were willing to reject the authority of the suburban synagogue, but they believed the deepest radicalism available to them was to be found in the authority of Jewish tradition, the Bible, and the rabbinic codification of law. They believed they had to transform these sacreds to make them relevant to their members' contemporary lives, though the core of traditional Judaism was thought to contain a critical perspective on their society. The counterculture led Jews to their own culture in order to achieve distinctiveness from America. They searched for alternatives in the past rather than the past itself.

What was potentially rewarding in the discovery of a historical dimension to cultural alternatives was that participants were tied to one another and to their organization in a different way than anything the New Left could offer. Paul Cowan, a journalist active in the New Left and in havurot, examined the similarities and contrasts between the New Left and the Jewish counterculture in his autobiography, *An Orphan in History* (1982).

> In the sixties the New Left and the havurah movement were both ideal places to find one's political or religious identity. They developed almost identical styles, which encouraged intimacy and virtually outlawed authority. For instance, members of SDS and the havurah movement sat in circles, not in rows. Both organizations insisted on a leadership that rotated frequently, arrived at all their decisions by consensus, not by votes or by the decree of some central committee. (1982, 214)

He continues by emphasizing their contrasts.

> But there was a crucial difference between the two movements, which emerged clearly as idealism ebbed, as conflict arose. The fights within the havurah were almost as bitter as those within the New Left, but since everyone involved was a Jew with some commitment to religion, personal conflicts and power struggles . . . couldn't be confused with ethnic prejudices. Ironically, the havurah movement's strength lay in the very parochialism that sometimes made it seem frustratingly narrow. It couldn't be Balkanized. (1982, 214)

Cowan notes a shared antithesis to authority and the creation of alternative forms of organization that lead to identity and personal visibility.

But he suggests that a shared history, a common sense of past, cut against the possibility of splintering havurot irrevocably. Alternative organizations for these Jews created not only social reform, but historically based community as well.

> Those quarrels could be painful, of course, but at their worst they led to the creation of another new minyan, not to the totally separate organization for the women, the blacks, the gays, the white men whose inability to cooperate destroyed the New Left. For, on a fundamental spiritual level, the worst enemies of the havurah movement had to cooperate. They all said the same prayers on Shabbos. . . . So because of halaha and tradition, their generational rebellion would endure, in one form or another, as the New Left's had not. (1982, 215)

New Left politics evolved from protest to alternative organizations. Activism became its own end. But, as Cowan notes, if the Left successfully undermined authority, its members also divided and redivided around alternative authorities, which splintered the movement into fragments never successfully reunited. Cowan believed alternative organizations united through a shared authority such as religious tradition might be parochial, but they enabled persistent community.

The havurah movement that developed out of the Jewish counterculture sought a new way for its members to be Jews in America. These men and women began their movement with a shared indictment of Jews, America, and the American New Left. They felt like outsiders to them all. Porter and Dreier describe the type of person who emerged from these experiences. "Only a special kind of a young Jew can survive and persist in this situation, a Jew who is willing to endure intense scrutiny from his peers and the Jewish establishment and to continually justify his stance without apology. He has had to create a role where none existed before" (1973, xlvi). The Jewish counterculture shared with the New Left a search for alternatives to society. They both imagined a new relationship to tradition as an antithesis of middle-class authority.

Their attacks on the synagogue and community did not go unnoticed. Rabbi Edward Gershfield addressed them in his remarks to the Rabbinical Assembly, the association of Conservative Rabbis:

> Our services of readings in fine English, correct musical renditions by professional cantors and choirs, and decorous and dignified rabbis in elegant gowns arouse disdain and contempt in our young

> people. They want excitement and noise, improvisation and emotion, creativity and sensitivity, informality and spontaneity. And they are 'turned off' by the very beauty and decorum which we have worked so hard to achieve. Of course the youth do not wish to go into the reasons why these aspects of our life had been created. . . . We seem doomed to having to watch as our youth relive the same self destructive impulses that we have seen long ago, and thought could not happen again (cited in Sklare 1972, 280–81).

The aesthetics defined by Gershfield, as well as his vision of authority, indeed were rejected by the havurah generation. For many Jewish youth, the modification of tradition that had worked so successfully for the second generation of American Jews was an anathema. One generation's vision of Judaism was uprooted by the next. The havurah would formulate the alternatives to save Judaism.

Havurah Judaism

Havurat Shalom (Fellowship of Peace), the first countercultural Jewish community, began in the fall of 1968 in Sommerville, Massachusetts, just outside of Cambridge. Its founder, Rabbi Arthur Green, explained to me why he saw the need for the havurah. He described a dramatic scene in 1966 at the Jewish Theological Seminary, where he was studying to become a rabbi. He, along with a few other students, attended a course in the office of their inspiring teacher, Rabbi Abraham Joshua Heschel. Father Daniel Berrigan, the Catholic peace activist, sat in on their class that evening. Rabbi Heschel announced, "Gentlemen, your assignment this evening is to help me decide if I should go to jail for political acts of civil disobedience, as Father Berrigan is urging." The students were immediately protective of their teacher because of his ill health and argued that he should not risk being jailed. They claimed that there were other ways for him to be politically effective. Father Berrigan responded by asking them, "We have the underground church, but what is happening in the Jewish community?" Rabbi Green recalled feeling "mortified" because he could think of nothing in the American Jewish community that was not "bourgeois and self-satisfied." He determined at that moment that he would begin a new kind of *yeshiva*, a school of Jewish higher education. It would challenge other forms of learning by its equality, mutuality, and love and would provide draft deferments so that his friends and colleagues would not be drafted. It would show that the Jewish community was able to generate a political and cultural response to America.[13]

Rabbi Green's plan for Havurat Shalom to become an alternative seminary ended almost immediately, and he, along with its first members, instead made it the model havurah. They were less interested in training rabbis than concentrating on building community. They made Havurat Shalom a place to study and to pray, "seriously and intensely." It brought together students and teachers as equals, allowing both to teach and to learn. And it spawned other havurot throughout the country whose members also spent Shabbat together, shared communal meals, and fostered what they thought of as serious Jewish learning in an environment of equality. Some havurot were politically active, participating in protests and organizing for social change, but, despite Rabbi Green's initial inspiration, Havurat Shalom was not one of them.

The ideological foundations for havurah communities cannot easily be put into social-science categories like "tradition" and "innovation" or "individual" and "community." Havurah members maintained elements of normative Judaism as well as fostered ritual experimentation and legal innovations in order to address what they thought of as the failures of American Judaism and the demands of countercultural "new age" views.[14] In these communities "tradition" often masked innovation, especially when traditional Judaism was invoked as support for a countercultural critique of American society. "Innovation" often maintained normative Judaism, particularly when a havurah insisted, as most did, on maintaining traditional prayer.[15] Havurah members wove together tradition and innovation as essential components of an authentic Judaism.

Tradition and innovation each implied an authoritative base for Judaism that on occasion did come directly into conflict. When individuals or a group contested the authority of normative Judaism—halaha—then they had to choose one authority over another. Overt conflicts of these kinds were not typical in denominational American Judaism. Lay domination of Judaism worked against the need to confront issues of authority because conflicts were not played out at the level of ideas for most Jews, and one simply could join or begin a new synagogue to avoid such conflicts. Institutions like the synagogue provided the aura of authority for any activity undertaken. The presence of a single authoritative rabbi, the apparent permanence of the congregation, and the existence of ritual committees always assured members of an apparent authority to which they could submit. It is not surprising, then, that Jewish jokes of the era of rapid growth in synagogue building emphasized the difference between private and public behavior. These jokes focused on such behavior as parking two blocks from the synagogue rather than in the parking lot, traveling on holidays that forbade travel, or smoking or eating in bathrooms on holidays that prohibited these activities. One did not openly challenge the tradition or the synagogue's designated authority, but ignored and accommodated to it.

Havurah participants attacked these illusions as proof of the absence of authenticity in American Judaism. They inevitably were drawn into conflict with authority systems. At the same time, havurah activists were not ideologues. Their ideologies, to the extent they existed, offered critiques of American Judaism, not platforms for alternatives. In the havurah, community negotiation rather than doctrine dominated. Their negotiation also took place in egalitarian, nonhierarchic settings. Negotiation occurred in the acts of naming and organizing Jewish life and in their definitions of what community life would be. While they eagerly abandoned the American Jewish community in its present form, they were unwilling to abandon other forms of community. Their claim to uniqueness in America rested more on their place among the Jewish people, an historical and mythical entity transcending space and time, than on their own havurah. The values and history of that people were the basis of their critique of their current world.

Havurah members found in "the People Israel"—that broader Jewish people—and particularly in its preimmigrant manifestation in Europe, "holistic community" and personal engagement. Both seemed to them absent from anything they had found in the American Jewish community or in American society. Men and women who wrote about the havurah often used the words *holistic* and *seamless* to describe what they sought and how they intended to make the havurah different from the synagogue. What havurah members meant by "community" was succinctly stated by a founder of the New York Havurah.

> The compartmentalization of our Jewish life was something that we wanted to end, or at least reduce. That we davened [prayed] with one group of people, did politics with another group of people, would be changed by bringing together a group that would share some of the cultural and social concerns that we had. To study with them and do Shabbos with them would be a high, and in fact it was. There was an integration of social and religious concerns and community.

This founder sought integration or holism in her havurah because different aspects of her life and interests were shared by her community. She perceived integration because these activities all occurred in a Jewish setting where they were understood as part of Jewish experience. The community created and authenticated a Jewish lens for her life. The havurah most resembled the cultural politics of the 1970s in this manifestation; the creation of community was an act of protest against the larger society. Such noncompartmentalized communities were inevitably intense, as a member of the Boston havurah maintained.

> When you are with a group of people dedicated to sharing things emotionally and practically and sharing a serious spiritual search, you get to places you can't go to in a different kind of context. Other communities are nice. It's nice to come together for a wedding or if someone suffers a loss; it's good to do that, and Jews do that. But that's very different from committing yourself to ten hours a week of study with the same people that you daven together with on Shabbos, that you go to the movies with.

When havurah participants formed these holistic Jewish communities, they overcame the split created by the Americanization that they believed had corrupted their parents' and grandparents' lives. Alan Mintz, a founder of the New York havurah, described the integration of Jewish values into his life.

> Being religious and political, for example, may no longer involve a schizoid treading of two divergent paths but might instead become a norm of the Jewish people. . . . Totality is the goal of Jewish existence. (1973, 77–79)

This totality, of course, always was contrasted to the childhood and parental worlds. One longtime participant in the New York havurah noted that synagogues were created for an entirely different time and generation and could not meet the needs of peers. He said, "synagogues were seen as a statement to our parents and the non-Jewish community. They existed to demonstrate that we Jews are here and we will remain." Such "statements" were no longer required by the third generation, he postulated. Havurah members, unlike their parents, did not seek Americanization as their ultimate goal. They took it for granted, as no other generation had, and now they wanted to express their difference and uniqueness in holistic communities.

What was evident to havurah founders was that authentic community was not attainable in large, highly institutionalized, impersonal structures epitomized by the synagogue. Rather, Jewish community was built upon the integration of religious values and observances with people whom one could also share intimacy, work, and leisure. The form the havurah took, then, was necessarily a small face-to-face group of peers. One shared an agreed upon approach to prayer and study with these people, as well as a neighborhood and a variety of interests. A man who belonged to havurot in Boston and New York recalled his Boston experience.

> Barely a day goes by when I don't on some level think, reminisce, or miss it, the intensity and quality of life. It was astounding. Many of us were single, and those of us who were married had no kids, and there was an awful lot of time and energy. The economy wasn't like it is now, and people had time to study together. This is what the group did. We had prayers together, ate together, socialized together, and yet it wasn't stifling. We didn't live together. Outside interests were legitimate. And yet it was the center of our lives. It was like being in this very exciting family.

The common denominator of every havurah founded since 1968 is its small size and idealized familylike quality of intimacy and sharing. *Los Angeles Times* writer Mark Pinsky labeled this denominator "a Judaism of scale" in his article on the havurah movement (1986). The havurah founder rejected the suburban scale and evoked the memories of immigrant or European storefront synagogues in their community scale. What was implied by that scale was the importance and visibility of every member. Everyone was an active participant or the group could not exist. In short, it was not institutionalized or depersonalized. A woman who was a longtime member of the New York Havurah described that sense of involvement. She said, "The havurah wanted to create a participant community rather than to be in a large impersonal institution in which culture or religion was dished out to us. We didn't want to be an audience, we wanted to be the *kahal* (community)."

Participant community meant that an individual stamp was placed on every activity from making meals, to leading services, to creating art objects. Havurah members did not call a caterer, hire a rabbi or cantor, or buy any object they could make themselves, such as prayer shawls, Torah covers, or the ark for the sacred scrolls. Imperfection in any form was preferred initially over professional and impersonal expertise. The presence of the person was necessitated by the scale of the community. The Jewish model for this "scale" of life was the preimmigration world of Eastern Europe, romantically pictured as the very unity of life experience so much of the Jewish Left longed for. The shtetel, the small Jewish town controlled by Jewish authority and tolerated by gentile authority, exemplified the ideal (Zborowski and Herzog 1971). Everyone kept the Sabbath, and everyone was responsible for one another. In the shtetels there were Jewish celebrations, Jewish music, Jewish prayer, a Jewish sacred and secular language, and Jewish commerce. The sacred calendar determined the lives of many. In addition, the urban and rural Jews of Eastern Europe were involved in politics. They identified with and joined the revolutionary and national movements of Europe. When these men and women immigrated, many formed the nucleus of America's nineteenth-century labor movement. Havurah founders refashioned and embraced their own construction of Eastern European religion, community, and politics.

Havurah members' romantic notions of the shtetel required them at times to overlook desperate poverty, internal conflicts, and class differentiation, as well as the excruciating oppression that led to the migration of Jews to the United States. But for them the shtetel's appeal lay in its indisputably Jewish character and the enforced interdependence of its inhabitants. Havurot members, who sometimes call themselves "neo-hasidim," also romanticized and admired the hasidim who lived in so many of these shtetlach (plural). Their appeal for havurah participants lay in their nonrational approach to prayer, their emphasis on experience and mysticism, and their early antirationalism (Jacobs 1972). Havurah romanticism also led members to sometimes overlook the authoritarian organization and dogmatic fundamentalism in the shtetel and hasidism. Their identification, then, was selective but real. Hasidism had been presented to these young men and women as one of the embarrassments associated with the ultraorthodox, which the first and second generation wanted to leave behind. It was not surprising that the third generation claimed kinship to them around issues of community and participation.

The havurah's key foci of community, authenticity, and scale are clearly variations on themes common to the counterculture and cultural politics of the 1970s. The havurah is an "exemplary social reform" of America and American Jewish life. Activists created lives that critiqued American failures. They achieved authenticity through the havurah. However, authenticity had at the same time another meaning that put havurah participants in direct opposition to normative Judaism. The tradition was to reflect the person. Judaism was to enable havurah members to express their commitments to equality, peace, spirituality, and social and cultural transformation. Havurah Judaism was to join person and tradition so that each reflected the other and reproduced a Judaism continuous with the People Israel. An authenticity, however, that reflected, rather than shaped, the person threatened to separate her or him from the People Israel. In fact, there were things halaha required that did not simply promote sixties values; the result was the need for constant compromise between the dictates of Judaism and the personal needs of participants.

The counterculture communities of people who shared the same need for authenticity did not normally require compromise. The self was the most important authority and only sought other selves who agreed to share community. The small-scale community rested on the like-minded. Michael Fishbane of the Boston havurah summarized the place of the person in the havurah.

> The responsibility for acting on the basis of the totality of what we had learned and felt made religious development deliberate and idiosyncratic. The diversity of issues with which we wrestled was integrated in the person of each one of us; each of us in our tensions was a Jewish "possibility" [certainly not an authority] for the others. (1976, 60)

It then followed from this relationship of "possibilities" that participants were eager to interpret, alter, and—to some extent—change Judaism with others in ways that would best articulate their own definitions of the world. In seeking out a "new" Judaism, havurah participants were eager, at least initially, to explore possibilities that others might have found. Communities could measure their degree of holism and active engagement precisely in terms of the variation different prayer services or discussion leaders would bring. Havurah members held variation at the core of their uniqueness and success. Different havurot experimented with traditional Jewish liturgy to varying degrees. All were likely to experiment earlier rather than later in their group's development. At the same time, all havurot were committed to active and meaningful services that implied their willingness to reflect on and possibly change, rather than simply accept, the entire liturgy. Study of texts often involved broadening the range of texts studied far beyond normative rabbinic texts, or selecting topics of contemporary concern at the expense of traditional problems.

Another long time member of the New York Havurah, now a congregational rabbi, described his personal experience with the havurah's commitment to tolerance for varying liturgy.

> In the havurah, unlike synagogues, people put forward their agendas. That was an important phrase. For example, you could say, "I'll

> run services this Shabbat," and it was expected that whatever you put forth, people would respect and give it a fair listening. One year, for *Shacris* [morning liturgy] on Yom Kippur, I played one of Paul Simon's songs on my guitar that was particularly upbeat. I said, "this is my agenda. I think Paul Simon is a modern poet and psalmist. Here's Paul Simon for Yom Kippur!"

Havurah members integrated the tradition with their immediate world. In this example, Paul Simon, a contemporary musician whose music reflected the ideas of the youth culture, was not simply a good musician, he was a modern psalmist. In that formulation Paul Simon was understood as visionary, and psalms were regarded as contemporary. Activists varied liturgy to integrate Judaism with the world havurah members loved, a world of contemporary music, ideas, and values, not just to keep prayer novel. If they integrated tradition with the contemporary world, a plural vision of Judaism emerged. Such pluralism and variation maintained an authentic Judaism by avoiding rote prayer and routine structure. Havurah members sought to keep ritual alive and potent and thus authentic.

Their refusal to compartmentalize Judaism from their lives, as they believed America had demanded, led them to maintain and change Judaism, to align themselves with the tradition against America and with America in order to alter Judaism. A long-time member of the New York Havurah described why she and her peers sought this type of Judaism.

> We had a self-conscious recognition that we were Jewish intellectuals, and we were not simply going to be Jewish without exploring what it meant. We were not going to be schizophrenic Jews whose Judaism was unexamined and related only to childhood loyalties. We were going to study and live Judaism with the same kind of vitality that we had picked up in graduate school and universities.

At times that examination could produce striking results. One man who had belonged to two havurot described a service he led in Boston. He remembered it particularly because it was unique and not the norm for the group. But he also remembered it because it was an example of what he believed a community open to variation and innovation could achieve.

> We went on a retreat and I was supposed to lead the service. I wanted to do something a little bit different than had been done.

> And there was a great deal of encouragement to experiment. I was basically going to do the standard service, but I wanted to start off with some body movement exercises. What happened was something totally unexpected with everybody claiming that I was responsible for it. But I was absolutely out of control; it was beyond me totally. The context of the group, and the fact that they had been together for so long and had lowered defenses, particularly their spiritual defenses, really made this an extraordinary experience. We started off doing some theatrical techniques of sound and movement. We were lying on the floor and I told them to emit a sound, a sound that was their sound in a particular moment. We produced a weird harmony, not as we understand harmony, rather sounds that form a harmonic range. From that I had people, still with their eyes closed, get up and move apart and together to form a circle and just make sound the whole time. And then I was going to say, "let the sound stop" and they didn't stop. From one part of the room someone started "shhhhhhhh-ma" [the first word of the liturgical creed Shma Yisrael]. Then someone went "Nishhhhhh-mat" [the first word of the morning prayers]. Each letter became vocalized and put together from letters into words, very slowly drawn out and coupled phrases. And a *niggun* [wordless chant] began after that that no one remembered having heard before and no one remembered starting. And we essentially did this for an hour. And then it was over and there wasn't any more davening. The depth of that experience I have never really touched with any group of people. The sound of Hebrew came out in a way that was magical because of the permission that was given in the group to let go and go with it.

The advantage, then, of an activist, pluralistic community was to create a Judaism that was more vital than any member had experienced. The vitality arose from "the right to fail," as Bill Novak put it, expanding and experimenting with the tradition in a tolerant community. Novak wrote,

> I have found something new in a religious group, something which affected me at least as much as the emphasis on community itself: the havurah showed no hint of religious intimidation. . . . We shared certain key themes: the Sabbath, and issues surrounding permitted and forbidden foods, to name the most obvious. But even within these broad frameworks there was room for a wide variety of opinions and observance. (1974, 110–11)

Activism enabled authentic community and engendered pluralism. The more of themselves people brought to a havurah to integrate the spheres of their lives, the more variation a service or discussion would reflect. Tolerating differences by encouraging uniqueness rather than conformity marked the havurot.

Outsiders to the havurah did not see tolerance. They saw self-enclosed communities abandoning the mainstream of American Jewish life. These critics challenged havurah activists to justify their Judaism and explain their changes and apparent inconsistencies. One havurah founder recalled the surprise of people who discovered that men and women lived together without being married, but kept a kosher home, or said the blessing appropriate for a Sabbath meal after passing around marijuana cigarettes. Even less dramatic juxtapositions raised questions by those not in the community. But those in the havurah rarely accounted for their changes to each other, let alone to outsiders. They simply did not feel the need. One member of the Boston havurah said that certain principles of normative Judaism were accepted, like keeping kosher in the group. However, nothing guarded against altering these principles at any point. By the mid-seventies one founder of the havurah movement remembered disparagingly, "In those days my Judaism was a delicate flower of the Diaspora, a kind of aesthetic religion based on values and symbols which sacralized personal relations" (Mintz 1976, 42). He claimed that there was no foundation to his havurah's Judaism, that the havurah had made community sacred without regard to its content.

Members' attention to their individual needs within the community threatened the connection of havurot to the Jewish people. If they vivified Judaism only to undermine it, they had failed. Activism, holism, and community were the essential ingredients of havurah Judaism. But where community stood, what constituted the limits of community, and how to ensure the essential peoplehood of Judaism, were defined and redefined. In seeking a new traditionalism, these tensions were inevitable because membership was based on a shared vision or on ideas never fully spelled out, rather than on a relatively given halaha.

Havurah Decorum and Authority

In their search for authenticity, havurah members faced a classic hermeneutic problem: how to interpret their texts. Their commitment to both normative Judaism and self meant that they had to change or retain and reinterpret prayers, the Bible, and praying. One foundation for their interpretation was individualistic; people tested texts against themselves. But they were also drawn away from individual interpretation and random alteration of ritual by the power tradition held in formulating the sacred calendar and the liturgical cycle. They inherited prescribed action, and changing it was an act not only of innovation but of denial as well.

Individual interpretation took place within particular communities. No two havurot were alike. Communities interpreted together, though surprisingly unsystematically. Their changes were rarely hammered out as a committee would formulate agreed upon rules and principles for an organization. If any single criterion existed among havurot for how to select which prayers to include in worship or how many sections of a weekly Torah portion must be included on the Sabbath, it was an aesthetic criterion. Because participants wanted to maximize the positive experience of prayer, they had to ask what effect excluding text had on the ritual life of the community. Aesthetic considerations dictated the styles, sounds, rhythms, and lengths of periods of concentrated praying, as well as the physical setting for prayer and study. Aesthetics, in the broadest sense, channeled and shaped the tradition, and both halaha and aesthetics were shifted in response to individual reactions. Decorum, the preoccupation of the laity in 1870 as well as 1970, took the form it did according to aesthetic evaluations. The Judaism that arose immediately after immigration was fundamentally shaped by an aesthetic of uniformity. The countercultural aesthetic that shaped the havurah depended on an expressive individualism that featured the activism of all participants. Expressive individualism, in turn, was the product of the American culture that gave rise to American Judaism and promoted Jewish secularism. Secularism and traditionalism acted upon one another through the individuals within havurot.

A havurah member expressed this sense of aesthetics himself when he reflected on his own experience. "I was moved to realize that we were developing our own style of ritual—deeply traditional and yet thoughtfully innovative" (Reimer 1976, 246). In this formulation Reimer suggested that havurah members were mindful of the tradition as they articulated the right and necessity of changing it. No havurah formally expressed precisely what was meant by either tradition or innovation. No principles defined either a minimum of observance that would constitute normative Judaism, or a maximum of freedom that would draw the limits on innovation. There was also variation from havurah to havurah and within any single group. In the early years, participants had only an implicit and changing consensus concerning what was tolerable. A man who participated in two havurot said when interviewed:

> There was never an organized theology. People were given a great deal of freedom and leeway, not only in how they would choose to lead a service, but in their own Jewish observance. So it was a group that combined a live and let live theology with a real traditional motivation and sensitivity. Hebrew was very important. People were Jewishly knowledgeable. Many of us were classically trained; some were rabbis. You had the two qualities side by side—liberalism and tradition. It gave you the right to fail.

Only in the havurah aesthetic then, could one find an articulation of authentic Judaism. Only by examining how members "would choose to lead a service," or how a "real traditional motivation and sensitivity" was articulated in the group could one discover the authenticity of Judaism. Members articulated tradition and service leadership through aesthetic forms. People knew a service had wandered too far from the halaha when it no longer "felt right." They also felt excluded from services when prayers were said in a way that simply fulfilled religious obligation and didn't take account of the worshiper. "Beauty" reflected tradition as well as a nonsynagogue atmosphere.

For example, during interviews with founders of havurot in New York and Boston, certain aesthetic issues were raised repeatedly: the appearance of the room where they prayed, the attention to melodies and ritual objects, and the care lavished on communal meals. Their aesthetic was always contrasted to members' experiences in synagogues or at home. One Boston havurah member described a Friday night service.

> Friday night was an incredibly sensuous, personal time in the group. We davened by candle light. The first service we went to at Havurat Shalom was a Friday night service. We walked into the house [where Havurat Shalom met] and then the prayer room. And in the prayer room there are no seats, just cushions on the floor. The candles were lit; it was dusk. It was really quiet and serene, people sitting around on cushions. After awhile someone began a slow niggun [wordless melody]; it was incredible. At the havurah there was an incredible consciousness of mood, of what constitutes mood, enhances and detracts from it, and a terrific sense of aesthetics, of Jewish aesthetics. What is appropriate and not appropriate to do; what enhances beauty and what detracts from it. I never understood that Jews could pray like that.

Her detailed description communicated what was important in the havurah, what contributed to prayer, and what differed from other Jewish experiences.

The values of decorum, aesthetics, and beauty were powerful issues for every immigrant generation. The transformations of tradition developed by each generation are not reducible to decorum, but visions of behavior and beauty in Judaism reflect succinctly the visions of self and the culture sought. The suburban parents wanted orderliness, harmony, and synchrony in ritual and formality. Their havurah children were equally focused on decorum, equally convinced that in their visions of Judaism lay the possibilities for maintaining an adaptable tradition. For them beauty implied spontaneity, disorderliness, informality, variety, and variability.

Disorderliness was the American counterculture's ultimate aesthetic. Loudness, multiple images, freeform movement and antiauthoritarianism all attacked the ordered constraints of middle-class America. Havurah aesthetics and styles were always inspired by disorder. An etiquette may establish order even if its inspiration is disorder. The home-baked *hallah* or personally made candle, while not disorderly, were individualized and unique. American culture made the mass produced product conterminous with order. In this context, disorder was uniqueness.

Each generation found that a new aesthetic was required. In both cases that aesthetic attacked the traditional authority. The parent generation's evident embrace of authority through the construction of denominations masked the extent of their innovation. The havurah members constructed an ideology that attacked authority but maintained the centrality of the traditional "sensibility." For both generations, traditional authority was questioned, whereas familiar aspects of tradition remained.

The suburban middle-class Jew's penchant for organization was repeated in the havurah generation's interest in new forms of organization. Both generations emphasized organization over theology. But above all, havurot were participatory. People were not members in name alone. They did not join so that their children, parents, or grandparents would be able to participate. And havurot members formed intense religious communities at an age normally marked by minimal Jewish attachment, precisely because most young adults have so few dependents. One need not obscure the real differences in the generations' visions of Jewish life in order to demonstrate havurah members' profound connection to American Judaism. They rejected synagogues, suburbs, and denominations because they sought a different, and what they believed was a more authentic, Judaism. They accepted decorum, organization and a traditional liturgy as the forms for their changes because they continued to synthesize Judaism, and American culture in that authentic Judaism.

Havurah activists differed from previous generations of American Jews because they rejected middle-class assumptions about the good life. They challenged those values in their romanticization of shtetel Jews, a group every other American Jewish generation sought to forget out of guilt, shame, or discomfort. Having grown comfortable in America, American Jews produced their third generation, who rejected the previous generation's choices. When Lucy Dawidowicz attributed the existence of havurot to a revitalization of orthodoxy, she misunderstood how deeply these communities were redefining their American heritage (1982b, 97). Because the dynamic that motivated a search for a past lay not in the immigrant experience but in the New Left's attack on "sham American pluralism," that search led the New Left to the creation of alternatives. They could build a new America alongside the old, one that joined "New Jews" both to American forms of protest and the Jewish preoccupation with decorum.

At the core of the havurah protest was a counter aesthetic, a means for differentiating youth from parents and young Jews from America. This counter aesthetic emerged within a generational context whose protests were made against a society organized to accommodate a bureaucracy rather than the individual. The Jewish counterculture sought uniqueness in a reformulated tradition rather than in the destruction of all rules, as did its secular counterpart. Both countercultures, however, produced counteraesthetics and alternative organizations in order to protest American domination of all minorities and difference. An aesthetic that fostered uniqueness was the initial cultural rebellion. The authority of the self rejected traditional forms of authority: family and national government. Within the counterculture, that self realized through aesthetics and organization constituted a cultural protest.

In their emphasis on aesthetics and their search for authenticity, what members often called "a traditional sensibility," participants in the havurah movement generated a flexible and innovative vision of authority. Their use of an English phrase indicated the extent to which that sensibility was American. A "traditional sensibility" implied flexibility within limits, staying within boundaries rather than being obligated to prescribed action. It made the self the chief arbiter of the sensibility. This authority, neither traditional nor arbitrary, was in fact well rooted in American culture. Indeed, by the 1970s Americans had devoted fifty years to promoting a cult of personality, emphasizing self-expressiveness and attacking traditional forms of authority. Even the "social ethic" William Whyte uncovered in the American suburbs of the 1950s was self-expressive and committed to promoting a well-rounded person, in contrast to the individualistic producer ethic of the Protestant ethic. The 1960s, then, did not so much constitute a radical change as culminate one long in coming. The counterculture wanted to dissolve normative structures and conventions in America to create an anticulture that urged people to make it all up (Fitzgerald 1986, 408). The only authority for this new culture was in the self. And that self was the product of values of self-realization, self-fulfillment, and self-gratification that developed after 1910 (Susman 1984, 280). Consumers are, after all, as anxious to express themselves as counterculturalists. The difference lies in the forms of expression. The 1950s emphasized a self-expression that conformed to a shared and chosen norm. The American counterculture emphasized a self-expression that rejected social conformity and sought uniqueness instead. Uniqueness was enacted within small-scale, alternative organizations that, while committed to community, did not define individual attitudes and rules. The power of the group was one of the defining contrasts between the old and New Left. In the New Left, authority was not even vested in a revolutionary alternative. People got along and accomplished political ends only because they wanted to.

Authenticity was assured by a sensibility or shared aesthetic. Authenticity was, in the view of some, a problematic basis for community particularly because it was nonobligatory and offered no guarantee of observance. Alan Mintz, a havurah member, reflected on this problem.

> Rather than struggle with halakah, prayer and study on their own terms, too often we gravitated toward what was most comfortable, least offensive, and closest to our agenda. The theological reasons for this emphasis are significant: the weakness of traditional belief . . . made such selectivity vis-a-vis the tradition necessary as it did the shift from God to community as the source of values. (1976, 42)

If community became the ultimate source of value, the foundation of all observance was what one member called, "interpersonal relations, a sense of groupness." He argued that the weakness of such a foundation was that "there was nothing in the group that some part didn't bring to the group." Because synagogues have the aura of authority due to their institutionalization, they represent ideas no one in the group need embrace. Law is superordinate. No principles, however, existed for havurot in Jewish law. The havurah's critics noted their circular seating arrangement for worship, claiming that it indicated their hostility to authority. They charged, "they pray to each other." One woman commented:

> I don't think it's an accident that havurot pray in circles. People say we pray to each other, and in some sense we do. But that's good, not bad. I think part of the problem of havurot is that we don't know how to pray to God. We're good at praying with and to each other. We're so into community and into interpersonal stuff it carries over into prayer, which is one sphere in which you think you can have access to a different vision. But instead we've made prayer harmonious when it's supposed to be schizophrenic. The community gives real power to prayer. But there is no question that what goes on in t'fillah is private dialogue, between the Ribbeno Shel Olam [a name for God meaning Master of the Universe] and the person. In havurot we somehow wrote out a part of the dimension. We're really good at the communal thing, better than anyone. But we don't give enough space for private dialogue. We don't know how to do it or talk about it, and lest the void be too awesome, we cover it over and pretend it's not really there.

The havurah sought a Judaism that would maintain community as well as a relationship to God. Sometimes the community's commitment to innovation got in the way of the spiritual quest. This woman poignantly noted that community was a more accessible goal than a relationship with God. Less critical than Mintz, she nevertheless worried that community alone was insufficient.

Their transformation of tradition was not to be an end in itself, not a self-serving process, but an authentic and enlivening one. Mintz's accusation implied the reverse, that change had only served personal ends—their desire to integrate relevant issues with the tradition or to find ways to redefine their lack of belief. Mintz at least worried that if havurah members tried to maintain a relationship between innovation and authority, they might end up abandoning all authority.

Ironically, their commitment to innovation was also threatened by tradition. Authority was still bound up with traditional liturgy and halaha. Hence, the renewal of the tradition was threatened by the tradition itself, which remained the script for religious experience and community. The much touted experimentation of havurot often was exaggerated. One member of the New York Havurah described that group's response to liturgical innovation.

> I remember one service in which a man who was leading it passed around flowers. For most of us I suppose that was nice in spirit, but

> it violated what was a much more rigid notion of what we meant by *t'fillah* [prayer]. In truth there was enormous resistance to creative services of any kind. People had much deeper needs and desires about what they wanted for t'fillah than they ever admitted.

Even in Havurat Shalom, where more experimentation took place, members believed that experimentation could be contained. As one man said, "There was a certain form to t'fillah that had to be maintained in some guise at least." The tradition had to remain recognizable to authenticate renewing it. The havurah, then, operated within the tension of "tradition" and "innovation." Their ideologies, by never clearly defining either, maintained both.

Redefining authority engendered a "sensibility" rather than a halaha (literally a way of life). The sensibility had to reflect the past and the present at once. Havurot emphasized aesthetic dimensions of prayer and ritual, placing experience over obligation, although members were anxious about their relations with God and other Jews and the meaning of authority. However, havurah members tended to judge the authenticity of their religious experiences against their childhood experiences. If one's Judaism was practiced differently from one's family, one was assured of being part of a changing movement. The dynamic between the generations was translated into Jewish worship. As immigrants had earlier distanced themselves from European synagogues, so Jewish youth disassociated themselves from the Judaism of their parents. One activist notes the centrality of this generational conflict.

> The Jewish Student Movement was prepared for cultural protest, but not cultural revolution. Pressing to the limit would have led to the symbolic commission of parentcide. It came as a jolt when I found out that I was being driven by Oedipal memories of corrupt institutions and leadership violating the Jewish life I longed to embrace. (Benjamin 1976, 51)

The "parentcide" that Jerry Benjamin feared lay for the havurah in transforming the synagogue, creating community, altering aesthetics, and keeping both tradition and innovation flexible. They welcomed that break with their parents. Not only did havurah members criticize the corruption of the past, they also altered their parental construction seat for seat, melody for melody, garment for garment. Middle-class values were excised and middle-class structures and authorities were toppled. Institutions were replaced with "communities." Professionals were replaced with peers.

Writers analyzing the American New Left have noted the continuity of this generation with its parents' norms and values (Keniston 1968; Flacks 1971; Friedenberg 1969). Rather than a rebellion, New Left protests, demands, and programs were a fuller realization of their parents' dreams for social equality and a fair society. The havurot members were no exception. "Parentcide" was not accomplished because they embraced values fundamental to their childhoods.

Though community was the havurah goal, members did not define a new communal authority. Individualism remained essential to the havurah's vision. A member of the New York Havurah summarized the centrality of the individual.

> When we made Shabbos it was in a traditional style. When you walked into the havurah it would look like an Orthodox shtibel [synagogue]. But the total framework, at least for the New York Havurah, was non-Orthodox. That ability to go in and out, to decide to observe in a very traditional way, but also to decide not to, was characteristic.

Individualism was a translation rather than a contradiction of suburban success. The "self-made man" became the self-expressive person. The Judaism that was to be kept neatly tucked in the affluent suburban synagogue as a badge of American success became, as one man put it, "an enormously rich resource that has the potential of enriching our individual, family, and communal lives." What Judaism could offer individuals changed; individualism was never undermined as the primary authority. The break with traditional authority had been made, and it was firmly maintained in havurot.

The havurot reveal the continuing vitality of American Judaism. Like their parents and grandparents, havurah members continued to create an American Judaism in their protest against America. The process of reinventing and maintaining Judaism is a continuous process only because Judaism or Jewishness remains a core issue of identity. For those who seek a place for a remembered, if unlived, past in the midst of the present, a ritual rehearsal of identity through a transformed tradition is inevitable.

Notes

1. L. Epstein's (1978) approach to ethnicity focuses on the affective dimension as well as the social circumstances that cast ethnicity in a particular form. Following Fischer, I suggest that Jewish ethnicity took on new meaning in the 1970s, though it was anchored

by the sentiments generated within the family. Epstein's emphasis on sentiment is consistent with this perspective.

2. I never found consensus among members on the meaning of the Minyan's name. The word *free* was interpreted by some to mean the absence of expensive dues and by others to suggest their relationship to religious obligation. The juxtaposition of "minyan" and "free" in their name suggests this very tension.

3. Over the last fifteen years a similar age group has been targeted for recruitment to extreme orthodoxy in the United States and Israel. Apparently tired of the relativism of American and modern life, increasing numbers of suburban assimilated Jews have become *ba'alei tshuva,* "returnees" to Orthodox Judaism (Aviad 1982; Jakobson 1986). But havurah members have even less in common with the ultra-orthodox than with their parents' generation. Havurot are predicated on members' willingness to alter a great deal of the Jewish tradition. They do not want to abandon secular society. They are neither extremists nor assimilationists. Like so many American Jews, they are planted firmly in-between. At the same time, unlike most Jews who succeed at Americanization, they are interested in creating new Jewish organizations rather than joining them.

4. David DeNola's (1974) article on the Jewish student press describes a number of these publications, their funding, and the press service that evolved from them.

5. Interviews for this chapter were conducted with Barry Holtz, Paula Hyman, Richard Meirowitz, William Novak, John Ruskay, Richard Siegel, and Sharon Strassfeld.

6. See the following works for a discussion of the American counterculture: Roszak 1969; Myerhoff 1969; Boskin and Rosenstone 1969; Keniston 1968; Flacks 1971; Clecak 1973; and Howard 1969.

7. Ultimately, steps were taken to build links between various groups. Yearly retreats were held at a farm in New York where members of havurot from all over the Northeast could meet. Then, in the late 1970s, a National Havurah Committee was formed. One of its chief tasks was to organize summer institutes for havurah members. At this point, havurot were also integrated into synagogues and no formal distinction was drawn between those inside and outside institutions. As of 1987, one institute was held in the East. In years prior, institutes were also held in the Midwest and West. Topics for the 1987 Institute included: Contemporary Human Rights: Issues of Jewish Concern; How We Imagine Ourselves: Treatments of the Human Body in Classical Judaism; Abstract and Concrete in Talmudic Law; Dialoguing Across Jewish Differences; Sensuality and Spirituality in the Poetry of Jewish Women; The Siddur: Structure, Content and the Spirit of Prayer.

8. A study of Jews living in Boston in 1975 found that 92.9 percent of Jewish males between the ages of thirty and forty-four had either attended college, graduated, or obtained a postgraduate degree. Seventy-seven percent of males between the ages of eighteen and twenty-nine fell into the same category. Eight-six percent of the women between the ages of eighteen and twenty-nine had either attended college, graduated from college, or done postgraduate work. Seventy-eight percent of the women between the ages of thirty and forty-four fell in the same pattern (Goldescheider 1986, 124, 131).

9. Paul Cowan's autobiography recounts his journey to what he would call a "havurah Judaism" (1982). As an active participant in the civil rights movement, he comments specifically about how that movement, its promises and disappointments, led him to a modified traditional Judaism.

10. A number of sociologists have written on the powerful connection between American Judaism and Israel. Leibman (1973) suggests that Israel provides the content of

American Judaism. Hence, Israel is a powerful ingredient in the Jewish identity of these men and women. But subsequent to the early years of the havurot, these same men and women founded organizations that criticized Israel's relationship with the Palestinians. *Breira* (Hebrew word for alternative) and New Jewish Agenda are national organizations of younger American Jews who maintained their positions as Zionists, but critically. The established Jewish community was particularly vociferous in its attack on Breira, a group that no longer exists. A *Commentary* article makes the attack (Shatten 1977), and in the subsequent issue many havurah members respond with letters to the editor (June 1977, 60–66).

11. Bellah, et al., describe the contemporary American form of community as a "lifestyle enclave." They are critical of the isolationism implied in the lifestyle of people who are joined by nothing other than common affinity, and note the lack of anything substantial out of which might develop commitment or longevity. They note that such enclaves are characteristic not only of the affluent and conservative but of the politically radical as well. The counterculture's approach to politics clearly moved the Left toward such lifestyle enclaves (1985, 71–75, 335).

12. See Michael Novak (1971) for a discussion of white ethnics in the 1970s. Novak's book not only describes the emergence of ethnicity but also illustrates it. He describes his own ethnicity, what it means to him, and how it makes him different from those around him. He emphasizes the cultural aspects of ethnicity and underlines the extent to which white ethnicity in the 1970s is a reaction to assertions of black rights.

13. There is no historical account of the havurah movement in print. Mintz and Sleeper (1971), Porter and Dreier (1973), and Neusner (1972) contain the most helpful documents and articles about the early years of the havurah movement and the two first havurot, Havurat Shalom (Boston) and the New York Havurah.

14. See Shils (1981) for a discussion of tradition in the social sciences.

15. See Sally Falk Moore (1975) for a discussion of how change and tradition can mask one another.

3

A Sabbath Minyan

Organization, Decorum, and Experience

> In the Minyan there is something for everyone.
>
> Aaron

The historical development of the synagogue and havurah demonstrates that religious forms are affected continually by social conditions. As Max Weber made clear in his study of why capitalism developed in a Western Protestant nation and not elsewhere, the conjunction of religion and social and economic relationships creates significant developments in each. Social relations are expressed in religion, in who participates and how they formulate a body of doctrine ([1904] 1958).

The emerging American middle class of the late nineteenth and early twentieth century, increasingly committed to leisure, discovered in Christianity and Judaism foundations for personal identity and social community. Immigrant Jews and their offspring wove together the manners and style of the middle class with traditional forms of Jewish ritual. The synagogue was the institution through which Jews rehearsed their identities. With changing social conditions, therefore, the relations between ritual and style were continually altered, often bringing generational formulations of Judaism in conflict. A great many American Jews, then, consistently have negotiated religious forms, social conditions, and Jewish identity within a Jewish ritual context. Indeed, they have relied on ritual within the family and the synagogue to formulate and authenticate their Judaism.

The Kelton Free Minyan was a setting for just such negotiation. As an alternative to both family and synagogue, it was an emerging generational formulation that responded to American post war suburbanization. Minyan members made a series of decisions in their first two years that reveal precisely how they constructed Judaism within a generational decorum. Members of the Minyan community incorporated into their Sabbath prayers ritual changes, reorganized social statuses, conflict with tradition, and their yearning for integration with Judaism as a culture and history. Most of these changes did not occur within the content of their liturgy, but rather in the ways they prayed together. The act of praying itself became a vehicle for identity construction within the Minyan, not just for what was said but for how it was said.

In the following chapters, I show how the Minyan channels the process of identity formation for young Jews. When they acted as feminists, liberals, or activists they did so within their Sabbath worship community, as well as in the other arenas of their lives. They were people searching to become who they were, not by creating identities but by integrating them. The Minyan was one important arena for this process.

The best introduction to the group may be the single material object they produced to mark the eastern wall (*mizrach*) of the room in which they prayed on the Sabbath. Jerusalem, the mythological center of the Jewish people, is in the east. Jews everywhere pray in the direction of the city where the temple, the center of Jewish worship, was constructed for daily prayer and sacrifices to God. Though the temple was finally destroyed in 70 C.E., its memory and the hope for its restoration remain central to observant Jews. Jerusalem is the subject of innumerable prayers and psalms and is physically recalled whenever a person prays and turns east. In American synagogues, the ark housing the Torah is customarily on the eastern wall.

During the Minyan's second year, women members created a unique mizrach. It was a blue cloth banner decorated with a young man and woman surrounded by sacred Jewish symbols. Gold cloth letters attached over the heads of the two figures read, "Worship the Lord joyfully," a phrase from the psalms. The group's banner reflected its desire to create a joyful and animated prayer experience. Their placement of the man and woman on the banner was unconventional in light of the Jewish prohibition on graven images, which forbids the use of a human form in religious art. This man and woman were direct reflections of the American counterculture. She wore a long flowered dress and held with assurance a Torah to her side, although in normative Judaism a woman has virtually no access to the Torah scroll because she is separated from the Torah and men during prayer. The young man stood, legs apart, wearing a casual shirt and pants with a prayer shawl around his shoulders and a *kippah* (head covering) on his head. On the banner surround-

Details from the Minyan mizrach.

ing the figures were three symbols. One was the braided loaf of egg bread (*hallah*) used on the Sabbath by Jews to make the blessing for bread. The lion, often associated with the Torah because its image frequently stands guard around the ark, was the second symbol. Sabbath candles were placed near the woman as a symbol of the festivity of the day. Women have the ritual responsibility for lighting them.

The mizrach juxtaposed traditional imagery with radically innovative forms. It pictured the selves idealized by the community: fully contemporary and at ease with Jewish tradition. They were dressed casually like their contemporaries, and they were surrounded and in contact with sacred symbols that embodied home celebration and the Torah, which required a minyan to be read. The person, the home, and the prayer community were embodied in the mizrach. Prayer and Judaism, then, were incorporated into the lives of Minyan members, and they in turn created their identities in relationship to the forms and idioms of Jewish life. The banner embodied and modeled the attitudes and counterdecorum that the community sought.

After introducing the Minyan and its members—describing in Chapter 3 their activities, their worship service, and their history—my focus will shift to two major conflicts in the group during 1973 and 1974. Conflicts about prayer and gender-based rules provide two case studies that reveal how Minyan members formulated their Judaism together as a community.[1] In these conflicts they alternately changed Jewish law concerning men and women and retained traditional prayer. Each choice represented a strategy for the creation of identity, community, and the practice of Judaism. The two opposite strategies (maintenance and transformation of tradition) also produced conflicts, which had to be resolved so that members could maintain the stability of their community and their ability to worship. To understand their resolution of these conflicts is to see how their religious lives were generated.

A Minyan Sabbath

Minyan members began their Sabbath morning activities some time before they prayed. They gathered together first to create the environment for the Sabbath and parted only after the space had been returned to its daily form. I begin by describing what members would consider a typical Sabbath in order to introduce these men and women who created the Minyan in its first years.

It was winter 1973 in Los Angeles. This Saturday morning was a pleasant, mild one. A breeze was blowing. In the university neighborhood of Kelton, the weekday buzz had disappeared and, except for the sounds of sparse traffic, it was quiet. At ten o'clock in the morning, at a large neighborhood intersection, voices were audible. At this hour, on this day, most observant American Jews have been at their synagogue prayers for thirty minutes to an hour. At this corner, the voices of gathering men and women offered Sabbath greetings. As they approached the University Religious Center, they greeted one another with the Yiddish or Hebrew phrases, "Gut Shabbos," "Shabbat Shalom" (Sabbath greetings). Clad in jeans, shirts, pants, embroidered blouses, and sandals, they looked like people attending an informal party, not a religious service. Alone, in couples, or in small groups they walked up two flights of stairs and entered the hallway outside the large rectangular room the Minyan used for Sabbath services. When eight or ten people gathered, the process of transforming this space into a place of worship began. No single leader directed the activity. A few people took a large red rug from a closet to cover the cold, institutional, linoleum floor. Enough couches and chairs to seat forty people were arranged in a rectangle around the rug. They took prayer books (*Siddurim*), books containing the Pentatuch and selections from prophets and other books of the Bible (*humashim*), head coverings (*kippot*), and prayer shawls (*tallitot*) from a cupboard in the library down the hall and placed them with care on a table in the hallway directly in front of the worship room; the table itself was to be brought into the worship room for the Torah service. People used one or all of these objects during the service. Finally, someone took the mizrach from the cupboard and pinned it to the eastern wall of the room.

The room was soon ready. By now, nearly thirty people sat together, near friends, or spouses. A few welcomed newcomers if they were present. They talked quietly, exchanging information or continuing conversations interrupted by the preparation of the room. This particular Sabbath, one small group of regular members exchanged information on vacations; Mark showed a postcard he had received from Jacob and Rachel who were vacationing. (Members of the Minyan will be listed for reference in Figure 2.) Mark and Jacob were colleagues at the University Hillel. Their offices were just a few feet from the room where the Minyan held its Sabbath service. Mark was nearly thirty and Jacob in his mid-thirties. Mark was unmarried and Jacob only recently married. Mark and Jacob began the Minyan together in 1971 and comprised the contrasts and commonalities of the membership.

Mark was ordained as a Conservative rabbi and Jacob as a Reform rabbi. Both of them observed the dietary laws, but Mark was the more

FIGURE 2

Some Members of the Kelton Minyan

Founding and Second-Year Members

Founders

Name	Age	Birth Place	Occupation	Religious Backgrund
Mark	late 20s	New York	Hillel rabbi	Conservative
Jacob	30	New York	Hillel rabbi	Reform
Ruth	early 20s	Los Angeles	rabbinical student	Reform
Susan	early 20s	California	graduate student	Zionist
Ed	late 20s	New York	Hillel rabbi	Reform
Harvey	mid 20s	Boston	graduate student	Conservative
Michael	late 20s	New York	profesor	Orthodox
Ellen	mid 20s	New York	secretary	Reform

Second-Year Members

Name	Age	Birth Place	Occupation	Religious Background
Jay	late 20s	Wisconsin	rabbi-educator	Conservative
Martha	mid 20s	New York	graduate student	Conservative
Beth	mid 20s	Los Angeles	graduate student	Conservative
Saul	early 20s	California	student-Jewish educator	Conservative
Doug	late 20s	Chicago	student	Reconstructionist
Rachel	mid 20s	Los Angeles	actress-singer	Reform
Aaron	late 20s	Philadelphia	sociologist	Conservative / Reform
Terri	mid 20s	Los Angeles	nursery school teacher	Conservative
Miriam	mid 20s	Chile	graduate student	unaffiliated with synagogue
Rob	early 20s	Los Angeles	rabbinical student	Conservative
Neal	early 20s	Indiana	rabbinical student	Conservative
Linda	early 20s	California	nurse	Christian
Joseph	mid 20s	Hungary	law student	Orthodox

rigorous in his observance of Jewish law. For example, unlike Jacob, Mark did not drive on the Sabbath. Both found all other Kelton neighborhood synagogues "depressing" for Sabbath worship, and both hoped that the Minyan would be the kind of community they sought for religious worship. Mark grew up in Brooklyn in an observant Jewish home. He had ten synagogues within walking distance of his house. He spent most of his adolescent summers at Camp Ramah, the camp of the Conservative Jewish movement. Jacob grew up in a New York City suburb in a nonobservant Reform home. Mark often said, "I made Jacob more traditional." Jacob said, "I made Mark think about the need to change the Jewish tradition." They were searching for a Sabbath experience where they did not have to be leaders, acting as *the* rabbi. They both sought a community of serious Jews, of intellectuals willing to pray and reflect on their Judaism. Rachel joined the Minyan when she and Jacob became engaged. Raised in Los Angeles as a Reform Jew, she attended Kelton University. She was an actress and singer.

Susan, another of the group's founders, described the camping trip she planned. She was in her early twenties and completing an undergraduate degree in English literature. She also took a minor in Hebrew literature, enrolling in advanced language and literature courses. Susan was raised in a small town in central California where there were not enough Jews to form a minyan. Her father was an ardent Zionist and encouraged the use of Hebrew in the house. Susan came to Kelton University to be in a large Jewish community. She was *Shomer Shabbat* (completely observant of all Sabbath laws). Like Mark, on the Sabbath she did not ride, cook, use electricity, or write. Unlike Mark, she did not grow up with such observances, but chose them for herself. She planned this trip with another Minyan member, Linda, Susan's roommate and a convert to Judaism. Linda was a nurse, educated at Kelton University. She was initially drawn to Judaism out of curiosity, took classes, and studied for conversion with Mark and Jacob.

In another group Doug was describing his progress on his master's thesis in urban planning. His focus on a Los Angeles Jewish neighborhood had given him a number of anecdotes he shared in informal conversation. He said, "There are several theories about the prominence of Chinese restaurants in this neighborhood." He explained, then wryly added:

> The fact is that American Jews have developed a taste for Chinese food and all Jewish neighborhoods have lots of them. Theories about density, multiethnicity, and other factors simply cannot explain it more effectively than that.

Doug was from a Chicago suburb. He was completing his education in Los Angeles and married a woman from the area. He did not live in the Kelton neighborhood as Mark, Susan, Jacob, and Rachel did. He drove to attend the services. He was raised in a family that was centrally involved in a Reconstructionist synagogue and was the only Minyan member from that denomination. He considered himself observant of the holidays, the Sabbath, the dietary laws, and other measures of Jewish piety. But he and his wife Beth drove to pray in a place they found most congenial. Beth was the child of immigrants and survivors of the Holocaust. She was raised in a family where more Jewish traditions were observed than in Doug's, but not one where women were given a formal Jewish education. Beth was pursuing a graduate degree in Jewish history at a local Reform seminary.

Beth and Doug were not Minyan founders, having joined the group when it was about a year old. They were nevertheless regular participants. They spoke with Joseph as they readied the room on this particular Sabbath. He had attended the Minyan regularly for six months. An immigrant whose family fled the Hungarian Revolution in 1956, Joseph's parents are survivors of the Holocaust that destroyed almost all of his extended family. He came to the United States with no idea what Jewish religious observance was about. As a six-year-old child he moved with his parents into the home of an Orthodox Jewish aunt. He attended a Jewish parochial school and, as he grew older, a public school as well as afternoon Hebrew school. He observed the strictest Jewish traditions. After high school he said he had "only disdain for Judaism. I was interested in embracing as many world views as possible." The radicalism of his college years led to an interest in Israel as he grew critical of the United States. He lived in Israel after college graduation and then returned to the United States. His time in the Minyan represented an interim period in which he was trying to decide whether to move permanently to Israel as a member of a *kibbutz,* (a collective farm) or to become a lawyer in the United States. He explained to me:

> The Minyan is a community I have always longed for. It has made prayer, a traditional form which was unpalatable, very palatable. Here is a group struggling and questioning forms of Jewish life and not simply accepting them.

Joseph thought of himself as "a faucet attached to an enormous water system which is all Jews in history. Sometimes I am onto the system and sometimes off. The Minyan allows me to be open to the system."

Paula is in another corner talking to a woman who is new to the group, generally welcoming her and asking her how she found the Minyan. Paula also joined the Minyan recently. On leave from law school, she worked in Los Angeles at a feminist art center. Raised as an Orthodox Jew in suburban New York, she was seeking a group to pray in. She explained:

> I want a traditional service, but one where I will belong. Women's participation is very important to me. But it also feels authentic here. I would be willing to relocate here permanently to be in this community.

Joseph and Paula were both twenty-four years old and unmarried. They each kept a kosher home, but also drove on the Sabbath. Although their practice was intermittent, their sense of Judaism was deep.

By 10:30 A.M. the Minyan began its formal activity of praying the Sabbath morning liturgy together. First, however, they held a discussion, instituted at the Minyan's founding in 1971 when the group had barely the required quorum of ten. Its purpose was to allow some time prior to praying for members to articulate doubts, questions, and insights about the prayers they would shortly chant from the traditional prayerbook. The discussion was called a "prayer confrontation." Before beginning the discussion, one woman in the room suggested that everyone in the rectangle give his or her name. Not everyone in the room knew each other.

Aaron led the discussion that week; he volunteered for the responsibility on the previous Sabbath. All tasks for a Sabbath were completed by weekly volunteers who took what members called "offices." Aaron chose to discuss a prayer called "*Aleinu,*" which is one of the closing prayers of all Jewish worship.[2] In the discussion led by Aaron, many but not all of the thirty people in the room participated. Men dominated, and the most dominant among them were the rabbi members and those with extensive Jewish knowledge. They disagreed among themselves and brought others into the discussion on different sides. No opinion appeared authoritative. Aaron opened the discussion with the following comment:

> I am critical of this prayer. When we read, "We therefore hope in Thee, Lord our God, Soon to behold the glory of Thy might. When Thou will remove abominations from the earth and the idols shall be wholly destroyed. When the world shall be established under the rule of the Almighty, and all the wicked on earth will turn to Thee," we are setting ourselves apart, even above all the other peoples and cultures of the world. We proclaim the superiority of a Jewish way of life, of Jewish worship, and Jewish beliefs. Even our God is set apart from all other people. This prayer is evangelical and I have respected Judaism because it was not an evangelical religion. I would like to know more about the circumstances in which it was written. What was going on that made it necessary for people to

> make a statement like this, a statement that frankly leaves me uncomfortable? How desirable is it to have a prayer that praises us to the exclusion of others and attempts to have all believe the way Jews do?

Their discussion was lively. Harvey said that Aaron misunderstood the prayer.

> The author of the prayer uses a framework that spoke only of the God of creation, not about Israel or the Jews' relation to God. The prayer does not claim that the Jews are superior. It claims that God is powerful.

Jay added: "What is dangerous in the prayer? Is it the exaltation of God the creator or the hope that all will recognize God as the only God and hope that 'his name would be one'?"

Ed offered a sociological insight:

> The answer is obvious. All social systems face similar problems. It is in the nature of such systems to assert their superiority over others. Jews are not unique in this and the *aleinu* simply mirrors that problem.

Mark adamantly disagreed:

> Pagan systems are entirely different from monotheistic systems. Pagan cultures never asserted that all humans must believe one thing over another. The Jews never suffered antisemitism under Pagan cultures because Judaism could be one religion among many. Frankly, I have always found this prayer difficult. I agree with Aaron. I can't see the point of asserting a wish to make all others like ourselves.

Doug agreed. "I am a Jew because I believed that implied respect for others. *Aleinu* undermines that respect."

The discussion continued as members took various sides in the debate. Mark, though a rabbi, questioned the prayer. Harvey, not one, upheld it. He was also a founder of the Minyan and an articulate spokesperson for tradition. At twenty-five, he was an advanced graduate student in modern Hebrew literature at Kelton University. His Hebrew was excellent. He grew up in Boston in an observant, Conservative Jewish family and was unmarried. He participated actively in Camp

Ramah in his adolescence, moving into leadership roles, and there met Mark and Jay years before he arrived in Los Angeles. Previously, Harvey participated in a minyan at the University of Chicago that resembled the Kelton Minyan. The Minyan began the year he moved to Los Angeles. His closest friends were drawn from the Minyan and the Kelton neighborhood where he lived. He was an excellent *hazan* (cantor) and widely admired for his skill and knowledge.

The sociological insight was provided by another rabbi and Minyan founder. Ed was thirty and a Hillel director at another university campus in Los Angeles. He was a consistent spokesperson for innovation, for altering prayers and challenging their contents. He was frustrated frequently with the preeminent role given to "tradition," which he believed Harvey and Jacob in particular "treat with kid gloves." He was raised in suburban New York in a minimally observant Jewish home. Though he was ordained in the Reform seminary like Jacob, he was less observant than other founders and inclined to bring ritual innovation to the Minyan.

Aaron, who began the discussion, was not a rabbi, but he was an important Minyan member. He was thirty-two, a professional sociologist in a local institution, who came to Los Angeles straight from the University of Chicago where he earned a doctorate. His studies were preceded by several years in the Peace Corps in Turkey. He was active in the Minyan because he believed he could express some of the very doubts and questions he aired in the discussion. Aaron felt uncomfortable in a synagogue. He said, "Before my first Shabbat in the Minyan, I hadn't been in a Conservative synagogue in twenty years." He did not believe that he fit into any of the denominations with which synagogues were affiliated. He found himself uncomfortable with the segregation of men and women during prayer, the norm of traditional synagogues, and the expectation of total observance of Jewish laws. Raised in a traditional Conservative synagogue in his early years, then in a Reform synagogue, both in the eastern United States, he always felt deeply attached to Judaism. Aaron told me: "There have been various times I tried to go back to Judaism, but I always felt uncomfortable. I always felt out of place because I didn't know the behaviors, how to recite prayers, how to step back and forth during prayer." He wanted, nevertheless, to find a traditional synagogue because of his warm memories of the Judaism of his childhood and his desire for a community of friends. Another reason for Aaron's discomfort in synagogues was his lifestyle. His hair was long and fastened by a rubber band into a neat pony tail; he usually wore jeans and casual shirts. He chose this appearance to differentiate himself from mainstream society. He recently married Martha, also a Minyan member, but they had lived together for some time prior to their marriage and would have been uncomfortable in a congregation that disapproved of their living arrangement. Many aspects of his life seemed incompatible with the conservative views and attitudes about lifestyles he assumed he would encounter in synagogues. Of the Minyan he said:

> In the Minyan there is room for everybody. I like the service that we pray in English and Hebrew. It is small. It blew my mind we were saying prayers that people had been saying for hundreds and hundreds of years. It still does.

Aaron was a valued member in the Minyan despite his rusty Hebrew, lack of expert knowledge of religious texts, and limited Jewish observance. He was thoughtful about what he read and did in a service. His personal observance was growing. He kept a kosher home and many precepts of the Sabbath since he began living with Martha. He combined the values to which the Minyan was committed: tradition, experimentation, learning through participation and active support for and involvement in the group.

The discussion ended with no summary or conclusions. The leader simply said the allotted time was up, and it was time to move on to prayer. Later in the morning this prayer was chanted in unison by the community. At this point some men and women, although not all of either sex, stood and put on their own or Minyan-provided prayer shawls. This was the only gesture of transition from discussion to prayer. Many members, in fact, recited the proper blessing and covered themselves with a tallit before the discussion, forging a symbolic continuity between discussion and prayer.[3]

With the beginning of the prayer service, the leadership shifted from Aaron to the two cantors or *hazanim* (plural; *hazan,* masculine singular; *hazanit,* feminine singular) for the day. The two cantors were Jay, who chanted the service in Hebrew, which is customary, and Jane, who simultaneously chanted in English. Her role was unusual in American Judaism; it indicated that English was a perfectly acceptable language for prayer and was almost equal in significance to Hebrew. The Minyan used the De Sola Pool Sabbath and Festival Prayerbook approved by the Orthodox rabbinate of America; it was printed in both languages, and the membership chanted in both languages. In most standard prayerbooks in America, English is printed in the Siddur, but is never chanted aloud. In a Conservative synagogue one or two prayers may be read aloud in English in unison or responsively, and in a Reform synagogue the majority of a service is conducted in this fashion. But to chant the language of America in the rhythm of ancient prayer is innovative and unique to the havurah movement.

In American synagogues the service is led by a rabbi who directs and guides the congregants through the prayers. The hazen leads specifically designated musical portions of the service. In Orthodox services, and in all traditional services in prewar Europe, the rabbi played no formal role in the service because all men were capable of leadership. A hazan was distinguished in that setting because of the beauty and drama of his voice; he might be hired for the holy days by several small or one wealthy synagogue. In America, the rabbi became the expert in the absence of a community of experts; as such, he acts as a leader, and his voice is often the only one heard, unlike the practice in traditional synagogues.

The Minyan self-consciously chose the European model, although all members were not equally capable leaders. They were proud of the communal yet individual nature of their praying, which was unlike prayer in synagogues, but resembled, they believed, "how Jews really pray." Minyan members musically chant rather than say words, and they sing some prayers and hymns of the service together. Their hazanim were "nondirective." They kept the group together by raising their voices audibly at the beginning and end of the prayers, thereby setting a general pace but allowing people to move autonomously within it. On the Sabbath in the Minyan, periods of song alternated with periods of chanting by individuals and the community.

On this Sabbath the hazanim represented the blend of skills and skill-learning that Minyan members believed distinguished them as a prayer community. Jay was a rabbi who directed a Hebrew education school; he had a fine voice and led a service expertly because of his command of Hebrew and music. He moved to Los Angeles directly after his ordination from the Conservative Jewish Seminary. He was born in Wisconsin and raised in a minimally observant family that attended their city's only Conservative synagogue. He related: "My family was positive about Judaism in general, not in particular. We ate pork sometimes on Friday night."[4] His attendance at the Conservative movement's Camp Ramah placed him on a course of Jewish observance. Jay explained: "In Camp Ramah we lived all week in the sweetness of Shabbat. I have a passion for Hebrew. My attachment to Judaism came from

A Sabbath service of the New York Havurah at a retreat. Retreats were occasions to pray outdoors. Not all members wear prayer shawls, and those who do wear them in slightly different ways.

these two sources." He lived in Kelton because he too was Shomer Shabbat and did not travel on the Sabbath.

Jane was a local secondary-school math teacher. She was raised in Los Angeles. Though she knew the prayers well, she learned as an adult how to lead them. She became accustomed to strengthening her voice to assert the melody and rhythm of the prayers at their beginning and closing sentences. The mix of Jane and Jay's skills symbolized for the Minyan a participatory Judaism that contrasted with the professional and expert-dominated American synagogue they wished to avoid. However, Jay, the expert, announced the order of the service, mentioned what would be included and where variation would occur. His voice was louder and surer. He was looked to more readily for the leadership of the service.

Jay and Jane met during the week to plan the service. From their first meeting Minyan founders established the liturgical order for the Sabbath. It essentially followed normative Jewish worship, with the exception of an additional service used on the Sabbath and festivals.[5] Though a matter of contention, the majority wanted to drop the service and did. The Minyan used a traditional Siddur that maintained that normative form, but rotating hazanim made innovation within the order of the service possible.

In their planning of the service, Jay and Jane's choices of which psalms to recite and which melodies to sing were based on personal preference. "We haven't said this for awhile," or "I like this melody" prefaced their decisions for which prayers would be included in the service. Those who were experienced exercised more choices and variation in the melodies and optional psalms. Newcomers were conservative, planning a service that resembled what they heard weekly and made them most comfortable. To begin the service, Jay briefly mentioned the pages and order of the service to be followed. Although the Minyan used a traditional prayerbook, it varied certain prayers, dropped some, shortened liturgical sections, and added silences, secular readings, and discussions. Its service was far more traditional than a Reform service and was basically a compressed version of an Orthodox or Conservative service. It was recognizable in every sense as traditional, if abbreviated, liturgy.

The Sabbath morning service included psalms and prayers of praise, core prayers of Jewish theology, a period of reading the Torah (Pentateuch), and concluding prayers. One distinguishing feature of Sabbath liturgy, as opposed to daily liturgy, is the absence of prayers of petition. Nonunison praying in the Minyan—that is, praying the same prayer at a different pace—is alternatively a jumble of hummed Hebrew, occasional complete silences, and sometimes unified song. The gestures that accompanied prayer included standing, swaying, and for those who wore the tallit, pulling it over the head, holding the fringes at specific points, or simply wrapping it more closely around the shoulders.

The various pages on which the prayers were printed in the prayerbook were announced by the hazan to allow members who were less familiar with the service to follow along. Though the hazanim led, other members still began a tune, or a particularly pleasant song continued because the group spontaneously sang more choruses. Overall, the impression of a Minyan service was of a smoothly run but little directed event. It was different than any synagogue service in America. There were fewer prayers, more interruptions to note page numbers of prayers, to read an English passage, or to offer other stage directions than one would find among Orthodox Jews. The informality and ease of praying was a real contrast to most Conservative synagogues. The traditional nature of the service made it radically different from a Reform service.

The services, of course, varied from week to week in intensity, enthusiasm, and music, but the prayers were virtually identical. Like most Jews, Minyan members called what they did by the anglicized Yiddish word *"davening"* (praying), a less formal and more physical sense of praying than is expressed by the Hebrew word *t'fillah,* which means prayer.

The Torah service began after approximately one hour of davening the prayers of the morning Sabbath service. The room was changed again. Unlike a synagogue, the Minyan had no ark, the permanent and richly decorated closet, typically on the synagogue's eastern wall, that houses its Torah or Torahs. The Torah used by the Minyan was kept in the cupboard of the Hillel library down the hall from the room where they davened. The table that held Sabbath paraphernalia was brought into the room to serve as a stand for the Torah. Because the sacredness of the scroll precludes its direct contact with profane objects, the Minyan maintained the Torah's sanctity through improvisations. The Torah was wrapped in extra prayer shawls when it was brought into the room, and the table where it rested was covered with more prayer shawls. Jay escorted the scroll into the room that day, while the group sang a liturgical song about the movement of the ark in battle, drawing an association between Sabbath Torah reading and the biblical Israelites' use of the ark. At the close of the song, the Torah scroll was laid on the table. In a synagogue it would be placed on a raised reading table after a procession through the sanctuary. In the Minyan, as well as the synagogue, the Torah scroll was ritually "undressed"; congregants were honored by being invited by the person in charge of the Torah service for that Sabbath to remove the velvet cover and waistband that held it shut. Any intimate contact with this sacred object is an honor. Then the Torah reader opened it to the appropriate sections for the Sabbath reading.

The ritual surrounding the Torah service and the actual reading of the scroll involved the Minyan in conflicts with both its own customs and Jewish law. The members' commitments to pluralism and equality broke down around the Torah. The Torah must be read in Hebrew, a difficult unvocalized (written without vowels) Hebrew at that, to a chant whose notations do not appear in the text. Few members had the skill and expertise to read directly from the Torah scroll. This service always differentiated those members who were well educated in Hebrew. Those who read Hebrew well were obliged to spend time in preparation each week. When members attempted to acquire this reading skill, their mistakes could not be gracefully overlooked. Custom dictated that mistakes be orally corrected because the Torah, God's word, must be accurately read. A newly trained reader could anticipate the public correction of every misreading. In most large Conservative, Reform, or Orthodox synagogues only experts read the Torah, and in some the Torah reader may be a paid synagogue position.

The Minyan upheld its egalitarian ideals in two ways, however. Members ignored the inherited designations every Jewish male receives through the male line, indicating whether he is descended from the priestly, assistant, or common classes. These designations determine the order in which one may come to the Torah scroll to offer a blessing (*aliyah*, meaning to go up) before and after the actual reading of the text and thus honor it. Orthodox Jews use these designators; more liberal synagogues may not. And men shared with women the handling, reading, and blessing of the Torah. Indeed, the Minyan contradicted Jewish law by counting women as members of the required minyan of ten and allowing them to lead prayers, something done infrequently at that time even by liberal synagogues. As visible participants in the quorum, the women were entitled to the same privileges and responsibilities as the men. They pronounced blessings over the Torah that accompanied each section read.

This Sabbath, Jay prepared the Torah reading.[6] His ability was evident. He chanted the sections flawlessly, using a beautiful melody. Although he was at "center stage" when he read the scroll, he was sup-

A Torah reader chants from the scroll. She uses the pointer to accurately follow the text. To her side is the person who has recited the blessing before the Torah reading (aliyah).

ported by various other actors. The entire event was directed by the *gabbai* (literally, tax collector), the impresario of the Torah service; today the role was performed by Frank. He prompted the reader from a printed, vocalized (written with vowels) version of the text in case of mistakes, and he called up other members to participate in the reading. He asked for volunteers for the various honors associated with the service. Miriam, Stan, and Bob requested *aliyot* (plural). Members followed Jay's reading in Hebrew or English, printed side by side in the humashim (the Pentateuch and selections from prophets and other portions of the Bible designated to be read on the Sabbath or festivals) owned by the Minyan. Sometimes members referred to the texts during the Torah discussion. When Jay completed the reading, David, asked by Frank, agreed to act as *hamagbiah* (lifter). He raised the open Torah above his shoulders, turned his back to the group to show the scroll, and then took the Torah to a special chair where he seated himself. He held it upright on his lap while Frank assisted him in rolling it shut. Toni, acting as *hagolelet* (roller, feminine singular) redressed the Torah with its waistband and cover. David continued to hold the Torah while Susan chanted the *haftarah,* the portion of scripture selected from the Prophets by the rabbis to be read following the Torah. These portions of the Bible were selected for each haftarah because they contained themes found in the Torah reading. Then the Torah was set down on the table and covered with prayer shawls.

With the completion of the Torah reading, the members regrouped for the second discussion of the day based on the text just read. The discussion generally lasted thirty minutes. Minyan members said this discussion was the reason they read only a portion of the prescribed sections of the Torah; there was not time to do both. The Minyan, in fact, recently had instituted two separate discussions during this period; to accommodate them, some members moved into the library across the hall. The larger number stayed in the room where the davening took place. The library group looked at commentaries on the Bible, and the larger group usually examined the Sabbath Torah portion.

The Torah discussion used to consist of a single, longer version of the preprayer discussion focused on the *sedra* (weekly portion). On this Sabbath one of the discussion groups read and reflected on the commentaries of the great eleventh-century French scholar, Rashi. His writings constitute one of the major commentaries on the Bible and Talmud.[7] The reading of Rashi's comments in English translation were not confined to the particular Sabbath Torah portion; rather, a single set of commentaries on one book of the Bible was read over the weeks. Participants made frequent use of Hebrew, as well as the Hebrew of the text. The Rashi group attracted the more observant Jews in the Minyan and the ones who considered themselves serious scholars of sacred text. This did not mean that the discussions were not punctuated with humor and delight in what they call Rashi's imaginative interpretations, "plain sense," and use of Hebrew. But it was an esoteric humor. Because not every member appreciated it, the humor tended to be divisive, setting one group off from the other members. Those who participated in the Rashi group recognized this separation, but said they had a right to "serious study." Unlike the Torah service, in which differentiation was inevitable, reading Rashi was an optional development at the end of the group's second year. On this occasion, six of the nearly forty people present attended the Rashi group.

The other discussion group had been meeting continually since the Minyan began. The idea was conceived by founders when the Minyan was a smaller and more intimate group. These discussions most often responded directly to the Sabbath Torah portion. On this Sabbath Linda led the discussion. She began by echoing sentiments often expressed by the group's founders:

> I do not simply want to repeat the same issues raised by others about the Exodus story and the ten plagues that we have discussed in other years. So I will try to raise some new concerns.

She summarized Parasha Bo (Torah portion, Exodus, Chapters 10–13, verse 13). This dramatic Torah portion continues the story of the negotiations of Moses with the Pharaoh to free the Israelite slaves from Egypt, allowing them to leave in order to enter the land God had promised them. God brings the three final plagues against the Egyptians because He "hardens Pharaoh's heart," and the ruler continues to refuse to grant freedom to the slaves.

Linda's issue for discussion focused on "the meaning of the tenth plague," which would destroy the first-born of all Egyptians, including animals and the child of Pharaoh himself. Linda said:

> In every other plague God directed against the Egyptians, the Israelites were passive. God acted and the people watched. They were simply witnesses. But they had to act when God explained the tenth plague. They were required to sacrifice sheep, take the blood, and spread it on their doorposts. In this way, their own first-born would be spared because they had given a sign to the Angel of Death. I find the act very dramatic, but also unsettling. It seems pagan rather

> than Jewish. Why is this the one act God requires from the Israelites? What does the blood mean?

Ruth, a second-year Reform rabbinical student, was the first person to respond. She offered an overtly political interpretation of the text.

> By this action, the slaves drew a boundary between themselves and others. With this act, they declared themselves not slaves and no longer part of Egypt. The boundary declared a commitment to God. It was an act they could not turn back from. It must have appeared to the Israelites that their God was fighting the gods of Egypt. There was no assurance the Israelite God would win, and they had taken a total risk if He lost.

Before the Minyan was organized, Ruth belonged as an undergraduate to a group that was dedicated to Jewish activism. They organized around, among other issues, the plight of Soviet Jews and their shared sense of Jewish identity and counterculture politics. Her interpretation was reminiscent of how they used biblical text in their politics. They interpreted the tradition as consistently committed to radical political action for the Jewish people. Ruth often, though not consistently, offered such political interpretations.

Minyan members came back to the subject of risk repeatedly in the discussion, noting that this action was dangerous. Beth emphasized the issue through an analogy. She said:

> Israelites' sacrifice of lambs would be like aliens slaughtering cows in India. They were slaughtering the gods of the host country. They risked everything to accept God.

Bill commented on why blood was smeared on the doorposts:

> Blood is an ambiguous substance and powerful symbol. It is a substance of both life and death. It represented the fact that some would die so that others would live. It focused on Israelite life and Egyptian death.

Neal then added his thoughts on Linda's question about blood:

> When I was younger I dismissed a lot of Jewish ritual because it was pagan, superstitious, or naive. As I have studied more, I understand that it is not a single ritual or symbol that is important; it is

> how they are interpreted. Passover, for example, was originally an ancient spring celebration, but it came to be interpreted as a celebration of Jewish peoplehood. These meanings set apart the ancient or pagan roots. Our participation in these events is about the Jewish people and our relationship to God, whatever the origins of the rituals may be.

Neal was a student at the University of Judaism, applying for admission to the Conservative seminary for the following year. After a period of self-defined indifference to Judaism, he "returned" both to religious observance and activism. Prior to joining the Minyan, he traveled to campuses throughout the United States raising funds for the United Jewish Appeal and for the support of Israel (see Chapter 2 for a description of the United Jewish Appeal).

At this point Harvey applied the discussion themes to contemporary America:

> In some way Passover continues to operate for us as the tenth plague did for them. It is a cut-off point. If you do not celebrate Passover, you do not count yourself as a Jew. Even if one's celebration is a family dinner, it is an act of identification.

Harvey's comparison evoked from several members their unhappy childhood memories of Passover. A woman complained bitterly about how brief the Seder ritual was made because of her family's impatience with observance. But Harvey persisted.

> Still, people do join together and attempt to express their identity as Jews within their homes and family. Even in a minimal form, it is a meaningful act of Jewish commitment. That is why the *Haggadah* (the liturgical order of the Passover home ritual) has been reworked so many times.

The discussion ended with Harvey's comments and without summary or conclusions. As with the morning discussion, the time allotted passed, and so it came to an end.

This typical Torah discussion is marked by three themes. First, there is biblical exegesis. The discussion leader and others look to the text for content and narrative form that requires interpretation. Linda noted that the tenth plague was different from the others, and presented it as a problem that required interpretation, often, though not in this case, by reference to other commentaries. Second, there is usually personal reflection, or even judgments. Linda labeled a biblical act distastefully as "pagan." Clearly this was no fundamentalist reading of the text. Individuals reflected likes, dislikes and opinions. Similarly, others then interpreted the text in the light of such judgments. Bill and Neal asserted the Jewish character of the acts. Interpretation then engaged not only their intellectual skills of exegesis but their personal reflections of interpretation. Because Linda personally reflected on the text, she showed that her originality was relevant to conducting a discussion. In these discussions, text was to be understood not solely through the eyes of experts but also through a personal assessment, which should be stimulating. Finally, members drew direct parallels between the text and Minyan members' lives as Jews. Harvey asserted that the tenth plague was like the Seder; both were identity markers. He made an explicit link between ancient and modern action.[8]

Minyan discussions, an embodiment of the unique characteristics of havurot, operated on several levels at once. They expressed continuity and discontinuity with the tradition, asserting individualism in interpretation and simultaneously requiring members to acknowledge the legitimacy of ancient texts. Minyan members understood their discussion to be Jewish "study," occasions for education about sacred texts that united them with the tradition of study as a sacred act.

Both the pre-prayer discussion of the Alienu and the Torah discussion of the Exodus verse use these modes of language and thought to establish members' link to Jewish texts. Their abstract interest in the text was insufficient for this purpose. Rather, interaction with the text, even disagreement, suggested an intimate and personal relationship to it. In the discussion of Aleinu, members' "discomfort," as some described it, linked them to a liberal and pluralist American tradition in which difference is unpalatable if it implies judgment. That very stance evolved for the ancestors of Minyan members in Europe whose advocacy of liberalism assured civil rights and religious freedom for Jews. The assertion of liberalism against the prayer is ironically an American Jewish position. In discussions Minyan members articulate these positions not in opposition to text or tradition, but as expressions of their Judaism they understand as compatible with that tradition.

In the Exodus discussion then, personal experience is repeatedly projected into the text. Ruth and Beth both imagine the anxiety of slaves by imagining a comparable act in a contemporary society or by expanding the biblical narrative to set the stage for the final plague. Neal's assertion of the primacy of interpretation over narrative asserts that the true meaning of the text rests on how it is understood for one's life.

The stance members assume toward sacred text demands their engagement with it. It is that very engagement that largely demonstrates that it is sacred. From that position criticism and disagreement are possible because the personal link is removed from question.

After this morning's discussion, the groups reconvened in the larger room for praying. The Torah service was completed when the Torah was re-dressed, marched around the room again and ritually returned to the table on which it rested, wrapped in several prayer shawls, and then finally removed to the library where it remained until the next week. The concluding prayers of the service were chanted together. Because the Minyan excluded the Additional Service, this portion of the service was short and dominated by songs. Their songs were sung in unison, often in harmony with the help of the group's more accomplished musicians. When they ended their final hymn, the service was concluded, and Minyan members removed their prayer shawls, folded and placed them either in a personal tallit bag, or piled them up to be returned to the Minyan cupboard. Everyone turned to a neighbor and shook hands or, more often, embraced and kissed, repeating the Sabbath greeting of "Shabbat Shalom."

The room was transformed again. The couches were moved back against the wall. The table was cleared of ritual paraphernalia and returned to the center of the room. The group prepared for the next portion of the Minyan Sabbath: eating lunch and discussing current issues to which the group attended. Lunch in the Minyan combined rituals surrounding food, informal socializing, eating, and discussing group problems or affairs. Each week two people assumed the office of bringing lunch, and the responsibility rotated among almost all members. The first ritual activity preceding a Sabbath lunch was sanctifying and drinking wine. But before the blessing began, members stood poised with wine in hand and volunteered for the offices necessary for the next Sabbath, which were solicited by someone who has participated that day. People were needed to volunteer to lead discussions, act as hazanim, assist in the Torah service, and bring lunch. Some offices were taken quickly, some with hesitation. Members were occasionally encouraged, shamed, or cajoled into volunteering. Today, volunteering posed no problem. If there was a delay, members told one another, "Someone volunteer or we won't eat lunch!" Minyan members recently decided to recruit for their offices at this juncture in the day's activities in order to pressure members into responsibility, a need that had not existed when the group began with a few dedicated members.

After people volunteered for the offices, they recited *kiddush* (sanctification) and drank the wine. At this point some members left the room to ritually wash their hands, as tradition dictated, before the ritual blessing over bread. This act distinguished the more and less religiously observant members. There seemed to be little tension between the two groups; differences in observance were taken as a matter of fact and personal preference, not moral worth. When all the members were assembled, they began a curious ritual unique to the Minyan. Instead of one person blessing the Sabbath loaf, which was customary, the Minyan divided into groups that held the loaf of hallah together in midair while all the groups recited the blessing over the bread in unison. People then twisted off pieces of bread to eat. Their informality fitted well into their counterdecorum.

Lunch was served on the table that previously held prayer books, ritual articles, and the Torah. Individuals moved through chaotic lines to fill their plates with foods that were acceptable even to the members who were the most observant of the dietary rules. Minyan members were respectful of the ritual needs of those among them who were most observant. If even one person would be offended by food brought to the Minyan, or by an act violating a Sabbath law, for example, no one did it. This accommodation around food, however, did not hold for prayer. They were far more willing to assert their different views around their central activity and, often, less willing to compromise.

During lunch the Minyan broke into smaller groups. Friends sat together, and the subgroups of the Minyan were visible. Informal groups were often homogeneous, separating, for example, unmarried from married people. Aaron, Martha, Doug, and Beth casually chatted about the week's events; they made plans to attend a play together the following week. A newcomer seemed unsure about where to sit until Mark talked to her. A few people left as soon as they finished eating.

After about forty-five minutes, members recited the "Grace" (*Birkhat ha mazon*) that follows a meal at which bread has been blessed and eaten. Most of the Grace was sung in unison, usually led by the "host" of that day's lunch. At the conclusion members made announcements. Today the upcoming retreat was discussed. Various people volunteered for food preparations for the weekend. When they discovered that five members were vegetarians, they concluded, as they do with ritual issues, that all members would share vegetarian food.

They quickly transformed the room for the last time. The wall and floor coverings were put away and the room was readied for its weekday uses. The group drifted out as casually as it arrived. The members who lived in Kelton or were visiting friends climbed the steep hills of the neighborhood. Some got in their cars and drove home, which may have been fifteen, twenty, or even forty-five minutes away. Some continued to observe the Sabbath until sundown; they did not drive, turn on lights, handle money, or prepare food. Others returned immediately to the secular world, indistinguishable from any other American, passing a Saturday shopping, visiting, or finishing school work.

Jewish Alternatives for the Alternative Community

Minyan members did not attend the group solely or exclusively to fulfill the commandments to pray set down in the Torah. Rather, the Minyan provided a setting and structure that enabled members to worship in their own ways. For all but a few, without the Minyan they would have had no satisfactory place to pray in a communal setting and no motivation to pray as regularly, or possibly at all. For some members of the Minyan who thought they could not pray because of discomfort and disagreements with the language and meaning of prayer, or contempt for the bureaucracy and lack of community in synagogues, the Minyan become an acceptable and exciting place to pray. Some members were from secular homes or were in the process of converting and found the Minyan a congenial place to learn how to pray.

All observant Jews and their communities are concerned with prayer, with making it aesthetically pleasing, lively, vibrant, effective, or perhaps "relevant." What distinguished the Minyan from all synagogues was its members' conviction that their primary purpose was to make possible a worship experience that could not be found elsewhere. It was ironic that Minyan members felt the lack of a workable alternative for worship. Kelton University is located in one of the major Jewish population centers in the world. Kelton, on the western rim of Los Angeles, is a complex neighborhood with three boundaries: Kelton University to the north, a freeway to the west, and a major boulevard to the south that runs from downtown to the ocean. The area is divided between a large, hilly residential neighborhood and a flat commercial "village." Both areas have become popular, dramatically inflating rents. Although there are student residences—cooperative, university-owned apartments, sororities, and fraternities, and of course apartments—official university housing is sparse. Rental prices, the proliferation of condominiums rather than rental units, and the rising property values of the area's lovely old houses, make living in Kelton proper unlikely for students. Although almost all the founders of the Minyan lived in Kelton, new members were increasingly recruited from outside areas where less affluent students and beginning professionals were likely to live.

Kelton has a large Jewish population, but it lacks the signs of a traditional Jewish community; there is no kosher butcher, kosher bakery, Jewish bookstore, or ritual bath (*mikva*). Virtually all Minyan members have cars and drive to areas with these services. But the most pressing need of an observant Jew is a place of worship that can be reached on foot because halaha prohibits travel on festivals and the Sabbath. For the people who began the Minyan, this was a major problem.

Kelton has two synagogues within walking distance: a large Conservative synagogue and a hasidic center. Minyan members found these options for worship "dismal" at best, and "unacceptable" at worst. Mark said he felt "depressed" on the Sabbath because he lacked a community in which to pray. For Minyan founders and subsequent members who were willing to travel to worship, either option would have been adequate if what they sought was authentic, traditional worship. Each option, however, was unsatisfactory in contrasting ways.

The Conservative synagogue is a few miles southeast of the campus. Its considerable success and wealth reflect a membership drawn from several upper- and upper-middle-class residential areas within and adjacent to Kelton. The lavish synagogue was built in 1961 in a modern architectural style; it takes up a whole city block. It contrasts stark angular lines with stained glass windows and spires. The three floors hold an immense sanctuary and a chapel, a kitchen, social hall, gymnasium, library, and an adjoining educational facility. The sanctuary seats one thousand worshipers and expands to a social hall that holds double that number. Like the churches in the city, the synagogue has a display case at its front entrance to announce the name of the officiating clergy, the topic of the weekly sermon, and special events (for example, the names of the children who will become b'nai mitzva). The Sabbath service is a well-orchestrated event. A choir and cantor perform the arranged liturgical music. The rabbi's sermon is the highlight of the service, but he shares the spotlight with the bar/bat mitzva who publicly reads from the Torah and sections of biblical prophets for the first time.

By any standard it is a successful, even major, Conservative synagogue. On any particular Sabbath, hundreds of people enter the synagogue: guests for the bar mitzva ceremony, active congregants, and a few elderly men who make up the dwindling minyan that meets there daily. Everyone is well dressed. Acceptable attire for Sabbath worship is comparable to formal afternoon wear. Women wear tailored suits, afternoon dresses, and expensive and subtle jewelry. Furs are worn on occa-

The conservative synagogue in Kelton's neighborhood.

sion, even in the warm climate. Men wear well-pressed suits or, occasionally, fashionable sports coats and well-cut slacks. Most congregants arrive at the synagogue in large, expensive cars; few walk.

The richly decorated sanctuary is all wood. Its *bimah* (platform where Torah readers and service leader stand) is carpeted and decorated with fresh flowers. The reading tables where the scroll is read are covered in velvets. Several beautifully adorned Torahs are housed in the modern ark. The atmosphere during the service is sedate and orderly. Congregants, male and female, sit and stand on cue, pray in unison, and read the liturgy responsively. The rabbi and congregation use Hebrew and occasionally English in the service. They use the Sabbath prayer book of the Conservative movement, which is modified and shortened; in only a few places does it actually alter the Siddur used by Orthodox Jews.

For all its beauty and success, this Conservative synagogue was unacceptable to Minyan members. To them it symbolized the American synagogue with its inauthentic treatment of Jewish worship. What disturbed them was not the prayer book that was used, the words that formed the prayers, the melodies the cantor chanted, or the relaxation of legal dictates that allowed men and women to sit together and women to be called up to the Torah; these practices were all shared by the Minyan. Rather, they were disturbed because to them the worship there was not Jewish and not theirs. "It is like a church," many said. The cacophony, movement, and spirit of what they believed was real Jewish worship had been channeled and limited; it had been replaced, Minyan members suggested, by a well-run spectacle. Within this and all other synagogues, Minyan members believed, worshipers had become consumers, and rabbis and cantors had become performers. The passive observer, active performer relation was responsible for transforming Sabbath worship and celebration into a less authentic, Americanized style of service. Individuals had given up responsibility for how a service should be run and turned it over to professionals. As Jews handed these personal responsibilities over to rabbis, they seemed to concentrate instead on buildings, status, and appearances. The Sabbath and Jewish community dwindled behind large buildings and superficial measures of success. In the view of Minyan members, a corporate structure replaced community at this and other such synagogues.

The Minyan members' desire for a less "Americanized" and "suburbanized" Judaism that moved the individual away from active participation in prayer was fervently echoed in the other setting for Sabbath prayer in Kelton. Habad House is in Kelton proper, across the street from one of the university's massive parking lots, only two blocks from Kelton Village's tangle of fifteen cinemas. The building is a converted fraternity house that was bought by the large and highly successful Ludavitch Hasidic movement.[9] In the sixties the movement became especially concerned with the assimilation of, and intermarriage and conversion rate among, college-aged Jewish youth, the vast majority of whom attend some institution of higher education. The Lubavitchers devoted a portion of their funds to support their rabbis in their work on campuses; the rabbis set up tables next to political organizations and evangelical Christian missions in order to find and recruit Jews to a Jewish way of life. They printed countless stories of rescuing Jewish students who were addicted to drugs or Jesus and of teaching them to keep the dietary laws, perform the daily prayer ritual of binding on phylacteries if they were males, or lighting candles for the Sabbath if they were female. The "house," which the Lubavitchers prefer to "synagogue," is explicitly intended to attract young, usually disaffected Jews, many of whom have been raised in Conservative or Reform congregations that may resemble Habad's Conservative neighbor in Kelton. Lubavitch Habad has long been critical of synagogue worship in America because it has changed or ignored some of the *mitzvot* of Judaism,[10] to which they are fundamentally and unequivocally committed. They believe these changes have ushered in a less rigorous Judaism than that practiced during the European epoch in which Lubavitch developed. Jews have moved away from Judaism because of their attraction to what Lubavitch calls "American values and assimilation."

The Habad house has none of the splendor of the nearby synagogue. It is a center for study and provides a kosher kitchen. A setting for prayer, its rooms are used for several different purposes throughout the week. One may pray and hold meetings in the same setting. Worship services are animated, cacophonous, and lengthy. There is no choir or cantor. The service leader is not necessarily a rabbi and gives no sermon. Bar mitzva ceremonies are neither lavish nor frequent events at the campus house. Men sway as they pray, their ritual fringes (*tzitzit*) in motion, hanging over their trousers and mixing with the fringes of their prayer shawls. All men are bearded, and all males wear long forelocks like the children and men in European shtetels. To honor the Sabbath, they dress in fine, long black coats and fur hats that resemble the garments worn by Polish nobles two centuries ago. Lubavitch welcomes visitors and seeks out any person who has expressed interest in being a Jew. They have more than an authentic Sabbath service to offer. They have endured with a success no other hasidic sect can match, and they believe that they have the ability to attract Jewish students that no other Jewish organization can. They have avoided the taint of Americanization and suburbanization. Their religion is timeless and attractive, they argue, because of its authenticity and truth.

Habad, where some Minyan members worshiped and continued to worship occasionally after the Minyan was created, was also unsatisfactory for all but a few members. Habad and the Minyan shared criticisms of the American synagogue and a concern with maintaining an alternative Judaism. Nevertheless, the Minyan's differences with Habad were substantial.

In hasidic and all Orthodox worship, men and women are separated by a divider or screen that gives men primary access to the prayer services. Women have few ritual privileges or responsibilities, and they are less prominent and significant in public life. In Jewish law women are different from men, although according to the apologists that does not make women less equal. One does not change Jewish law to include women in the service, however, because one does not change or tamper with Jewish law; it is God's divine and perfect word. One tries to live one's life in complete accord with the letter and spirit of that law. Rabbinic courts can change the law, but it is a privilege they rarely exercise.

No one in the Minyan embraced such a perspective on Judaism, not even those few who closely observed the corpus of Jewish law. Change, interpretation, and even critical judgments informed by the secular world were important to Minyan worship. Of course, opinions among members diverged. For example a subgroup in the community favored adherence to the requirements of the most traditional members, particularly about the rules concerning prayer. Nevertheless, pluralism was still uppermost.

Although members of the Minyan were drawn to the informality of Habad worship services, they also were aware that Lubavitch Habad is an international, hierarchic movement, led by a *rebbe* who is a lineal, cognatic descendant of the founder of the movement. Such hierarchy was not congenial to Minyan members. Identification with the movement through regular worship at Habad house was thus an unlikely possibility for Minyan members, even if its services were rich with the sounds and physical movement of traditional Jewish prayer because Minyan members believed the fundamentalism of Habad narrowed Judaism and discouraged the analytical, critical, and thoughtful processes that they wanted to bring to worship and tradition.

Minyan members were committed to worship that was traditional and derived from halaha, but flexible and pluralistic. They wanted prayer to be responsive to questions, problems, and difficulties with tradition, though respectful of the tradition itself. They believed themselves unique in these goals, and they believed that in embracing them they forged a Judaism that was fully authentic and meaningful.

The Minyan Developed

Initially, the Minyan founders defined themselves in opposition to the synagogues and American Jews around them. Once they agreed to meet regularly, then they had to define their own plans and program. From the start they had to confront various conflicts and needs. In two years Minyan membership more than tripled. Though the group developed without a well-established vision, members shared certain assumptions. Like other havurot, the Minyan founders agreed to focus their greatest attention on achieving successful prayer by restructuring the worship community and decorum. Initially, generating new structures seemed the best solution to all problems. They created a continually negotiable organization. This organization became the necessary condition for praying, differentiating them from synagogues. Their ability to separate themselves from other Jews was central to their religious experience, as noted in Chapter 2. In Chapters 4 and 5, I will examine how this organization related to prayer constituents. I turn to decorum/organization in order to describe the significance of their context for prayer.

In the group's first year its members agreed on how to accomplish Sabbath tasks in the Minyan without formal leaders. Members established that the service would combine traditional Sabbath liturgy and two discussions.[11] They agreed upon regularly meeting each semester to evaluate their satisfaction with "how things are going," and to solve any problems about the service. They formulated, in practice, their alternative. When shared assumptions were breached, conflict ensued. These conflicts continually reappeared during the time of my research. The following brief group history makes clear how these issues were initially formulated and what kinds of solutions resulted.

When I began my research with the two year old Minyan in 1973, its founders were beginning to look back on the first year as paradise lost. Often I was wistfully told that I "should have seen the Minyan in the old days," two years previously, when barely a minyan gathered in someone's home in Kelton. After the service they would open a few cans of tuna and share lunch around a folding table. At these lunches they discussed "how the service had gone," what needed improvement, and encouraged a shy member, or one whose Hebrew was either rusty or newly acquired, to lead a service. If someone new volunteered, others tried to take offices for the upcoming week so the service would maintain some balance between learners and experts. If a newcomer attended either as a guest or, more rarely, if someone came who had read the Minyan's advertisement for Sabbath services placed in the Kelton University newspaper, he or she would be welcomed and encouraged to return, on occasion even called during the week.

This description by its founders of the Minyan in 1971 was not the Minyan I found in 1973. Their growing numbers necessitated their move to the University Religious Center. As more people came regularly, the founding members still took primary responsibilities for the service. The founders did not think they were attracting enough people like themselves. Some newer members, the founders argued, had become spectators. They did not take offices, and they were not involved in shaping a vision for the group. Susan described it this way.

> We [the founders] had an idea of what we wanted, and it wasn't a clear idea. We were willing to feel our way toward it. It was a concerted, united effort. And I think we resented or were upset that our vision was being sabotaged, not maliciously, by other people. I don't think you could call them ideological issues really. Most people didn't seem to have ideologies, except for a few like Martha and Aaron and Beth and Doug. It seemed like a dilution of the whole thing. That essential tension just couldn't be captured. They affected it and they were very upsetting.

From 1971–1973 the membership explosion necessarily and dramatically transformed the group. To that point it operated solely on consensus. Every decision, every change, and every action taken represented shared agreement among those people (first ten then twelve then fifteen) who considered themselves active Minyan members and came every Sabbath. They not only never took a vote on an issue that year, they considered it inappropriate to do so. As consensus was the model for governance, accommodation was the model for religious life. Their ideology of pluralism translated into their personal relations in the community. When they discovered that one woman in the group knew no Hebrew and found the service difficult to follow, another member began to daven the prayers aloud in English. They began their bilingual praying in this spontaneous fashion. When another member expressed anxiety and doubts about the truth and values of prayer, they began prayer discussions. When some felt a service dragged on too long, they all agreed to modify some of the prayers.

Over the first year, the founding members shared many occasions when individuals had questions, doubts, or discomforts in their community. They believed that they had translated each such occasion into a triumph. In short, they demonstrated their ability to accommodate to one another's needs while maintaining the authority of traditional Judaism.

Jacob summarized the pervasive feeling shared by Minyan members throughout the first year:

> The Minyan was something we had all been looking for, and all needed, and suddenly it happened. I remember after the first session, there was a wonderment. "Wasn't it lovely? "Yes, it really was." As it went on in the first year it was tremendously stimulating. It never had birth pains; that was an incredibly easy delivery—a fast pregnancy and an easy delivery. I think that really helped it. The struggles really came afterward, but it helped us work them out because we didn't feel it was something we created, but something we found.

The Minyan seemed simply to grow. It began in ways so informal they were only barely remembered. Mark and Jacob invited a few others to pray together in order to establish a regular Sabbath minyan. Harvey's father donated some money. The Hillel Foundation, headed by Mark and Jacob, also provided funds with which they were able to purchase a few prayer books and humashim. They borrowed a Torah from a synagogue and moved their services and all their necessary books and ritual objects from one member's house to another for each Sabbath. At the conclusion of their first Sabbath together, they spontaneously danced and sang. They were a community! As the weeks wore on they found themselves able to accommodate one another's needs without difficulty or stress.

Mark held as a minimum requirement for the community that it attract like-minded participants.

> My thing was to start off with a few people, decide what we're going to do, and then invite people to join. I didn't want us to come together to vote on what we wanted to do. I wanted people of similar minds to build on consensus. I didn't want to lead it.

Mark's experience in Jewish groups led him to conclude that community depended on shared assumptions. He wanted to start the Minyan with people who agreed with him. The Minyan had attracted, at least initially, people who could make religious compromises and maintain a commitment to tradition.

By the fall of 1972, the beginning of their second year, the Kelton Minyan had changed. After the first few services of the year, one member, Susan, wrote to Ruth who was in Israel studying.

> Our community? It has grown—or should I say mushroomed. Those of us from last year—Mark, Harvey, Jacob, and I sometimes catch each other's eyes in wonder. After all, we wanted to share our experience with others, and it is only right and natural that as others come it is their community too. But quite selfishly speaking, it is no longer ours and no longer fulfills our needs.

Another member, Ed, described the founders' sentiments in the following way:

> There was an ego involvement in both the survival of the group and its form, and these now came in conflict. It was the feeling of one whose baby grows up and separates from you. "Oh good it's getting on; oh bad, it's different from what I wanted." The growth led to depersonalization, institutionalism, bureaucratization, and all of these were symbolized in the move to the University Religious Center. It represented moving down the road of being establishment.

Others came who the founders found insensitive to the Minyan's style of worship; they led services poorly, dominated discussion, did not participate, and even criticized the group for its unfriendliness or its failure to be what they thought it should be. The group could not accommodate so many people with such diverse Jewish knowledge and ideas about Jewish community. They were losing the consensus that Mark indicated was crucial for a successful community.

The founders were also aware that the Minyan was not the intimate community of neighbors it had been. People drove to services from all over the city. Arrangements for each service were becoming more formal and complex. In size and other respects it increasingly resembled a large organization. Dues collection necessitated a treasurer and tax deductible status, arranged by a lawyer in the group. They mimeographed a small directory of members' names and phone numbers. Worshiping in homes became difficult. Mark lamented, "We've become a synagogue."

The newcomers became aware that some people in the Minyan

seemed to have more authority than others. Even being a rabbi did not guarantee such authority. Rather, it was the group's founders who comprised this special elite. Newcomers also realized that some established members were friends who spent time together outside the group. One newcomer said that people were always aware of an "inner circle" and not being part of it.

Within the inner circle of founders, matters were also changing. One member had married and another was living with a woman. Both women were outsiders to the Minyan and joined because of their relationships. A man and woman in the inner circle began a relationship and then broke it off, leaving all concerned uncomfortable for some months. The one married couple made other friends in the city, and the woman was expecting a child.

The founders were all pulling away from a Minyan-dominated personal life. The Minyan no longer provided them the intimacy and intensity of the previous year. As the inner circle in fact expanded, on occasion inviting a newcomer "like them" for a festival dinner or a Sabbath meal, the people invited commented that they learned that "in the inner circle there was nothing there." The intimacy and warmth of the first year community had been transformed, as had the community itself.

None of the founders ever desired a group that institutionalized a set of leaders or undermined an egalitarian organization. They persisted as the strongest proponents of shared communal responsibility and flexibility in defining membership in the group. They were its indisputable leaders; it was made immediately clear to me and to newcomers that these were the people to meet, to seek advice from, and to listen to in meetings. They spoke with authority. They wanted to pray with people like themselves because that would enable them to live an integrated Jewish life.

The Minyan in its second year was characterized by Aaron and Martha as "in search of an identity." Members were no longer neighbors. The age range broadened. They could not operate on consensus. The Minyan was a success, but not quite sure where it was going. Founders had recruited some members like themselves who were expanding the leadership group. But as Harvey said to me with dismay, "The Minyan runs itself." The question had become, where is the Minyan "running"? Diversity was established; points of connection were harder to find.

The conflicts of the second year were summarized by a simple phrase used by a newcomer at the first Minyan Sabbath retreat. "You," she said, directing her comments to founders, "have a founding father complex." Later the phrase was altered as it was more widely used. People began to refer to the "Founding Mother and Father complex." It implied that the founders' sense of ownership posed difficulty for the group. Nonfounders were constantly made aware that there were some people who were more entitled to membership than others. Each person's suggestions did not carry equal weight. While all people were expected to participate, the group was far from egalitarian.

By the end of the second year, just prior to my arrival, they reached a series of agreements about how to solve problems. The evaluative discussions of the first year were expanded in a variety of ways. Members held their first weekend retreat in spring 1973 to examine their purposes and goals. They instituted occasional discussions after Sabbath liturgical services to allow people to express satisfaction and dissatisfaction with the group. Newer members became more assertive about things they wanted: more social activities, more variation in prayers, more creative services, where additions of new liturgy would be welcome. These issues will be discussed in the following chapters, for they emerged continually throughout the Minyan's third year. Both the issues and occasions for raising them came out of the meetings held as a result of the membership explosion. They no longer discussed the minutiae of successful davening. Now they discussed who they were. The Minyan's membership generations became a matter of self-conscious discussion. There were continual references to founders and newcomers and constant fights over tradition and changes. Founders even held informal study groups, which led newcomers to charge them with elitism.

Beginning in the second year the Minyan developed a core and peripheral membership. The core consisted of founders and regular members. Both core and periphery were flexible and changing. Core members came most frequently, but not every Sabbath. Peripheral members came irregularly. Some came for several months, then not at all, then back again. People who made friends in the group were most likely to stay. The Minyan functioned for them as both a social and a religious community.

Three Minyan founders left the group in 1974, the Minyan's third year and my period of fieldwork. Ed, as well as Michael and Ellen, a married couple, stopped coming. The couple remained in Kelton and maintained close personal ties with other founders. They left the Minyan because they believed it had changed too much from what it had once been. Its growing size, expanding membership, and, to Michael, its turning away from tradition, made it less desirable. Michael prayed with or without the Minyan. He continued to observe the Sabbath, but not in the community context. He and his wife left the city for a new academic post during the summer of that year. He simply attended no service for about four months.

Ed left the neighborhood, and though he remained cordial with founders, he did not remain friends. His disaffection from the group coincided with his relationship with Miriam. She joined the group through Ed, and stayed in it somewhat longer than he did. But when they moved to the other side of the city, neither of them attended, though they did continue to see various members socially. Ed left the group for reasons that were opposite from Michael's. He found the community too sensitive to tradition. In addition, the group had not only grown larger, but he believed that little meaningful interaction occurred even between founders. Their dogged attachment to all of the tradition, according to Ed, revealed a lack of sensitivity to the needs of members. As a rabbi, Ed continued to participate in the services led at his Hillel, but he had no ongoing community for prayer. He found himself increasingly uncertain of what prayer meant for him.

Many members took "vacations" from the group when experiencing some conflict over Minyan decisions. When the community agreed to my study, one founder withdrew for many weeks. Other ritual or community decisions sent members away for brief periods.

However, what struck me was the persistence of attachment: so few people permanently cut ties with the group. The flexibility of the group worked to include most people. That two founders should have left over opposite interpretations of the community seemed consistent with the plural and apparently nondogmatic nature of the group. Those most intimately tied to the group found it the most difficult to sustain more casual relations.

Minyan Organization—An Experiential Decorum and Aesthetic

In all their conflicts, Minyan men and women inevitably returned to the issue of how the group was organized. They consistently sought to reorganize their setting for prayer as a response to any individual's difficulties with the experience or the group. That is why as the Minyan developed it did not revise or rewrite Jewish liturgy, though it did initially exclude some prayers. Rather, decision after decision led them to revise their organization of the prayer experience. In both form and content lay the foundation for group prayer, not only the meaning of prayer but the authority for it. In understanding what is unique about the Minyan's organization, one can understand how the member's responses to different generations constituted their Judaism. The Minyan's various decisions about their communal organization revealed what prayer meant for them.

Organization and Decorum

Organization in this context refers to manifestations of decorum. As decorum regulates relations between people as well as between people and the physical space in which they pray, the organization of any liturgical event also involves decorum in the realization of the worship experience. Decorum was manifest in different ways in the American synagogue, in the preimmigrant European synagogue and in the Minyan. Specifically, the organization of the liturgy, as well as the community relations in which prayer occurs, reflect rather different prayer experiences. In the European small-town synagogue, the community's organization was replicated in the house of worship. Community relations were enacted in worship, and prayer united the individual with the community and both with God. The people with whom one prayed not only symbolized the people Israel but the people with whom one lived one's life. Those most respected in the synagogue, the rabbi, the scholars, and the wealthy, also held sway over community life. The values of the Siddur were supported, at least in part, by the community. This unity and redundancy of relations is not so much an ideal as an inevitability in a culturally homogeneous enclave. Community organization and decorum mutually reflected one another.

The American synagogue after 1840 had, by contrast, an elaborate and specialized organization whose effect was often to separate persons from worship and whose large size made it unlikely to draw people together in community. The synagogue reflected the diversity and disconnection of its community. In a bureaucratized synagogue, prayer often emphasized the division of labor that made the laity passive and experts active. The synagogue replicated the institutional relations of modern society and emphasized organization at the expense of community and prayer. Indeed, America's great rabbis of the fifties and early sixties often wrote about the failure of the synagogue to get people actively engaged in prayer rather than passively listening to the clergy (Heschel 1953; Borowitz 1969). The institutional apparatus reflected American Jewish status, but did not engage its members in a prayer life. Decorum expressed the organization of the larger society and distanced participants from prayer.

The Minyan faced quite another set of problems. Though its organization preoccupied its members, it was so unelaborated and consistently negotiable that it could not satisfy all the functions members assigned to it. The essential Minyan prayer experience consisted of Jewish prayer conducted in a way that emphasized equality, informality, and beauty within an egalitarian division of labor. The Minyan's decorum, unlike the previous generation's, was not expressed in architecture, its board of directors, or the solemnity of the service. Members sought an egalitarian organization capable of solving any problem a person had about prayer. Decorum resisted the organization of the larger society, and members hoped that decorum would substantially contribute to altering their prayer experience. The conflicts prayer generated in the group, which are laid out in the next chapters, testify to the burden that this ephemeral organization was made to bear.

Initially they seemed to succeed, as their brief history proves. If, for example, one found difficulty with the Hebrew language for prayer, then the Minyan created an "office" called English hazan, and prayers were led simultaneously in two languages. One could pray in a familiar language. If the contents of the prayer raised questions, then discussions were instituted to voice those problems, and secular readings were incorporated into the service to express subjects of immediate concern. Over two years the Minyan succeeded, members believed, in solving every problem through reorganizing the structure or offices of a Minyan service. These "solutions" were given names (Hebrew hazan, prayer confrontation) and sometimes assigned committees. As a last resort, Minyan members used discussions to express feelings of personal failure about praying or to articulate frustration at what they felt were inadequacies of the text to respond to problems of the modern world. Such discussions proved that members were what Harvey called "religiously honest." They understood these revisions of organization to be compatible with the Jewish tradition; at the same time, the conflicts generating them were thought appropriate and were taken seriously.

I postulate that there is a link between organizational specialization and the extent to which the prayers engage the participants. A decorum that emphasizes distance between participants and ritual specialists and restraint in the worshiper, appears to distance the laity from the texts of prayer. There seems to be a "fit" between the dense ties of Jewish communal life in Europe, or among the ultra Orthodox in the United States, and the capacity for prayer to speak for participants' experiences. Any follower of Emile Durkheim's view that the social order and the symbolic order are normally linked in traditional societies or enclaves would find certain proof here for that assertion. Social ties and religious beliefs are reinforced in the act of prayer.

However, the other two examples, of Americanizing synagogues and the Minyan, provide alternatives that are typical of religion in modern society. In these cases there is the consistent threat of a "misfit" between worshiper and worship. Minyan members believed that bureaucracy failed to create the possibility for communal prayer to articulate important values for participants. Their observation led them to conclude that an organized bureaucracy was the primary obstacle to creating the proper fit between community and prayer life, between wanting to pray and being able to pray.

What second generation Jews sought in large synagogues was the effective integration of Judaism, American success, and the Jewish family. They pursued a different set of goals for their religious lives. The integration they appeared to achieve was bureaucratic. The size of the building, the size of the membership, and the synagogue staff communicated a massive, permanent presence of Jews in America. For a generation that conflated Judaism with America, a synagogue succeeded best when it emulated American institutions and structures. Its bureaucratic aesthetic, however, distanced the worshiper from worship, from sacred texts, and from the content of prayers whose purpose is to underline Jewish distinctiveness. Second generation Jewish identity was forged on bureaucratized institutions.

Minyan members sought an experiential decorum and aesthetic. Every relationship they altered was meant to achieve the opportunity for "equal access" to sacred texts, praying, and participation. The degree to which this decorum mirrored the status relations of American society for these young, largely middle-class (soon to be professional) men and women may not be the most relevant question. The meaning of the prayers for them is best understood not on the Durkheimian model but as the reflection of social relations, a point I will discuss at length in Chapter 4. Their approach to religion certainly expressed their fuller integration as Jews in American society, but rather than increasing acculturation, it led to their demand that Judaism reflect their identities more completely. Prayer, then, was not a formulation of the world as it was, but of the world that they wanted. It communicated generalized meanings focused on the integration of members' identities into a single symbolic framework.

These meanings are most visible in the structure, organization, and decorum of the Minyan. They defined the basis on which Judaism could be integrative of the self and made integration the central issue for the third generation. Their need to create an activist Judaism, rather than reflecting successful professionalization of status, involved restructuring decorum and appealing to decorum and organization, rather than liturgy, as the basis for enhancing that activism. Engagement implied creating the proper context for prayer. Hence, structure was constantly negotiated as much to achieve engagement as to constitute it. The more members maintained a flexible organization, the more certain they could be of avoiding bureaucracy and compartmentalization.

Community, then, not only symbolized social unity and differentiation but also, more importantly, personal integration with Judaism. Because the group was voluntary and placed within a bureaucratic society, their capacity to symbolize engagement in every medium of religious activity, including organization, made them hope prayer could be effective. If they could solve their uncertainty about traditional prayer by discussing it, for example, then the Minyan was a community more than an institution because it could solve each person's problems. Both the problems they solved and the means by which they addressed them demonstrated their ability to integrate rather than compartmentalize Judaism within their lives. At the same time, the very negotiable features of organization made it difficult to sustain that effectiveness. Unlike preimmigrant Europe there was virtually no redundancy in the Minyan community. One prayed with some of one's friends, but the organization was so unelaborated that its complete flexibility failed to encompass much of the person's experience. Placed within a plural society, little of the Minyan was reflected elsewhere in the work world. The decorum mirrored the style of the generation, but had no capacity to draw in members and demand commitments that would ensure a fit between their vision of Judaism and the rest of their lives.

Until the emancipation of Jews in nineteenth-century Europe, the daily minyan was embedded in densely integrated communities. Links of neighborhood, kinship, guild, and belief tied people together who prayed. As that social world was ghettoized or set apart, prayer and the ritual cycle provided a profound explanation for that ghettoization, endowing social links with sacred meaning. Community events, the outcome of a harvest and the prosperity and well being of that community were the concern of, and explained in, liturgy. This symbolic and social density was absent from the Minyan's experience of prayer. They aimed to achieve integration, but it was apart from, and in conflict with, their society.

In Chapters 1 and 2, I introduced voluntary organizations as critical settings for developing the values and norms for an emerging American white and ethnic middle class. Similarly, to understand the Minyan I suggest a close look at the nature of their organization. In the constitution of group organization, we can see how a unique ethnic identity is actually maintained within the dominant culture. In the Minyan, as against the synagogue, integration was achieved by all elements of prayer, and members articulated Judaism in a decorum that demanded continual adjustment. The fact that Minyan founders experienced their group as "given" rather than worked for intensified their sense of participating in a group that was authentically their own. They discovered a Judaism within a community that responded to their needs. Not only prayer, but how they solved problems, maximized their ability to integrate and assert their identity as Jews. On the other hand, unlike a synagogue their organization was so negotiable that it was difficult to sustain prayer as integrative when new members of the group could unbalance that sense of success.

Why should issues of decorum in general, and organization in particular, preoccupy Minyan members? From the perspective of the group, what is the significance of differentiating between changing the content of prayer and changing the setting for prayer or the division of labor? What is being constituted? Members' focus on organization allowed them to criticize the failure of the synagogue without suggesting that the content of Judaism was fundamentally problematic for them. Minyan members' dichotomy between organization and prayer is explained in part in an argument made in *The Homeless Mind,* where Berger, Berger, and Kellner examine the connection of meaning and organization. They suggest that "homelessness" and "underinstitutionalization" characterize modern life (1974, 186–87). Homelessness is the product of modernization processes in which work and meaning are separated from one another (1974, 186–87). As production was separated from kinship units and became increasingly specialized and rationalized, individual life was disengaged from the collective and lived within varied, nonoverlapping institutions. One worked, interacted with intimates, played, and reflected on the cosmos and one's place in it, in often separate and always separable institutions. Berger, Berger, and Kellner argue that meaning has become the province of nonwork, hence, the private sphere and the concern of myriad voluntary organizations. *Underinstitutionalized* is the term they applied to these voluntary organizations that inevitably fail to provide meaning, because "meaning" implies a coalescence of all aspects of oneself through unified symbols, beliefs, or groups. There is no holism in modernity because meaning is private and located in underinstitutionalized, voluntary organizations.[12] Hence, Jewish prayer could not express for its members what it meant for European Jews living in a homogeneous community, because meaning is not integrated within all realms of one's life experience. Meaning is embedded in the interstices of structure, like the voluntary association. Minyan members' rejection of bureaucratized worship was a rejection of a bureaucratized society. Their search for identity and meaning was articulated, in part, through issues of organization, which itself was a protest against society and a source of identity. For Minyan members and their generation, meaning and scale of society were connected because the society they lived in had separated them.

They were determined that the Minyan would be what the synagogue could not be; organization would save them because organization had failed them. They would not compartmentalize prayer from the rest of their lives, afraid to reflect on it or to associate new experiences with it. They would not recreate a synagogue that simply provided people with prayer services and offered secular activities without creating community. They would bring their intellect and personal commitments to prayer and find organizational solutions to handle whatever contradictions that emerged. They were part of a decade of American history preoccupied with fragmentation, structure, and meaning. Inevitably they would associate the "emptiness" of synagogue prayer with the lavishly elaborate voluntary organization that they believed the synagogue had become. It followed that if the synagogue was a bureaucracy, they would emphasize "antistructural" features like equality and deny the necessity of separating life, experience, and text (Turner, 1969). Prayer within a new organization could challenge modern values and provide an integrated Judaism of their own design.

How can such a vision for organization sustain prayer and integrate identities? If organization is the form through which a decorum and aesthetic of experience are established, then the relationship between them and prayer will allow us to understand not only what Minyan prayer is, but what established its authenticity.

Notes

1. In my doctoral dissertation I rendered these conflicts as social dramas. Victor Turner labeled long-term conflicts in tribal and national settings "social dramas" (1957, 1974). He emphasized their phased and regular stages, leading from a breach of norms through a period of crisis to a period of redress and final resolution. For Turner the period of redress was the most potentially creative in society. In this period, cultures and groups often turned to their rituals and symbols, not only to use them in the resolution of conflict

but to innovate, create, and invent from these resources. In my dissertation I noted that the definition of the crisis often determines what occurs in the phase of redress. In the Minyan's open-ended structure, major conflicts often turned around simply defining the crisis. The form of redress—ritual, discussion, or denial—inevitably followed however a crisis was defined (Prell-Foldes 1978b). I have not used the social drama model because I no longer seek to make a social-structuralist point or analysis. Turner's model, nevertheless, remains a significant one for the analysis of conflict at virtually any level of social interaction.

2. *Aleinu* (Upon us) is recited standing.

It is for us to praise the Lord of all,
to acclaim the greatness of the God of creation
who has not made us as the nations of the world,
nor set us up as other peoples of the earth.
Not making our portion as theirs,
Nor our destiny as that of their multitudes
*For we kneel and bow low before the supreme
king of kings

Acknowledging that He has stretched forth the heavens
and laid the foundations of the earth.
His glorious abode is in the heavens above,
The domain of his might in exalted heights.
He is our God, there is no other,
in truth our king, there is none else.
Even thus it is written in His Torah:
"That the Lord is in the heavens above and on the earth below.
There is none else."

We therefore hope in thee, Lord our God,
Soon to behold the glory of Thy might
When Thou wilt remove abominations from the earth
and all mankind shall invoke Thy name,
and all the wicked on the earth wilt turn to thee,
May all earth dwellers perceive and understand
that to thee every knee must bend, every tongue vow fealty
and give honor to thy glorious name.
May they all accept the rule of Thy dominion
and speedily do Thou rule over them forevermore.

For the kingdom is Thine, and to all eternity
Thou shalt reign in glory,
as it is written in Thy Torah,

"The Lord shall reign forever and ever."
Yea it is said,
"the Lord shall reign over all the earth;
On that day the Lord shall be one and His name one."
(De Sola Pool 1960, 336)

*It is customary on these words to bend the knee.

3. The *tallit,* or prayer shawl, is worn by adult men during morning prayer. The injunction to wear the garment is found in the book of Numbers (15:37–41), where God commands men to wear a fringed garment. Reform Jews typically do not wear these garments, as they were thought of as unnecessarily foreign. Men and women both cover their heads in traditional communities, but men wear special caps called *kippot* (*kippah* singular; in Yiddish, *Yarmulke*). Women have no special head covering. Jewish women interested in equality have appropriated both the tallit and the kippah. Not all women in the Minyan wear these prayer garments. All men cover their heads, and most wear prayer shawls. In some communities it is customary for a man to wear the tallit only after marriage, in others, after he becomes a bar mitzva and is called to the Torah for the first time.

4. Pork is prohibited in Jewish dietary laws.

5. The additional service is called *Musaf* in Hebrew. It involves the repetition of the Amidah, the central prayer of the liturgy. During Musaf a paragraph is added that prays for the return of animal sacrifices as they were practiced in the Temple in Jerusalem under the supervision of the priestly cult. Some people object to the Musaf because they do not want the return of such sacrifices. Others simply do not want to repeat the Amidah, a long prayer, which has been recited once previously during the morning. Musaf was a prayer service that most havurot discussed and many altered or rejected entirely.

6. In a traditional service the entire Torah portion, consisting of seven sections from the Bible, is read. One reader may chant all seven parts, or several people may act as readers. Conservative synagogues, following an old custom, often read the Torah on the triennial cycle, reading one third of each Torah portion every year. In the Minyan about one-third of the Torah portion was read each Sabbath, but they do not read on a formal triennial cycle. The Torah is read in the morning three times during the week. The new portion is begun at the Sabbath afternoon service. Only during Sabbath morning prayer is the entire portion for the week read.

7. The *Talmud* ("study" or "learning") is defined as "teaching derived from the exegesis of biblical text" (*Encyclopedia Judaica,* 750). The word most often implies commentary. The Talmud is codified oral law with rabbinic analysis and commentary. Torah is written law.

8. Minyan discussions are not themselves acts of biblical criticism, though their exegetical character has been influenced by that tradition. Joel Rosenberg suggests that biblical criticism is both analytic and synthetic. The analytic side emphasizes rhetorical and stylistic features of the narrative, focusing on meanings unique to the character of that narrative (1984, 34). The synthetic side of the criticism places any single narrative unit within the larger context of the entire narrative (1984, 35).

This Torah discussion is more analytic than synthetic, but both approaches may be found in Torah discussions. Such approaches are the result of two factors: First is the familiarity of many members with biblical criticism, who, when using this approach, provide models for others for how to lead discussions. Second, critical approaches assume the truth of the text without requiring a faith statement. The biblical text is approached as a literary text, rich and complex and amenable to interpretation. Issues of truth or falsity, in contrast to personal assessments of the text, evoked different types of interpretations by members.

9. Lubavitch Habad was founded in the mid-eighteenth century in northern Russia. It is an international organization and includes Jews all over the world; its headquarters are in New York. At the head of the organization is a rebbe, the descendant of the first rebbe, who is believed to have divine and miraculous powers. Habad is the name of the system of thought that Lubavitch developed. It is an acronym of the Hebrew letters that

stand for wisdom, understanding, and knowledge. It is a unique hasidic group and certainly the most successful, because it created a "systematized mystical philosophy" (Wiener 1969, 155–96). An indication of the popularity of the movement is the fact that in 1985, *The New Yorker* ran a three-part series on Lubavitch excerpted from *Holy Days: The World of A Hasidic Family* by Lis Harris (1985).

10. *Mitzvot* (commandments) are the obligations incumbent on Jews. The system of 613 mitzvot are encompassed by the halaha (tradition).

11. When I asked members how they formulated their liturgy in their first few meetings I received the same answer. They modeled what they did on the services they had at their Conservative summer camp, Camp Ramah. Though not all Minyan founders participated in that camp, they followed the lead of those who had. As noted in Chapter 2, this denominational camp played a major role in establishing a view of Judaism for people throughout the United States who would create havurot like the Minyan.

12. *The Homeless Mind* by no means exhausts the literature on the relationship between meaning and scale of society. Virtually all sociological theory on modern society address just such problems. I find Berger, Berger, and Kellner of particular use because they focus on the voluntary institution and why it should be a province of establishing meaning.

4

The Constituents of Minyan Prayer

Community, Interpretation, and Halaha

> When the Minyan began I expected it to be a traditional service, a place where we could daven with a traditional mode, and I could daven with people I could also talk to. When I lived in Israel I was not comfortable davening with people who didn't share my assumptions, who saw the Torah as given on Sinai.
>
> Harvey

Decorum and organization provided the context for Minyan prayer, but they did not constitute it. Looking back on suburban synagogues, we have a visible record of how that generation envisioned Judaism. Minyan prayer, in the absence of buildings or rewritten prayer books, provided that vision for its members. How members prayed, with what attitudes and aspirations, revealed what made prayer effective for them. Their ability to integrate themselves with prayer was their primary task, and it was one that turned out to be constantly vulnerable to the community and tradition that created it.

Prayer united people even as it continually evoked conflict within and between them. As a group committed to pluralism and tradition, they compromised without much discussion in matters having to do with dietary laws, Sabbath restrictions, and accepting members' different attitudes toward tradition. But when it came to prayer, every alteration or reflection upon its effectiveness provoked not one but many discussions and rediscussions. Indeed, traditional Jewish prayer—what it is, what it should be, and how it should be conducted—framed the questions that most preoccupied community discussion and was the issue on which they found compromise the most difficult.

When asked, most Minyan members seemed willing and able to describe what occurred when they prayed. Beth described her prayer experience in a typical fashion.

> Prayer is first and foremost the most important way I connect myself with the Jewish people. I don't examine if a God is listening or not at the other end, because I really don't care in some sense. Somehow I feel that there is a God only because of the view of God I have. When I pray a lot of the words, I let them be experiences for me. When I read about angels, I don't see them dancing on the head of a pin. I just know there is an angelic experience in the world. When I read about victory or famine, I think that there are ups and downs in life. If I am a good person, if I observe the mitzvot, not all 613, but in general, then the world can be better. And sometimes I just have fun seeing if I can understand every word of the prayer. I want to see how good my Hebrew is getting. And I think I understand this prayer and that's something I have in common with Beruria and Rabbi Akiba.[1]

Beth said several things in her description of her prayer. She emphasized that prayer connected her to the Jewish people, and by that she meant the historical people, the mythological community of Israel that finds its origins in the Bible and in all living Jews in the world. Her link to those overlapping groups took a liturgical form, which she described as nondiscursive. The words were neither facts nor information; she was constantly engaged in interpreting them. By calling them "experiences," she did not imply that she stopped at each word, thinking about whether or not she disagreed with it or searching for a more appropriate definition. Rather, the prayer language allowed her to locate herself within the text as she reflected on it. Angels, famine, even the legal requirements of Judaism were to be grasped "symbolically," standing for something other than their literal meaning. The content, nevertheless, linked Beth to the Jewish people, so that though she understood the words in a variety of ways, they still evoked an experience she recognized as Jewish. She reflected on her ability to achieve that link by her mastery of Hebrew prayer and her ability to identify with the people that said the prayers many centuries ago. Finally, she clearly eschewed the need to have God "listen" to her, finding that less essential than the link she felt with Rabbi Akiba and Beruria.

Beth's comments in turn, raise questions about prayer. Why did she pray in a language she struggled to master? Why was prayer the most effective means to connect her to Jewish history and its great leaders? Why should she bother to pray words that require interpretation? The only self-evident answer to these questions is that prayer was a fundamentally different experience from making statements with which one agreed or disagreed. Prayer engaged a different type of experience.

Why Beth did not simply assent to the prayers can be explained by what social scientists of religion call the process of secularization, the diminishment of religious authority in the collective and personal life.[2] These theorists seek to understand how a changing social system undermines religious belief and participation. These theories offer a great deal to our understanding of why religion has changed, and the differences between twentieth-century American and nineteenth-century European Judaism. Though they may explain why Beth and others believe what they do, they have been unsuccessful in explaining why they continue to participate and what religion means in modern, plural social systems. Indeed, Beth's statement showed little evidence of a religious or, specifically, Jewish world view. Neither religious institutions nor religious ideas controlled her action or her consciousness. She chose religious activities, rather than being bound by religious authority that put God at the center of her experience, and she emphasized her individual choices to do and to say what she believed, a stance associated with secularism, despite her use of traditional prayer.

American Religion and Secularization Theory

Secularization theorists argue that the basis of religious and social life has changed unalterably. A series of economic revolutions produced social differentiation in the societies of the Western world, resulting in the loss of shared rituals and shared beliefs. Every social sector became specialized and distinct so that the family, the work place, religious institutions, and political relations now serve different and disparate functions. Underinstitutionalization, described in the previous chapter, is one direct result. This differentiation created specialized knowledge so that people no longer shared common ideas about life and experience. Religion is typically thought of as the source of that very store of knowledge about the world. Indeed, the term *world view,* often thought of as synonymous with religion, cannot be so global or encompassing in a society whose institutions are highly differentiated. Without that shared knowledge, there is no shared world view. Without a commonly held world view, society no longer produces what Peter Berger has described as "plausibility structures," social supports such as institutions and official doctrine that legitimate the reality that religion claims (1969, 45). Religion is certainly a matter of individual consciousness, but that consciousness cannot be maintained, according to secularization theorists, without the support of a social system that institutionalizes religion and gives it the aura of the factual. Indeed, in secular society people may well have no need for a religious explanation of the world. Technical and scientific explanation may suffice. Max Weber used the term "disenchantment" to characterize this neutral and technological view of the world.

Secularization not only transforms society, but religions will also change and often be fundamentally transformed. The relationship between Christianity and the larger society has been central to the forms these transformations have taken. In the West, various forms of Christianity have either come to terms with secular culture and society or abandoned it. Troeltsch's ([1912] 1966) early distinction between Church and sect articulated these paths. His typology differentiated accommodation and rejection by associating the former with a charismatic, lay, egalitarian, voluntaristic religion, and the latter with a hierarchic, institutionalized one.

Max Weber ([1904] 1958) further demonstrated that sects themselves hastened secularization processes. Protestant sects, unlike the church, focused on beliefs and communities of believers. Baptists and other aescetic sects required that believers take their other-worldly impulses into the marketplace. An ascetic life focused on the rational planning of all activities in response to one's ideas about God created a style of entrepreneurship consistent with capitalism. Sacrifice in the marketplace was good for business. Therefore, sects led to altering the organization of the economic sphere that led to the reorganization of society.

Richard Niebuhr (1957) pointed out in the early twentieth century that sects tend to be the province of the lower classes with the least stake in society. If sect membership leads to a more rational and controlled life affluence may well follow. Sects tend to become part of establishment churches as their members' affluence increases. Sects, then, are developing into churches and churches are continually splintered by charismatic sects. The process is continuous, but within the framework of a pluralistic society neither church nor sect defines the experience of most citizens.

The process of secularization has taken different forms in different nations. The United States is of particular interest to these theorists because of its structure—separation of church and state—and the resulting pluralism. Ironically, in this manifestation of secularization, religious adherence turns out to be remarkably high. Sociologist David Martin suggests, therefore, that the American pattern of secularization has focused less on institutions or beliefs than on "ethos." (1978, 5)[3] He seems to follow Peter Berger's conclusion that in a pluralist society religion becomes a matter of choice and must vie with all other meaning systems within a kind of competitive market of symbols. The more choices available, the less able any single competitor is to claim a monopoly on meaning and the less likely any individual is to sustain an exclusive commitment to one system of meaning. Secularization and pluralism, then, work hand in hand; choices make more choices possible. Each individual, rather than the social system, decides what is plausible, providing uniform structures of authentication. Every Sabbath each American decides not just where to go to worship, but whether to worship and what form worship will take. One is equally free to go to one's childhood church or synagogue, to go to a newly created or borrowed Eastern cult, or to jog for several hours. Each activity may make claims to provide a world view and offer a program for living one's life.

Indeed, Thomas Luckmann (1967), a sociologist and frequent coauthor with Berger, concluded that the world view or available shared cultural assumptions, are "invisible," with no connection to institutional religion. Churches cannot convey that world view because they are committed to doctrinal differences. He effectively describes the voluntary nature of institutional religion, demonstrating why it cannot be an encompassing world view. He is less successful, though, at accounting for what religion is today and the ways it synthesizes the tenets of modern society. The world view, or invisible religion, he describes focuses on mobility and achievement as the most widely shared values and that family, love, and loyalty all serve these ends. Luckmann never explains why these Western ideas do not look like religion, lacking ritual form, community symbolism, or effective mechanisms for transmission.

These secularization theorists argue, in effect, that a revolution has taken place in the social basis of human interaction. Where there was uniformity in experience, now there is difference. This revolution included a transformation of knowledge, making it difficult for modern men and women to accept claims of biblical truth because of scientific developments.[4] Secularization theorists explain that religion becomes entirely "privatized," a matter of choice, and American religions increasingly must "market" themselves to continue to capture devotees who had been theirs alone at an earlier point in human history.

What theorists have overlooked is what religion means to those who do participate. If cultures no longer generate cohesive world views, how is meaning constituted? What authorizes religious participation when the structural support from society has been withdrawn. These questions suggest that secularization theory can provide an understanding of how homogeneous small-scale societies generated world views and identities for their members. However, faced with religion in complex society, these theorists postulate that religion is not a world view, but they do not explain the nature of meaning that people like Beth found in Judaism.

Indeed, until recently scholars generally accepted secularization theory. But many of its assumptions have been called into question, (Hadden, 1987) as these theories have failed to account for the rise of Islamic fundamentalism in the Middle East and the spread of the American religious Right. Religion seems more powerful and persistent than any of the theorists of the first half of this century would have predicted. Their evolutionary sequence, which postulated a linear development from "tradition" to "modernity," left all things traditional, such as religion, behind. Hence, secularization theory is in no position to explain, for example, the dramatic shift in denominational affiliation patterns among Christians from liberal to fundamentalist churches that only fifty years ago appeared to have little promise for the future.

The new voices of dissenting scholars often seem simply to emphasize different issues about religion than those who focus on secularization. Other contemporary sociologists of religion tend to ignore theory and argue empirically that people continue to behave as though they were religious. They attend church; they give to charity, and they identify with religion. Therefore, secularization cannot be said to have occurred (Stark and Bainbridge 1985 for example). Without specifying the content of these acts, such scholars nevertheless point to their persistence. When confronted with Gallup polls indicating that Americans decreasingly believe in the Bible or other religious doctrine, they must claim unconvincingly that such attitudes may also not affect religious belief (Hadden 1987, 602). Secularization theorists, on the other hand, discount religious activity, dismissing it as meaningless from the point of view of the society, and finding in it little more than psychological support for the individual.

David Martin is one of the few secularization theorists to specify the limits of his model. He suggests that his analysis of how secularization works in various Western countries only examines institutions, and he acknowledges that such an analysis must be partial because religion focuses on "symbol, feeling and meaning" (1978, 13). Martin implies that something may well be missing from the discussion if we do not understand the worshiper's experience and how it is created within the religious context. Knowing what happens in activities that are thought of as religious is as yet a largely ignored resource for understanding what provides the "plausibility structures" for modern men and women's beliefs.[5] Secularization theorists do not find religion in macroinstitutions. The quantifiers fail to extend their inquiry about religion beyond the question of whether people "show up."

There are other questions to ask that will allow us to examine what generates the authority for individual participation and allow us to overcome the dichotomy between "meaning" on the one hand and activity on the other. Without denying that historical social changes have affected religion, we still can accept the validity of religion as a social and cultural system, leaving open questions about the sources of its power and the significance of its system of meaning. In the first three chapters, I argue that changing social relations did alter religious forms, and I describe some of the decorum and aesthetics of different generations' Judaism. Now I ask, what can we learn from those forms about the meaning of, and authority for, the prayer of Minyan members. Rather than ask how often they attend prayer services and whether such services represent their world view, my focus shifts to what allows them to pray and what does it mean to them.

The Constituent Elements of Prayer: Performatives, Form, and Context

In the last decade a number of scholars concerned with religion have addressed the issue of prayer, bringing to it a new interdisciplinary approach. Though secularization theory was aimed at describing institutions, it had significant implications for understanding individual prayer experience. Similarly, while those interested in work on prayer address the seemingly more narrow concern of ritual, their ideas may help us to reconceptualize religion in a pluralistic, complex society. How prayer is constituted as an experience in modern society is a question only recently addressed.

Sam Gill (1981, 184) suggests that the near silence of scholarly disciplines on prayer is a direct result of dilemmas faced by nineteenth-century theorists of religion, E. B. Tylor and Frederick Heiler. They posited an evolutionary sequence in the development of religion in which humans moved from prayer expressed through given forms to spontaneity. Spontaneity, they argued, represents a higher expression of human relationship to God. Prayer was confounding for them because "higher" religions had liturgies that did not wither away to be replaced by "sheer spontaneity." The result of this apparent discrepancy was an early and lengthy silence on the subject by scholars.

More recent literature, however, discusses prayer in a way that is helpful in overcoming the dichotomies created by the secularization debate. The starting point for this interdisciplinary work is the presumption that prayer is both a text and a ritual; one must study both prayer and praying. If prayer can be understood as a ritual and a text, then its emotional force, its ideas, and above all, its status as a cultural and social activity stand to reveal important insights concerning its significance and persistence. Judaic scholar Lawrence Hoffman attempts to define a "liturgical field" in order to understand Jewish prayer (1987). The field encompasses historical themes and events and "master symbols" inherited and created by the social communities that pray the liturgy. When people worship they find and create what Hoffman calls their self-definition. The entire liturgical field, not simply the text, must be understood in order to learn the meaning of the prayers.

This view is articulated also in an earlier work by Sam Gill on Navajo prayer (1981). Perhaps because he was working with a less fluid body of prayer than Hoffman, his approach to prayer focuses somewhat less on its content. Indeed, he claims that the message of the prayer is so well known that its purpose cannot be to inform or educate worshipers. Rather, he focuses in large part on the physical and emotional aspects of prayer that signal to the participant that a special frame of interpretation is to be engaged. The worshiper does not look at prayer content as empirical or as "encyclopedic" knowledge. Instead, in the prayer situation, redundant and well-known messages are combined with a performance style so that the emotional mood of the worshiper is transformed to accept what Gill calls "meaning-giving messages." Performance, in other words, persuades the participant of the truth of the prayer message by evoking emotions and moods that make the values and ideas embodied by Navajo cultural symbols convincing. For Gill, like Hoffman, prayer mobilizes a cultural field of meanings and emotions that shape and reflect the experience of the worshiper. Both of them move far beyond the text for an analysis of prayer and explain worship by understanding the significance of both prayer ideas and performance-evoked emotions. Their approaches might be called a contextual analysis of prayer.

Explicitly ethnographic studies of ritual that rely on contextual analysis exist. For example, Ronald Grimes' (1976) study of ritual symbols in Santa Fe, New Mexico, provides a comparative analysis of Protestant, Catholic, and Pueblo Indian forms of worship and ritual, and their connection to public and civic ritual. Grimes isolates what he argues is the "fundamental pattern" of Santa Fe's public ritual system

(1976, 46). At the same time he devotes his book to the study of the overlapping symbols and communities that define the public ritual system. Indeed, he understands the rituals as a "selection of symbols whose meanings evolve" (1976, 50). Grimes searches out system and process. His discussion of Protestant and Catholic liturgies, as well as experimental Catholic masses, takes up the problem of ritual beyond text and how these performances knit together sacred and secular meanings.

Grimes' comparison is reminiscent of Lloyd Warner's analysis of ritual in Yankee City, the site of his intensive analysis of an American community (1959). Both Warner and Grimes pay close attention to the form worship takes in order to understand its messages. Each emphasizes the value in ritual form for the analysis of religious meaning. Though Warner was less sensitive to context than subsequent writers, he did embed his discussion of form and meaning within actual practice.

Contextual analysis then, understands religion in general, and prayer in particular, as dynamic processes capable of change. Because the experience they create locates the worshiper in a cultural and historical system of meanings, as social context changes, meaning will too. Neither Hoffman nor Gill understand the content of prayer to be primarily informational. Hence, its power rests more on the context in which it is prayed. Contexts are altered, but their emotional power cannot be removed solely because structural relations are transformed. The meaning messages depend upon the liturgical field: the form of the ritual, the symbols containing shared meanings and shared history. Secularization affects the structural underpinning of the liturgical field. It does not remove the symbols or ritual forms that must be understood in light of change. Beth's emphasis on the emotional power of the prayers because they locate her in Jewish history, even in the absence of understanding them literally, illustrates this point.

The contextualists make clear that religion is experienced through rituals that formulate meaning and action together. Without understanding how these rituals work, we cannot understand how they affect worshipers, or how they are affected by the changes that concern secularization theorists. In the last decade several anthropologists have written about the significance of ritual form. They have all been influenced by the idea of ritual as a "performative," a concept of J. L. Austin, ([1963] 1962) a philosopher of ordinary language. They look to ritual form to explain how ritual works, that is, how it affects people's attitudes and actions. Most of these scholars are interested in traditional society, yet none attribute the effectiveness of ritual exclusively to the integration of world view, society, and ritual. As such they offer a useful alternative to secularization theorists for interpreting how ritual integrates person and society.

They derive their ideas from J. L. Austin because he offered a model of language that emphasized that the efficacy of ritual depends on the conditions under which it is performed. Form creates efficacy. Austin was interested in a peculiar form of language whose utterance was not amenable to verifying its truth, as one would a statement of fact. Performatives are utterances that constitute doing. With such a statement as "I pronounce you man and wife," "I bet," or "I christen this ship" (Austin's now classic examples), one has done the very thing one purported. Performatives cannot be true or false, but they can be "felicitous" or "infelicitous." If the circumstances are improper, then the performative will be infelicitous, that is, void. A person without ordination cannot marry people no matter what words are stated. Or if the intention of the person is insincere, as in an already married person going through a marriage ceremony with another person, then the performative is hollow. In the first case the performative has "misfired," and in the second it has been "abused," but in neither case is it true or false.

Roy Rappaport (1979), Stanley Tambiah (1985), and Wade Wheelock (1981) have found Austin useful for the interpretations of ritual, liturgy, and prayer, because he emphasizes the "constitutive" quality of the act. That is, rather than focusing on the text as a source of information, they examine what constitutes the act of prayer (Wheelock 1981, 56; Gill 1981, 185–87). In all cases they pay attention to how prayer can create or "simulate" intention and how its formal properties aid in communicating its messages and attitudes (Tambiah 1985, 132–33; Wheelock 1981, 58, 60). Though Tambiah and Rappaport disagree about the extent to which one can understand ritual and liturgy by separating form and content (Tambiah 1985, 143; Kapferer 1983, 239), both see in form (the performative) one of the central foundations of prayer, indeed, a constitutive element. All of the scholars cited agree, to some extent, that what appears sacred, convincing, or truthful is in part derived from the form that liturgy takes.

Prayer is not, of course, like all ritual acts. In the marriage ritual, for example, the act evokes a different kind of certitude than prayer. Particularly when prayers are petitionary, it is difficult to define them as unqualified performatives.[6] Prayer still cannot be falsified, but the potential failure that results from an unanswered prayer does in fact affect the performative quality of the utterance. Tambiah has such an exception in mind when he labels certain ritual acts as "regulative" (1985, 136). He argues that healing or rain-making rites, for example, are intertwined with, and often replaced by, practical alternatives. Regulative rites have a "constitutive" element, but that alone does not exhaust the activity because of the implications of their producing a result. Tambiah concludes that uncertainty does not "undermine their performative validity" (1985, 137). In the case of prayer in a plural society, by contrast the performative quality remains an open question. The market place of meaning does consistently offer alternatives whose competing claims in part rest on their efficacy. Some claim they are likely to produce better results than others. Hence, systems that compete with petitionary prayers for health, rain, or a desirable change in life directly attack the effectiveness of others. Results cannot be ignored. Therefore, as appealing as the performative model is, prayer cannot be understood exclusively in those terms because some prayer can be experienced as ineffective; its message and content are not exhausted by its form.

The very reason that prayer cannot be defined solely as a performative speaks to a general and unfortunate dichotomy drawn between the content and form of ritual. Austin overcomes that dichotomy through the performative model because he claims it does not exist. The form of the utterance, "I christen thee," and the content are the same. He focuses instead on how alteration of constitutives—false intention, inappropriate speaker, or problematic context—can affect a felicitous performance. Formalists within anthropology are particularly drawn to this approach because they claim that ritual content is irrelevant, and ritual's work is accomplished through its external forms. In Rappaport's example, a message of invariance is created by repetition and an unchanging form. Indeed, formalists attempt to compensate for decades of anthropologists who examined ritual semantics alone and ignored the contribution of form to ritual. Because they collapse medium and message, however, they ignore the complexity of ideas and messages communicated within ritual, comparing them to Austinian utterances. Formalists also ignore how ritual messages are affected by the variety of media encompassed by form. Media and message are interdependent but not the same, a problem I will address in Chapter 5.

These questions are particularly significant for understanding religion in a plural society. Secularization theorists posit that meaning evaporates, or is radically personalized, in a plural society. They do not examine the relationship between form and meaning, nor how to understand any change from, or any continuity with, traditionally ascribed meanings and forms in a plural context. Nor can theories of prayer ignore form, or the way form is crucial to its message. Though much of prayer is well described as a performative, not all of it can be. It can only be understood through a model sensitive to the relationship between form, content, and context, understanding that on some occasions these processes are unified in the worshiper's experience, and on other occasions they are not.

What performative theorists have in common with contextualists like Hoffman and Gill is their interest in how ritual elements integrate the prayer experience and the impact of the context upon that experience. What a performative approach asks is what makes prayer felicitous, its context and its structure. Contextualists are more concerned with the cultural and historical meanings expressed by the prayers and how the ritual form effectively communicates those messages. The contextualists do not understand the content of prayer to be any more informational or falsifiable than the Austinians, but they do argue that content requires explication. The performativists emphasize ritual form alone. The contextualists look to social and cultural circumstances for culturally relative interpretations. Finally, both those concerned with context and those committed to a performative view look at prayer to understand how it situates its performers in a world of meaning. Both approaches seek to understand what conditions make prayer possible, or even successful. All of these scholars go beyond Austin by looking at how effectiveness is linked to an expanded sense of context.[7]

Questions about the constituents of the prayer experience—context, form, and performance—give us that middle ground previously ignored by secularization theorists. Those theorists sought to understand, as noted, how religion gains objective status in society, capable of providing "truth" and defining meaning for men and women. They therefore concluded that when religion competes to define the world view with other systems of meaning, it no longer monopolizes truth or plausibility. Those scholars who look at prayer and ritual on a performative model, or wish to contextualize ritual performance within a social and cultural field, are asking significantly different questions and explaining different phenomena. They try to understand how an experience, whether it is aimed at establishing the sacred or communicating cultural values, is created and maintained and what its constituent elements are. They all place the ritual within a social context, but unlike secularization theorists, for them the social and historical context does not exhaust what there is to know about the ritual in general, or prayer in particular. What these performative theorists have in common is understanding how ritual and prayer shape and create certain attitudes and emotions and the authority or plausibility that generates them. Their analysis of the ideas, symbols, values, or meanings articulated depends on understanding the constituents of the ritual act, *as well as* the various contexts in which the act is performed. In short, they are interested in how ritual expresses and shapes action, not just in how it reflects institutions. Similarly, they find plausibility for religion, in large part, in its ritual components, whose forms, for some of these theorists, are the products of social relations.

The advantage of this broad and encompassing theoretical position rests not in abandoning the study of the relationship between society and religion, which it does not do. Acknowledging that form and content affect one another, as the Austinians argue, suggests that as social relations change so form is affected, which has consequences for the meaning of religious participation. Instead of abandoning either the study of social relations or institutionalized religion, scholars can understand contexts, form, and the relationship of form to meaning to interpret the religious life of modern men and women. Hence, when David Martin suggests that he can only study institutions—yet "ethos" has been secularized in America—we are left wondering what secularization theory can contribute to our understanding of the persistence of religious life. What creates the ethos that modern society secularizes? What makes it plausible for people to continue to pray? The most important question to ask is how do we understand what occurs within ritual performance? What generates its effectiveness and connects it to ordinary life? Then we can understand how prayer created a world of relationships for Beth, joining her and Jewish history to one another.

The works of Hoffman and Gill, whose theoretical interests are parallel but whose subject matter is rather different, provide a useful contrast. Gill examines Navajo prayer to understand how an unchanging form can be applied to many different circumstances, so that prayer, rather than being a mechanical variation on a structure, synthesizes and symbolizes Navajo culture for its worshipers. Hoffman demonstrates that changing liturgical fields lead to changing liturgies that combine Jewish symbols, historical events, and current social circumstances. One emphasizes stability and the other change. Yet both explain how prayer depends on a larger cultural system, that it continues to exemplify key cultural notions and is capable of expressing essential messages, if not, in Hoffman's case, a world view. Both Hoffman and Gill focus on the relationship between form and content and their integration with other "themes" or "symbols."

The performative element of this approach, which emphasizes particularly the constitutive nature of certain utterances, is a valuable alternative to secularization theory for another reason. Austin himself was concerned with the infelicity of performatives. He wanted to understand what made these utterances ineffective. Tambiah and Rappaport, the anthropologists who have applied Austin to ritual, both look at the structure of ritual to understand its suitability for "lying," or "rigidity." The formal properties of liturgy and ritual enable them to communicate messages that are beyond question, but the conventional, redundant, and symbolic language that conveys messages as cultural truths is also capable of communicating banalities or lies. Because language is so important for praying, prayer is vulnerable to emptiness or "ossification." As a fixed form, liturgical language is constantly repeated without necessarily communicating much beyond words. That is what differentiates liturgical and every day language. The more conventional a set of utterances is, the less likely it is to communicate intention. In addition, liturgy is ultimately both reliable and unreliable. Its unchanging language, a reliable formulation, posits relationships with unseen, transcendent beings, whose responses are unreliable. Hence, those who pray are constantly at risk in their experience. Roy Rappaport argues this point well.

> While participating in liturgical performance may be highly visible, it is not very profound, for it neither indicates nor does it necessarily produce an inward state conforming to it directly. But for this very reason it is in some sense very profound, for it makes it possible for the performer to transcend his own doubt by accepting in defiance of it. (1979, 194–95)

Again, to explain ineffectiveness or failure, Rappaport and Tambiah look to the ritual form, rather than social context alone, to explain infelicities and how they may be overcome. While one would never want to exclude social institutions or social relations from understanding occasions of ritual uncertainty, this analysis also allows us to see how ignoring form makes our understanding of ritual or religion partial at best.

In order, then, to understand what makes prayer felicitous or infelicitous, effective or ineffective, I will examine the constitutive elements of Minyan prayer. I begin with its three most salient forms: that it is public and communal, that it is interpreted, and that its words are prescribed by halaha, Jewish law. How members' perceptions were integrated with the demands of the form will be explored in an analysis of an important Minyan event, an evaluation meeting. The conflict between members at this meeting about their prayer experience explains the significance of their concern for the form prayer should take. To this point I have concentrated on members' concerns with structure, organization, and decorum. These were especially important to the community members in their first two years together. In the Minyan's third year, members shifted their attention to the form of ritual, indeed, to prayer itself. This shift not only reveals the changing issues for the group that came with expanding membership, but also demonstrates the affect of the ritual form on the members' ability to pray.

Minyan Prayer Forms: Community

Through prayer Minyan members interacted, and, in turn, their prayer was affected by those interactions. Because public Jewish prayer requires a minyan, it was an inherently appropriate vehicle for community. The Minyan's desire to create an alternative to the synagogue arose out of their intense interest in truly communal prayer. They all valued forms of prayer that intensified community. They sang prayers together, prayed aloud to be heard by one another, arranged their prayer space, and moved their bodies while praying in a way that made them visible to one another. The Minyan sought to achieve an experience of prayer that was nonunison, yet still synchronized. That type of prayer has been compared to jazz, with its emphasis on improvisation within unity (Heilman, 1983). The strongly communal aspect of Jewish prayer is illustrated by the fact that if an individual prays alone, he or she should attempt to pray at the same time the synagogue does, using the same liturgy, except for those prayers that require the quorum. Prayer is not only prayed within a community, it takes a communal form in the use of some plural language, and its subject often concerns the community. Hence, the first constituent of Minyan prayer is that it is public and communal.

No one in the Minyan was clearer in defining the communal basis of prayer life than Saul, a college student in his early twenties. He was a member of the group for less than a year in 1973, but had prayed regularly his entire life. As a Jewish educator and a child of a Conservative rabbi, he had grown up with considerable consciousness of what prayer should be like and how to achieve that end. I asked Saul if he prayed to someone, and his answer emphasized the connection between prayer and community.

> You mean God? No. Do you mean is someone in the Minyan listening to me? That's pretty important. I like the feeling that other

> people are being affected by my mood in their prayers. The people who sit around me when we pray can tell my mood and concentration. People look to see if other people are concentrating. If a lot of people are, it helps me to concentrate. And when I am hazan I want to mobilize something that's going on in the group and get that in synch with the prayers that I particularly like and find powerful.

He articulated how closely people were linked in the community through prayer, even though they prayed individually for the majority of the service. Prayer could be, and often was, tied to the moods and emotions of participants. To listen to others praying was part of prayer. In this sense prayer was quite appropriate to the articulation of communal sentiments. The halahic requirement of a quorum for prayer indicates that the tradition itself recognizes that community is an integral part of the prayer experience. Mark explained to me how he understood the relationship to others in prayer.

> I need prayer to connect me to others. It's easy to pray in isolation, to find a beautiful spot in nature. But confronting nature isn't confronting others. The Amidah says, "Keep my lips from speaking evil." That prayer recognizes that prayer itself connects us with other people.

Though Mark was anxious to be united with others, he believed that prayer made a contribution to maintaining such relationships by acknowledging the difficulties involved.

In the Minyan, one might argue that the communal focus was primary. Mark, one of the Minyan founders, even questioned the balance between the communal and other constituents of prayer.

> It's seeking for community that brings people to the Minyan for prayer. We all know we want to be together. But we all know we want to have some Sabbath experience. Now, we don't have in our system of projects anything that is better than prayer. Part of the passport to community is reading these prayers. The price you pay for being a Jew, certainly within this community, is prayer.

Mark's tone was cynical. He expressed this view at a time when the group was in the throes of reevaluating its purpose and goals, events to be discussed in Chapters 5 and 6. Nevertheless, he articulated another sense of communal prayer in contrast to Saul. For Saul, the communal form of prayer implied that the presence of other Jews at prayer affected his prayer and he in turn affected theirs. Prayer was an individual act made different by the presence of a community. The significance of the connection between those who prayed was a "variable" in the prayer experience. Mark, by contrast, understood community as separate from prayer. In the Minyan one prayed in order to be with others; he did not address the issue of whether being with others had an impact on prayer. Mark's rather harsh appraisal expressed a tension set up by prayer's communal nature. The worshiper is in danger in two ways. He or she may merge entirely with the community, losing the private experience of prayer necessary for creating a relationship with God. Or the individual may stand in isolation from the community, leading to alienation from praying, at least within a particular minyan. Susan articulated this tension more positively than Mark when she described her prayer experience.

> I have a very personal relationship with the Siddur. I feel very strong about it. It is both dear and familiar. And it's an experience worth struggling for. It has dual elements, the comfort, familiarity, and community, and that level of experience that is very difficult to reach and we're struggling for. Without the comfort it wouldn't be worth the struggle.

Susan, in describing the conflicts she sometimes experienced in praying traditional Jewish prayer, counts community, those with whom she prays, as an asset, a familiar and predictable assistance to her praying.

Because prayer is activity as well as text, its communal form influenced both aspects. Its content addressed the community, and it was enacted communally. But at the same time there were concerns about worship that arose out of differences in how members understood the role of community and its place in the prayer experience. The communal form of prayer was one of its constitutive elements. The gathered community was essential for public worship. The Minyan existed to pray and its communal form articulated messages about the value of community.

Minyan Prayer Forms: Interpretation

Prayer was not exclusively a text, but neither could it be understood apart from its written form. The text of prayer engendered the most problems for group members. In response they developed the single most unique feature of a Minyan prayer service. Their statements of potential dissent were an integral part of the liturgical service. At points in the prayer service where one might want to "study," to examine classical rabbinic texts about Torah or prayer, Minyan members most often raised or responded to questions about whether or not Jewish liturgy adequately reflected or illuminated their life experiences. On those occasions the text might also be used as a starting point for a discussion about contemporary events to see what insight it might provide. In either case, the liturgical service intertwined the recitation of traditional liturgy with comments upon or criticisms of its relevance. As in Beth's description of her prayer life, the worshiper's relationship with liturgy in the Minyan was to make the prayers speak for and to him or her. Members created periods of reflection that, by their position in the liturgical order, made prayer a performance of a given text and a weekly comment upon it. This sequencing and juxtaposition were consistent with the practices of other havurot and unusual in normative Judaism. As sociologist Samuel Heilman asserts about Orthodox Jews, particularly the non-intellectual laity, "Even the most modern among the Orthodox would prefer to leave their doubts unspoken and disattended" (1983, 65).

Minyan interpretations differed markedly from normative Jewish interpretations of texts. The source of traditional commentaries purports to be the Bible itself. Classical interpreters subordinated themselves to the continuity of tradition, rather than bringing new ideas to that tradition (Holtz 1984, 13–14). Innovation certainly occurred, but it was often presented as in keeping with tradition. Minyan members' analyses of prayer were based neither exclusively on traditional commentaries nor on a simple rejection of them. Unlike most analytic processes, they expressed feelings of anger and pleasure as well as ideas in their assessments. Nor was their interpretation without consciousness of the impact of their group or culture on their comments. Their remarks reflected values and ideas derived from their peers, their educational training, and American ideas of justice. This analytic approach is what Minyan members associated with the discussion formula "I have a problem with . . . ," as well as their more purely textual discussions.

Interpretation necessarily distanced the self from prayer. Members believed, however, that by expressing their personal feelings they would be less alienated, and those feelings would genuinely become part of prayer. By interpreting prayer it would yield a place to them. A shared communal interpretation or a heated discussion of a text were sufficient proof of the group's success at achieving engagement with ancient tradition, according to members.

The normative Jewish liturgy created a dilemma for Minyan members. Their commitment was to tradition. Yet this tradition alone did not formulate their ideas and feelings about life, community, and the cosmos. They wished to reinterpret the tradition without altering its liturgy, precisely because that tradition powerfully evoked authority and emotion. Praying was simultaneously highly persuasive and alienating. As an activity, it drew members into the enactment of the tradition and created conviction about the truth of the act. As content and information, expressing not only acceptable truths but embraceable ones, it was alienating. Their solution to this conflict lay in constantly interpreting what they did. This perspective was embodied in the epigraph for this chapter. When this Minyan member described his frustration about his prayer life in Israel, it was evident that he lacked the opportunity to interpret what he was saying and a community to do it in. His need to interpret seemed as great as his need to pray a traditional liturgy.

Minyan members' willingness to critically reflect on prayer and halaha suggested that they chose a traditional Jewish arena for individual and collective disclosures of their conflicts about Jewish tradition. Their choice was embedded in their assumption that the minyan, the community of prayer, was the appropriate setting to experience oneself as a Jew in America. They prayed and they examined their prayers. Their examinations were both intellectual assessments of the content of the tradition and personal reactions. Praying, then, expressed one's Judaism as well as evoking conflicts about it, conflicts that were not resolved simply by no longer praying. Doug offered his view of how this was accomplished.

> In the Minyan we are attempting to integrate the past and near past, which get remote from us, with what we are and feel. We are searching for something we can't find in other communities. Prayer is a way of coming to terms with remaining a Jew. One of the things I like about the Minyan very much is that not only are members generally successful at it, they are engaging in academic careers and other professions. They're very modern and "with it." Yet they can do it through the medium of these age-old prayers and then in terms of the twentieth century. Many synagogues are dealing with the early twentieth century. They haven't really progressed. The Minyan is more appropriately placed at this point in time.

Doug noted a contrast between the Minyan and other synagogues, who, at the beginning of the century, were simply trying to prove by their architecture and decorum that they were American. For Doug that was a settled question. A later "twentieth-century" congregation had to be concerned about interpreting prayer texts, discussing, questioning, and even disputing them in light of contemporary life. The twentieth century is represented by interpretation, a constituent of the Minyan's prayer experience.

Discussion is neither prayer nor performative. To the contrary, it is the exact opposite. Yet within the Minyan's liturgical service, discussion became part of every single performance of the liturgy. Then, contrary to a normative sense of prayer in which a statement of blessing God's name constitutes the act of blessing, something more is at stake. In the Minyan, prayer involved both performative utterances and falsifiable statements. Both seemed essential to create prayer as an act for a group "placed at this time." Hence, in this context, discussion (a nonliturgical form) became a part of prayer because these men and women made discussion a key form of interaction within the prayer experience. Therefore, I call it a necessary condition of prayer like community.

Minyan Prayer Forms: Traditional Jewish Liturgy

Community and interpretation constituted components of the liturgical experience. Liturgical content, however, was traditional prayer. When members talked about prayer being difficult or an "experience worth struggling for," more often than not they were saying something about conflict with prayer language, what it said and what it asked worshipers to say. Virtually all people who came to the Minyan, with few exceptions, came precisely because this was the liturgy they wanted to say. The Siddur was "authentic," a word members used often. Its authenticity allowed Beth, among others, to remark on her connection to untold generations of Jews, who she believed used basically the same words. Were they to write a new liturgy, a more relevant one, even in Hebrew, it would destroy that authenticating link between themselves and others. The fact that Minyan members, as well as havurah participants throughout the country, did not set about writing or modifying the liturgy sets them apart from other Jewish movements. Hoffman (1987) contends that every American movement modified the liturgy or created a new one. The havurah did not, and it does not seem likely its members will do so.[8] Although some havurot members may well have written prayers or created innovative services, these were never disseminated. The National Havurah Co-Ordinating Committee has never circulated these prayers, and it is not likely to appoint a liturgy committee given its continuing negative attitude toward a bureaucracy. Those as-

In private Jewish prayer.

sociated with the havurah were committed to spontaneity and innovation and were reluctant to determine the experience of others. Bureaucracy alone, however, did not deter them from such changes. They could articulate their rejection of American culture through their liturgy only if they maintained its traditional form. Similarly, their claim to cultural uniqueness depended on their maintaining a continuous liturgical tradition. Ronald Grimes notes a similar resistance to abandoning "historicity" in Liturgy in Santa Fe, a nongeographic parish (1976, 31–32).

For Minyan members, prayer, mandated by halaha, implied the obligatory, authoritative, and historical force of the tradition. Mark's view that Minyan members pray "because that is what is done on Shabbat" implied that prayer was the natural requirement of the day:

> Prayer is the thing you do Saturday morning. It is tied to time. You could have a study group any other time, but you can't have Saturday morning services any other time. Now the Sabbath comes as a day of rest, a day of a natural sort of communal event. You could substitute a morning of study for it, but there's no definite reason why one should study that morning. But there is a definite tradition of praying that morning.

Like many adherents of halaha, members are unwilling to change prayer or alter its language. Unlike other adherents, however, their sense of obligation is voluntary. Most pray for only one of the Sabbath liturgical services. Few pray daily. Their sense of requirement and obligation is voluntary.[9]

The History of Jewish Liturgy

The history of Jewish prayer makes evident that modernity is not the sole cause of difficulty with prayer. The prayer's formal components work to make it alienating as well. Hence, the development of Jewish liturgy itself attests to the impact of form on the prayer experience. This discussion of that prayer history focuses on how the Jewish tradition confronted the worshiper's experience of prayer. This history of the development of Jewish prayer is filled with examples of worshipers' fears that they lack sincerity or engagement, rendering their prayers unsatisfying and reflecting the realization that prayer is a difficult and often inadequate expression of Jewish life (see Millgram 1971; Garfinkel 1958; Petuchowski 1972; Idelsohn [1932] 1967).

That history, of which many Minyan members are aware, corroborates the assertion that prayer must be understood in light of its form as well as social context. Secularization alone will not explain the difficulty of praying. For prayer always engages both angst and promise, possibilities that transcend the modern situation. The complexity of prayer as a performative is particularly evident here. Though prayer is constructed as an invariant liturgy that emphasizes its certainty, its content postulates innumerable possibilities for failing to achieve its end, contact with God. Saying is doing in prayer, but saying efficaciously is at once promised by the form and undermined by the content. The words of the prayer may be the opposite of the worshiper's intentions, or they may articulate emotions that the worshiper does not experience. My discussion of Jewish prayer focuses on this very dilemma because it is in many ways its most salient feature for Minyan members, since they were committed to prayer but also to self conscious interpretations of it.

Jewish prayer evolved and changed under the sectarian movements, diverse cultural settings, and historical periods, resulting in considerable variation in Judaism and Jewish liturgy. What the Minyan finds in its Siddur dates largely, though not exclusively, to the rabbinic period and is prescribed in the Mishnah and Talmud. Indeed, the rabbis understood prayer to be a commandment, a mitzva. Like the commandments to study, to honor parents and teachers, and to do charity, prayer was a requirement embedded in the daily cycle of an observant Jew. In other historical periods, such as the Hellenistic or Late Antiquity, rabbinic prayer was not considered normative. Indeed, most non-Orthodox denominations of Judaism in America have taken some degree of liberty with that tradition, Reform being the most extreme. Hasidic Judaism, as well as other Jewish movements from the nineteenth century on, willingly changed the liturgy. Nevertheless, observant Jews who are descended from Europeans think of their liturgy as an orthodoxy that cannot be changed without violating Jewish law.[10] Yet a core of the liturgy persists.[11]

Prayer flourished as an important ritual of Jewish life only after the destruction of the sacrificial center of the Temple. The final destruction in 70 C.E. at the hands of the Romans dispersed Jews from their own land and from worship in Jerusalem. There were two precursors to, and influences upon, Jewish prayer: spontaneous prayer and sacrifice. The Bible records the spontaneous prayers of several figures: David and Hannah among them. Sacrifice is the organized activity that precedes prescribed and formal prayer in Jewish history. Sacrifice shares with prayer the intention of building a bridge between, or ladder to, a divine source. Hubert and Mauss, the French social scientists who wrote about sacrifice, argue that the sacrificial victim was a mediator between human beings and the divinity to whom the sacrifice was addressed. Humans and gods were never in direct contact ([1899] 1964, 11)

The sacrificed animal was replaced by the words of liturgy when the destruction of the sacrificial center in Jerusalem brought sacrifice to an end. Words now had to mediate the relationship between humans and God. Jewish prayer retains many connections to the sacrifices. Like sacrifice, prayer is required in the morning, afternoon, and evening, with special additions on the Sabbaths and festivals. The prayer services have maintained the names of sacrificial services, and sacrifices are mentioned and described in portions of the liturgy. In Hebrew, sacrifice is called "service of the altar," and prayer is called "service of the heart." One continues to "serve" in creating a relationship to God, but the locus, setting, and methods for service have changed. The second-century rabbis who developed prayer and made it obligatory, as the sacrifices had been, claimed that the contact created by one could be maintained by the other. They legitimized prayer by asserting a relationship between it and sacrifice. In contrast to sacrifice, the language of prayer carries more complex messages. The complexity of the messages, now combined with a discursive form, makes prayer more sensitive to uncertainty and to questions about the performer and performance. The rules that accompanied the proper execution of a sacrifice could never be as concrete for prayer.

This transformation of forms for contacting God was revolutionary. Prayer became appropriate for each individual in a way that the priest-dominated sacrificial cult was not. Prayer occurred at special times, and lacking a single sacred geographic center, Judaism became attuned increasingly to time rather than space (Heschel 1977, 8). The sacrificial victim was replaced figuratively by a standardized liturgy. The drama of the temple was replaced by the considerably less dramatic community, the minyan with which one prayed, studied, and heard the Torah read. Above all, prayer, even in its prescribed communal setting requiring the individual to participate in the community, to recite certain prayers, to say "amen" to the prayers of others, and to hear the Torah read, was an individual act. Hence, Jewish prayer was built on a tension between the private and the public, the individual and the communal, the spontaneous and the standardized. That tension is maintained rather than resolved in the worship service.

Over time the developing liturgies of Judaism incorporated the growing experiences of the Diaspora Jewish people. Since the language of prayer could communicate more varied and complex messages, prayers changed and liturgies included new prayers. The corpus of prayers reflected the different sentiments, interpretations, events, and theologies of many historical periods and prominent rabbis. Liturgical allusions to the sacrifices appeared near personal statements of praise and love for God, and those appeared after statements of creed mixed with petitions for individual health, freedom from personal and political enemies, and the ability to follow God's commandments. The move from sacrifice to prayer, then, engaged individual actors more intensely through a liturgy that is historically inclusive. It created a private-collective relationship, not necessarily in opposition, but in tension. In the prayers, one speaks to God, ideally desiring a personal relationship, but using a standard language and being surrounded by one's fellows who both invade and support one's attempt at contact.

This standardization and publication of a common book of prayer were long in coming because the rabbis dreaded canonization (Petuchowski 1972, 3). In the ninth century, Spanish-Jewish scholars appealed to the head of the Babylonian academy of rabbis that developed in the Diaspora to compile a standard prayer book and unify the growing variation in Jewish prayer services. Though the core prayers of the service remained constant, anxiety had grown about the order of the prayers. The resulting codification of oral traditions and knowledge of actual practice constituted the first prayer book.

This standardization did not stem the accretion of new prayers and material through the middle ages. The prayerbook grew unwieldy. The addition of prayers was commonplace, though deletion was not. Only in the nineteenth century, with the development of classical Reform Judaism, were excisions made. In 1818 Reformers published their own Siddur. The Reform Siddur went through a number of changes after 1850. The Conservative and Reconstructionist movements printed their own prayer books in the twentieth century.

That the Jewish prayer book is called Siddur, or "order," indicates that prayer is amenable to ordering and hence creates orderliness. That very orderliness is embodied in the structure of the prayers. They follow a set order, are made up of sections that follow a similar structure, and even blessings follow a certain formula and structure. One prays the same words in the same order. The variation that does exist is the result of the time of day, day of the week, and festival of the year.

Precisely because of the certainty and orderliness of prayer, the tradition prescribes a proper attitude for certain prayers, requiring worshipers not to fall into rote repetition of a familiar liturgy. It is not sufficient to simply say the words of central prayers. That proper attitude is *kavvanah* (from the Hebrew root "direct"), a form of concentration. With kavvanah the "worshipper is conscious that he stands in the presence of God and thus his mind is aware of the meaning of the word he utters" (Jacobs 1972, 79). I. Epstein described it as combining "the meanings of attention and intention—attention to what is being said, intention to perform the commandment" (1947, 77). Kavvanah opposes the rote repetition of prayer. But kavvanah also contrasts with the normative form of prayer, *keva*, which means fixed form, routine, or tradition (Petuchowski 1972, 7). The development of the liturgy suggests an emphasis on both keva and kavvanah. All prayers are said according to keva; only a few prayers require kavvanah. The rabbis acknowledged that they could not require kavvanah for all prayer, as few would be capable of such concentration.

The tension between keva and kavvanah, recognized by rabbinic scholarship, reiterates a point made in a context-oriented approach to ritual. Rituals are fixed forms and performed events. Jewish prayer is not only a liturgy but a performance as well, requiring an attitude and often necessitating the support of a community. The meanings of fixed forms will change given the context of performance. As Jacob Petuchowski argues, one generation's kavvanah is another's keva, and one generation's keva may be another's kavvanah (1972, 9–13). What is liturgically fixed and routine for one generation may provide the source of intense spirituality for another. For example, the poetry of individual Jews became fixed liturgy over time. What began as the product of intense personal feelings about God ultimately became keva.

Indeed, this complex relationship between form and spontaneity in prayer is recognized in the Talmud, which demands that only certain central prayers—those that remain the core of Jewish worship—be said with kavvanah. These prayers were crucial in second century Jewish liturgy. By the medieval period, Jewish thinkers were stressing "greater inwardness" as a requirement for more of the prayers. In the eighteenth and nineteenth centuries, mystical interpretations of Judaism gave kavvanah a meaning beyond concentration on the plain sense of prayers and envisioned worshipers focusing not on their needs, but rather on the significance of even the letters and spaces of liturgy (Jacobs 1972, 28). The common concern throughout these historical periods demonstrates that religious leaders were aware that prayer is a communicative act of uncertain efficacy. Simply repeating liturgy never has been the sufficient end of prayer. At a minimum, praying must include the intention of fulfilling one's ritual obligation. Ideally, it always concerns communication and formulating relations within a community that represents the Jewish people, and formulating relations with God, who creates that community.

The psalms relate ideal models for prayers, "all my bones shall say 'Lord, who is like thee,'" because of their awareness that such a form of concentration is rarely achieved (De Sola Pool 1960, 76). The psalmists idealized total engagement with prayer, even in one's body. In the Jewish tradition rabbis' prayers record the desire that they may pray. Jacobs cites the rabbinic admonition not to pray unless it is with concentration, and then translates the rabbi who argued in the nineteenth century:

> Nowadays we find it so hard to concentrate adequately, the older rule, that if prayers have been recited without kavvanah, they have to be recited again, no longer applies, since the likelihood is that the second time, too, they will be recited without kavvanah. (Jacobs 1972, 3)

This passage voices the common view, articulated particularly by the anti-hasidic orthodox of nineteenth- and twentieth-century Europe, that those who pray well are few and that no one can pray as the great rabbis and leaders of old could. Humans are far removed from the revelation at Sinai, the temple, the great rabbis and, as a result, are simply less spiritually vital.

The sectarian conflicts in Europe between Mitnagdim (nonhasidic traditionalists) and hasidim in the nineteenth and twentieth centuries laid bare the conflict over the relative significance of prayer in the Jewish tradition. Hasidism gave prayer priority over study and, in so doing, challenged normative Judaism. As central as prayer is to the normative tradition, the study of Talmud in particular is more highly regarded, though both are required. The tradition even dictates that if in a crisis such as a flood or a fire in which a community must choose which to save, it is more important to save a school of learning than a synagogue. Jacobs illustrates this view when he writes about prayer in the *Encyclopedia Judaica.*

> Prayer stands high in the world of values. God Himself prays, His prayer being that His mercy might overcome His judgment. Nevertheless, the study of Torah occupies a higher rung than prayer. . . . A rabbi who spent too much time on his prayers was rebuked by his colleagues for neglecting eternal life to engage in temporal existence (*Encyclopedia Judaica* 1971, 981).

Acknowledging that the tradition itself regards prayer as a less solid basis for religious life than study invites a comparison of the two activities. Though there are questions of law with contradictory and equally valid interpretations, and dissenting opinions have been retained, study is simply a more predictable activity than prayer. Difficulties and questions can be decided by rabbinic courts. The end point of law is translation into practice. It does not lead to constant questioning about efficacy. Its purpose is not unselfconscious, though standardized, communication with God. If, as Mintz argued, prayer often translated the values of the Talmud onto the spiritual plane, it did not communicate those values as rigorously, hence as concretely, as law. In reality, however, every observant male can pray three times daily, but few men can study full-time rather than work. Observant Jewish men are more likely, then, to pray regularly than to study. Nevertheless, the ideal is important to understand.

As hasidism elevated prayer to the preeminent Jewish act of piety, hasidim altered prayer by making it a more "mystical" experience. The plain sense of the language became virtually irrelevant. Petition was appropriate only insofar as it was understood metaphorically to concern the needs of God, not humans. Prayer had as its end point the juxtaposition and ordering of various names of God used in the liturgy, which were interpreted as "vessels of great power." The meaning of communication as the end point of prayer was entirely transformed and mystified in a tradition that made prayer preeminent.

It is worth noting that not only Jewish liturgical traditions generate conflicts in worshipers. The scholarship on liturgy notes these ubiquitous tensions. Prayer, ideally, promises a great deal. At a minimum, one may have contact with the one to whom it is directed, articulate the key ideas of a culture, perform prescribed cultural dramas that may idealize reverence or penitence. Precisely because what may happen is significant, what may not happen is distressing. Individuals may not feel their prayers are being heard or they may believe their prayers are not being answered. They may feel disconnected from God, cut off from the community. Even in a less differentiated society where religious rites are universally shared, one may well experience the power of the gods in the collective society, as Emile Durkheim argued ([1912] 1965). But as he did not note, one may feel more isolated in the absence of contact with those gods because one imagines that others succeed. All prayer raises the problem of efficacy.

The unique possibilities and anxieties engendered by prayer are attributed by sociologist Robert Bellah to prayer's place in the development of "non-primitive" religions (1964). In these societies, he argues, human "communication systems" (prayers) are needed because the gods are increasingly out of reach and distinguished from humans, yet must still be accessible. He writes of prayer and sacrifice:

> No matter how stereotyped, [it] permits the human communicants a greater element of intentionality and entails more uncertainty relative to the divine response. Through this more differentiated form of religious action a new degree of freedom as well, perhaps as an increased burden of anxiety, enters the relations of his existence (1964, 365).

Bellah then, places this anxiety in an evolutionary sequence. Prayer is inherently a form of ritual that carries more messages, makes more claims, and signifies more meanings and relationships than nonverbal, simpler forms. Jewish liturgy illustrates this view.

This history of prayer underlines the importance of understanding the complexity of the link between prayer and its social context. As I explained in Chapter 3, prayer is created through decorum and organization. Synagogue, Minyan, and European prayer were not the same because they were embedded in different social structural relations that affected their meaning. Nevertheless, the form of prayer itself affects worshipers, forcing them to understand prayer in new ways, or lower their expectations of what one can accomplish in prayer. Prayer cannot be understood apart from social relations or reduced to them.

Focusing on what constitutes prayer within a particular community requires setting out its essential conditions. Prayer requires a text, a context, and activity. Scholarly research on prayer, or even ritual in contemporary society, tends to emphasize one constitutent at the expense of the other. Because Minyan prayer, like all ritual, communicated a set of ideas, each constituent embodied these ideas and enabled the worshiper to internalize them.

Prayer and Covenant

At its most general level, Jewish prayer addresses the central event of the Jewish people, the covenant made between God and humans at Mount Sinai when God gave His laws for the people to Moses. That covenant reasserts the first covenant made between God and the biblical patriarch Abraham, rewarding Abraham's faithfulness with God's blessing on all his descendents. These covenantal acts established a relationship between God and the Jewish people, allowing each partner in the convenant to ask and expect things of the other. Remembering the events of the covenants, promising a relationship of loyalty and love to God, and asking in turn for God's blessings are expressed in innumerable liturgical forms in the Siddur. Though theologians recognize the tensions inherent in prayer, they argue that prayer is nothing without a personal relationship with God (Heschel 1953). Prayer within the Minyan, with its interpretations and adjustments, already puts Minyan members at odds with this theological view. Yet even the many members who said that God was not necessarily the primary listener still understood prayer to create a relationship. All of them sought a relationship with a self-transcending entity called the People Israel. Hence, the form of worship and even much of its content was directed to a covenantal end continually interpreted in prayer discussions and within the creation of the community itself. Though no havurah member ever wrote or said that a suburban Jew misunderstood the covenant, their continual concern with finding an authentic Judaism indicated their need to recreate Judaism and that sense of convenant.

Prayer articulated this timeless covenantal relationship. It signified the authenticity of the "eternal People Israel" by binding living Jews to that people. For members who understood Hebrew, and for those who did not, the most important use of the language was its antiquity. What was relevant about its contemporary use was that it embodied the reality of the continuing covenantal relationship between God and humans, as well as between all Jews in space and time.

For those who prayed regularly, and have prayed over a long period, prayer joined the self quite personally to the covenant by the association of prayers with one's own maturation. Saul suggested this connection to me when he said:

> I've prayed for a long time. I was brought up with it. There are so many subtleties to my personality that it brings out. At different stages of my life it's always meant different things. I'm really playing on a whole backdrop of my existence when I pray. Some of the prayers I really like, I've said hundreds of times. Every time I come back to it, it brings up all the inflections and feelings that have gone into saying it, in parallel with that prayer.

Here is an example of a virtuoso who was able to integrate personal experience into prayer and prayer into his Judaism. The content of the prayer was often a backdrop for his focus on his own development as a

Jew. The covenant placed the person who prayed in webs of relationships with God, with all periods of Jewish history, and with family and community. Not every Minyan member experienced every such relationship, but covenant stood for the entire range of possible ones.

Prayer meant many things theologically and historically, but its most profound meaning was a very general one—relationships that constitute Judaism. This meaning was formulated through the constituent forms of Minyan prayer. Each form expressed and transmitted covenantal meanings, joining members to these relationships. The link made to others through prayer recreated commitment to the Jewish people and the maintenance of Judaism. Community, maintenance of tradition through prayer, and the integration of the self communicated nothing so powerfully as the capacity for prayer and therefore covenant. Community prayer created and preserved that covenant.

Ideal Minyan Prayer

Minyan members shared a consensus about who among them prayed well. Thus, despite many differences between members, they did share a vocabulary about effective prayer when they described others. Virtually everyone mentioned Jay, Jacob, Mark, and Harvey as models of how to pray. The language used to describe them varied. People spoke of their "comfort with davening," "acceptance and understanding of traditional Judaism," "integrity," "searching and spirituality," "lack of self-consciousness" and "love of the Siddur." The way these men moved their bodies while praying, used melody and song, led services, and represented traditional Judaism strongly modeled praying for most of the others, many of whom were less educated as Jews and were newer to the tradition. Members emphasized knowledge of the text, attitudes, and ease when they described virtuoso daveners. There were interesting tensions in these descriptions. Words like "searching" and "integrity" implied struggle. The ideal was not the rapid rote davener who could pray the whole service by heart at a lightning pace. At the same time, they valued a "comfort" or ease that indicated a person who was fully competent at the skills involved. Attitude, spirituality, and love for the prayer book were mentioned, but classical descriptions such as piety and belief never were.

By contrast, some Minyan members reflected on their own difficulties with prayer as the opposite of ideal prayer. Doug described to me his distress about his ability to pray.

> I am very easily distracted. The color of the page of the Siddur, if the ink is smeared or if someone moves, can distract me. Sometimes I get really hung up on how I look. Do I look like I am bowing too low? Am I bumping into somebody with my elbow? But some Saturday morning, for twenty minutes, I read the words, I move my body, and I think, "Ah, this is really what it's like." And then my mind wanders and I think, "Am I the only one who is not into it?"[12]

For Doug prayer was poignantly self-conscious. He constantly reflected on his own ability to pray "correctly," to be engaged by prayers, and to do them properly. He occasionally achieved what he thought was the proper prayer experience, only to have it evaporate. Doug did not have a classical Jewish education. He grew up in a suburban Midwest synagogue where his parents were active members, and he received an American Reconstructionist Jewish education, including the study of Hebrew, prayers, Jewish history, and the festivals of the year. His family and synagogue anticipated that he would be adequately educated to mature successfully into a full member of the Jewish community. But Doug apparently had doubts about that possibility as he recalled a high-school Jewish camp experience where he encountered a European rabbi who embodied an alternative vision of what prayer should be. "I had a feeling it was a private world he created all by himself, wrapped in his tallit. Yet it was in the midst of many people. He cut off distractions." Doug saw and recognized the prayer he wanted. His inability to achieve that seemed to him his own isolated problem, which he was less willing to describe.

Both through positive example and self-criticism Minyan members idealized that very tension that both social scientists and Jewish scholars find in prayer: that it is uniform yet spontaneous. What Minyan members sought in their prayers was an experience that was fully Jewish (unselfconscious, expert, comfortable) and at the same time critical and interpretive. In the Minyan that religious experience, as well as the critical interpretation of it, were constitutive of prayer.

Understanding these prayer constituents leads to the Austinian question about whether such prayer is "felicitous." In the language of liturgy, is it effective? Do Minyan members integrate the form and content; do they interpret and pray with success? What is the source of their willingness to pray, especially with the many doubts they express on any occasion? Rather than presenting a somewhat abstracted picture of Minyan prayer to answer these questions, I turn now to ethnographic events in which people, in the course of a Sabbath meeting, addressed the success of the group and the group's purpose. In the last chapter, I looked at the structure, organization, and decorum of the Minyan, arguing that through these elements of community life members articulated their uniqueness and authenticated their Judaism without substantially altering the Siddur. In this and subsequent chapters, I address the constituents of the prayer experience. The former elements—structure, organization, and decorum—articulated the generational formulation of these men and women. Community, interpretation, and the Siddur were constitutive of their activities. Understanding the felicity of their prayers depends on understanding how and, more importantly, why these elements were linked. In that linkage we have the components of the Minyan's liturgical field.

Conflicts About Forms of Minyan Prayer

One of the constituent forms of Minyan prayer is interpretation, an unceasing willingness to examine and question prayers and to refuse to compartmentalize them from cognitive analysis. The community itself was open to identical scrutiny. In their first year, founders recalled asking questions weekly about the effectiveness of the davening. As the group grew larger its members held meetings every two to three months called "evaluation meetings." The purpose of these meetings was always vague, and their contents were often explosive. Rarely held on the Sabbath, so that they could discuss commonplace issues about their treasury, the tone of the meetings differed from the Sabbath. Members disagreed more, complained more, and expressed individual needs more readily. The tone was critical and evaluative. "How can we as the Minyan do better? What do we need to do better about?" In the American discourse of the counterculture, they most readily spoke about "needs" not being met. The wide variety of needs expressed could never possibly be met, but neither did anyone censor them. Usually everyone spoke and then an interpersonal politics prevailed. For in this entirely egalitarian group no leader determined whose needs were the most appropriate. The personal power or respect individuals commanded, and the subjects they addressed, determined whether their concerns were attended to. Though many people expressed a wish for more intimacy or more socializing in the group, those needs were never addressed. Those who complained about prayer, often for the opposite reason that it was not made the group's primary concern, were usually taken seriously. A vast array of members' needs were to be answered by prayer. These discussions made clear what prayer was to facilitate, to symbolize, and to achieve.

The subjects covered at the meetings were far-reaching, emotional, and intensely critical, but in the end inevitably involved virtually everyone stating their satisfaction with the group. Their intense self-scrutiny was matched by public statements of satisfaction with the group, consistently modified by its imperfections. These evaluation sessions, then, were democratic, used the language of personal needs, and paralleled their interpretive sequences about prayer. In both instances their scrutiny was directed to efficacy. Did they pray well? Did their prayers express the values, sentiments, and ideas they thought authentic and appropriate? One form of scrutiny was linked to Jewish text, the other to the Minyan itself. The very act of such scrutiny convinced them that they were visible in the tradition, able to express their concerns and remain fully Jewish. That is what Minyan organization and structure made possible. As they criticized tradition, they were drawn to it. As they performed the tradition, they criticized it. Particularly in evaluation discussions, members expressed all they wished the Minyan might be, all their disappointments and hopes about what might happen in the future. Because what the Minyan did together was pray, inevitably these sentiments were expressed around prayer, and comments about prayer were directed at the Minyan.

Although some members were less anxious for such examination to take place, others always insisted on it. For example, Harvey in particular urged that such discussions occur. He believed that the group would succeed only through "rigorous religious honesty" enabled by constant evaluation of what and how they prayed. He initiated an evaluation meeting in the late summer of 1973, coinciding with most members' return from summer vacations. Harvey suggested during one Shabbat lunch that it was time for a meeting and volunteered to chair it. Though there was some discussion about the appropriateness of holding such an event on Shabbat, Harvey prevailed, arguing that more people were likely to come following services than on a Sunday night.

The Sabbath Evaluation

Though Harvey may have initiated the need for an evaluation, others must have agreed because forty members attended. All but eight stayed for the evaluation following the obviously hurried lunch. There was a sense that a discussion of consequence would occur. All the members pulled their folding chairs into a circle and looked to Harvey to begin. "Our discussion today has to deal with whether or not the Minyan is meeting our expectations," Harvey said. "What is it that we want? I think it would be best to bring both positive and critical remarks about the Minyan to our discussion. I want someone else to begin." Martha suggested that "each person should have a chance to make a brief statement in answer to your question, Harvey. Otherwise, only a few people will say anything."[13]

Members' comments that followed addressed a wide range of issues. Two themes were unifying: an affirmation of the value of the group, and a series of individual needs that members wanted the Minyan to accommodate. Saul introduced a subject that concerned several people.

> I enjoy the Minyan very much. I'm excited about davening in this group. But we need to create a mechanism to bring new people into the group to teach them the melodies we use and familiarize them with how we daven. We are davening much too fast. I like a slower pace and this is disrupting me.

There was mumbled approval throughout the room. Saul had raised two issues that were repeated in the discussion, the quality of prayer and the formation of community among Jews with a variety of religious backgrounds. As Saul experienced a direct link between his prayer and community, his interest was rather personal. The approval for his comments indicated that forming community, and its impact on prayer, was an issue. Then Aaron spoke, reflecting similarly on his membership:

> I also feel very good about the Minyan, very positive about being here. This is a context in which I can express my Judaism, which is not God centered. That makes me feel like I belong, that there is a place for me here that I have never felt in a synagogue. I would like to see us have more regular retreats, to get away from the city several times a year for a whole Shabbat. I think that would be a good thing for us to share.

Aaron, by contrast, looked to community in a way that was less systematically linked to prayer. He was unusual for disclaiming God so openly in his remarks. He emphasized his desire to strengthen community, which in turn solidified his sense of Judaism, but he did not emphasize prayer as integral to that process. Mark spoke next and shifted the topic to the specific quality of their prayer.

> I think it is fantastic that the Minyan is in its second year. Frankly, I find it unbelievable that there are forty people here. When we started the Minyan none of us would have imagined davening with forty people. But perhaps it is time to start talking about some structural changes. I find the lateness of the service very difficult. We are lax about when we start. My body, the time of the day, and the prayers I am davening have to be synchronized. If we don't say *pseukey de zeimrah* (Psalms of praise) until eleven o'clock, I am already a little tired and hungry. The liveliness and the force of the prayers feels inappropriate. Then, standing through the Amidah comes even later and feels wrong. We need either to shorten the service, read fewer Psalms or take some measures to make the service more appropriate to these needs.

After a mixture of positive reflections on participating in the group and random criticisms, several people turned their attention to the issue of what they called "discussions" and I have described as "interpretation." There was a general sense that the discussions were not sufficiently stimulating. They had become predictable. This was one of the problems Mark had in mind when he said "structural changes" should be considered. Jean suggested that everyone break down in three- and four-person groups and all discuss the same thing at the same time. Larry suggested simply that they should institute several discussions on a number of topics each Shabbat. Martha commented that the group should no longer divide into two groups but meet as a whole again. She urged using more general topics for discussion. "We might discuss issues about Judaism, moral and ethical behavior even." Finally, Don suggested that the Rashi study group be more open to more people. "Can't someone announce anyone is welcome to join. It doesn't feel very accessible."

Jay took his turn next. Having come to Los Angeles several months before for his first job since becoming a rabbi, he said:

> I have ended up in the right city. I cannot imagine any place more desirable than the Minyan to spend Shabbat. I would like to see a retreat as well from time to time. I wish we could spend more parts of Shabbat together. There are other portions of Shabbat than the morning service. I also would like to see us study together during the week.

Then Harvey finally took his turn.

> I agree with Jay. I feel great satisfaction with the Minyan and this is the best possible place to worship. But I do not like what is happening to our davening. We sing too much while we worship; the melodies belong at meals or parties. We need a tone for the service that recognizes there are right ways to say certain words and phrases. We need more subtlety and more concentration and less singing.

Rob, who had passed his turn, now spoke up.

> Harvey, you are wrong. Singing may be the means by which we establish religious or Shabbat feelings. You cannot dictate a right way to pray. This way is appropriate.

Other comments were briefer, agreeing or disagreeing with earlier remarks. Harvey then summarized what had occurred.

> Two basic issues have been raised. One concerns the retreat and the other is structural changes, how we are doing things. I want some concrete suggestions to come out of this feedback session.

Members agreed to a retreat, setting a date, establishing a planning committee and subsequently choosing the topic of the "ritual structure of the service."

Then the group again discussed structure and experimentation in the Minyan service. Many members reiterated their desire for change or experimentation in the service. Jay said, "Our davening is becoming so predictable that I know the speed any particular hazan will daven at. It's the pattern of the davening we need to alter." Martha added:

> When I davened at a minyan at the University of Chicago, services always had themes. Once I organized a service around Franz Rosenzweig's notion of the Sabbath as the day of revelation.[14] Why don't we select themes and try that. We should devote one Sabbath a month to an experimental form.

Harvey, who also had davened at the Chicago Minyan retorted: "I do not want this minyan to be like that. One day I arrived to discover that for the service we were to listen to taped music. The Siddur is central and essential and nothing should change that." Martha's voice rose in anger as she said to Harvey: "There is a lot of variation possible within the Siddur. It is the laziness of people in the Minyan that keeps people committed to the same form Shabbat after Shabbat. It takes effort to be creative." Jay mediated the conflict by saying:

> I trust and know the Minyan well enough to know that no one will do a service that is too outlandish. Even if one service is a disaster I can sacrifice a Shabbat and tell the people who organized it why I think it failed.

When Joseph reiterated that he wanted to do things differently, Martha said: "I hear Joseph say that he wants to do an experimental service and I volunteer to help. Who else will join me?" Several people raised their hands. That seemed to draw the discussion to a close.

The Minyan had once again taken a hard look at itself. Members had set goals, agreed on concrete changes, and intensified their commitments to one another by agreeing to a retreat to look even more closely at these issues while they shared an entire Sabbath together of prayer, singing, eating, and relaxation. Harvey suggested that the retreat theme should be prayer.

The wide-ranging comments at the evaluation discussion covered the central issues that concerned Minyan members. Harvey's question "How is the Minyan meeting my needs?" was responded to in three ways. First, many people discussed the Minyan as a community. How successfully had the Minyan incorporated newcomers as well as including those present? Was it a good setting for Jews who came to join? Were people friendly enough and sensitive to one another's needs? In addition, many expressed the wish that more activities would be shared, that a greater sense of community could be forged. The second issue raised by many members concerned what I call "identity." Several people commented that this Minyan is a place that made them feel really Jewish, or comfortably Jewish, or properly Jewish. Comments about the openness of the group, the flexibility of members concerning degrees of observance, and shared notions of prayer all focused on members' sense that the group represented them in a way consistent with the identities they sought to forge.

Finally, a number of comments, mostly from the group's founders, focused on prayer itself. Several people commented on prayer aesthetics: how prayer felt, how it met the needs of those who wanted to create a good environment for prayer. These comments were the widest ranging. Several people spoke about the rhythm, timing, tone, and mood of prayer in the Minyan. Discussions of speed and type of music were particularly frequent. But another set of concerns described "staleness," "predictability" and "lack of innovation." In brief, a number of people commented that prayer was boring, unsatisfying, not working. Even those who said that the Minyan was the best place to be for Shabbat said the Minyan had to change or their prayer was endangered at worst or boring at best.

Harvey also complained about the group's prayer life, but he proposed that the Minyan move in another direction. He argued that prayer must conform more strictly to its traditional form and intent. Others argued that the intent of prayer might be better met by experimenting with the Minyan form of prayer. Members had as many suggestions concerning discussions as they did the organization of the service. Though their positions seemed polarized, in fact they both spoke to a real and powerful fear about how well prayer functioned in the community. Both sides insisted that praying required attention and care. Those who favored experimentation felt that Minyan prayer was stifling under the order of service that the group had established, that they were moving toward a routinization of prayer that troubled them. Their concern was, to use the terms of Jewish tradition, that keva dominated. While Harvey and those in sympathy with his position also feared routinization they were equally concerned about how serious the Minyan members were about prayer. Harvey and others feared experimentation in such an atmosphere. Would members abandon the liturgy if given the opportunity in favor, for instance, of popular music?

At stake in this discussion, which occurred as the Minyan began its third year, was, in social scientific language, the relationship between form and content. Could they achieve an authenticating traditional experience if they altered any of the Minyan constructed forms that they associated with normative Jewish tradition? How could they, as individuals and as a group, address the problem of the rigidity and invariance of worship and of Minyan forms of prayer? Most of them acknowledged that their carefully crafted form for worship was not doing what it should be doing. They expressed high regard for the community, but questioned its efficacy. Indeed, community was brought into the problem of efficacy when Jay claimed that changing the forms depended on trusting others in the Minyan. Harvey was obviously finding that difficult to do. He apparently felt that his ability to pray was endangered by others.

Both perspectives revealed members' anxiety that the purpose that created the Minyan as a unique setting for traditional Jewish prayer might no longer sustain the community. In that case prayer threatened to become an empty activity, resembling too closely the synagogue and the Judaism of other generations of American Jews. The Minyan needed to take prayer seriously to remain the Minyan, but no consensus existed about how that might be accomplished.

Minyan members' fears that prayer could become an empty activity was matched by their desire to fill prayer with an abundance of meanings. The evaluative statements made by members about what the Minyan should be included the demands that prayer enable identity, that it provide community, that it be interesting, and that it be fundamentally traditional in character. It was not so much that prayer needed to be the excuse for community; then people could simply have prayed the required words and gotten on with the sociability they desired. Rather, prayer was to provide a liturgical field in which community, identity, and the conviction of oneself as truly Jewish could be formulated and rehearsed. It was to provide private contact with God, with the historical Jewish people, and with the members of the Minyan. If prayer failed in that, and members understood that prayer was difficult under any circumstances, then what they aspired to be as Jews was brought into question.

As a community of Jews, Minyan members found in their liturgy a link to their collective pasts; an authentic language for personal expression; comfort, discomfort, awkwardness and ease; an alienating language; and exhilarating truths. They resolved the contradictions by creating a decorum that was not only familiar but unique to their generation. They wrapped an ancient language within a contemporary one of sound, sight, and personal relations. The continuity between the two depended on a small and homogeneous group. As membership grew and changed, not only were both languages challenged but so was their compatibility. In matters of both prayer and law, various members wondered what the tradition held for them. The questions challenged the community as well. Could this group of people continue to offer one another an authentic and personally significant Judaism?

From Minyan members' statements it was apparent that the efficacy they sought from prayer was "covenantal." They wished to achieve connection and relationship to several communities simultaneously. Their questions about efficacy, then, suggested that those relations were not always created in prayer. In Chapter 3, members' frequent recourse to organizational change is explained; the evaluation discussion led to the same forms of resolution. For example, suggestions regarding the number of discussion groups and the timing of prayer were potential "structural changes," as Mark called them, that might bring about the ends they sought. If form is in fact essential to accomplishing a desired end for prayer, then it was unlikely that structural changes could make a significant difference. Indeed, precisely because there was so little social or institutional support for ritual, the form took on increasing significance for supporting its own claims and providing its own plausibility. Interpretation and discussion, so critical to the Minyan, undermined form by continually examining it.

The Minyan was itself a creation of its liturgical field. Its approach to Judaism was created by developments within America that welcomed Jews into a bureaucratic middle-class that was eroding religious observance and rewarding minimal religious participation. Prayer, even if it was only to represent and transmit a general sense of Jewish identity, relied increasingly on its performative form over and against a world of social relations that did not reflect its values. Minyan members were committed to prayer within their community, but were in conflict over how to make it efficacious. At the same time that they attempted to reorganize and restructure their community, which was their typical response to perceived problems, they also addressed prayer forms. Knowing that prayer forms were increasingly important to delivering their messages and creating their efficacy, it seemed inevitable that Minyan members would begin to address the issue of form.

Chapter 5 describes the Sabbath retreat that was precipitated by this evaluation, where Minyan members talked about prayer. On this occasion, each member spoke personally about his or her own feelings about a prayer life.

The questioning of forms in the above discussion was followed at the retreat by questions about the very possibility of praying. These discussions, taken together, make it possible to lay out all the constituents of prayer in order to understand why they were apparently unravelling. As in any diagnostic model, we are better able to understand how a system works as it begins to work less effectively. To this point we know that the Minyan depended on the interrelationship of its community, its capacity to interpret, and traditional Jewish worship for any liturgical event. Further, we know that its form promoted certainty at the same time that it promoted the very ossification to which Minyan members referred. The context producing these constituent forms was modern American life, in which all of these young Jews were situated. They lived in a secular, bureaucratized society, which they were about to participate in because of their careers. The same society made them yearn for distinctiveness. Though that yearning led them to seek out integrating rituals and communities, such possibilities were inevitably under-institutionalized. They were compelled to find in prayer forms possibilities that would continue to elude and frustrate them. Their attempts were consistently judged by their efficacy, often defined as the ability to meet personal needs. Chapters 5 and 6 address the unraveling and reweaving of prayer in order to explain how it is made plausible for the group.

Notes

1. Beruria is a figure conflated from two texts. She is named as a learned woman in second-century B.C.E. texts. Her name is also associated with an unnamed learned daughter of Hananya ben Teradyon. The texts are contemporaneous. The strands are drawn together in the Babylonian Talmud, which dates from the third to the fifth centuries A.D., and she is mentioned as a scholar in her own right, as well as the wife and daughter of learned scholars (Adler, ms.). Rabbi Akiba was a first-century rabbi and leader of a major school of thought. He was instrumental in organizing a rebellion against the Roman control of ancient Israel.

2. Secularization theory is both widely discussed and increasingly controversial in the social sciences of religion. Its ideas date back to the foundations of sociology and the social sciences in the United States and Europe in the nineteenth century. Martin (1978) attempts to refine the theory and provides a good bibliography. Karel Dobbelaere (1981) provides an excellent overview of the key positions in the development of secularization. Hadden (1987) criticizes the theory, arguing that it is not in fact a theory, but a set of value judgments. He lays out recent literature that contradicts it. My own position will be discussed in this chapter.

3. Martin never defines ethos, but appears to mean a style of relating or a cultural form of interaction. Hence, I assume that he suggests that institutions maintain religion while the wider American culture undermines it.

4. Paradoxically, religion in America enjoys widespread support but limited credibility, rendering it incapable of obligating adherents to action or belief.

5. Mary Douglas is the only anthropologist I know who has directly addressed the problem of a "plausibility structure." Beginning with her book *Natural Symbols* (1970), she claimed that the ability to compare religion in different societies at different scales of complexity is an important task, hampered by evolutionary assumptions that society moved from the tradition-bound to individualist-dominated. She takes up this theme again in a critique of Berger's work, suggesting that his attention to plausibility structures is useful because it looks at the social basis of belief (1983). However, she takes Berger to task for his assumption that religion is always integrative and that individual choice did not emerge with modernization. Douglas criticizes Berger for retreating behind the notion that modern religion is ultimately subjective, not tied to social experience.

6. Austin goes into some detail differentiating types of speech acts and distinguishing between varying degrees of performatives. Evans (1963) has argued that liturgical forms are most likely to be found within one of those differentiated forms. For my purposes that detail is not essential. Rather, I wish to focus on the contrast between performatives and statements of information and the importance of the form for conveying the message.

7. There are other theorists of ritual who address the form-content dichotomies, but none of them have written specifically about prayer. Their work is nevertheless relevant. They emphasize performance, how the ritual text is brought to life within social activity. Bruck Kapferer has made a particularly significant contribution to this approach in his study of Sri Lankan exorcism (1983; 1984). Kapferer argues that the ritual text (what I

will call content or semantics) not only takes its shape from performance, but is inseparable from it. Actors within ritual are brought into a relationship to the text only through performance that creates their subjective experience and meaning. Schieffelin's work on ritual seances in New Guinea (1985), Mac Aloon's edited volume on performance (1984), Turner (1985) and Tambiah's work all reflect an interest in how form and content work together, rather than one effacing the other, to create a cultural experience through performance. I will return to performance in Chapter 6, where I discuss authority.

8. The modern Jewish movement that is beginning to create liturgy is Jewish feminism. Its activists feel the need for new liturgy because of the masculine language used to refer to God, and the masculine imagery of the Siddur and the absence of rituals relevant to a woman's life cycle. Most havurah members have made use of some new life-cycle rituals, particularly around the birth of daughters. The P'nai Or community, which draws people throughout the Northeast, prints examples of some of these liturgies.

9. In his discussion of contemporary religion, Louis Dupre understands the difference between secularized religion and traditional religion to be one of adherents "perceiving" as opposed to "holding" their convictions (1983). By holding he means that individuals adhere to doctrine only after they have chosen to do so, a decision made from "within." The person does not experience the power of the system from "without," not amenable to choice. As a result, he contends that contemporary American religion puts considerable emphasis on spirituality and mysticism.

10. Tzvee Zahavy explained this periodization of the liturgy (personal communication). For a recent article on the subject see Reif (1983).

11. These core prayers are recited at the three daily services. They are the *Shemah*, the Jewish creed that asserts the oneness of God, and the *Amidah*. The Amidah is a rabbinic prayer that on weekdays consists of eighteen blessings. It so epitomizes Jewish prayer that it is sometimes referred to in Hebrew as "prayer." The form of the Amidah is altered on the Sabbath and festivals to exclude prayers of petition, though it retains the same structure and theology as the weekday version. In concluding his discussion of the form and meaning of the Amidah, Alan Mintz writes: "The liturgy was a vehicle for expressing the central value concepts of Talmudic civilization: teshuva as the daily act of self-revision, the commitment to the establishment of justice and to the active pursuit of peace, a profound sensitivity to the power of rumor and slander in human community. . . . That is, in prayer the task of the mind and the soul is not to work out the why and the how, but to form a personal link of acknowledgment and responsibility in these fundamental categories" (1984, 417).

12. Doug's self-description is interesting to compare to that of Milton Himmelfarb's. Himmelfarb, the well-known editor of the *Jewish Yearbook* wrote about the daily minyan he attends: "Not many of us have or attain kawwanah—inwardness, concentration, the merging of the pray-er with his prayer. They say it used to be common. Whether or not that is so, I cannot recite a verse of six or seven words without my mind wandering. (I can hardly listen to three bars of music at a concert without my mind wandering.) Besides, kawwanah, decorum, singing and pace and every other occidental propriety are trash. . . . If we have to do without kawwanah, we may as well have niceness" (1972, 158). It is Himmelfarb's lack of anxiety over his mind-wandering, coupled with commitment to attendance at a daily minyan, that provide such a striking contrast to Minyan members. His plea for "niceness" is a request for a positive community to pray with where the pace of prayer is slow enough to make the experience meaningful. He shares that desire with the Minyan, whose members believe that fast-paced davening, typical of many traditional

synagogues, is pointless. But what is assumed by Himmelfarb to be normative—a large institutional setting, fast-paced praying, and less than competent laity—forms the basis for an alternative community that rejects and wishes to transform such norms. In addition, Himmelfarb feels utterly at home with Jewish prayer and that seems sufficient for his participation, even if he feels distracted.

13. Martha's suggestion was not simply democratic but particularly reminiscent of feminist consciousness-raising techniques derived from a group therapy model. In the therapeutic model everyone should be encouraged to articulate feelings, and no one should censor or disagree. In the Minyan these techniques did enable wider participation, and they were consistent with the "decorum" of the counterculture.

14. Franz Rosenzweig, a contemporary of Martin Buber, was an eminent German Jewish theologian and scholar who lived in the early twentieth century.

5
The Prayer Crisis

> We in the Minyan are like a tribe trying to get back its traditional way of existence. We've lost the magic formulas and we're trying to come up with them ourselves. The only thing we remember about the tribe is that we really did have the formulas and magic symbols. We can read all we want, but we can't find the formula to do the old magic work.
>
> Mark

The ideal prayer experience for Minyan members, whatever differences there were among them, involved taking the prayer text into the self. Then the text was voiced as a product of the self that was also a product of Jewish tradition. In prayer the self and the tradition are joined in reproducing each in the image of the other.[1] Jewish tradition was reproduced through prayer when Minyan members achieved that relationship between self and text. Whether this experience happened for only twenty minutes for Doug, or more consistently for others, it was what constituted effective prayer. When prayer was ineffective for some of its members, the Minyan turned to organizational solutions to achieve this reproduction of tradition. The self was linked to prayer through discussion so that praying would not have to be the only way to forge the self's connection to tradition. Or they understood Jewish tradition as changeable, so that including women, in violation of halaha, was nevertheless defined as the reproduction of Judaism. These changes suggested that the relationship between self and prayer was the significant issue for a community that existed to pray together. Understanding how the relationship was created is a problem suggested by an approach to prayer that emphasizes the relationship between form, content, and context. Only by understanding that each area formulates the relationship of self and tradition can we learn how prayer can articulate protest and covenant. Neither incomplete belief nor frustration with prayer can explain why people look to Jewish prayer to find a self.

We have seen, however, that members often found the interiorization of prayer difficult. What affect did the prayer constituents have on that difficulty? Because those constituents of prayer articulated a rather wide range of possibilities for what self, prayer, and tradition were, contradictions between them were inevitable. The American countercultural self of Minyan members was expressed in all the prayer forms. The traditional texts of Judaism were not equally apparent in interpretation or in the community, prayer constituents that often contradicted halaha. Those texts, for example, were placed in tension with the interpretations that were so often external to them. Hence, every effort to create a link between prayer and the self was usually mediated through a form that was set in opposition to the tradition. Members' willingness to share the rejection of a literal reading of prayer text, for example, also undermined their ability to reproduce a Judaism dependent on it. Often their recourse to organization was in lieu of their reproduction of traditional Judaism. Such struggles, mediations, and innovations would be necessary in an Orthodox community where the self works to subordinate its will to the tradition. Minyan members' ability to achieve effective prayer depended on, and was undermined by, the need to reproduce the tradition as a product of the self. When halahic prayer was prayed within the Minyan and interpreted by its members, then what should have followed was the reproduction of Judaism. The covenant with all its meanings was expressed in the act of praying.

Meaning in Complex Society

When I suggest that the text is external to the self, I am addressing the problem of meaning in complex society. Traditional societies have been pictured by social theorists as having a shared world view, a perspective central to secularization theory. Some recent studies have attempted to understand or conceptualize what happens to religious meaning, in particular, in the absence of such a shared world view. Louis Dupre, whose work I referred to briefly in Chapter 4, distinguishes between "holding" a conviction and "perceiving" through it (1982, 6). By "holding," he not only implies a more voluntaristic notion but also emphasizes that the authority for such convictions grows out of the self. The primary difference between what he calls "genuine religion" of the present and the past rests upon how it "integrates" religious authority with individual conviction. Dupre argues that religious authority operates only insofar as it has been previously experienced and "interiorized" (1982, 7). Conviction may be strong, but it is chosen on an individual basis.

Anthropologist Peter Stromberg advocates a similar view of contemporary religion in his ethnography of a Swedish Pietistic church, *Symbols of Community* (1986). Like Dupre, he makes fine discriminations within classical faith words to communicate ways in which meaning is different in traditional and plural societies. Stromberg describes the deeply committed church members as people who share a "commitment system" rather than a "consensual culture" (1986, 4–9). Persons in complex society, he argues, become "committed" to an outlook because they find it "uniquely meaningful." They do not "accept" the outlook, that is, "perceive through" it, in Dupre's terms. Because not everyone in the same society shares the same commitments, Stromberg concludes that there is no "inherent meaningfulness" in these systems (1986, 9). He advocates understanding contemporary religion in terms of how believers appropriate and apply the outlook to constructing a view of themselves. These "cultural resources" have truths to offer about the relationship of the self to the world. His study demonstrates how various members of the Swedish church constructed their identity through Christian symbols that drew them into community with one another. For Stromberg these meanings are not shared. They are neither entirely private nor public. The "common discourse" of the church that draws together Christian political activists and conservatives is forged out of many meanings rather than from those shared by cultural consensus. Because they lack the consensus of commonly held meanings, these modern men and women, according to Stromberg, do not so much "believe" as "believe in" (1986, 17), a phrase he uses to emphasize the emotional component of their faith. Religious symbols are meaningful insofar as they reveal important things about the self, who then chooses to adhere to church community and doctrine.

Both Stromberg and Dupre address the relationship between the self and what they call belief or perception and what I call interiorizing tradition. The challenge Minyan members faced, in part, is faced by all adherents of modern religion. Because of the way social life is organized, each person chooses belief systems that are created as externally authoritative. Since the choice is private, the interior experience increasingly dominates the way religion is formulated. Inevitably, modern religion must work to keep adherents' choices alive so that they will not look elsewhere. Minyan members are made constantly aware of their choice by their struggle to interiorize the prayer text in order to reproduce the tradition. Their consciousness of the struggle reflects their awareness that the system is grounded in choice. The notions "holding," "believing in," and "commitment" are all examples of the process by which an external text is interiorized and reproduced as authentic religion. Dupre and Stromberg both note the effect that these approaches to religion have on the religion itself. They do not note the weight it places on the worshiper to continue to make the choice and to experience the potential lack of connection between self and commitment. How does the demand for the worshiper to increasingly personalize the meaning of religion, to interiorize it, affect the process of praying? How do these issues present themselves to American Jews in particular?

Minyan members are different from Stromberg's subjects in a crucial way, more because they are Jews than Americans. The Swedish Pietists inherited an intensely individualist and self-scrutinizing Christianity from their forebearers. American Jews have a different sort of inheritance. Upon immigration, their task was to refashion a cultural and communal world view into a denominational religion. In the first two chapters I argue that American Judaism developed around decorum and prayer aesthetics, noting that for the laity in particular such issues were preeminent. Aesthetics carried and communicated messages that content initially did not. Changes in liturgical content came only slowly through denominational channels. A new decorum, realized at the local level in the synagogue, took hold more rapidly and frequently. I argue that the sorts of messages decorum and aesthetics carry are not classically cosmological. As such they do not detail issues of good and evil, punishment and reward, or justice and injustice. They are not readily amenable to "holding" or "commitment." They are overwhelmingly concerned with identity. What kind of person prayed in this setting? How was the nature of worship—formal or intimate—tied to ideas about God and community? While rich in detail, ultimately the aesthetic messages were very general. In Jewish terms, they were not halahic; they did not offer a concrete and specific way of life. Instead, they provided general guidelines for how to live as an American Jew. Aesthetic messages seemed appropriate for men and women entering a new society and for their children and heirs, who were to continue to negotiate their uniqueness within a society in which they sought acculturation. In short, meaning was general rather than particular, as I discuss in Chapter 4. The array of Jewish symbols adapted to American life articulated only general meanings. Adherents who found themselves choosing among fewer and fewer obligations tailored their religion to make minimal demands upon their time and resources.

It was in this environment that covenant and the sense of a Jewish people, rather than detailed observance, flourished as the most significant referent of any Jewish symbol for the majority of American Jews, particularly because Judaism was more a statement of identity than a religious world view. Covenant was the most generalized Jewish meaning to emerge from American Judaism, because it was the religious articulation of community and responsibility for other Jews. If one continued to pray a relatively traditional liturgy, then prayer and song articulated general messages in a traditionalist language and in traditional categories. The dramatically altered liturgies of Reform made even more explicit the general significance of the tradition.

Covenant was addressed to a community where decorum was the dominant concern. Though decorum articulated a set of middle-class prescriptions concerning the form of interaction, neighborhood location, and kinship relations, as well as a minimum degree of religious observance, and an emphasis on marrying within the faith, it did not articulate cosmological themes as such. Rather, both decorum and its aesthetic forms—uniformity and expressive individualism—have largely been responsible for carrying the messages and meanings of Jewish ritual and prayer—the centrality of sacred relationships—in America.

Decorum, because it concerns the regulation of social relations, is thought of as nonreligious. If religion addresses the sacred, decorum speaks to personal relations. In Chapter 2 I suggest that when religion is the expressive medium for community and social relations, then decorum and religion intersect. I argue in light of this twentieth-century conjunction of the sacred and the social that aesthetic formulations are the most powerful for articulating Judaism. Then American Judaism is "held" or "believed in" insofar as it maintains identity or covenant within American life.

Personal meaning and emotion, key concerns for Stromberg, are brought about for Jews through the maintenance of tradition and the link to the People Israel. Placing the self within that history, via prayer in the case of the Minyan, is at the center of their "commitment system." This commitment is partially achieved by interiorizing experience. It is fundamentally achieved by participation, by literally being counted within a Jewish community. Minyan members were certainly conscious that whether or not they "believed in" Judaism, their reproduction of the Jewish tradition kept the People Israel alive. When Joseph, the child of Holocaust survivors, described himself as a faucet who was "turned on to the whole Jewish people" in the Minyan, he articulated just such a statement.

Minyan members, then, were vulnerable to three problems in their effort to interiorize prayer. First, American Judaism was built on general meanings transmitted through aesthetics that make it difficult to support the precise world view of the Siddur. Second, as outlined in Chapter 3, there is virtually no cultural or social structural grounding for Jewish texts in American life. As in the Swedish example, emotion must play a major role in generating commitment. However, as Stromberg notes, Swedish Pietists are Swedes. He is able to find a shared view of the world between the films of Ingmar Bergman and the church he studied. This is not the case for the Minyan members for whom Judaism in large part played a crucial role in differentiating their identity from the culture around them. The ability to interiorize text was made difficult by their participation in American society.

Of course Minyan members, like most educated American Jews, were active consumers of American Jewish culture. They virtually all read the novels and short stories of Saul Bellow, Philip Roth, Bernard Malamud, and were beginning to read Cynthia Ozick. They knew the films of Woody Allen, whose more popular film, *Annie Hall* had not yet been made. They, and many of those in the Jewish counterculture, were decidedly ambivalent about these popular figures. They did not want to be identified with the assimilationist culture—the Jewish family, or the aspirations and activities of its characters—most of these writers described and represented. Articles in havurah journals and newspapers debated the authenticity of these writers' Jewish outlooks. In contrast to most American Jews, they were more interested in modern Israeli writers who have subsequently grown in popularity in the United States. They were also drawn to the Yiddish language, music, and literature. They praised Isaac Bashevis Singer over Bellow or Roth. However, when the mainstream Jewish community attacked Roth or Bellow as "self-hating Jews," writers for *Response* were quick to point out their contributions to getting the work of Yiddish writers translated into English. Ironically, the more American a Jewish writer or artist might be, the more these Jewish counterculturalists and intellectuals were anxious to deny his or her authenticity. As American Jews they sought literary and artistic expressions about their lives in the past or at a distance in Israel.

Finally, insofar as identity is successfully forged with the texts, there are, as noted above, inevitable contradictions in the fashioning of the self. The expressive individualism of the counterculture worked continually against the text. Even though Minyan members "chose" prayer and modified observance, they constantly modified what they chose because they were trying to live Judaism within America. Hence, they were still engaged in their grandparents' practices of transforming culture into religion. This process is nowhere more difficult than in maintaining a regular prayer life because of the need to articulate the world view of the prayers.

Ritual Poles and the Problem of Prayer

Religion in contemporary Western society is fundamentally affected by the relationship between the person and religious authority. Only when the self authorizes belief for her or himself can it hold any power. From Stromberg's work we can assume that prayer is efficacious as long as it continues to reveal relevant insights about the self.

I argue in the previous chapter that much of what is assumed as the result of secularization can only be explained by also examining ritual as performative, or studying ritual as a performance. It is equally important to ask how the problem I have described as interiorization results from the structure of ritual and prayer, as well as from its social context. I concur that a significant change in Jewish practice and belief has resulted from a lack of consensus in modern Western culture. However, it is equally important to recognize the impact of ritual on the problem of creating a link between text and self in contemporary society. Indeed, were we to ignore the inevitability of ritual form distancing participants, we could not adequately understand the impact of contemporary society on religion.

Anthropologists who have written recently about ritual have noted its peculiar tendency to evoke both intention (engaged participation) and "ossification," a dulling routinization. Ritual, in all settings then, may evoke distance, routinization, and alienation in participants. Rituals embody ideas and truths, but are performed in social settings where the interests of various groups may well be served by them. Hence, they will communicate both cosmology and status concerns, often at the expense of one another. This point is made with exceptional clarity by Stanley Tambiah.

> All the substantive features which nourish the formalism of ritual also conspire to empty it of meaning over time. Cosmological ideas, because they reflect the epistomological and ontological under-

> standings of the particular age in which they originated, and because they are subject to the constraint of remaining accurate and invariant, are condemned to become dated over time and increasingly unable to speak the minds and hearts of succeeding generations facing change and upheaval. During these periods of ossification, rituals may increasingly lose whatever semantic meanings they previously had and may carry primarily indexical meanings which derive from rules of use and from pragmatics or functional considerations. (1985, 165)

Tambiah understands the poles of intention and rigidity to result from the inevitable link of ritual form to ritual content, which results in cultural messages being communicated through redundancy and formality. He imagines these meanings to be a "bouquet" held together by ritual forms. Hence, ritual meanings are capable of taking on radically different significance over time.

He suggests, nevertheless, that one must be cautious in assuming that ritual is inevitably more functional than meaningful. He points out, as does Bauman (1975, 298), that in periods of religious revival semantics (meaning or cosmological truths), attached to ritual, emerge again and dominate political and social interaction. Every word of religious discourse can be made relevant to a particular moment of political upheaval by leaders and followers. In my terms, ritual may be interiorized and thought to speak personally to and for the self. Tambiah notes, nevertheless, that in time the demands of everyday life will reassert themselves, tethering rituals to the social positions, interests, and commitments of practitioners, which results in ossification. Ritual, in short, oscillates between poles of revival, in which semantics dominate and new possibilities are articulated and rigidity, in which rituals will largely serve the interests of those in power, and rote repetition will dominate. Tambiah argues that ritual is most likely to rest somewhere in between these extremes, articulating both types of meanings in light of one another.

It is important to exercise care in comparing the causes of the ossification of ritual. I suggest two different sources for the alienation of a person from ritual. First, his or her disbelief in text or activity may lead to experiencing the ritual as "stale" or unconvincing. Secondly, following Tambiah, ritual may become routine or empty because it is associated with power and status relations. Though the causes of ossification may differ, the effect may be substantially the same. When worshipers are distanced from ritual in traditional society, we may argue that ritual meaning has changed. When worshipers are distanced from ritual in contemporary society, meaning and behavior may have changed.

The ability to interiorize the prayer texts for Minyan members determined whether they understood their prayer to be routinized, lacking meaning and sincerity, or vital and effective. Routinization had a different significance for Minyan members as contemporary worshipers. They did not live in the societies that concerned Tambiah, in which ritual is part of normal social discourse, including relations of power and status. Minyan members found in prayer a literally alternative language to secular and non-Jewish society. Its purpose, however, was to sanctify an identity for members that differentiated them from the larger society. Minyan members could not link their prayers to society and a culturally shared daily life because they lived in a pluralist world. As non-Orthodox Jews they did not live in a Jewish enclave where ritual was the primary medium for social interaction. As a result, the meaning of prayer was radically limited. It lacked indexical or functional significance. Its primary referents, then, had to be cosmological, but narrowed to the covenantal ones I described in Chapter 4.

Effective or vibrant prayer was full of meanings that placed the worshiper within the text of prayer, making believable the link between text and self. Ossification implied something more devastating than rote participation. In this context, ossified prayer was ultimately alienating because the worshiper felt him or herself to be disconnected from the text. Their inability to interiorize the text resulted in experiencing prayer, community, and interpretation in conflict.

At the retreat, suggested at the evaluation meeting, members came to define themselves as overwhelmingly at odds with prayer. Most of them thought of themselves as unable to pray effectively. They formulated their failure in a series of dichotomies—between content and form, aesthetics and content, and authentic and empty prayer—that offered insight into the very processes that alienated them from prayer. Further, their self-perceptions revealed the circumstances that evoked alienation. Minyan members' formulation of prayer reflected the conflict in the very prayer constituents that formed the linkage between self and text. And their attempt to resolve their prayer problems also suggested that each constituent itself embodied an approach to interiorizing text that was not equally effective. Interpreting texts, relying more on community relations, or changing halaha, each had different implications for the resolution of the problem. Felicitous prayer, then, depended on interiorizing prayer by being able to synthesize its constituents.

The Minyan Retreat

A series of cars drove along the Pacific Coast Highway leaving Los Angeles on a Friday afternoon in September. They made their way from the coast up the foothills, carrying twenty Minyan members to a camp one woman located for their Sabbath retreat. The Hilltop Camp, forty-five minutes from Los Angeles, was the improbable setting for a Sabbath devoted to prayer, celebration, and discussion. Its main lodge room was covered with snake skins, bear heads, and various animal furs. It looked more suitable for hunting than for the praise of God. But Minyan members, as they do at the university and in one another's homes, altered the space to make it their own.

A planning committee—Harvey, Martha, Jacob, David, and Jean—drew up plans for the retreat. They understood the focus on prayer, agreed upon at the evaluation meeting, to mean several things and planned accordingly. First, they scheduled a discussion for members to freely express their feelings and attitudes about prayer. They wrote and distributed questions about the differences between verbal and nonverbal forms of prayer and the direction and focus of their prayer (see Figure 3). They also appointed leaders for Friday night, Saturday morning, and Saturday afternoon and evening prayers. In the place of Torah discussions, to precede prayer they designed two hour-long classes on the history and structure of the Siddur. Jacob, Harvey, and Mark would lead the classes. They also decided that a Saturday afternoon meeting would allow Minyan members to decide what to change or retain in the traditional liturgy in forming their own official liturgy. They planned again to discuss the future of creative services in the group. It was to be a Sabbath of many textures: prayer, analysis, study, discussion, song, and meals.

The planners also organized the meals for the weekend. They appointed a committee of volunteers to clean the oven and stove of the camp kitchen to make it kosher. Preparation of vegetarian meals, out of deference to the group's few vegetarians, was distributed among members so that no cooking would actually take place on the Sabbath. The camp's kitchen would be used only to reheat food prepared earlier. All food was brought to the camp before sundown. They planned a completely observant Sabbath; lights would not be turned on and off, cooking would precede the twenty-four hour period, and travel would be unnecessary.

The Minyan retreat occurred in what V. W. Turner describes as a "liminal period," a transitional time "betwixt and between" periods of

FIGURE 3

Kelton Free Minyan Retreat

As we did at the first Minyan retreat, we shall go around the room on Friday evening, this time asking each person to express briefly her and his feelings on prayer—questioning, doubting feelings as well as positive, affirmative feelings. Here are some questions you might wish to think about in preparing for this discussion (please don't feel you have to address all—or any—of them!), as well as any others you might wish to add or substitute:

- Do we pray primarily for the benefit of ourselves, of others, or of God?
- What do we want to say when we pray? Do the words in the traditional Siddur say what we want to say? Does the Siddur reflect our own world view? Should it?
- What is the best language for prayer? Why do we need language at all? Can song or dance be prayer?
- How personally should we address/speak about God in prayer? How shall we talk about God—in the second or third person? In the masculine or the feminine? In other ways?
- Are images like "king," "Father," "throne," etc., a help or a hindrance in entering prayer? Are there other images that might be more helpful (e.g., "lover," "companion," "energy," etc.)?
- What is the discipline needed to get into praying? Is there a difference between praying and davening? Between davening and meditating? Between prayer and group singing?
- What are the advantages/disadvantages of spontaneous prayer over against prayers prepared by others? Of prayers in the Siddur over against prayers written by our contemporaries?
- How do we feel about praising God? For what can we praise Him? How do we feel about petitioning God? What are valid requests? What is the role of love and fear/awe in praise and petition?
- How much of our prayer is an intellectual experience? An emotional experience? A bodily experience?
- If we have theological problems with certain prayers, is it hypocritical to say them anyway? What values can we find in prayer beyond the words? How far is it "legitimate" to go in reinterpreting theologically difficult prayers?

regular work, status relations, time, and place (1967). Though the Minyan normally met for a ritual period suspended from daily interaction and requirements, a retreat was a further separation from even the characteristic Minyan Sabbath. Similarly, at the Minyan retreat normal interactions were intensified by physical closeness and extended time together. Members prayed three times a day, not just once, and sang for hours, not for thirty minutes. They took long, ambling Sabbath afternoon walks, not short ones home. They observed the religious requirements of the most observant, not for two hours, but for twenty-four hours. During the retreat their time together was structured by a traditional observance of the Sabbath, punctuated by prayer services and meals. All participants experienced their community and their Jewish observance in a more focused fashion than normal. Turner maintains that such intensification of relations and activity in a setting removed from ordinary routine allows and encourages the opportunity for group introspection, for assessment and scrutiny of its basic norms. The Minyan retreat facilitated this process. The Sabbath, the suspended day between the end and the beginning of the week, took on heightened significance during the retreat.

Upon arrival they gathered in the large multipurpose room of the camp, which was to be the site of meals, discussions, and some praying. Their communal sleeping quarters were directly off this room. Only two women shared another dormitory at the other side of the multipurpose room because they were uncomfortable about the arrangement. The bathrooms were sex segregated. The kitchen lay behind the central room and both men and women moved in and out of it, sharing in food preparation.

As the sun began to dip behind the mountains, most of the women initiated the Sabbath by lighting candles placed in candlesticks and sang the blessing over them. It was an unusual moment in the Minyan, whose members never gathered on Friday night, to hear only female voices, to watch only women act in a ritual capacity. When the candles were lit everyone turned to each other saying "Shabbat Shalom" and "Gut Sabbos." The atmosphere was warm and familial. Many minutes were spent in Sabbath greeting among people who had previously been standing together for more than an hour. There was something new about their interaction when they welcomed the Sabbath, and the embraces that followed the ritual marked that change.

They prayed the evening service. Harvey acted as Hebrew hazan. He was judged a fine hazan partially because of his ability to lead songs and create a spirited tone for the service. Saul acted as English hazan, consciously praying loudly to encourage those who wanted to pray in English, which he usually did not. The service planners included, in addition to the liturgy, a number of additional readings of poetry and comments by rabbis on the Sabbath. These additions were intended to enhance the prayers by adding insightful and beautiful descriptions of the Sabbath. These readings carried two messages: that liturgy was open-ended and to be added to and that people could bring poetry and prose to enhance the experience of the whole community. These additions, though the source of conflict in discussions of "creative services," were consistent with the community's emphasis on "experience" and on their own activist participation. With the conclusion of the service, members again turned to each other with Sabbath greetings, warm embraces, and familial kisses.

Then all the members sat down to a large and festive meal preceded by communal blessings over wine and bread. For an hour after the meal, they sang *zmierot* (table songs associated with the Sabbath), which, while they varied in tone, pace, and melody, were all spirited and created an atmosphere of unity. Various members even argued over melodies, reflecting the variety of settings in which such songs were learned: camp, home, synagogue. People advocated their own familiar tunes and some enjoyed learning new ones. The arguments were playful and proceeded with relish. These people liked to sing. The meal ended with the Grace blessings, *birkhat ha mazon,* which were also sung almost in their entirety.

After the dinner dishes were cleared, members drew their chairs into a circle. They again made jokes about the snake skin and animals decorating the walls. But a rosy glow pervaded the room—shared by people who ate good food, drank good wine, and shared hours of fellowship in prayer, music, and conversation. Jacob introduced the discussion, saying that the Planning Committee designated this time as the occasion to talk about the "meaning of prayer to the individual."

> We chose this topic because of the evaluation session we held several weeks ago. We want this Shabbat to really focus on prayer, what it is and what it means to us. The previous Shabbat you all received the questions we raised to allow you to think about these issues for this conversation. Harvey, why don't you begin?

Harvey did begin and his lengthy comments surprised virtually everyone and clearly affected much of what followed. In fact, he ignored the majority of the questions the committee had carefully written and answered only those questions that focused on the direction of prayer—to whom is prayer directed and what do we say when we pray? Harvey's comment set a therapeutic tone for the discussion. He emphasized his feelings, his conflicts, and his pain regarding prayer. The impact of this presentation was great precisely because in the Minyan he increasingly presented himself as a traditionalist, as the spokesperson for prayer rather than singing and for the Siddur rather than innovation. His introspection and doubts, expressed in a circle of equals, seemed to set a pattern for the remainder of the evening that overshadowed the questions the committee, of which Harvey was a member, wanted discussed.

> Jacob, you're getting even with me for making you introduce the discussion. But in fact I would like to begin. When I was young I was influenced by a number of teachers who were Orthodox Jews. They changed my behavior. I became an observant Jew. I prayed three times a day and I observed the mitzvot as fully as I could. I became so good at rote and rapid morning prayers that I was able to sleep late, daven *Shacharit* (the morning service), and still make the bus. Praying, for me, was perfectly normal and completely comfortable. The prayers were my language; the Hebrew came with complete ease. I have never lost the sheer comfort of prayer. But when I went to college I had a crisis in meaning, at least that is the way I think about it now. I no longer could see God out there as a transcendent force over me. I continued to daven, though less regularly, because I came to see prayer as metaphoric, as I would see literature. I never again could look at prayer literally, as the truth it had been for me as I rotely repeated it each morning of high school. I am comfortable with prayer, with the Hebrew and the tradition, but I am uncomfortable with the content and the meaning of the words. I am searching to find how I can keep the tradition embodied in a form whose content I can never understand as true. I do not know how to bridge the gap between my childhood and my adult life. Metaphor lacks the power, effectiveness, and importance that prayer once had for me.

In his lengthy and reflective comments, Harvey voiced a paradigmatic dilemma for some Minyan members: "Prayer is important to me, but it is not true." He suggested that everything about the prayer experience was personally appropriate. Words such as *comfort,* and *normal* particularly underscored Harvey's ability to live as a Jew within American society, comfortable in two languages and two cultures. However, normality and comfort were ineffective responses to the young adult "crisis" of which he spoke. As he redefined prayer as "metaphoric," his behavior changed. He could not pray as often. His experience of prayer was also altered, for he contended that he was searching for something to help him continue to pray.

In abstract terms, one would say that Harvey no longer derived "semantic" meaning from prayer. The *meaning* of the prayer became remote to him when he could no longer envision God as a transcendent force in his life. Harvey, however, continued to find prayer meaningful, but he shifted his definition of meaning to "metaphorical" meaning rather than "truth." His contrast between literature and prayer indicated that prayer should be believed, not merely studied as literature. In short, Harvey polarized "comfort" on the one hand and "meaning" on the other. He claimed to be a competent Jew, but an alienated one.

Other members who grew up as observant Jews expressed parallel sentiments. They echoed Harvey's dichotomy between comfort and meaning. Mark, for instance, made a related statement.

> I confronted the meaning of prayer very late in my life. I prayed without thinking because it was expected and it was right. Now I am just beginning to think about what the prayers mean, if I believe them, or how I feel about what they say. I have stopped compartmentalizing. Even though prayer is familiar and beautiful, I am worried about what those conflicts do to my ability to pray. Prayer is pleasant for me; the familiar tunes and the words move me.

Mark talked not only about comfort but about obligation. His family was more observant than Harvey's. It was not the teachers' but his family's expectations that induced him to pray. When Mark stated that thinking about meaning came late to him, he suggested that he lived within a system he never questioned through his entire education and rabbinical degree. Now, as a Hillel director, those questions emerged. He noted the evocative, affective dimensions of prayer for him that are triggered by music and language. However, by language he did not mean semantics as much as sound, rhythm, and the Hebrew language. He also indicated, though less forthrightly than Harvey, that questions about meaning and belief were threatening to prayer. He could not welcome those questions without acknowledging his anxiety that he might not be able to continue to pray.

Martha was also raised in a home that was religiously observant. Her Jewish education, facility in Hebrew, and regular participation in synagogue prayer assured her competence in Jewish ritual. But she also dichotomized her competence and her prayer life.

> In the world I grew up in, if you are Jewish you do certain things. If you don't do those things you are not Jewish. There are no questions or choices. As a result of attending Yeshiva day school, I too am comfortable with prayer. I know how to walk back three steps and bow during the Amidah. I know what happens if a holiday falls on a Sabbath, and for the second day whether you say *Havdalah* (a ritual) first before you light candles to begin it. But a lot of my

> religious feelings are guilt motivated. I have a love-hate relationship with Judaism, some of it out of love, but mostly guilt. I want to know what the prayers mean and I want them to mean something for me. I don't want just to do it correctly, but with feeling.

Martha did not state that she found prayer difficult. She asserted though that prayer could not simply be rote repetition as she, apparently like Mark, had been raised to believe. She wanted prayer to have meaning, to speak to her situation personally, and without that quality she felt her tie to it was motivated by what she alternately called "hate" and "guilt." She declared that her expert knowledge of its rules could not be a sufficient basis for prayer.

Harvey, Martha, and Mark envisioned their prayers as a disjunction between form and content, lacking cosmological truths. Though all willingly acknowledged their difficulty with prayer content, all eagerly wanted to maintain the traditional Siddur and paid close and detailed attention to its aesthetic forms. Rather than form and content working together, they experienced the opposite. They described the form of traditional prayer with great satisfaction, using words such as *pleasure* and *comfort.* It was meaning that was problematic. Neither competence nor pleasurable familiarity appeared to sustain prayer semantics.

Their questions about meaning are best understood as a version of an Austinian infelicity. Saying prayers according to a proper form was not sufficient for creating a prayer experience. The "hollowness" or problematic intention involved in their prayer, however, seemed less at fault than some members' inability to integrate form and content, a problem of prayer context. They could not take prayer in to speak it as their own because what had enabled them to do that previously had changed somehow. Although meaning, as we have seen, is inevitably at risk in ritual because of the formality and invariance of the medium, it had not emerged previously in the Minyan as a widespread problem. No one regarded the content of prayer as literal truth; hence, statements of the truth and falsity of the prayers, or disagreements with them, did not normally stand in the way of praying. The prayers, conflict aside, retained their ability to ignite an experience of sincere praying; that is, people continued to participate, retaining traditional prayers with all the conflicts they raised, because something happened to them that *elicited* their sense of a proper prayer experience. In this discussion, their conflict with meaning, narrowly defined, was brought to the center of their prayer experience rather than remaining to the side.

Another group of Minyan members, who were raised in minimally observant homes and in Reform synagogues where they had virtually no contact with traditional Judaism, addressed a dramatically different set of problems. They expressed little conflict over the semantic significance of prayer, but focused primarily on their emotions. However, by the evening's end the two sets of comments came to be identified with one another. Rae, an occasional member, then a graduate student in her early twenties in a suburban college, made a comment that was echoed in a variety of ways throughout the discussion circle.

> I grew up as a Reform Jew. Yet I take real comfort in tradition, and the sound of Hebrew, which I do not understand. Last summer I went to Hawaii. While I was there I visited a synagogue. I felt a real tie with those people, with Jewish peoplehood. It is the tradition which matters to me.

Rae's attitude toward prayer made semantics irrelevant. Prayer itself was a mnemonic. Its sounds reminded her of Judaism, invested her with the sense of her own Judaism. Her view was echoed by Miriam who said that though she did not understand Hebrew, it was only that language that gave her the "emotional" meaning she sought in prayer. Other members spoke of envying Martha because of her ease and facility with prayer. Alan, for example, a young psychiatrist raised as a Reform Jew, claimed that the struggle for him to pray in Hebrew was alienating, though he wanted to pray in a traditional form.

What made these comments representative of so many others was their emphasis on those aspects of prayer that elicited emotional responses. These three people focused on Hebrew. In addition, others talked about the music and the rhythm of prayer as essential. Rae, Miriam, and Alan did not present themselves in crisis. They suggested that prayer content was irrelevant and that the form of traditional prayer elicited, or had the potential to elicit, the effect they desired. Other members held this view, but some chastised themselves for it. One woman called the primacy of her "pleasure" in prayer a failure. In a manner that was reminiscent of the evaluation, she despaired of any effort to pray that was a mere pretense for a social gathering. Terri, one of the Minyan's most active members, said:

> Prayer makes me feel guilt more than anything. All my life I have been told to pray to reach God or to pray to God. God should be in front of me where I can see Him. Instead, I always think of Him at the back of me. Is He there? I'm looking. The fact is I have never been in a prayer situation for any reason other than my enjoyment

> or because it seems interesting. I like the music and singing best of all. I feel very guilty about that. I often feel like a failure. I'm afraid I am lazy and that's what keeps me from praying more.

Terri was by no means the only member who associated prayer with failure. She was critical of her own individualist motivation for prayer and her attachment to music. She worried that she "was not reaching God." Terri's use of the label *failure* implicated others who prayed just because it pleased them. No one disagreed with her, contending that their prayers were adequate or successful as a result of such a motivation. The label stuck so effectively that at mid-point in the discussion, Aaron found a way to summarize everyone's comments that, albeit humorous, put the whole reason for prayer in question.

> After hearing these comments I find myself wondering why we don't get together on Saturday mornings to daven the *New York Times*. [And Mark added, "As long as we do it in Hebrew and add music and rhythm."] I share these problems too, of course. I love the Hebrew and the group praying together, but these words don't mean much to me. I disagree with them.

The problem of the meaning of prayer presented itself differently to this group of members, for whom prayer was less familiar. They raised questions about their motivation and discipline. They knew precisely why they prayed, seemingly with less conflict than the group's members who grew up within normative Judaism. They prayed because it made them feel more Jewish. The whole group, particularly in Aaron's terms, saw such a reason for prayer as unacceptable because it made any content consciously irrelevant.

When members contrasted these two sets of personal assessments of worship, the aesthetics of prayer emerged in the discussion as the most significant constituent element of their experience. One group claimed that aesthetics and competence were not sufficient for prayer. The other group claimed that, lacking competence, aesthetics was all that sufficed, even if in one case it induced guilt. The effectiveness and rigidity of prayer were both articulated in aesthetic terms. What aesthetics achieved seemed to be a dangerous question for Minyan members. If it allowed them, as they saw it, to dichotomize intellect and ritual performance, or community and Judaism, then they had failed. Aaron made them aware that they may have really believed that the great tradition of Jewish prayer was interchangeable with the daily news of the *Times*, as long as it provided a basis for community.

Though the second group of Minyan members came at the problem from the opposite direction, they too were made to understand that their prayer "misfired." However, as they had less competence and experience at it, they seemed to rely primarily on an emotional sense of belonging as their test of prayer effectiveness. Their praying was less authentic and less Jewish.

Two comments that came near the end of the discussion represented two different responses to what several members perceived as a developing crisis. The members who offered them, Ed and Jacob, were both Minyan founders, both Reform rabbis, and both Hillel directors. Yet despite these similarities, the vision of prayer they each offered, for themselves and the group, differed radically. Their statements focused less on their familiarity with prayer than on the form of belief required for praying. Because of their high "expert" status as rabbis, neither man was in a position to envision prayer as the second group of Minyan members did. Ed and Jacob could not simply articulate their problems and doubts, hopeful that if others succeeded in praying well, perhaps one day they would too. They could not imagine that with a little more Jewish education, or a new angle on the matter, they might pray well. Ed spoke with sincerity about his difficulty with prayer.

> The Siddur is a source of great pain for me. The fact that I am fluent in Hebrew makes the problem considerably harder to deal with. I do not know how to say prayer in any form whatever if I cannot find meaning in those words, let alone the prayers that I completely disagree with for their values or world view. The tradition and the beauty of the music just are not enough.

Jacob's comments were entirely different, and only he and Jay, another rabbi, described prayer as inducing no conflicts for them.

> I have been on vacation for the whole month of August. I had some excellent and beautiful experiences with prayer in the Southwest by myself, outside or in my motel room. But being back I realized that I missed the Kelton Free Minyan. It was not just the people who I have seen, but the davening experience. I am surprised because I am a rather private person who does not usually become attached to groups. But in addition to loving the Minyan, I also love the Siddur. It is a document that contains everything. I have never felt it needed to be made relevant. I approach it as if it were a play or novel, but I am a character in this piece of literature, not simply the audience. As a piece of literature there are certain questions I do not

> ask of the Siddur. I don't scrutinize the language in search of literal truths. I seek interpretation, subtlety of language and levels of meaning. Tonight I am very sad because I do not know how to bring together my two good friends, the Siddur and the Kelton Free Minyan.

The contrast between Ed and Jacob could not be more obvious. One essentially advocated abandoning the Siddur for prayer. The other described an attitude he felt was essential to prayer. Jacob claimed that his prayer experience did not rest on belief, but on placing himself within the prayer and suspending other questions.

Why Meaning Took Center Stage

That most Minyan members felt prayers lacked meaning for them is undeniable. It was a powerful assertion, but also a complex one. People's willingness to express their "crisis," to define others as "in crisis," and to continue to pray suggests that they were not making a simple statement of fact. They were expressing needs and concerns; they were not saying that prayer was meaningless if that meant that the appropriate action to follow was to stop praying. Ed, the person who came closest to that position, dropped out of the Minyan a short time after the retreat and never returned. Though he had many conflicts with the Minyan, none was as intense as his view that the group had an unyielding attachment to traditional prayer. His attitude, one of total alienation, led him to an action no one else took.

People's conflicts with prayer were expressions of, above all, a disjunction between themselves and the texts. I noted above that interiorization was difficult for Minyan members for three reasons. First, American Judaism developed its meanings primarily through aesthetics, which were not well suited to the detailed cosmology of prayer. Second, that American society, as both pluralist and secular, provided no "indexical" meanings related to status and political relations. No secular authority beyond the self-sanctioned prayer. Finally, Minyan members' desire to link themselves to the tradition involved articulating a basic resistance to tradition, because they constituted themselves very much as individuals who "chose" obligation rather than individuals who felt subordinated to it.

These three stresses on prayer are linked rather straightforwardly to the three prayer forms that Minyan members evolved to constitute prayer. They were successfully linked in the Minyan's first two years. In this discussion those links seem not to have been effective. What made their modified commitment system so vulnerable? First, the communal nature of prayer was a halahic form as well as one unique to the Minyan. Perhaps the most significant context of this discussion was a dramatically changing Minyan membership. There were more "newcomers" than founders at the retreat. The evaluation meeting suggested that there were many differences among members about how prayer should be conducted and what was valued. The founders had lost control of the group, though they remained important leaders. The community in which prayer was supposed to work, indeed, that stood together against the larger society, seemed to be in danger of no longer providing a proper environment for prayer.

Community and prayer have always been linked. Prayer meant different things in America than it did in Europe, and different things in the Minyan than it did in the synagogue. But because the Minyan was a quintessentially ephemeral group, the members had to be particularly sensitive to one another's views of prayers to be able to pray together. Taking together both the retreat and evaluation discussions one cannot miss how closely "meaning" was tied to "community," and as community was undergoing dramatic changes, meaning suddenly became a distressing public problem. Hence, the communal form of prayer was vulnerable to the changing and unstable nature of Minyan membership that could alter the group formulation of prayer. Some judged the prayers of others insufficient. Others judged their own prayer inadequate. These judgments were mirrored in the members' disagreements over the best way for the community to conduct its praying. Prayer might appear meaningless if the community itself did not share a vision of prayer.

The second prayer constituent, unique to the Minyan, was members' use of interpretation within prayer. Externalizing the prayers by reflecting upon them promised to allow members the opportunity to internalize them as well. The process of interpretation juxtaposed the self with the text. The contemporary countercultural self was entirely visible in interpretive discussions, and community was created by members sharing these like-minded selves. That they never had to cut off the self from prayer seemed more important than ignoring conflicts around prayer while continuing to perform it. However, this strategy for interiorizing the prayers was risky because it made connection dependent upon opposition to the text. Though interpretation created visibility for the self, it put prayer and other texts at risk.

Indeed, the retreat discussion was similar to prayer and Torah discussions. The Retreat questions asked about the relationship between the self and prayer. What was implied in the questions was whether or not the self could be adequately represented or articulated through prayer. The first question asked, "Do we pray primarily for the benefit of ourselves, of others, or of God?" All the other questions followed it, concerning form, discipline, and theology. Discussions of text often took precisely that form, especially about prayer.

The language of need, satisfaction, and feeling is a psychological discourse ultimately concerned with the development of the self (Rieff 1963). It is not the classical religious discourse that inevitably subsumes the self to the obligations that follow upon belief. Even the style of the Minyan's discussion, the discussion circle, is a psychological or therapeutic model of interaction. Psychologists pioneered an approach to group process through group therapy and the human potential movement. Therapeutic techniques have been built into all types of group processes, ranging from management seminars to consciousness-raising groups. The hallmark of the process is the right of each person to speak and of no person to censor or criticize. Indeed, during this discussion the members were respectful and empathic about each comment, even when there was complete disagreement. Community, in this instance, implied the right of the individual to believe what he or she wished. Even if the comments became patterned, they were voiced individually with no fear of censorship or disapproval. The individual was entitled to all feelings and expressions, even, as in Aaron's case, the rejection of God. People spoke of themselves as failures, never of others.

The retreat discussion was neither purely evaluative, hence functional, nor text-based, hence necessarily embedded within Judaism. Therefore, it revealed, as no other discussion had, the tenuous link between self and text. When these men and women understood taking prayer within to mean that traditional Judaism had to speak to them personally and discursively, they found themselves formulating their religious lives psychologically. All members had legitimate feelings, an equal right to believe as they wanted, and needs that had to be met by the tradition. It was a language that authorized only self-understanding through ascertaining truth free of attachment and illusion (Rieff 1966).

The essential need to link the self to prayer, often reinforced through interpretive discussions, had the opposite effect at the retreat. Not only was a changing membership reflected in members' difficulties with meaning, but the constitutive prayer form of interpretation no longer served as an integrating function in the discussion. The prayer form most sensitive to this interiorizing process turned out to be the most vulnerable. The focus on need seemed to render prayer meaningless. Hence, interpretation was vulnerable to its psychologizing formulation, which cut directly against the ability to interiorize prayer.

By far the most significant issue of the discussion concerned aesthetics, all the elements of prayer that made it effective, satisfying, familiar, and powerful. I describe aesthetics above as the primary medium for transmitting meaning messages in American Judaism. As such, aesthetics, which varies in Jewish communities throughout the world, always attaches to halaha or tradition. Therefore, although halaha is a crucial constituent of prayer, the aesthetic form halaha assumes in specific groups synthesizes all others. There is no halaha without its aesthetic expression: music and prayer decorum, which make it possible to perform what halaha requires. That, I would argue, was why the aesthetics of prayer were so powerful for Minyan members. I will return again in this chapter to a fuller discussion of aesthetics. For the present I note that aesthetics not only integrated other constituents—community and interpretation—but mirrored them as well. Hence, a prayer aesthetic expressed how the group constructed their prayer experience. The very dichotomy members articulated during the discussion, between aesthetics and prayer, demonstrates this mirroring or dependent status of aesthetics. Their stated frustration, that they could experience beauty but not truth in prayer, indicated their inability to internalize the text; they prayed nevertheless.

The statements of crisis that focused on meaning were unprecedented in the Minyan but, at least in retrospect, not unpredictable. The elements that constituted prayer were all liable to separating self and text. Community usually joined the worshiper to prayer, but served here to undermine this relationship. Interpretation mediated the worship experience attempting to join the worshiper to prayer through a strategy of opposition, but here interpretation psychologized prayer and emphasized personal needs. Finally, aesthetics, reflective of the other constituents, were a sensitive instrument of the very forms of separation prayer attempted to overcome and, hence, reflected the separation of self and text. The Minyan's resolution of this apparent conflict about the meaning of prayer revealed the available strategies for synthesizing these constituents in order to avoid a "misfire" and meaningless prayer.

The Minyan Responded to a Crisis

When the formal discussion ended, the group quickly dispersed into private conversations, then went to bed. Jacob brought together one group of members that talked for some time. He rounded up Jay, Mark, and Harvey, people he believed capable of "making something happen in the Minyan," he later recounted. Jacob told them that he was alarmed about what he had heard that evening and sensed great danger for the Minyan from these comments. Though two of those present, Mark and Harvey, voiced identical concerns to the rest of the group, in this private context they shifted roles and became "protectors" of the Minyan's well-being. They felt the need to respond to a crisis that the group precipitated by their public acknowledgment of personal doubts, confusions, and anxieties about prayer. As protectors, they laid aside their own conflicts to conclude that the solution to what they heard lay in Minyan members' need to educate themselves about the history and meaning of traditional prayer. The crisis, they argued, would be handled in the same way they themselves handled it as individuals. As each of them understood prayer "metaphorically" to circumvent a crisis in belief, others must do the same. They concluded that "metaphoric understanding" would result only from education, from learning the intentions of those who constructed prayers. Such knowledge would provide a framework to either supplant personal belief or enable it. Harvey described their private discussion and the decisions they reached that night.

> I had the sense that we got much deeper into the problem at the retreat than we had expected. Initially it seemed people ought to understand the prayers that they were saying. After the problem was brought to the surface, I talked to some people. We felt that the goal really had to be now to try to understand the traditional form of davening from the inside and to try and bridge that gap between us [and the Siddur]. We had never, at least the group had never realized such a tremendous gap, and we were so conscious of it. And there was the feeling that we were going to have to start having certain kinds of discussions.

The Friday night upheaval had no immediate impact on the retreat. Everything proceeded as planned. The Minyan seemed to have enacted another successful compromise. They could express their gravest and most far-reaching doubts within their community, which was committed to tradition. In the morning, following a hurried breakfast, they met in small discussion groups for unusually directive lectures by Jacob, Harvey, and Mark on the history of the Siddur. These discussions were didactic, emphasizing the structure and history of the prayer book. Those who had described struggles with a prayer life during the previous evening now demonstrated their knowledge and competence.

Because of the length of the Siddur discussions, morning prayers did not begin until eleven o'clock. They had no other discussions during prayer. The service was conducted outside on the camp's grounds. Members sat beneath a large tree on chairs brought out for praying. Again, the planning committee chose a particularly good hazan to maximize the pleasures of the service: Jack Gold, one of the first people who initially left the Minyan over the issue of the equality of women (see Chapter 7). He had returned to the group. He did not have many friends in the Minyan, but commanded great respect for his exceptionally fine voice and his willingness to teach others the skill of reading Torah. He and his service were warmly appreciated.

A long lunch followed in the main room and once again more than an hour was devoted to singing zmierot with all the usual arguments and some attempts at harmonizing. They recited the "Grace After Meals." For an hour people rested or walked around the camp.

The group reassembled, and Martha was asked to chair a meeting, which Jay had characterized ironically as "How much do we leave out?" Members would decide the content and form of future liturgical services in the Minyan. They were to make one of the most significant decisions in the group's two-year history. Martha began.

> We will go through the whole Siddur section by section. People are to bring up what they like or do not like about a particular section and we will discuss it. If we do not want to say certain portions then some people must come up with appropriate substitutions.

But Mark stopped the event before a single word was uttered about the siddur. Mark, who conferred the previous night with Jacob, Harvey, and Jay, offered an alternative proposal.

> Your agenda is unnecessary in light of what we said last night. Let's stop praying altogether and simply meet for lunch and singing. That is what we genuinely like and what we ought to do.

There was a single moment of stunned silence. Then Martha retorted, "Because we have problems with prayer doesn't mean we want to give up praying. Who said anything about not praying?" Jay seized the moment to offer the alternative discussed in the small meeting the night before.

> Then let's really talk about prayer and confront the problem. We can study the Siddur seriously if we give up our regular Torah discus-

> sions and prayer discussions. We can move through the Siddur section by section and try to understand it as well as discuss our feelings about it.

The group needed only minimal discussion. Every member who spoke basically supported the idea. Their only hesitation was that the book of Genesis, which was soon to begin in the Torah cycle, often provoked the best conversations during regular Sabbath Torah discussions. But they agreed it was a price worth paying. They even decided that an optional study group could meet after lunch to discuss the weekly Torah portion, which would still be read but no longer discussed.[2] The possibility of such classes was greeted with real enthusiasm, and a number of people volunteered to meet the next night in the city to plan the curriculum of the "prayer classes."

Minyan members went on to make several other decisions, none of which concerned the traditional liturgy. They endorsed continuing the creative services, as often as, but no more than, once a month. Martha volunteered to organize one, and the women who volunteered eventually planned the women's service, the subject of Chapter 7. And Minyan members, as they do at every other business/evaluation meeting, exhorted one another to begin each Saturday promptly at ten o'clock in the morning, and to have the Hebrew and English hazanim work together more effectively by meeting during the week before the Sabbath service. They promised one another they would volunteer more readily for Minyan responsibilities.

The solution to the crisis was prefigured in the Saturday morning classes. Members were to be educated about prayer, to learn the basics, and the integration between self and prayer would result. At the same time, in the later Saturday afternoon discussion, they assented to the controversial creative services. What Harvey initially rejected, he now said he looked forward to with "real enthusiasm." Ironically, members agreed to adhere more closely to tradition, through classes, while in their creative services they agreed to keep their distance from it. They seemed once again to have accommodated all needs while maintaining the primacy of what they thought of as the traditional sensibility.

Then they davened the final services of the Sabbath, ate their last meal together, sang yet again. The prayer services were without strife. As the sky darkened they joined for *Havdalah,* the ritual of separation at the close of the Sabbath and festivals. Members stood in a wide circle. A braided candle of many wicks was lit and held. A cup of wine was blessed and passed from member to member to sip. They passed and

Havdalah.

blessed aromatic spices, each inhaling them to linger for one last moment in the beauty of the Sabbath. As they extinguished the braided candle in the wine cup, they sang in one voice for the coming of the Messiah. They all embraced for the last time during the weekend with good wishes for the week, "Shavuah Tov." But no one lingered at the dark hilltop camp, and within minutes cars were packed and winding down the mountain road for the return to Kelton and Los Angeles.

How to Pray

The Minyan, poised on the brink of changing its liturgy, retreated to what appeared to be an organizational solution, typical of all such responses to potentially transforming challenges. They would have more and different types of discussions that would recast the way they understood prayer as well as themselves. However, beneath that solution lay an approach to prayer that emphasized one prayer constituent at the expense of another. It represented the conceptions of one particular group, and articulated one view of what prayer is. The cognition underlying their entire solution to their problems with prayer was to work directly against what normally made prayer authoritative and effective.

From their retreat comments it seemed that what Minyan members most wanted from their prayers was a desire to pray. When they prayed, their Judaism took on a different and more intense significance. Wanting to pray indicated that the self had engaged and was engaged by the prayer; meaning was made internal, and self and tradition reflected one another. The result of the desire to pray and praying was to create a link to the Jewish people, thereby reproducing Judaism as well as creating a community with each other. As Rob, who was studying to become a rabbi, said at the retreat discussion as he reflected on what prayer meant to him: "The whole act of praying traditional prayers in Hebrew is historical. It says 'I'm here, but I'm back 3,000 years. Not only do I have a past; I also have a future. I'm not cut off, and when I die not all of me dies.'"

Interestingly, Rob did not mention "meaning" as much as the ability of the prayer to locate him in an historical relationship with the Jewish people. Meaning, in a nondiscursive sense, is closer to "commitment system," as described by Stromberg. It is a resource, a set of symbols to be applied to the self, and in the case of Judaism, to connect Jews to the People Israel. The meanings are openended, but less amenable to a form of belief than casting one's self with a people to whom one is obligated in some sense. Prayer is one of the bonds between all generations, and it articulates the covenant.

Effective prayer was what members sought and felt they could not achieve. Effectiveness had not appeared previously to be dependent on belief or assent to the truth of the Siddur. Normally the attitude of members was best summarized by an infrequent member who described his prayer experience to me:

> Praying is like driving on the freeway. I am sometimes at my destination without being fully conscious of how I got there. Sometimes, when I pray, I pause at a particular phrase, or wonder why the rabbis included that phrase in that place but, more often, I simply say the familiar words without conscious reflection. Prayer has an artistic quality for me. The more I understand the more beautiful and more complex I know the prayers are, and that deepens my appreciation.

This man judged his prayers effective because they were "authentic." Saying traditional words in a prescribed way allowed him to achieve effectiveness rather than a dispassionate analysis of content. He was typical of most Minyan members, exceptional only by his degree of competence. Effectiveness was the product of being able to "mumble" prayer utterances with an ease comparable to a frequent freeway traveler, though his knowledge of Judaism was also helpful. While praying may result in numbing routinization, this was not necessarily the case. This Minyan member's attention was sometimes caught by an idea that intensified his sense of being rooted in the beauty of the prayer. The general significance of the content and meaning, in the Minyan's case, was to make a worshiper able to worship, to underscore and emphasize a message carried as much by Hebrew as by the prayers' ideas.

What Minyan members rejected at their retreat in their interpretive discussions about prayer was an aesthetic formulation for prayer. Aesthetics were isolated from meaning and content and implicitly judged as inadequate bases for community or worship. My analysis of aesthetics in worship suggests that aesthetics are always the most integrative force in ritual, able to unite the self with the ritual and with other participants. Members' rejection of aesthetics constituted a negation of group prayer because it appeared to reflect a view of the community some rejected.

Aesthetics and Interpretation-Strategies for Linking the Self and Text

Minyan members defined prayer aesthetics as virtually all ACTIONS performed in the process of articulating the contents of the prayer. It was what they did rather than what they said, how they voiced prayer, brought it to life, and made it beautiful. Minyan members thought of their group prayers as unique from prayer in synagogues because of their active involvement in praying, which was made visible in their use of their bodies to rhythmically sway and in the use of their singing and their nonunison chanting. For their music and body movement made them different by aligning them with both the counterculture generation and hasidim.

Theories of aesthetics posit that the aesthetic is satisfying and unique because it is valuable in itself. It is noninstrumental, not for the achievement of an end (Saw 1971, 55, 204). Aesthetic considerations filter experience by emphasizing nonutilitarian ends. One contemplates or performs what is beautiful for the sake of that beauty alone (Saw 1971, 61; Dickie 1971, 49). Aaron's remark at the retreat about the *New York Times* points to the classically aesthetic state of Minyan prayer. If the primary purpose of praying is to create beauty, it need not be directed to God nor performed, because it is obligatory. The pleasure in prayer arises from its intrinsic satisfactions. "It feels good" is the Minyan refrain. This aesthetic perspective is the opposite of obligation, which is ultimately interested in and trained on an end, fulfilling the law. But it also stands in opposition to the therapeutic nature of the retreat discussion, which is ultimately self-critical, incapable of transcending the self because it is radically introspective.

Though the aesthetic element of prayer works through the individual, it is simultaneously unifying—unifying the self to the aesthetic form (interiorizing) and the selves participating with one another. The aesthetic enables self-transcendence by intensifying experience. Bruce Kapferer's seminal work on ritual aesthetics emphasizes how music and dance within demonic healing ceremonies in Sri Lanka both frame and form a context for the immediate subjective experience of the individual (1983, 191). Participants frame their experiences and are united to one another through their relationship to the aesthetic, even if there is variation in their interpretation of the experience. Conscious reflection does occur during the healing ritual when certain ideas are presented that reconstitute a healthy self from a sick one, but not during aesthetic forms such as music and dance, where attitudes are experienced non-cognitively.

Aesthetics in general, particularly music, Hebrew (whether or not it is understood), and to some extent body movement, worked together to integrate the forms of prayer within the social and historical context of the Minyan. Hence, members experienced the maximum integration—the sense of themselves as interiorizing and reproducing Judaism through aesthetic media. As they sang, chanted, moved and swayed they brought the text within, experiencing it as self-transcending.

Aesthetics, then, were integrative of the constituent elements of prayer. They articulated prayer for the community as collective, active and self-transcending. Chanting and singing continuously moved Minyan members between collectivity and private experience, between inwardness and focus on the community. And aesthetics conveyed to Minyan members integration primarily through maintenance of ancient language, hence history, within what they experienced as a unique form. They understood aesthetic form to be both more contemporary and more authentically spiritual than that used by acculturated American Jews. The countercultural aesthetic was active, hence integrative, because its effect was to internalize experience by emphasizing worshiper involvement. The worshiper sang, rather than listened, shuckeled rather than stood motionless, and used a language of continuity. By that activism he or she prayed a tradition that was mutually reflective of self and Judaism.

Those anthropologists concerned with formalist properties of ritual often rely on aesthetics to explain the ritual's meaning and purpose. Unlike Kapferer, however, they oppose meaning and form, arguing that ritual messages have virtually no relationship to their content. For example, an invariant ritual form communicates a message of unchanging truth. Invariance is often aesthetically expressed through word repetitions. Anthropologist Maurice Bloch (1974) argues this point in service of his idea that ritual is incapable of communicating meaning. Rather, ritual exists solely to support the claims of traditional authorities who control it. Bloch follows Austin in suggesting that there are two types of meanings, propositional and performative. He uses linguistic theory to demonstrate why ritual, like political oratory, cannot be propositional, that is, amenable, to falsification or capable of transmitting information. Ritual uses what he calls "impoverished language" (1974, 60). As a formalized language, it always follows the same logic, evokes no novel questions or connections from its speakers, and offers no new connections between units. He boldly concludes that it is therefore incapable of offering "semantics." (1974, 66). The meaning that ritual or political oratory offers is the support of traditional authority, since it is a language that as a result of its extreme formalization, is inappropriate to challenge or create alternatives. He concludes that ritual is always fused with its context, providing no language apart from it, and is a useful agent in shielding the truth from those who do not control it.

Bloch is particularly interested in chanting (sing-song) and song and places it on a continuum with political oratory, sermonizing, and ritual language, all examples of impoverished, that is, formalized and repetitive language. The "one act of will" in singing involves the choice to take part. After that, the actor experiences song and all other ritual "from outside himself" (1974, 70–71). This genre of language is not to be "explained," because it is incapable of transmitting information or complex messages. One must simply understand what it is trying to convince participants to do. Hence, Bloch places the origin of religion in the exercise of political power. Traditional authority works by making its own hierarchy appear natural, and often priests speak for that authority by employing an atemporal language that only allows its spokespersons to assent.

Bloch's argument is intriguing. He understands how critical aesthetics are to ritual. Yet for him ritual aesthetics create oppression by their close tie to a single political context. The argument is difficult to support empirically. One only has to think of the place of the spiritual in the American civil rights movement to understand that religious song is capable of producing radical resistance to political authority. The use of spirituals in demonstrations, in political meetings that incorporated prayer, and in prisons among those arrested for civil disobedience gave eloquent testimony to the fact that such music involved more than the assent to sing; it placed contemporary racial discrimination into a mythological system of oppression and deliverance described in the Bible. As such, the music coalesced participants and delivered a message of the righteousness of the cause and the certainty of victory over powerful oppressors. Political oratory of opposition was supported by traditional black church music.

Bloch argues that though ritual units are constantly "drifting out of meaning," they remain in a dialectical relationship with "new units," reintroduced from outside by revivalist movements (1974, 76). Bloch does not acknowledge how often ritual takes on new meaning and new interpretation within changing historical contexts, as in the civil rights movement. Were he to acknowledge that possibility, he then would have to affirm that ritual had meaning that was not entirely formal, hence impoverished, and that the dialectic that produced religious change grew from within the ritual, which, as Tambiah noted, involved both semantic (cosmological) and indexical (functional) elements. The pole that dominates can only be understood within a culturally and historically relative setting. So it is that the havurah movement could primarily maintain traditional liturgy particularly because their cultural protest was against cultural homogenization.

Rather than prayer drifting out of meaning, it took on altered, general meaning—embodied in the covenant—that was relevant to the community in which it was prayed. The fact that the meaning of prayer was in question only underlined that Minyan members had more choices than to assent or reject it. Bloch did not describe a complex society, of course, but it is unlikely given his view of ritual that he would imagine any circumstance in which it could be meaningful or capable of articulating identity in opposition to society. I suggest that aesthetics cannot be separated from ritual messages. When Minyan members themselves perceived that to be the case, they expressed alarm.

Aesthetics, then, enabled the interiorizing of ritual messages more effectively than any aspect of the ritual, not to oppose ritual meaning but to communicate it. At the retreat, however, the Minyan quite clearly chose a version of their interpretive constituent—neither prayer discussions nor retreat discussions exactly—to describe and then resolve their relationship to prayer. In so doing they underplayed an active formulation and selected one that suggested that their "needs" were best met by cognitive understanding of prayer. Interpretation, that prayer constituent most free from rigidity and formalism, was least amenable to synthesis and was, of course, the least aesthetic. Ideally interpretation created a connection between the self and the text. In the therapeutic discussion, as well as regular textual ones, discontinuity tended to be emphasized. Aesthetics were sensitive to group relations because prayer messages were interiorized within community.

The result of these choices will be discussed in Chapter 6. My point here is to contrast the two approaches and note that the interpretive/cognitive one appeared to carry the power of constituting the contemporary expressive self. Aesthetics, linked to halaha, created inclusiveness. One was potentially authenticating and unifying, and the other was cognitive and potentially individualizing.

Prayer Misfires

In the last chapter, I emphasize the Minyan's prayer forms or constitutive elements because I claim that prayer has performative qualities. I modify a classically Austinian stance by emphasizing a broader sense of context than is normally associated with Austin. I take the context for a felicitous performative to be social and interpersonal. Prayer is effective when particular words are said in a particular context in a particular way. The measure of their effectiveness is not based on truth claims, but on being performed under the proper conditions. Minyan and havurah members considered prayer effective when it differentiated them from their parental generation and created a sense of their authenticity as Jews, in short, emphasized their Jewish identity.

However, at their retreat Minyan members judged their prayers ineffective, offering their lack of meaning as the cause. The concept of meaning represented the conditions that were making it impossible for prayer to be effective. These conditions, of course, were tied directly to their prayer constituents. As the group grew larger, members did not agree on the meaning of prayer. What was the nature of interpretation or its limits? Could everything in prayer be discussed, changed, or eliminated? Neither could they agree on the nature of their aesthetics: the relative balance of singing and chanting and rearranging the prayers and maintaining them in invariant order.

Prayer appeared not to work from the point of view of worshipers because the community wasn't working. Hence, the founders and traditionalists of the community determined that an aesthetic motivation alone was insufficient, regardless of the remarks of members. Others argued that they felt pulled into a formulation that did not represent their attitude toward prayer, but reflected the evening's dominant voices. Indeed, more than one Minyan member was suspicious that the comments in the circle became ritualized, following a form presented by the first few participants. Saul stated:

> The discussion became a ritual. "I have a problem with prayer" started every statement. I went into the formula also and I didn't even feel it. I was annoyed with myself. It was the God conflict and the problem of belief and none of that is a problem for me.

And finally, even those who had most powerfully expressed their own "crisis in meaning" immediately moved to define the nature of the resolution of the crisis by offering a solution most compatible with their own approach to Judaism—learn the traditional formulation and it will suffice. They turned away from their regular interpretation, aesthetics, and community toward a reliance on traditional prayer utterances and study. A group committed to egalitarianism was increasingly split by the learned and unlearned, newcomers and founders, those in favor of experimentation with prayer and those who opposed it.

The misfire, then, rested in large part on the connection, or lack of it, between the social context and the integration of the prayer constituents. The rigidity or vibrance of ritual not only is an abstraction but is experienced in particular terms by those who pray. In the Minyan ritual rigidity produced alienated feelings about prayer; vibrancy was the opposite. Both poles rested specifically on how effectively members were drawn into praying by the group's prayer aesthetics. However, these aesthetics, so central to their uniqueness as a community, no longer articulated prayer personally and vividly. If music was too slow or too fast, if prayer timing was wrong, if failure to reorganize services indicated predictability, as these people maintained in the evaluation discussion, then their meaning crisis was surely related to these complaints. Each of these aesthetic judgments was tied to the change in the Minyan's membership. The failure to generate intention in prayer grew out of a new conjunction between aesthetics, decorum, and community. The Austinian "misfire" at work here reflected their changing perceptions about the ability of the community to share an aesthetic and a decorum. They could not contextualize prayer. Covenantal meanings apparently were not expressed through communal and traditional forms of prayer. They found prayer meaningless. Their move to resolve the crisis reflected how prayer was linked to its constituents. Prayer misfired because the group could not unite its constituents; hence, it necessitated a renegotiation.

In my discussion of contemporary scholarship on prayer and ritual, I noted three perspectives, each of which emphasizes different aspects of the experience: the context of prayer, prayer's formal properties related to its status as a performative, and finally, the performance of prayer. Each illumines what makes prayer effective and how worshipers are engaged by the different aspects of the experience. They are not necessarily exclusive, though some theorists oppose one another. Emphasis on the social and cultural context of prayer, the first area, makes evident why in the Minyan meaning is formulated "in general." Aesthetic messages emphasize identity and covenant. Prayer in the Minyan is rooted in neither a cosmology nor a dense social system in which status is articulated. America as a plural Christian society that allowed the acculturation of Jews had a direct effect upon the messages transmitted by prayer. Semantics were constrained, certainly. But the same society that generalized prayer meanings also enlivened them as the articulation of differentiation and uniqueness.

I noted, however, that context could not exhaust the meaning of the prayers. Understanding the pluralist nature of society could not explain the impact of the formal properties of ritual on the prayer experience. That prayer experience seems universally to move between poles of rigidity and significance indicates that Minyan prayer would always be susceptible to these problems. Yet understanding the poles within the Minyan setting indicates that rigidity and emptiness were articulated as prayer, as "mere aesthetics" or the "price for community." This was the condition that created a misfire for worshipers. Ritual inevitably has a cultural and organizational definition. In the Minyan, aesthetics, the most effective expression of prayer, was falsified because of changing social relations within the group. Prayer could not represent covenant because the community could not function as a homogeneous collective. In the Minyan, not only were form and content at odds, they may well have been in conflict precisely because community and aesthetics were at odds. As surely as the German Jews of New York's Temple Emanu-El required agreement about an aesthetic formulation for their sacred and social relations, so did the Minyan. That consensus was breaking down.

Form and content pulled apart because of their interdependence within a functioning community. That members' statements should affect one another demonstrates how closely community and private experiences interpenetrated. Prayer was as much or more a group experience as an individual one. Prayer reflected community relations, hence covenantal relations, so that the purely rote pole of the prayer experience articulated the lack of consensus that defined the prayer experience.

Performance is the final element of prayer to be addressed. The Minyan's resolution of its conflict was made possible by performance. Aesthetics were recast through performance, where the integrative potential of prayer was reasserted.

Notes

1. Don Handelman suggested to me this formulation of the self-text relationship.

2. In fact, only a few such discussions took place and were soon dropped because of poor attendance.

6

Praying in the Minyan

Performance and Covenant

> People are frightened about patterns. They hunger for order and they hunger for change. We are not asking the question why pray at all. We are asking questions that explore what there is in prayer.
>
> Rachel

Minyan members agreed upon a plan to resolve some of their shared and individual difficulties with prayer. Their proposal to study about prayer together appeared to be particularly sensitive to integrating prayer with their own life experiences. They defined their problem as the disintegration of self and prayer; any solution would, therefore, have to reflect themselves within prayer. It appeared that praying together was insufficient to create such a bridge. This chapter examines what makes that bridging possible and impossible within prayer ritual and the Minyan classes. How are the strands of meaning present in all rituals gathered together so that they can be experienced personally by the worshiper? Does the "general" nature of meaning for Minyan members affect how the self is made part of prayer? The Minyan's experiment with classes underlined the important link between aesthetics and praying and put the question of belief and meaning in a new perspective.

Planning the Organizational Solution

On Sunday night, upon returning from their retreat, several people gathered in Mark's living room to discuss how to implement the prayer classes. Once again, Jacob, Mark, Harvey, and Jay joined together, but now they no longer met privately, as they had on Friday night. They, along with Saul and Miriam, represented the formal interests of the Minyan as the Planning Committee. Saul was a Jewish educator and an undergraduate psychology student. Miriam's interest in these problems in part derived from her graduate work in religious studies. Mark's book-lined room was a good setting for establishing what they called a "curriculum," a course of study members believed was necessitated by the retreat's Friday night discussion. Jacob commented that this group must find the best way "to educate Minyan members."

They made what appeared to them an obvious decision. The Minyan should study the Siddur, examining it section by section and major prayer by major prayer. They would meet each Sabbath morning in small groups prior to praying to "maximize the chance for discussion to be meaningful," as Jay put it. The classes were to maintain stable membership for the duration of the curriculum. Their stability would increase people's willingness to share their thoughts, they reasoned. These planners decided the purpose of each group: "to go prayer by prayer, read each and make the content clear. We will look at the prayer's structure, its values and the connotations and implications of the Hebrew words that make up the prayers."

The group planned their course of study to do more than educate. They were filled with enthusiasm and a sense that their project was "entirely unique," because "What we must do," said Jay, is "move the prayer experience to the life experience to see prayer as a door between the experience of praying and life." He offered an example.

> I like to donate blood each year. It makes me feel very good, helping people in such a small way. When I give blood I say the prayer from *Birchot Hă Shachar* [morning blessings] about bodily functions. So I turn it into a Jewish experience. I would like other people to see that these connections can be made in the Siddur. The Minyan is a nice experience from ten to twelve-thirty. But the prayer experience doesn't spill out. As we grow more comfortable with the Siddur, we will get closer to what Mark calls "the prayer praying itself."

Jacob responded by suggesting the following:

> Why don't we start each group by asking people if they have had an experience during the week that directly relates to prayer, a time when prayer would be appropriate or they would like to say a prayer.

Mark responded, "that feels fundamentalist, asking people to witness some experience. I feel uncomfortable with that suggestion." Harvey agreed.

Jay and Saul, however, sided with Jacob. Because they were both Jewish youth educators, they were more likely accustomed to eliciting such experiences from their students. They argued that this approach was what Saul called "genuinely Jewish." Jay said, "What other way is there to get inside the values of the prayers, to integrate them with our lives?" Jay suggested that each Minyan member could keep a notebook to record experiences during the week in which prayer would be appropriate. Members might bring the notebooks to the class for weekly discussions. The prayer classes, then, had as their goal to "bridge the gap between the culture we live in in 1973 and the era of the Siddur in our own terms," as Harvey finally put it on Sunday.

The planners had no difficulty achieving consensus about the content of the classes, the need for four small and stable groups, and a commitment to try this curriculum for eleven weeks. They all expressed their hopes that such discussions would even continue past the designated time. The planners also agreed that "teachers are needed to direct each group." They "will transmit knowledge required for an intelligent discussion." Nevertheless, the committee maintained that the teachers had to share responsibility, and they concluded that he or she would invite another class member to help plan and lead the group each week. They envisioned "nonexpert" class members raising questions different than the teachers'. For example, "the impact of the mythic and ritual meanings of the prayer on its content" was raised by Miriam as an example of such an issue. They anticipated issues "separable from Jewish content." By the evening's end, Jay asked Miriam to help plan one of the classes.

The planners' enthusiasm was briefly diminished as they began to draw up a pool of qualified teachers from the group. They found themselves quickly cutting down a long list of names to a short one. Some, they argued, were capable but not too interested, such as Ed. Some, on second thought, seemed only marginally qualified. Some did not come often enough. They were finally left only with Mark, Harvey, Jay, and Jacob. But Jay was unavailable on a weekly basis because his job as an assistant principal of a Hebrew school took him out of town for several Sabbaths during the year. The planners compromised by organizing three rather than four groups. Mark and Jay agreed to share responsibility for one. Harvey called Martha during the meeting and persuaded her finally to share responsibility for a class with him.

The prayer curriculum planners reflected with pleasure on their accomplishments of the evening. They had designed something they believed was innovative and exciting. They were giving themselves and all

Minyan members the chance to confront, rather than hide from, the problems they described at the retreat. They were disturbed that so few people could lead the classes, but believed that they had devised a way to remain democratic. They concluded when Harvey said, "We have matured and grown as a group because we have ceased to be afraid to acknowledge that some of us know more and can be teachers." Jay added, "I hope Minyan members are as mature as the group."

The Prayer Classes

During lunch on the following Sabbath, Harvey described the prayer curriculum and communicated the planners' enthusiasm. He circulated "tentative procedures for prayer study," a mimeographed sheet setting out "general procedures," "content," and "curriculum" (see Figure 4). Three weeks later, the classes began. The first day of the Minyan classes was reminiscent of the atmosphere of the first day of school. Most members seemed optimistic, anticipating with a little anxiety the changes in the Minyan: formal classes and no Torah or prayer discussions. Minyan members all arrived on time, remarkably, because lateness had recently become a point of concern.

Aaron began the morning by describing how he selected the membership of each class. The task was assigned to Aaron because he was a sociologist. The great seriousness with which he described his methodology for grouping class members, combined with his substantial qualifications for doing so, was sincere. This event was important to all the members.

> As you asked, I have randomly selected the class participants who will stay together for the next eleven weeks in groups. I took an alphabetical listing of all of us. I reshuffled the names to balance gender. I separated couples and known friendships to divide them between groups. I did this to bring people out and get the talkers evenly distributed.

Aaron solemnly read the names, assigning each class to a different room of the University Religious Center. Aaron also assigned anyone who was new or whose name did not appear on the list to a class.

The pomp and circumstance of simply moving into rooms and into classes signaled the seriousness with which the Minyan undertook this new task and structure for the group. Nevertheless, Aaron's concern about whether or not members would participate equally and share the

FIGURE 4

Tentative Procedure for Prayer Study

10–11 A.M.

The purpose of the prayer study groups is to understand the Siddur on its own terms and to explore the possibilities of integrating our own perspective with that of the Siddur in order to be better able to use the Siddur for our own religious expression. (Or, as Jacob would put it, to make the Siddur our friend.)

General Procedure

- There will be four groups.
- Each group will be led by a person with Hebrew and traditional Jewish knowledge.
- The leader will prepare for each session with another member of the group, who will provide another perspective.
- Each group member will keep a notebook in which she/he will record experiences of each week which relate to the prayers discussed.
- Short readings will be prepared from time to time on the nature of prayer, religious symbolism, etc., which will be read at home to enrich the discussions.
- A bibliography of additional optional reading will be compiled.

Content of Discussions

A. Experiences of the past week related to previously discussed prayers.
B. Consideration of prayer for that week from the following points of view:
   1. Historical background and context of the prayer.
   2. Place of the prayer in the overall structure of the Siddur.
   3. Meaning of the prayer: inner structure, symbolism, rhythm, sound, value concepts, experience it responds to, connotations of Hebrew terms, etc.
   4. Experiences members of the group have had which have some relationship to the prayer.

Tentative Curriculum

A listing week by week for twelve weeks of the prayers to be discussed.

feelings and ideas that were essential for the success of the groups was indicated by the need to appoint a "professional" simply to divide the groups up. Obviously, members were already suspicious that though everyone assented to the prayer curriculum, not everyone would bring to it and get from it what the planners anticipated.

The three prayer classes were remarkably different, given that they shared a single curriculum. They remained different throughout the months they met. Jacob's group was so classroomlike that Minyan visitors for the day took notes, clearly not realizing that this behavior was not allowed in the Minyan, though no one asked them to stop. Mark also used a lecture format for his class, though he raised specific questions for discussion and waited for responses. Harvey and Martha took a different approach. They jointly prepared their class focusing on the themes and issues connected to the prayers and anticipated responses from class members. They were disappointed when few people responded during the first class. These formats held throughout the prayer classes. Detailed examples of each class at three different points in the semester demonstrate how the prayer curriculum was enacted.

Martha and Harvey's Class

Martha described the process she and Harvey used to plan each of their classes. "We attempted to raise every possible issue for discussion and then take these issues and formulate a theory of what the prayer communicates." At midpoint in the class sessions, they discussed two prayers that constitute the introductory section of the Sabbath morning liturgical service. They are called *Barehu* (Blessed is He) and *Yozer* (God who forms light and darkness). They began with *Yozer,* a naturalistic prayer that examines God's attributes as creator of the world, of light and dark in particular. Martha began the class by proposing an interpretation of the prayer: "Darkness and light are images in this prayer of good and evil. They establish a duality in life which, through its orderliness, makes it possible to understand the world as orderly." Next, Harvey and Martha examined the grammatical form used in the prayers and the structures of the prayers. Harvey discussed the "world view" and "historical context" of the "framers of the prayers." He asked class members: "How did the authors understand light and dark? Did it have symbolic meaning for them that differs from our own?" Harvey remained committed to seeking members' participation, their comments, responses, and accounts of relevant experiences. Nan helped them prepare that day's discussion and particularly focused on male and female qualities in the prayer.

Harvey and Martha also wanted to move the class through a set curriculum that required that they cover certain material each week. They interrupted discussions that they considered "overly long," and tried to discourage too many comments. People willingly participated in the classes. In retrospect, one of the members of Martha and Harvey's group remembered a great deal of discussion and disagreement and a lively atmosphere in classes. But no one expressed either private doubts or agreement with prayer values or issues. The subject matter of the class was the prayers, apparently not themselves. They all approached prayer as if they were in a class in college that was taught by people who were close to completing their doctorates in literature and the philosophy of education, as were Harvey and Martha.

Jacob's Class

Jacob's first class was very much like the one he led at the retreat. He described his intentions.

> My interest was in having them see both the different kinds of relationships possible with God and to understand the various levels of meaning in the words, including humanistic understandings. I wanted to encourage them to play at opening themselves to the meaning of words and of prayer.

He offered a general introduction to the Siddur, its structure and history. He focused primarily on the principle Hebrew blessing form, "Baruch Atah Adanoi" (Blessed are You Lord), which begins most blessings. Jacob first analyzed the *bracha* (blessing) within the siddur structure, discussing where such blessings were most likely to occur in the liturgical service. He spent the majority of his time translating the nuances of the three words: "Baruch is normally translated as 'blessed,' but in fact it is a far more powerful concept that is associated with a gesture of humility expressed in the presence of power, bending the knee." He then contrasted "blessed" with the word *to praise* and finally to God's name, Adonai.[1] He compared the person uttering the "blessed are you" phrase with theologian Martin Buber's concept of the I-Thou relationship. Jacob suggested that the connection Buber envisioned between people and between people and God was available in prayer. The rabbis conceived of prayer enabling an unmediated intimacy and connection. He underscored the tensions between intimacy and awe implied in the blessing formula, but contended that connection was ultimately the goal of this relationship of an I and a thou. Someone asked a question. Jacob often asked participants if they had any questions. During the class he said: "It would be very helpful for people to share their personal experiences at any time. Please add any questions or comments." But they did not. Jacob lectured. People listened appreciatively and the class ended. In retrospect he commented, sighing, "I talked way too much." Jacob believed that his own understanding of prayer grew in the Minyan after his rabbinical ordination. He wanted to use that process as a model for how to teach others. He described to me how he believed his praying matured.

> My feeling about words, the importance of the limited number of words came out of realizing how frequently a small number of words recur in the siddur. My way of discussing a particular prayer was to analyze it very closely, to tie up the whole thing, to try to make some sense out of it, and out of doing that I would find a theme in a few recurring words.

Minyan members' comments about Jacob's class often reflected their awareness that he was acting as a model. When I asked Aaron about Jacob's first class, he answered, "I don't know if it helped me exactly, but just seeing that prayer works for Jacob gives me hope." Jacob was able to communicate his great attention to the language of prayer and his seriousness about it. Members of his class, as all members of the Minyan, respected that attitude, but like Aaron found it difficult to translate into their own experience.

Jay and Mark's Class

Jay, part-time leader of the third group, began to teach his class near the middle of the curriculum. Mark had led the first classes. Jay's group spent several weeks on the prayer *Sh'mah,* the major creedal statement of God's oneness. His discussion concerned the second paragraph of the prayer, which commands men to wear a fringed garment. When Jay asked for a review of the previous week's class because he had not been in the city, he discovered that only one person present had attended it. Jay had obviously planned to combine his discussion with the content of the last class; it was unnecessary. During the class he presented a series of ideas about the paragraph. First, he offered information about the ritual object the paragraph describes, *tzitzit:* how they are knotted and dyed.[2] He also described the blessings one says while actually holding the fringes, an act performed while reciting the Sh'mah paragraph in the morning. Jay discussed the theological problems raised in the paragraph, which he referred to in Protestant theologian Paul Tillich's terminology as matters of "ultimate concern." He asked, "Can one truely believe and remain critical?" The question engendered comments about tolerance and pluralism. He closed with two stories from rabbinic literature. One concerned where to find the required color of the dye for the fringes. The second described how the ritual fringe, brushing against the leg of a young rabbinical student, saved him from adultery and led to the conversion of the prostitute he initially sought. His many ideas were taken up by participants in his class.

Jay's class appeared more like the regular Minyan prayer discussions than a well-integrated part of the study program. Participants offered a wide range of comments that did not build on previous discussions and were not well connected. One might, for example, have given a personal opinion, a secular scholarly comment, or a traditional Jewish interpretation of the passage. There was no continuity in this group between successive classes or members. The discussion focused entirely on the leader's provocative comments for the day.

Some months after the prayer discussions, Mark described to me what went on in his group. He and Jay had "different teaching styles," he said, and didn't work together on planning any of their sessions.

> In my group I was very much a teacher, with people giving reactions to what I was saying. My goals were to give information and interpretation and to show the depth that these prayers run into. I tried to show how many levels exist in the prayers. When people have spent some time with prayer they come to certain things. There are things to come to. One of the things I did was to give possible interpretations that came to me as associations when I pray. Once, when we discussed the *Ahava Rabba* (the prayer preceding Sh'mah describing God's love for His people), things just kept on coming—word associations and all kinds of ideas, and people really appreciated that.

Mark reflected on what he did and did not do in his group.

> I did not provide an example of how to pray, that's for certain. I did show that prayer is a repository of meanings. Those are two very different things. Perhaps we were seeking both, but I couldn't do them both.

The style of each class reflected the leaders' ideas and theories about prayer and learning, which in some cases differed from one another. In addition, it was immediately apparent that neither participants nor leaders focused on the experience of praying. Their sense of despair or indifference at the retreat was never directly addressed. Some discussions had more erudite references, while others reflected a detailed analysis of sections of the siddur. But none addressed or responded to the problems raised about members' alienation from the content of prayer or their feelings of incompetence in its performance.

The Classes Effect on the Minyan

Members began to complain immediately after the first class. Some people did not like the individuals who were randomly selected to be in their group. Others did not like the format. As Frank put it: "There were lists and groups and people saying 'you don't belong in this group.' And I didn't like this." The atmosphere of anticipation rapidly changed to distrust. In turn, the leaders immediately began to alter their expectations. They all decided to drop the idea of writing personal reflections in journals. None of the members wrote journals. The leaders took this step without publicly discussing that this was not working.

People's reactions to the discussions were mixed. Doug was one member of Mark's group who found the experience genuinely satisfying. He said:

> Once prayer was explained, what the ideas were for those who wrote them, like understanding the agricultural cycle in the Middle East or why the sun was symbolized as coming up through a window, then we could talk about our images, and those were just as valid. I feel better about the Minyan now because I have more understanding in my own eyes as a participant. What is in my prayers feels valid now.

But others expressed displeasure. Susan was in Jay and Mark's group as well. She characterized the experience quite differently.

> Mostly it was an intellectual experience and not even one of integrity. It was a cleverness game, a game of one-upmanship. We were doing literary analysis. Who could find the best interconnections and symbols? "Look at the alliteration here and the assonance there." There were a few people that would have really wanted to talk seriously and honestly, but the circumstances were wrong.

Of Martha and Harvey's group, Frank said:

> I cannot recall saying anything, not more than six words. I wasn't sure about it, having leaders. It was a learning experience. I did learn about prayers. I think more about prayers, about their meaning, rather than about their sound now.

Saul, who had helped plan the curriculum, also participated in Martha and Harvey's class. He found the classes "interesting," but felt the whole approach was doomed from the start.

> What happened was an intricate delving into the prayers to the point that people were spending a whole discussion period discussing the *shin mem ayin* [Hebrew letters] of the Sh'mah prayer, just the word! Then, the idea was that through that discussion we would get to the ideas. Integration was going to occur by moving from the *bet* [Hebrew letter] of *baruch* [blessed] to expression of feelings around prayer. We are not really aware of the connection of our lives and prayer, so I don't see how this extreme form of dissection could do that.

Terri was also in Harvey and Martha's group. Her reaction was positive. "We took each word and analyzed its meanings and connotations, all the possibilities that could be involved in the word. We expressed our feelings." However, when asked what impact this had on her davening, she said: "None. It was just interesting, a good group. Nothing has ever changed my davening. I've always felt the same about davening." Her experience had little to do with the intention of the classes. These comments, elicited during formal interviews, were the members' only public discussion of their reactions to the classes. Their reactions, however, were expressed powerfully in what actually occurred on each Sabbath during the period of the prayer classes.

In the few weeks following the initiation of the curriculum, the Minyan began to change. Some people began to stand in the hall of the University Religious Center during the prayer classes. They did not join in until the davening started. Others clearly and purposely did not arrive until after the classes were finished in order to pray and eat lunch without participating in the groups. Their arrival disrupted the classes as they walked through rooms where the discussions were in progress in order to wait.

At no other time in the Minyan did people come for one event rather than another. Certainly people consistently arrived late, entering a discussion while it was underway, but this occurred during the Minyan's first thirty minutes. Now a sizable and growing number of people ceased seeing all parts of a Minyan Sabbath as integrated. Saul commented: "In my mind I completely dichotomized discussion and prayer. I never wore my tallit during the prayer classes as other people did. I put it on only when we actually began to pray."

Members held a brief meeting at lunch on the fourth week of the classes. Martha stated that there was a real problem with people arriving so late and disrupting classes. They agreed to switch the prayer classes to the end of the service in order to eliminate disruptions. This infuriated members who arrived on the fifth week only to discover that they had missed half the praying, thinking they would only be late for discussions. In addition, others felt the tempo for the Sabbath was destroyed by discussing after praying. In the sixth week the classes again began the Sabbath morning.

That same fifth week the size of the Minyan dropped dramatically. Twenty people attended instead of forty. Because far fewer people attended, the pool for recruits for Minyan offices was drastically reduced. In addition, because those offices associated with prayer (the two hazanim) required high skill, there were even fewer members able to lead prayer, in the midst of a Minyan seemingly preoccupied with it. It became harder to find people to do what had to be done. Over the next few weeks it became even more difficult. Only four people were willing to act consistently as hazan. Three of them were not considered good at it. As a result the services had changed. There was no spirit or intensity and little music. The Torah readers were decreasingly prepared and their readings were constantly corrected. The dwindling numbers made it difficult to recruit people to take responsibilities. Lunch was often the scene of angry interchanges and accusations about who had taken a role recently and who ought to be helping more.

On the seventh week of the classes, Harvey sent a message with Martha that he was no longer interested in teaching his class. He asked her to tell others that he did not want to carry the burden of planning and preparation because it was too demanding. At the same point, Jay took over his half of Mark's classes. The result was two groups with new leaders and there was little continuity in the classes.

It was December and the academic semester was drawing to a close. Only half of the regular number of members attended consistently. The three classes dissolved into two, then one. On December 8, a gray, dismal, rainy Saturday, one member said, "There are so few of us because it is rainy and everyone is studying for final exams." But Rachel retorted, "Last week we said it was sunshine and finals that kept people away." Martha asked if the discussions should be switched again. Another man sighed, saying, "It won't matter." Finally, Jacob somberly concluded: "It is time to end the classes. Martha will be leaving Kelton soon to move to New York and there aren't enough of us to continue." That day no one had even remembered to bring lunch. The Minyan's future looked bleak. There was a palpable sadness in the room. Then Terri said:

> Since we don't need so much space for the classes, why don't we meet at my house next week. We don't have to stay at the University Religious Center at least.

The following Sabbath attracted very few people because the University Hillel was holding its annual snow trip, taking two rabbis and many student members to the mountains for Shabbat. Terri explained why she volunteered her house.

> I think it's lousy and cold at the University Religious Center. It's a building, a place for administrators. It lacks warmth, which is what a home has.

Jay attended the Sabbath service and acted as hazan, something he rarely did. Terri was English hazanit, and she and Jay had practiced during the week in order to synchronize their praying and to make careful choices about what melodies they would use. They wanted it to be a good Sabbath service. Jay described the Sabbath in retrospect.

> There was a low that hit the Minyan. The Minyan seemed to be pallid. Then Terri said, "For a change let's have it at my house." We had to wait a while for a minyan, which of course created a feeling of our being *halutzim* [pioneers]. It was fabulous! We had only one discussion, and it was nice. The whole Shabbat was uncluttered. Then we had lunch together around only one table. Then I said, "Let's have it at my house next week." By the time people reached my house the next week they had all heard what a great time we had. Jacob led the service and that made everyone participate. Terri's house solved the whole thing.

Indeed, the Sabbath at Jay's was a remarkable contrast to dismal December. His large living room was filled to capacity with many members who had not been there for a month. At the end of the service, the offices for the following week were rapidly filled. People seemed to grab the opportunity to participate. It was a Minyan with a great deal of singing and voiced, melodic praying. Beth led a regular Torah discussion and people participated avidly. The room was filled with obviously happy, involved people. At the end of lunch, Harvey once again said, "It is time for a regular Minyan evaluation." Susan volunteered to have the group to her apartment on the next Sunday night.

When they convened nine days later, the meeting was unusually well attended and enthusiastic. Everyone seemed to have an opinion about everything. During their discussion about their Sabbath lunch, Michael, a Minyan founder who now only rarely attended, suggested that the group stop having lunch after the service. "Look," he said, "we are getting too big to have lunch together. Bringing the food is a burden. We break down into lots of little groups. What's the point?" No one agreed. In fact, the group held an animated discussion, not about whether to have lunch but about what to eat. Again, everyone had an opinion. They debated at length the relative merits of various foods for lunch, discussing the suitability of starchy Jewish cuisine such as noodle pudding [kugel], which was easier and cheaper to make, but "not healthy," "too fattening." Only one topic failed to capture the attention of at least ten people. When Jacob said, "We agreed to talk about prayer classes tonight," one member laughed uncomfortably, and the rest were silent. No one demanded any further comment and there was none.

Once again the Minyan made a series of decisions that restructured their Sabbath. A whole new type of discussion would precede prayer, neither the classes nor the previous "prayer confrontations." They spontaneously called them "free play," to be on any topic of each leader's choice.[3] The Rashi group was disbanded because members concluded it was too divisive, separating people from one another. Instead, they would have two concurrent Torah discussions on the weekly portion. Size alone compelled division of the group. Members also agreed to share responsibility more equally and to meet at least once a month in the few Minyan members' homes large enough to accommodate them all. Their meeting in January 1974 turned the tide of despair. The new year held great promise for the Minyan. They attributed the bleak last month of 1973 to the normal drop in attendance associated with the end of the academic semester.

I pondered how to understand these events that stretched from September to January. How did the touching enthusiasm of men and women about to enter a new phase in their community development turn so quickly to feelings of anger and disappointment and to a barely functioning Minyan? In turn, how did a single Sabbath attended by only eleven people turn the whole process around, moving members out of the lethargy that shrouded every previous Sabbath?

The classes obviously had a powerful, if unarticulated effect, on every aspect of the Minyan. Individual expressions of dissatisfaction soon became the general attitude. The group's antagonism toward the classes was evident in prayer. As fewer people agreed to serve as hazan, those who assumed the burden came to resent the job. Jacob was one of many who characterized the praying as "awful." The malaise led to

A New York Havurah discussion to "process" group activities and ideas.

uneasiness about the group as such. Would they continue; would they be able to recruit a weekly minyan, the clear measure of minimal success for any Jewish religious community? When members switched the classes from before prayer to after prayer to before again, some lost confidence in their ability to even predict what would occur on any particular Sabbath. They could not anticipate events.

The classes created a division between leaders and followers. The decision taken to alter their formal equality seemed a benchmark of maturity for the curriculum planners, yet even one of the leaders stopped participating. The longer there were leaders, the more unwilling the followers were to join in. When Jacob stated that the prayer classes should end, in combination with Harvey's withdrawal, it seemed that the leaders no longer wanted to lead.

Relief from this situation came in a peculiar form. It derived simply from the reassertion of the Minyan's normal structure, a small number of people meeting in a home. Gathered at Terri's house, in addition to her and Jay and a few of his out-of-town visitors, were Susan and Harvey. They experienced the Minyan as pleasant, and they had a large network to whom they could communicate the day's success. By the next Sabbath a great many people were willing to participate, demonstrating that a successful revival of the Minyan was indeed underway.

What occurred at that transitional Minyan was, in addition to a normative Sabbath, an emphasis on the community's central and unique features. First, for them the personal, familial home setting provided a marked contrast to the perceived sterility of the University Religious Center. Second, the smallness of that Minyan Sabbath necessarily put great value on each participant who attended because of the importance of "making the minyan," that is, being assured of assembling ten members. When Jay said they felt like "pioneers," he meant that each person was critical to making a unique Sabbath happen. Their small numbers powerfully reasserted egalitarianism. Third, Jay called the Sabbath "uncluttered." A real fluidity in the Minyan Sabbath reemerged. The jagged break between classes and prayers did not occur. Discussion took place only during the Torah portion, which was associated regularly with study. Prayer was the primary activity of the day and little disrupted that. Finally, they sang a great deal, reinforcing a strong sense of unity, participation, and community. In short, every activity of that Sabbath provided a contrast to the Minyan dominated by prayer classes.

The prayer classes, which began as a way to bring the self in a closer relationship with the text, accomplished the opposite. The Minyan's regular interpretive discussions, which were potentially alienating for the worshiper, did have one important quality; they were pluralistic and democratic. They included many opinions, all of which were tolerated by community members. The variation in the discussions grew directly from the many perspectives represented in the group: political, liberal, feminist, literary, Judaic, and others. These discussions led to prayer because they were occasions to reflect on the connection between the tradition and one's life—values, ideas, and principles. The ideal Minyan self brought his or her personal and intellectual uniqueness to traditional texts and hoped to see each reflected in the other. One also reflected on text at his or her own level, without fear that those perspectives would be rejected for not being sufficiently erudite.

These classes were monolithic rather than pluralistic or democratic. Each group had a leader, and the leader had a point of view sanctioned by expert knowledge about the Siddur. There was a correct interpretation that required experts. Expert analysis necessitated structural, theological, and literary methods. Members who joined with the formal leaders, and those were few, usually added another expert point of view. The unique and self-expressive selves of the community were in some sense irrelevant to the class, other than to learn the proper approach. Some members appreciated the knowledge they gained, but their role had been altered. Certainly no one intended this result, but it was inevitable because the need for a proper approach to prayer initiated the classes. Consequently, prayer and class discussions became polarized each Sabbath. The Minyan could not obligate its members to attend and fewer came each week.

The prayer classes were "deconstructing" in nature. They pulled apart the service as well as the letters, words, phrases, and sentences of prayer. Prayer was fragmented and cognitively assessed. Classes were neither democratic nor did they heighten the participation of any Minyan member by showing a connection (even by virtue of producing lively argument) between the issues of the Siddur and one's own life. Interpretations were offered, but only specific canons of interpretation were authorized.

It was Saul, an undergraduate, who brought my attention to the implications of Minyan members attempting to solve prayer problems by analysis. He considered me among the overeducated and believed I would have difficulty understanding his alternative view of how to solve problems about prayer.

> How did the Minyan react to all the problems of prayer? We never said, "Let's do more intensive praying—a longer time of silence, a

> longer Amidah. Or let's do Amidah twice, once silently and once together and see the individual responses and the group response. The group reaction was "Let's divide it up. First we have the *Barehu*. What does *Baruch atah* mean? Then we'll do one of the three prayers that precede the Sh'mah each week. Then maybe we can get to the Amidah." You know, that's an unusual thing. There were never discussions of an ALTERNATIVE way to do things. What I'm suggesting is harder to plan. If you want to DO something, it is easier to study. You know what you're going to do. I don't think anyone would say after a discussion, "Now that I know that Baruch means the power of God, that has cleared up my spiritual problems." The only reason people thought it would is because there is a lot of education there. You make things like a classroom.

The analytical approach to prayer, as the classes came to define it, was a cognitive, hierarchical one. It enshrined a set of interpretations that standardized the prayer experience. It made motivations, such as the desire for community or emotional satisfaction, appear banal.

In the previous chapter, I note that the retreat was dominated by a psychological vocabulary of needs that cast prayer as an activity requiring self-scrutiny in order to determine whether or not one agreed with its content and if it met the needs of each person. The classes, however, were dominated by a vocabulary of "oughts," a classically religious discourse. They were predicated on a problem of personal belief that required new information in order to be resolved.

In the classes, a distinction emerged between one's ideas and opinions on the one hand, and one's feelings on the other. Normative discussions in the Minyan involved statements of opinion and points of view, disagreements with or interpretations of traditional texts. Such discussions embraced the secular work world and the values and beliefs of American culture (Prell-Foldes 1980). For example, criticizing the book of Genesis for its problematic visions of women, as troublesome as that may be for some, is not as personally revealing an experience as expressing a loss of faith in the omnipotence of God. The retreat discussion spontaneously gave public voice, for the first time, to such concerns. The prayer classes were intended to continue to demand private reflection, not in the context of a liminal period, but in the context of a classroom, which was for them the essence of daily life. As the result of a virtually impossible demand on members for self-exposure, they retreated into formal classes, which as a result of being hierarchic made any revelation unthinkable. The result was alienation from prayer.

The prayer classes prescribed responses for what was normally unspoken and were a constant reminder of statements of alienation made at the retreat. This approach narrowed members' discussions from an expansive and ideally integrative process to a hierarchic and excluding one. Both the retreat, which rejected prayer as lacking meaning, and the classes, which rejected the pluralism of expressive individualism, failed to create the interiorization of prayer for Minyan members. They returned to what they normally did in order to create that elusive bridge between themselves and prayer.

As comfortable as virtually all members were with discussion, reflection, and interpretation, the Minyan's founders and educated elite were most proficient at it. They defined the retreat discussion; they determined what issues in that discussion required resolution. And then they planned the curriculum and course to facilitate that resolution. The prayer classes may be seen as their strategy to regain control of a group that was moving in a new direction unsupported by its founders. In other discussions and decisions, Harvey often held a position opposed to those of newcomers; he spoke against their proposals for creative services and their desires for more singing in the davening. The founders asserted an approach, the classes, that allowed them to literally maintain control over the group, though they soon tired of it when it proved not to be what they had envisioned.

The transforming Sabbath at Terri's home had very little analytical activity associated with it, though several founders were there. The absence of classes led Jay to think of that Sabbath as "uncluttered." The special qualities of the day were associated more with what I characterized as prayer aesthetics, such as music. Terri described her efforts with Jay to produce a beautiful service, one that was well synchronized, and included a great deal of music. The service moved smoothly and without apparently extraneous events. The aesthetics of the day contributed to the pervasive sense of unity and community. People communicated with one another on a face-to-face basis. Members had one lunch table, one lunch conversation, one Torah discussion, and felt their participation mattered. The service was far more communal, and communal activity resulted—song, conversation, and discussion—which led to a satisfying experience of prayer.

Members were alienated from the prayer performance as a result of the classes. Attendance fell and people were less engaged or willing to be involved in services dominated by analysis. Their emphasis on aesthetics had the opposite effect. Members eagerly flocked to Jay's house for a Sabbath that promised to be satisfying, that would not probe and question. The pleasure derived from praying, even if it was, as Jay said, "with partial satisfaction and partial fulfillment," moved people to continue to pray and remain in the Minyan.

Following these events Ruth explained to me what she expected from the Minyan. Her description echoed what members came to conclude themselves.

> Prayer itself is the mainstay of the group. I know pretty much why I come to the Minyan or why on a particular day I do not. But if I really stop to hassle every time with every word in the Siddur or my relationship toward God and prayer I would go nuts. Maybe it's a given in a sense that the basis of the Minyan is prayer, and that maybe other social relationships will grow out of it or certain discussions and knowledge might come from it. That's the meat of it.

Performance and Covenant

The transitional Minyan Sabbath succeeded, according to members, because everyone was an active participant, and prayer was judged excellent because of its beauty. That day Minyan members appeared to link themselves successfully to prayer. In the terms I develop in Chapters 4 and 5, Minyan members' connection to the prayer texts was an expression of their participation in the covenant. Praying the text as one's own words—successful prayer—was an expression of their participation in the Jewish people. All the synthesizing elements of ritual aesthetics, such as music and swaying, joined the worshiper to covenantal relationships. Minyan members could be placed in those relationships only through the performance of prayer, and a felicitous one at that. As we have seen, simply reading the words was not sufficient for prayer to succeed for its members. Covenantal relationships were expressed when community, text, and performance were all united in a common purpose. Chapter 5 describes how important aesthetics were to ritual in the Minyan. Aesthetics communicated ritual messages that were made effective through performance. When one enacted prayer and ritual, one activated and embodied its messages. Performance was not simply translating a text into motion, but creating its message as well. Covenant was realized in prayer. Bruce Kapferer understands ritual to be "an emergent phenomenon" because it translates cultural forms into action. (1983, 154). Without performance ritual could never have personal and immediate significance for its participants, and could not join self, text, and community.

Within prayer, then, Minyan members created three covenantal relationships: a relationship to the Jewish people who preceded them, a relationship to the community in which they prayed, and a relationship reflexively to the self. Praying surrounded Minyan members with their own history. To have said the words of the Siddur as one's own was to experience what Beth and others noted: Jewish men and women said many of these very words for thousands of years. As so many in the group sought authenticity, which is why they insisted on Hebrew prayer, then praying was authenticating because it appeared unchanging. In prayer performance, the worshiper made the relationship to history active, hence one's own. The connection was indisputable; the performance sufficed to make the point. Since the covenant was made in history, it could be authenticated by creating a relationship with the makers of that history. One of the most reliable links to history has always been established through a relationship with Jewish texts. The all-important and authenticating relationship with the Jewish people has always been made directly through prayer.

The second covenantal relationship created in prayer was between the worshiper and the praying community, one that had been problematic in the Minyan. While differences in their knowledge and in their views of the Minyan had not disappeared, after the transitional Sabbath people were no longer willing to press them. The near demise of the group, and the founders' abandonment of projects to transform the Minyan, intensified their willingness to compromise. The differences between members became less important after the abortive prayer classes. No one wanted to abandon the Minyan, even with its imperfections. They emphasized their commonalities in prayer, rather than their differences in classes.

Members' commitment to praying only underlined what the community and prayer expressed about one another—authenticity. Their strongest tie was their ability to see and validate one another's Judaism, as well as the tradition. The third covenantal relationship between the self and God or the Jewish people depended on that authenticity. The requirement for the minyan emphasized the impact that community had on individual prayer. As one prayed, one was seen by and watched by others, and this affected the experience. Minyan members were particularly committed to communal prayer, often praying only in that setting.

As anthropologist Gilbert Lewis astutely notes, performing and beholding in ritual are equally ambiguous. Because neither stance is absolute, each leaves open a freedom of interpretation and discovery that makes it possible to perform ritual meaningfully even without having created it (1980, 38). Lewis, in contrast to Maurice Bloch, finds in the ritual act the constant opportunity to make these actions personally meaningful. By seeing others act, or acting oneself, one is, within an "arena of constraints," able to discover and interpret the significance of what is being done. This process offers continuity as well as what he calls "enrichment" to those who participate in rituals designed for circumstances and experiences far removed from their original setting. In ritual performance one becomes a creator, because as one participates, interpretation of some sort is inevitable. Seeing one's contemporaries pray successfully makes it possible to pray despite the doubts one might experience. As audience, as well as actor, one's participation is intensified as the possibility for personal interpretation is heightened. "I see myself in my intimates as I see them in me when we pray." Minyan decorum regulated social relations, which emphasized informality, expressiveness, and democracy. Prayer was organized in such a way as to emphasize these same features. The historical covenant was translated into contemporary relations in the Minyan. Praying with Jews like oneself heightened the sense that prayer expressed the self. Insofar as prayer created relationships between peers, it intensified the ability of the worshiper to pray. Communal ritual usually works in this fashion. But in contemporary America, where few communities reflect anything integrative about the self, the burden on such groups is intensified. Each prayer performance underlined the covenantal relationship among members. Decorum and the sacred intersected as community worship was linked with individual worship through prayer performances.

Ultimately, the covenant included the person only insofar as he or she experienced the reality of that sacred relationship. The contribution of aesthetics to prayer, as discussed in Chapter 5, was to transform the person so that covenant was made real. When Mark spoke of his "associations" with prayer, or Saul described prayer "playing against the backdrop of his personality," they clearly noted how in the act of praying personal links were made between the self and the text; the text was interiorized. Only then did prayer have the quality of reality for the self. Covenant, then, had a reflexive dimension in prayer performance. Prayer reflected the self to the self, as it reflected the self and community to one another.

In short, covenant in the Minyan rested on three fundamental relationships that were also articulated through prayer. For some members all these relationships reflected an ultimate connection to God. For others, though few said this publicly, God was irrelevant to that issue. The God to whom prayer was addressed meant for them Jewish tradition or peoplehood. If covenantal relations were best articulated and even realized through prayer, then that returns us to the fundamental questions raised by secularization theorists. What authorizes prayer? If it is not society, or agreement with the content of prayer, or possibly God, what allowed Minyan members to pray?

Prayer Performance

Each covenantal relationship described above allowed members to interiorize their prayer. Voicing prayer with the conviction that it was one's own words within community reproduced the culture or tradition that created the prayer. Conviction cannot come without a sense of one's own involvement in creating a ritual, an involvement that comes largely from performance, as either spectator or participant. Covenant, then, was closely connected in the Minyan to performance. We can surmise that the real difference between Minyan prayer with prayer classes and Minyan prayer without prayer classes was the group's reorganization, which emphasized performance. During prayer classes members continued to pray, of course, but for that period the community emphasized prayer as an abstracted body of knowledge rather than an interiorized experience.

Performance is all the more important in the religion of complex and pluralist societies because of the loss of the functional, if routinizing, elements of ritual that obligated people to action. Obligation, nevertheless, embedded ritual and prayer in normal social life. Freed from social obligations, women and men turned to religion to define the self, often in opposition to the surrounding society or in order to reform it. The individual self, no longer secured by institutional requirements, depends increasingly on performance itself, to take a greater share in making ritual effective as well as authoritative. The scholars of religion, who note the in-turning that often accompanies religion in pluralist societies, are seeing religion emphasize interior experience. Performance, whether it involves meditation or davening, is experienced powerfully within the person, joining form with personal experience.

The absence of obligation is not a social-structural issue alone. For related reasons, there is also no single or unifying domain of meaning in complex society. To the contrary, there are contradictions between domains of meaning. There are few interrelationships between family and work, or politics and religion. There is little equivalence among the institutions and relations that fragment the lives of men and women in complex society.[4] Insofar as synthesis between domains occurs, it is more likely to take place within the person than within the culture as a whole. Since the nineteenth-century transformation of American society and the creation of its urban-professional middle class, discussed in Chapter 1, individuals have tried to make such integrative statements through religious organizations. Judaism, however, only intensified the sense of alienation for its adherents, because it is predicated on the notion of Diaspora, that the Jewish people have been separated from their homeland and live as outsiders wherever they are. Mark suggested this problem to me as he talked about what was difficult about prayer. "The Diaspora fills us with a sense of incompleteness. Whatever you do has very partial significance to a standard of what is real. There are few occasions for repentance, joy, sadness, or happiness integrated through a relationship with God in America." Jews must work all the harder to create covenant in America and to make those covenantal relations synthesize and reflect their experiences. Performance, then, assumes a powerful religious burden in complex society.

In the Minyan, community and a general sense of Jewish tradition were created by the performance of prayer. Each such performance was reflexive, a metastatement on Minyan members' success at praying honestly, in an engaged fashion, as they believed their parents' generation failed to do. They were persuaded of their identity and the rightness of their "choice." They constructed a religious community that, though untypical, still persuaded them that they were praying as Jews. They *achieved* their tradition, emphasizing the "material that has continued to be relevant to the ethos of the community" (Hymes 1975, 71). That "material" was to be found in the maintenance of their traditional liturgy and particularly in covenant, though they were still compelled to stamp their unique organization and aesthetics upon them. Halaha, community, and interpretation were woven into a single fabric of experience. Minyan members said in their organization, in their discussions, and in their praying, "We are Jews." Praying was possible, that is, persuasive, because the Minyan emphasized those aspects of the experience that best expressed who members were, particularly through performance.

Ritual performance, in the context of a specifically defined decorum, was effective in creating the integration and synthesis that produced successful prayer. Performance on its own, however, cannot motivate a person to participate. Without "believing in" or "holding" the covenant, there would be no reason for performance. Members came to the Minyan more or less convinced by their families, by camp, by educational experiences, or by some relationship or private realization that praying and being Jewish were related activities. Active participation in American society largely determined that Judaism would be generally, rather than specifically, meaningful. Nonetheless, covenant and performance were intrinsically linked to one another, dependent upon one another in prayer life.

Quite literally, Minyan members could not say prayers if they could not perform them. The prayer performance enabled reaffirmation of the equation that to be Jewish was to pray and to pray was to fully express oneself in the covenant. A mutual relation existed between praying and the traditional formulation of the prayers in the Minyan, which may be true for most who pray in the modern world. Performance generated form. To pray as a Jew was to make oneself and the prayers believable. Acting, doing, praying, and speaking the words of tradition as one's own words created the sense of the rightness of the ritual form. Their performances were persuasive for them precisely because they made use of traditional forms. The arbitrary use of just any set of words in any particular language failed to evoke the emotions that these Jews required as the condition for ritual enactment and the expression of their Jewishness and Judaism. Various Minyan members described their associations with prayers. The more observant and better educated described feelings, thoughts, and reflections on their own Jewish lives evoked during prayer. Others simply noted the value they placed on the sound of Hebrew, which held deep emotional or aesthetic value. Intoning an unknown language, not an unusual activity in religious practices throughout the world, created a sense of attachment and connection to the ritual and to a general sense of identity or purpose. As Sam Gill remarked about Navajo prayer:

> While it is not irrelevant to the situation, the message of prayer is highly redundant and the encoded information is well known. The style of the performance and the physical and emotional aspects of the performance seem to greatly overshadow any concern with the message. (1981, 185)

Doing enforced believing, because doing in a particular context made the form believable. As Saul stated the matter, "Praying is more important than prayer for me."

However, the process did not end there. It was not a matter of simply rotely enacting a given liturgy. For form generated performance as well. Prayer necessitated praying. The texts came alive and were made acceptable and believable because the performance made them that way. Doing what Jews do made one a Jew, and being a Jew moved one toward Jewish activity. The prayer performance enacted in the Minyan community was part of what generated the process of maintaining identity, creating visibility, and personally claiming the tradition as one's own.

That the Minyan flourished in its prayer performances and withered in its prayer classes demonstrates that the reasons why members pray are not as significant as the fact that they pray together. In retrospect, Jacob himself recognized this obvious point. "When they were asked, members were more than willing to criticize prayer, but praying was what makes us a group, and no one asked how they felt about that." Jay made a similar point.

> No one, by the way, offered any alternatives when they complained about their difficulties with prayer. There wasn't an overriding outcry, "Teach us, correct us, change us, substitute meditation or trances for prayer." The discussion was an expression of pluses and minuses and an emphasis on real happiness with the Minyan.

Praying worked quite adequately to maintain what they associated with Jewish liturgy and join it with the personal conviction generated by the actual performance of the words. When Terri explained why the prayer classes had no effect on her davening, she also described what did.

> I'm the kind of person who needs a lot of reinforcement from the congregation. I like good feelings all around and I daven much more serenely and pleasantly. When people drag when they sing or daven, I feel lousy. When there's unity, a strong bond between people, it makes a difference. Once I was hazan and some people were bored with the songs I picked out and it spoiled it for me and for others.

What pleased Terri and attached her to the Minyan was the support of others in her praying. In the retreat discussion, she described herself as a person burdened all of her life by her failure in prayer, her fear that God was not in front of her and not able to hear her. But in describing her davening, we see another picture. Here is a woman moved by the community's support of her, caught up in song and music, fully engaged with the tradition and Sabbath prayer. She was confident of the experience and of herself. She achieved a successful performance of prayer and experienced herself and those around her as Jews. In doing that she made the words of prayer her own.

Performance and the Power of Aesthetics

What performance does, in short, is to allow the person to interiorize prayer, thereby reproducing the tradition in general, and covenental relations in particular. The covenant authorizes prayer, that is, grounds Judaism in a theology, history, and requirement for communal relations. However, praying recreated the covenant weekly for most Minyan members and made it convincing for them. Without that conviction, members would not "believe in" Judaism, as Stromberg put it. They would not be emotionally invested in the religion so that the self was connected to it.

Performance occurs within certain constraints and forms. I noted at the outset that not any performance would do. In Chapter 5, I identify aesthetics as the synthesizing feature of ritual and prayer. Without it the person cannot be drawn into the ritual, cannot be unified to others and to the ritual event itself. Though the ritual communicates messages to participants, the point of aesthetic forms, such as dance and music, is to unify the person with the rite, altering his or her experience as a result.

Aesthetics are, to state the obvious, culturally variable. In the plural world of American society there are cultural, generational, religious, political, and many other varieties of aesthetics. A synagogue performance did not "work" for most Minyan members because of those differences. Particularly for the majority of members who did not feel "obligated" to pray, aesthetics were virtually determinative of participation. The same words voiced in a community with the "wrong" decorum or an inappropriate aesthetic made prayer almost impossible and undermined a sense of covenant. Aesthetic media of song and movement, as well as aesthetic styles, all contributed to the capacity of ritual to convince worshipers of their ability to pray.

The aesthetic aspects of ritual enable people to enter the altered world created by ritual, where "the world as lived and the world as imagined, fused under the agency of a single set of symbolic forms, turn out to be the same world" (Geertz 1973b, 112). Doing is believing. Seeing one's fellow "doing" is even more potent in making action believable. To pray with a particular aesthetic, to say words, to put one's body in motion as one davens, is to be a Jew. As Dell Hymes suggests, "Tradition itself exists partly for the sake of performance. Performance itself is partly an end" (1975, 19). Performance is persuasive; it provides the intensely felt, highly affective sense that what one does is right because he or she is doing it. Clifford Geertz (1973a, 1973b), Sherry Ortner (1978) and Barbara Myerhoff (1977) have commented on the persuasive dimension of ritual. As Geertz argued, authority flows from it.

Performance translates knowledge into action. In fact, Minyan members had not only imperfect knowledge of the tradition but arguments with it. All of them sought to change, to some extent, what constituted the bedrock of Jewish law. But they all shared the desire to take responsibility for the performance of that tradition. They did not want to be mere observers in their own religious lives. Though their prayers may not have constituted what Hymes calls the "breakthrough to performance"—that is, authoritative performance authorized by the most conservative definition of the tradition—their performance was nevertheless convincing to them as an authentic enactment of Jewish prayer. As such, they internalized a general Judaism.

What results from such authoritative performances? In the case of the Minyan members, the reproduction of tradition oriented their lives and intensified their identification as Jews and, hence, as something unique within America. The more seriously one participated in the Minyan, the more likely one was to observe dietary laws, to expand Sabbath observance to all twenty-four hours, and to participate in the cycle of Jewish festivals throughout the year. If one came as a traditionalist, the liberalism of the Minyan also sanctioned lessening observance, but without feeling it was impossible to remain fully Jewish. The general, rather than minutely defined, nature of tradition made it possible for members to experience their Judaism as authentic without requiring fundamentalist belief or total observance.

The Minyan emphasized authenticity within pluralism. Judaism served as a repository of meanings, but the members emphasized the ones they found most valuable. Of course members fought over prayer content. For instance, as a result of group decisions that did not please all members, they did not pray for the return of animal sacrifices in the Additional Service on festivals and the Sabbath. They did not even pray for victory and the destruction of modern Israel's enemies. In the Minyan, however, as in America, no values were stronger than the extremely general ones of community and tradition, as opposed to the particulars of cosmology and theology or, in the end, ideas about gender. For some, the general nature of prayer specifically oriented activity. They read directly from prayer to their behavior. Jay, one of the Minyan members who prayed daily, noted the general sense of what prayer was likely to mean for him.

> Davening is cracked up to do a lot more than it really does on a regular Shabbes minyan basis. I am convinced that at certain peak experiences in a person's life, prayer can have a major role. But for the most part, as a friend of mine says, the prayer experience is a "down holiness," an earthly kind of thing that provides a cue in our life. It provides us certain categories to think with, certain symbols.

In the rather abstract language of "cue," "category," and "symbols," he asserted that this daily ritual provided him with an outlook on life. Jay's entire life as a rabbi and educator was devoted to Judaism. The cues were encompassing.

Doug, who by contrast told me, "I never pray alone; I need the community," also found cues in prayer, though not as precise as Jay's "categories" or "symbols."

> Prayer is not just petitionary. It's somehow a celebration of life and a statement of being Jewish. I work in a Jewish organization, but that doesn't go anywhere near fulfilling my needs. I'm not sure I draw on prayer for my life, but I do on things of Jewish culture.

Doug appeared ambivalent. Even in a single thought, he indicated that prayer allowed him to celebrate his Judaism, but at the same time he was not certain he drew on prayer in the way Jay described. He seemed willing to continue to struggle with the meaning of the prayers because it did something for him that all other arenas of Jewish life did not.

Ruth reflected on prayer in order to explain what happens to her while praying.

> When I think of davening in the Minyan I never think of anybody out there listening to me. I just always think of it as me and a renewal of my commitment. In a sense a check-off list of things that I want to try and dedicate myself to and try and remember to give direction to my own life. But there are times, mostly of pain and trouble, where I just quietly hang my head and think, "Please don't let there be war in Israel," knowing it's not going to do anybody any good. And I guess at Havdalah, in the quietness and the darkness, I really for two seconds can believe the Messiah is going to come and somehow make it all better. That goes away as soon as the candle goes out and the lights go on. Just trying to get in touch with your insides is a very cleansing experience; to get in the rhythm and to accomplish something. I really feel good after we finish Adon Olam [the closing hymn]. The book closes and it's Shabbos; it really dedicates Shabbos.

Ruth, Doug, and Jay, all with different levels of Jewish education and observance, and with different ideas about a God without and within, found in the prayer performance cues, guides, and occasions for reflections that no other private or organizational setting made possible. In their performances, their Judaism was made real, dedicated and rededicated and "rehearsed." As text and performance created and generated one another, so they made the individual's participation compelling.

These men and women described the internalization of the prayer experience. It was a unique experience, different in quality from others, neither divorced from the great tradition of halaha nor disconnected from an idiosyncratic approach unique to the community. Understanding and didactic knowledge were not its primary result. In all cases prayer provided a frame for what they, as Diaspora Jews, thought of as Jewish experience. For the most observant prayer offered the expression of key categories and concepts. Mark quoted verses of prayers to me when he expressed, for example, the importance of community. Less observant members were more likely to speak in general terms of identity or peoplehood or history. But those meanings and values were directly evoked by the prayer experience, which involved a powerful link between self, text, and performance.[5]

Felicitous Prayer

Borrowing J. L. Austin's vocabulary in Chapter 4, I ask what makes prayer felicitious, that is, how does prayer work. Particularly in plural and secular society, where virtually all the standard conditions rooting ritual to society no longer exist—obligation, homogeneity, connections to status relations, and uniform ideas—why does prayer work? Why do people continue to pray? Prayer proposes to be about contacting God and the expression of belief. In the Minyan there are many examples of people who neither believe nor are preoccupied with contacting God. Then what is their prayer and what does it do? In more general terms, what constitutes prayer for modern women and men?

The constitutive elements of prayer vary. Though prayer resembles performative speech in many ways, its context is far more complex. All prayer has a liturgical field, including history, current social relations, and inherited forms. Within that field, in the Minyan, prayer involved a required social group (community), an inherited form (halaha), and, uniquely to them, reflections on the process (interpretation). Not only must these constituents be present for prayer to be effective, they must be synthesized, that is, joined together. All constituents are unified only within the prayer performance. The worshiper takes prayer in to express it as his or her own only when they are unified. When action and community are linked, that is, when prayer and minyan are linked in the act of praying, then prayer is felicitous or effective. Judaism is reproduced as the product of self and text reflecting one another. The worshipers can continue to pray knowing that prayer speaks to and for them.

In the Minyan, because both community and praying were voluntary, the prayer constituents were inevitably sensitive to one another because they existed in a somewhat closed system. Halaha, for example, was not mirrored in either a political system or even in an ethnic enclave. It, then, only articulated a system of obligation that basically was negotiated by people according to their individual needs. In Minyan prayer, discussions and texts consistently reflected upon one another. Interpretations of texts in discussion could lead to the ability to pray. Praying could recast certain interpretations. They flowed in and out of one another in both the structure of any liturgical service and in creating intention and the ability to pray. Similarly, as I discussed in Chapter 5, community, halaha and discussions reflected one another. Changes in the group were reflected in what could be discussed and how the obligation to pray was understood. Prayer in the Minyan was felicitous, then, when these constituents could be mutually reflecting and drawn into the person through performance.

Prayer performance, on its own, was insufficient to keep members from distancing themselves from prayer in their therapeutic retreat discussion, which led to the prayer classes. In the Minyan, prayer was infelicitous, that is, judged meaningless by worshipers, when it did not allow them to participate in the covenant. The retreat discussion occurred at a time when the community was reassessing and reorganizing its approach to prayer. Increased negotiation about prayer intensified differences and undermined people's conceptions of prayer. Normally assumed difficulties with prayer took on greater significance as the community became ineffective at reflecting its members as either competent Jews or Jews with appropriate needs.

The problems created by the prayer classes were resolved through praying. In the end, the primary authority for prayer rested in recreating the covenant anew through praying. It articulated a message of sacred relationships, which was reflected in the communal, interpretive, and halahic constituents of prayer. That "general" message translated into attitudes, cues, and behaviors for members who brought them back to prayer. The aesthetic elements that were critical to effective performance aided that very process of unifying community and prayer to create what I have called throughout this book "intention," "belief in," and "holding" beliefs. In summary, felicitous prayer unified the constituents within prayer performance to remake covenantal relations that authorized participation.

The "plausibility structures" that Peter Berger understood to be essential to religious life exist in a radically different form in complex society. Voluntary associations, particularly religious ones, have a long history in American society of being vehicles for authorizing and authenticating a religious experience tied closely to the development of communal and individual identity. They have moved into the vacuums created by conflicting values and institutions to provide enduring forms such as ritual, as well as novel interpretations and applications of the traditions transmitted by such forms. Religion, then, is an individual matter, but one formulated through traditional frameworks that require interaction with community and activities that carry the stamp of tradition and continuity. The extent to which ritual and community can combine disparate elements of the culture within traditional frameworks is essential to the development of identity.

Because secularization theorists have ignored the formal features of ritual, as well as failed to explore the messages communicated by contemporary religion, they have not examined what makes the religious experience plausible. They have not looked at what constraints traditional forms place around identity formation. Nor have they paid attention to the mutual relations between traditional forms and how they are enacted in order to see the impact of one upon the other. Only when one combines an analysis of the formal properties of prayer and their contribution to the prayer experience can one understand the effect of secularization on those forms. Similarly, one must understand the impact of ritual forms on secularization. Fischer and Epstein, among others, have pointed our understanding of ethnicity toward an analysis of how ethnic identity grows out of the relationship between traditional forms and pluralistic society. Their interests parallel this attempt in order to understand the link between performance, context, prayer, and community.

The Minyan's prayer classes were ultimately about a mistake, though not an arbitrary one. Communities, particularly fragile ones whose voluntary membership makes them less stable, experiment in formulating themselves. They do not have the generations of experience and the wide-range of activities that would allow them to develop a flexible but fixed form. The prayer classes were just such an experiment. They were the vision of one group of people, who because they started the Minyan, had the hardest time watching it change. Their prayer curriculum was designed to create Minyan members that the founders felt would resemble themselves. But the classes did not work. A few weeks of classes could not create for others what these founders experienced as Jews.

The prayer classes were a mistake in a much deeper sense than the temporary control of the group by a handful of teachers. They pushed people from the community and from prayer because the classes changed the nature of the prayer experience. They polarized discussion and praying, making performance appear second best and analytic considerations primary. They pulled aesthetics out of interpretation, and interpretation out of praying. The constituents of prayer were further broken apart. The retreat discussion reflected a separation between community and praying. The classes only further disengaged prayer, community, and interpretation. Prior to the prayer classes, Minyan members had reflected on the problematics of their prayers. Prayer seemed meaningless. But during the prayer classes, prayer was not worth doing at all for the majority of members. Doubt was tolerable, but abandoning prayers spelled the group's end.

Minyan members had no interest in reflecting on their prayer classes. They simply moved back to the Minyan they had created, a carefully controlled, weekly performance that emphasized the continuity between prayer, community, and interpretation, synthesized by aesthetic performance. Indeed, the Minyan moved back to performance as the primary focus for their shared time, which persuaded members by sentiment, and aesthetics, rather than didactics.

The conflicts of these months only underscored how precise the Minyan's organization of prayer and of social relations was. Decorum without performance, like the sacred without the social, was impossible. Their performances were consistently vulnerable to misfire because their constituents were so closely reflected and interrelated. Conflicts in community affected prayer. Their solution to this problem remained organizational. They continued to redraw the lines of their time together to harmonize the prayer constituents. Maintaining the balance between prayer, community, and interpretation and all that those processes represented, allowed them to pray. Each person was willing to sacrifice needs and expectations for the group, though that discovery was a difficult one for the Minyan. Their visibility to one another through prayer remained essential.

In the event described in Chapter 7, community itself was divided in a new way, by gender. That division raised more than personal problems to be addressed by organization. The very possibility of both Judaism and the Minyan incorporating women was raised by women members, who turned to ritual to address their exclusion. In the prayer crisis, the classroom was used to address intensely personal problems. In the women's ritual, prayer was used to address exclusion. The classes provided no identity and no possibility for resolving prayer issues. Chapter 7 will show how prayer, which appeared tenuous in so many ways, was made to carry new and contradictory messages and provide visibility for women members, and how it revealed its further significance as a source of identity formation.

Notes

1. Jews pronounce the four Hebrew letters *Yad Heh Vav Heh* as Adanoi, translated in English as "Master." This name of God was revealed to Moses at the burning bush in two passages in the book of Exodus (Chapter 3 verse 15, and Chapter 6 verse 5). These two verses are at the center of a scholarly controversy concerning whether Adanoi is a name previously known by the Jewish people, or one revealed on this occasion. The sources tend to suggest two different possibilities. Adanoi is not an accurate pronounciation of these letters. The name is so powerful that to say it correctly would bring death. In fact, rather than saying Adanoi, a Jew might simply substitute in its place, *Ha Shem,* "the name."

2. *Tzitzit* are the knotted fringes on the four corners of the prayer shawl. They are also placed on a garment worn daily by completely observant men. The latter garment is worn under the shirt and the fringes are worn exposed over the pants. These fringes are mentioned in the paragraphs of the Shmah taken from the book of Numbers (15:37–41).

3. Several men in the Minyan subsequently referred to this discussion as "foreplay." It was an interesting image for the activity that implied both its preparatory function and their sense of the intimate and even erotic nature of prayer. The pun was never made public and was treated as an off-color joke.

4. Roberto Da Mata discusses this phenomenon (1984).

5. The general sense of cultural knowledge is advocated by a number of anthropologists interested in focusing attention on cultural performances per se. Schieffelin (1985), for example, noted that in each seance that occurred, members of a New Guinea society had the opportunity to fill in additional information to a system that was rather open-ended. Hence, performance becomes the occasion not only to express cultural ideas but to elaborate and create them. That creative aspect of ritual performance is implied in Kapferer (1983) and Mac Aloon's (1984) view of performance "transforming" ritual participants.

7

Community, Visibility, and Gender In Prayer

> The logical response of a feminist to Judaism is to stop being Jewish. When you decide you cannot stop being Jewish, it is much harder.
>
> Deborah

In the previous three chapters I examined the Minyan's "prayer crisis" which appeared to develop out of members' claims that they did not "agree" with or find meaning in their liturgy. Their crisis emerged when in one particular context, prayer was cast by some members as statements requiring agreement. The ultimate solution to the crisis involved restoring prayer to a setting that integrated its constituents so that it would express and allow worshipers to remake the covenant.

At the same fall retreat, another conflict was in the making. This one concerned gender relations in the Minyan, in Judaism, and particularly in prayer. This conflict also divided the community, this time along gender lines, in a way that threatened to undermine their unity and their prayer. The prayer crisis was defined by some members who despaired that prayer could not be appropriately voiced as their own. If this first formulation of the problem was "I disagree," the other was "I am invisible." Women asserted that they were absent from the imagery and the content of prayers and, hence, could never be reflected in texts.

In the first series of events, the link between community and prayer was never articulated by Minyan members, and no one acknowledged that the prayer classes caused conflict. In the second series of events, women made explicit that community was directly problematic. In the end, however, their greater concern was with the texts of prayers, which seemed equally to neglect them. These women chose a radically different solution to their problem than the prayer classes. They created a ritual to address the problem of prayer and their connection to it. In this ritual they altered the prayer constituents. They refocused Minyan community, altered halaha, and more narrowly defined what interpretation allowed.

In the prayer crisis, the text-self relationship was undermined by disconnecting the prayer constituents and then redefining prayer as cognitive rather than aesthetic. In the women's ritual, the text-self relationship was undermined by defining prayer and community as exclusionary. Each case evolved forms of resolution that were directed to reorienting the prayer constituents in order to reformulate the connection between self and text. The events surrounding the women's service revealed how any formulation of the self in light of tradition rests on creating a tie between performance and covenant. Precisely because the women's challenge to tradition was so far-reaching, it demonstrated that as meaning became more general in Judaism, its most significant referent was to the formulation of the self through relationship to others. The strands of meaning in prayer were abstract and exclusively cosmological and increasingly reflected identity. But as this chapter's epigraph notes, when staying linked to the Jewish people is at the core of one's identity, then prayer must work to articulate change as much as to maintain tradition. Performance can create conviction only when constituents are reformulated. This chapter, in contrast to the analysis of the prayer crisis, examines how performance can resist the text, though not the tradition, and can redefine successful prayer. The cases taken together show different uses of prayer performance in the formulation of identity.

The Women's "Problem" in the Minyan

Men and women in the Minyan faced two problems concerning women. First, halaha forbade their full and equal participation. Second, though the members agreed to ignore halaha in favor of gender equality, women did not fully or equally participate during the community's first two years. The women began to experience this as a problem in the third year of the group. The first public recognition of this problem on the part of men and women came at the fall retreat. When Martha asked who would like to join her in organizing a creative service for a forthcoming Sabbath, only women raised their hands as volunteers. Men laughed loudly and nervously. Though no one said anything for a moment, everyone seemed to take it for granted that the theme of this service would surely focus on women. Issues about gender equality were prevalent in America in 1973, among Jews and in the Minyan. Martha did say soon after the laughter subsided that they would address the halahic inequality of women and men. Several members, besides the initial volunteers, met regularly over the next few months, during the period of the prayer classes, to plan an event that took place in March 1974. As unequivocal as the group was about the importance of equality for the genders, women nevertheless felt excluded and wanted to organize a Sabbath service to make that explicit.

It was to avoid that sense of exclusion that Minyan members originally made their boldest transformation of halaha.[1] From its beginning, the community included women in all ritual activities and simply ignored any halahic limitation on women's participation. The Jewish tradition is unambiguous about the role of women in public worship. They may not sit with men or be visible to men during prayer. Their voices may not be heard by men in public worship. They may not even count in the prayer quorum, the very word the community took for its own name. The absolute distinction between men and women is ever present. In Europe, therefore, the synagogue was the male domain par excellence.[2] Women attended synagogue for prayer briefly and infrequently. They never participated in study. Their religious education was minimal or nonexistent, and they were rarely taught Hebrew. They took responsibility for child care on all ritual occasions. Even their brief periods in synagogue behind the *mehitza* (the divider that separated men and women during a service) were full of the distractions that attention to children creates.

American Judaism, however, was not primarily framed by halaha, and gender relations were dramatically changed as a result of immigration. Virtually all denominations transformed male-female relations in the synagogue in the early twentieth century. In 1851, Rabbi Isaac Mayer Wise, a German Jewish Reformer, introduced radical change with integrated seating at the services of his Albany, New York, synagogue. Integrated seating was an ideal of classical Reform, but it was only realized in America. Wise emphasized the importance of what he called "family worship," obviously facilitated by integrated seating (Philipson 1907).

Throughout the twentieth century, as new denominations developed, each responded to issues of gender equality. None were as radical as Reform, but each found ways to integrate women, whether in synagogue seating or in lectures and programs that allowed men and women to participate together. The model for the integration of services and social events was American churches, where women were not ex-

This curtain is the mehitza of a first settlement Los Angeles synagogue. Women sit in pews behind this curtain.

cluded from worship, and sanctuaries were not the domain of one gender. The degree of involvement of women in American synagogues varied widely, and their participation in Reform, for example, was never equal until contemporary feminism, but the walls of male-dominated synagogues had been breached by early leaders of the developing denominational Judaism.

The Americanization of Judaism and its family orientation created an expanded educational system that trained girls and provided rituals parallel to those for boys marking the culmination of their various stages of education, particularly among the non-Orthodox. Though Jewish education was not extensive for most boys and girls in America, it was increasingly, though not fully, equal throughout the fifties and sixties. The more traditional the denomination, however, the more persistent was educational inequality. Nevertheless, Jewish girls received messages about the importance of their competence as Jews that would have been unthinkable even fifty years before.

Insofar as Minyan members wanted a traditional Jewish community, halaha stood against gender equality. They discovered, however, that changing the law was not sufficient to include women completely. Though gender-related changes constituted the Minyan's boldest break with tradition, its members felt the most vulnerable about their failure to accommodate the needs of women members. Women consistently felt like less than full participants. Over several years, many women in the Minyan came to think of themselves as invisible in the eyes of the community and the tradition. They felt excluded because men dominated the discussions and the leadership of the services. But they also felt excluded because their prayer texts and Torah readings included no women with whom they could identify. They felt doubly marginalized by community and tradition, resulting in an invisibility that was both social and symbolic.[3]

Their constant consciousness of incomplete equality was engendered by contemporary feminism, which provided Jewish women with a systematic vocabulary for articulating their anger at continued marginalization and exclusion from the public arenas of Jewish life, particularly in the synagogue. By the early 1970s, the term *Jewish feminism* had been coined to describe the efforts of women in particular, but some men as well, to address and transform Jewish law.[4]

The period of the first half of the seventies, when the Minyan began, was one of intense public activism for women in America. A contemporary women's movement had taken shape. Feminist writings were widely available. The "Judaeo-Christian tradition" presented an early target for feminist criticism and analysis. Both academic and political feminists saw in that tradition the foundation and support for the fundamental Western conceptions of male and female roles in the social and cultural order. They examined every aspect of religious tradition, from the language of prayer and theology, to the gender of the clergy, to history, to the Bible and liturgy.[5] Most American denominations responded to these concerns in the subsequent decade. Jewish feminists joined their voices in the debate. Their writing and political action were also obvious in the Jewish press as well as in the *New York Times*.

From the start, the issue of gender equality was crucial in the Minyan. Without equality, members believed they could not integrate tradition with a countercultural decorum or succeed at establishing a unique community. The men, in particular, could not explain why women would not participate more actively in the Minyan, other than the differences in their Jewish educations. At that time only one woman in the country had been ordained as a rabbi.[6] Few women in America had substantial Jewish educations because of the traditional view that discouraged educating women, and those few would have been unlikely to participate in this Minyan because of its liberalism. Rather than altering Judaism, as had been their hope, it seemed that the Minyan was replicating it. They were all intermittently frustrated about why things had not changed. In the Minyan's third year, men and women came to define the problem, each with his or her own definition and solution. Though they struggled with great sincerity over those issues, their differences indicated that interiorization of prayer required different experiences for men and women. If that was the case, then community, one of their prayer constituents, was not the same for men and women. The most important function of community was to mirror the authenticity of all members' participation. Men and women had not equally participated in the Minyan, and women had begun to question their place in the community.

How the Minyan Responded to Jewish Law

When Jacob and Mark had their first meeting to discuss the Minyan, they invited a woman student who was active in Hillel. She never became involved, but offered some ideas and participated briefly in the planning. They involved a woman immediately because it seemed evident to them that women would be equal partners in the Minyan. Jacob had attempted to organize a minyan two years previously, and the male and female students had insisted on separation and inequality of the sexes, because of halaha. Jacob was uncomfortable with this attitude and was somewhat relieved when the group stopped meeting. They failed to recruit ten men so that they could form a minyan. According to tradition, of course, women could not be counted.

The original participants at Minyan planning meetings finally discussed Jewish legal issues about women at their third session. Jacob described the tense moment of public decision.

> I think the Gold brothers raised the question, "Did we want women to be full members?" Paul came out very strongly opposed to it and said he could not be in a minyan where women were full members. My fear was that because both of them were valuable members, people would give in to keep them. The exact opposite happened. People were very firm. No one argued with him I think. They just said, "This is very important to me and that's how I want it to be."

The result was that the brothers left the group. They stated that there were many deviations from custom they could agree to, but they would not reject laws that forbade women's public participation. The new Minyan had lost essential participants. They were knowledgeable Jews and fine hazanim. The Minyan's early members never formally voiced their commitment to equality. Jacob noted that no one made strong ideological statements about their beliefs or aspirations for the new group. Though a fundamental premise of the group, it was rarely verbalized. Susan, a Minyan founder and undergraduate student, described why equality was a given of the community.

> Near the end of the Minyan's first year I traveled in Europe and worshiped in synagogues where it did not seem particularly unusual or wrong to sit separated from men and not be able to participate. But because we created the Minyan ourselves, it would have felt strange and wrong to have built inequality in, despite the halaha.

Without rancor or recourse to a developed set of principles, Minyan members followed a general sense of what was appropriate to them as Jews. They created an egalitarian minyan built on a tradition in which such equality was unthinkable. As such, their radical decision was treated as what I have referred to as an "organizational" issue. They simply appropriated a traditional male status for women. Women were made full participants. Just as there could be two hazanim, there could also be a new group of people—women—allowed to participate fully.

The direct result of this organizational, as opposed to ideological, approach was, in effect, to treat women like men, hence neutralizing the gender of both. As a result both men and women were invited to wear all prayer garments, use all prayer gestures and participate in all worship. Women acquired the symbols associated with males and clothed themselves with them. The group's intent was not to make women men, but to set aside the questions of gender and keep halaha basically intact.[7] Maintaining the tradition was the essence of the organizational solution, and it was one that reflected what Jewish feminism, indeed feminism in the early seventies, called for. But its effect was experienced differently by men and women, making it virtually impossible for women to interiorize prayer.

Integrating Women

The Minyan's first years abounded with examples of women's apparently successful integration. Ideological polemics on equality were absent. Rather, the rituals and roles performed by women spoke eloquently for what the members believed an egalitarian Judaism should be. For the first time in their lives, many women put on prayer shawls and skull caps historically associated exclusively with men. Many women, for the first time in their lives, said Torah blessings, putting them physically close to a sacred object. Religious activities familiar to any preadolescent boy became accessible for the first time to women who were already in their twenties. These women expressed awe, pleasure, anxiety, and appreciation.

One Sabbath early in my fieldwork, I watched a woman receive an aliyah (Torah blessing) and put on a prayer shawl for the first time. Miriam indicated at the start of the Torah service that she would like to say one of the blessings at the Torah. Though she lacked a formal Jewish education, she had participated in innumerable Sabbath services as a young child in Latin America and in college at her university's Hillel. In addition, she had attended the minyan for eight months. She was called to the Torah by her Hebrew name, which she had told to the gabbai (organizer of the Torah service), and went up to the bimah where the Torah was read. Jay, who was the Torah reader that Sabbath, explained all the behavior required for saying the Torah blessing. Such public prompting in the middle of a service was not unusual in the Minyan. First, Jay asked Miriam if she wanted to put on a tallit. (Some in the Minyan believed that no one, either male or female, should bless or be near the Torah without one. Others disagreed). When Miriam said

"Yes," he helped her put it on. Jay then showed her how to perform the Torah blessing. He demonstrated how to put the fringes of the tallit to the first word on the Torah scroll to be read and then to bring the fringe to her lips to kiss it. He showed her where to stand while he read and at what points to recite the blessings: Prior to his reading, she was to say:

> Bless the Lord, the blessed one.

(The community responded with the second sentence she repeats.)

> Blessed be the Lord who is blessed for all eternity. Blessed art Thou, Lord our God, king of the universe who has chosen us from among all peoples and has given us His Torah. Blessed art Thou, Lord, giver of the Torah.

Following Jay's chanting of one section of the Torah she said:

> Blessed art Thou, Lord our God, King of the universe who has given us the Torah of truth and planted among us life eternal. Blessed art Thou, Lord, giver of the Torah.

Miriam did as instructed, saying the blessings in English, though in the Minyan as in normative Judaism, they are most often chanted in Hebrew. After the Minyan service Miriam said to me:

> I have heard people say those blessings literally hundreds of times. But as I got close to the scroll, I suddenly felt very apprehensive. Then, as I did all those things that were at once familiar and new, I felt I might cry. I was unprepared for what a moving experience I would have.

Miriam, without any knowledge of Hebrew, found her participation powerful despite how commonplace the event was for her as an observer. In her switch from audience to actor she experienced the intensity of engagement. Clearly direct participation heightened her sense of involvement with ritual activity.

For women who came to the Minyan with a Jewish education from homes where observance and tradition were well established, the Minyan presented the opportunity to acquire and use skills never previously allowed. Women became activists in synagogue worship as their fathers and male relatives had been, but they never imagined it would be possible for them. Women would, for the first time, publicly lead services, read from the Torah, and chant special books of the Bible associated with Jewish festivals. They used the skills that mark an educated Jew. These more educated women, however, often commented on their intense anxiety around performing these skills. Before the Minyan service began one January morning, for example, Ruth told Terri how nervous she was about reading from the Torah that day. Terri nodded her head, corroborating all the symptoms. Ruth said:

> I'm so nervous this morning. But the Shabbat morning nervousness is different than the nervous stomach I have all week long after I volunteer for the Torah reading for the next week. Now I have the "morning of" aches which aren't nearly as severe as the five minutes before going on panic.

These symptoms seemed extreme. Ruth and Terri had Jewish educations. In fact, Ruth was a rabbinical student at the local Reform seminary. She returned to the Minyan after her first year of rabbinical school, which she spent in Israel. She was from a minimally observant Jewish home and became involved in Kelton Hillel activities when she was an undergraduate. Inspired by Jacob, increasingly interested in Jewish observance and prayer, she decided to become a rabbi. Yet she felt very aware of "how much more the men know." She did not want to embarrass herself publicly. As a female rabbinical student she was constantly aware of her minority status, and she was concerned about becoming a competent rabbi.

Terri grew up in a suburban Los Angeles, Conservative Jewish home. She was in her mid-twenties and a nursery school teacher in a local Jewish synagogue. She received a Jewish education, but was prohibited from participating in synagogue leadership of services because she was a woman. In the Minyan she was one of the women most likely to volunteer to lead a service or to read the Torah. Despite her apparent competence, she still expressed overwhelming anxiety about each role. She did not call herself a feminist and always refused, with horror, to put on a tallit, which she saw as a male garment. Nevertheless, she wanted to be an active participant. Earlier she had attended the hasidic center in Kelton, but finally left, frustrated by her inability as a woman to participate fully.

Certainly the embarrassment of public correction of mistakes during the Torah reading is awkward. However, I heard poorly practiced men read Torah who were corrected constantly, and none of them expressed such anxieties. Some of the younger men were intimidated by the prospect of reading publicly, but every woman in the Minyan articulated real fear. They always presented themselves as anxious newcomers to Judaism, whether or not their command of Hebrew was excellent and despite the aspirations of some to the rabbinate. Jews all of their lives, their roles in the Minyan were new. In the Minyan they were more than members of a synagogue sisterhood, or even participants in an adult education class; they were full participants, and none of them had seen Jewish women fully participating in prayer. At a point in American history when women were being made conscious of their right to equality, as they assumed those rights, these women found themselves struggling with the intimidating power of the tradition. There were occasions when they felt like outsiders to the Judaism they felt was important to their own identity. That outsider status must have only been heightened by their need to assume traditional activities and symbols that had been associated with men.

The successful integration of women into Judaism, as well as the Minyan, was highlighted by a birth ritual in 1973, near the Minyan's second anniversary, in honor of the first baby born to active Minyan members. The ceremony enforced the community's sense of itself as both unique and unequivocally committed to gender equality. The child's parents, Michael and Ellen, were Minyan founders. Michael, a Kelton University professor in the natural sciences, was the Minyan's strongest spokesperson for tradition and halaha. He was the least compromising, though committed to equal rights for women. His wife had no Jewish upbringing or training. When she married Michael she found herself responsible for a kosher kitchen, for observing the Sabbath, and for participating in worship. The Minyan proved an excellent compromise for them. It was Ellen's lack of Hebrew fluency that led Jacob to suggest English praying and to establish the "office" of English hazan.

When Ellen gave birth to a girl, they decided to ritualize her birth far more extensively than is usually the practice among traditional Jews. The normal custom is to simply give a daughter a Hebrew name on the Sabbath following her birth during the Torah service at the synagogue. The child, rarely present, is given a blessing and her name is announced. The father is invited to bless the Torah in honor of her birth. This celebration pales by contrast with the rituals that mark the birth of a son. His Hebrew name is given on the eighth day following his birth at his *brit milah* (ritual circumcision), which is followed typically by a large and lavish party for friends and relatives.

The distinction in ceremonies is related to the reproduction of gender roles within Judaism. The circumcision is the sign of the continuing covenant made between God and Abraham. Hence, the ritual not only names the boy but brings him into the ancient relationship established between God and men. Women have no ritual that marks their relationship to God. The baby-naming ceremony has no ritual significance beyond the naming. One may find proof for this difference in the blessings bestowed upon each child. At the brit milah, the community wishes that the parents will "rear their son" to marriage, to study, and to the performance of good deeds. The wish for the daughter is that she be reared to marry and to do good deeds; there is no mention of study, the most significant responsibility of the mature Jew. The new ceremonies that were being developed for girls in the early seventies did sometimes address the issue of covenant, in addition to acknowledging that the daughter born was worthy of celebration.

Michael and Ellen made their daughter's naming a major Minyan celebration. In addition to giving her name during the Torah service, they asked the members to communally recite biblical Psalms. These passages formed an acrostic derived from the first letters of the sentences spelling their daughter's Hebrew names. Following the service Michael and Ellen hosted a festive lunch and invited the whole Minyan.

One month after the birth, the child's parents invited Minyan members to an adaptation of the ceremony *Pidyon ha Ben,* the redemption of the first born son, for their daughter.[8] Upon introducing the ceremony, the *Pidyon ha Bat,* redemption of the daughter, to all his assembled friends Michael said:

> Our daughter was as important to us as a son at her birth. After living with her for thirty days, her importance is more so. Therefore, we could not imagine not celebrating her birth in exactly the same way.

Their ceremony, except for gender references, was identical to the redemption ceremony for a son. Michael made a statement that explicitly appealed to the need for equality despite the dictates of halaha. That statement, and the ritual itself, were more powerful because of their association with people who most firmly upheld the Jewish tradition.

The Results of Women's Integration

Events such as these suggested that women members had found an ideal community. They were free to participate as equals. Publicly, however, women tended to be silent; women privately complained to one another that they felt silenced because they were overshadowed by men. Though the women founders were a crucial part of the Minyan fabric, for a number of reasons they were not aggressive participants. As new members joined, they commented on women's minimal participation and silence. Jacob summarized women's involvement during the first year in the community when he said:

> That was also a problem the first year, the place of women. Yes, of course women were equal. But it became very clear that first year that women were not participating in discussions in the way men were. Some men participated more than others, but almost all the women did not participate. There were no women who knew as much as some of the men. There were just no women with enough education.

Jacob presented the standard analysis of why women did not participate actively. They could not because they were not sufficiently educated. They were at an inevitable disadvantage. At the same time, and privately, women acknowledged the difference in their knowledge, but thought more was at work. They felt they could not compete with men and were not given the opportunity to participate actively. Like the larger culture in which they lived, they felt silence was expected from women, otherwise men would work harder at listening to them. For example, one woman member led a controversial discussion about the value of the laws of keeping kosher, for which she believed she was aggressively attacked by male traditionalists. The participants in this conflict did ultimately discuss the incident and dispelled lingering bad feelings. Nevertheless, women remembered that incident and did not want to be open to that kind of aggressive conflict if their position was unacceptable to some men.

The membership explosion that transformed the Minyan at the close of its first year brought with it two new women who became different kinds of participants. Beth and Martha not only shared a Conservative Jewish background, but had the interest and competence to lead services. Martha was Hebrew hazanit (female form of hazan) at the second Minyan she attended. At the close of the service she remembered: "I was surrounded by people congratulating me. 'Gee I'm really impressed,' they said. 'I'm glad you are a woman and you did it.'" She had not been the first woman to lead a service, but by the Minyan's first

FIGURE 5

Women Participants in the Women's Service

Name	Joined Minyan	Occupation	Religious Background
Miriam	1972	graduate student	unaffiliated with synagogue
Susan	Founder	graduate student	Zionist
Ruth	Founder	rabbinical student	Reform
Terri	1972	nursery school teacher	Conservative
Beth	1972	graduate student	Conservative
Martha	1972	graduate student	Conservative
Debo-rah	1973	rabbinical student	Reform
Nan	1973	graduate student	Conservative
Jean	1973	secretary	Reform
Sarah	1973	professor	secular
Ellen	Founder	office worker	Reform

anniversary her ritual role was still an event. Beth and Martha were interested in feminist issues, and Beth in particular considered herself a Jewish feminist and wore a tallit, one of the first women to do so consistently.

Throughout the Minyan's second year, they were joined by a growing number of women with ritual skills and interests in more active participation in the Minyan's religious life. In this period Terri joined and regularly took several offices. Women who joined with minimal knowledge, such as Miriam, were often motivated to try to acquire skills or to take honors and roles because they were identified as feminists. They were consciously creating a new pattern of religious life for Jewish women. The women without higher Jewish education often had secular ones. Miriam, for example, was pursuing a doctorate in religious studies and led impressive discussions about Torah portions from the point of view of her scholarship.

In 1973 and 1974, three more women joined the Minyan (see Figure 5 for women Minyan members). They expressed their feminism more boldly. While different in many ways from one another, their shared commitment to feminism, to a focus on women, and a concern for women's participation in Judaism was widely discussed. Deborah had just moved to Kelton to begin her third year at the Reform seminary. She had lived in Israel and New York and moved to Los Angeles to join a boyfriend of many years. She attended an Eastern undergraduate college where she majored in religious studies, and chose to begin rabbinical training and to become one of a tiny number of Reform women rabbis. While participating in the Kelton Minyan, she also acted as a rabbi-intern at Kelton Hillel where she worked with Mark and Jacob. Like Jacob, she too was influenced by Mark's more traditional Judaism and considered him one of her most important teachers. As a woman rabbi, she was conscious of being a "role model" for members. She was a relative newcomer to traditional Judaism because she was raised as a Reform Jew, yet as a rabbinical student, she believed she represented the tradition.

Nan came to Kelton to study music as a graduate student. She had lived in the Midwest, grew up in a Conservative home, and attended religious school and Jewish camps. She was interested in acting as hazanit and Torah reader. She was also concerned that women be active participants in the Minyan and was committed to the Minyan as an egalitarian community. She frequently expressed these opinions publicly.

Jean joined the Minyan with no Jewish education. She was waiting to enter law school, and in the interim she worked as a secretary at Hillel. In the Minyan she had become romantically involved with Harvey. Such liasons were infrequent. Her intermittent participation emerged out of her interest in understanding the tradition that was so important to Harvey. She brought feminist issues to the Minyan in order to make the tradition consonant with her own life.

A fourth woman joined the Minyan who was to become actively involved for the academic year 1973–74. Sarah was on the Kelton University faculty as a professor of Yiddish. She had moved from New York, where, as the child of Holocaust survivors, she was raised as a secular Jew. She introduced Yiddish material to the Minyan, including a number of women's prayers. She did not identify herself as a feminist, but was nevertheless interested in changing Jewish law to allow men and women equal participation.

The Minyan women active from 1973–75 represented a wide-range of Jewish educational backgrounds and aspirations. They were representative of the same variation in Judaism as the men. They nevertheless shared a more intense concern about the place of women in the Minyan.

These overtly feminist members led Torah discussions whose topics increasingly focused on "female role models in the Bible" and "a lack of female imagery in texts." In winter 1974, when the Minyan had been meeting for two years, Torah discussions on women in the Bible were initiated by women on the average of once a month. In addition, some women frequently shifted the discussion topic to include women. The Minyan's feminists kept women and their place in the tradition a central concern. And other Minyan members acknowledged their significance by entering into exchanges and discussions.

In January, for example, Nan led a Torah discussion in which the whole group participated. She focused on the verses in Exodus that tell the story of the infant Moses surviving the Pharoah's command to kill all male Israelite babies. She commented:

> This passage is unusual. The mother and sister of Moses, as well as Pharoah's daughter, are all very positive models. They are courageous and act independently. They are compassionate. Though enemies, the Israelite and Egyptian women cooperate. Perhaps their roles are so positive because of their association with Moshe [Moses]. Because they preserve the greatest leader of the Bible, the normal criticism and contempt for women becomes approval.

In February Beth led one of the two women-led Torah discussions that month, again on the book of Exodus. She took a single phrase as the subject for her discussion, "God is a man of war." She remarked:

> We face a definitional problem in these words. The attributes of God are male. God himself is referred to as male. We know God has no gender. Yet we think of God in male terms. War is not associated with women. The Bible alienates me, constantly causing me to be aware that I am after all not like God. I do not share the attributes or images associated with God.

These comments were typical in 1974. Several women brought a persistent set of questions about the tradition and their own place in it to discussions. They scrutinized the texts and made their scrutiny public rather than private. "Who were the women of the Bible?" Feminism had affected members' participation by providing a vocabulary and a series of questions through which traditional texts were to be studied.

The Minyan was beginning to feel and look like a different group. The increasing presence of women in the Minyan led one male founder to comment in 1974:

> There was even a time, by the way, when I had the feeling that the women were going to take over the Minyan. They had become so

> together and so confident, and so many of them could do so many different things, that if one took a count of who in the Minyan could fulfill all the offices there might be more women than men.

Women appeared to be better integrated into the group.

An actual count of who held offices for nine months in 1974 does not reveal a group dominated by women. From January to October, forty-two men and women took roles in Sabbath services, ranging from bringing food to reading the Torah. Twenty-five of that number were men and seventeen were female. Men, however, dominated the two most important offices, Hebrew hazan and English hazan. For thirty-five services, including Sabbath morning, three additional festivals, and one extra Sabbath evening service during a retreat, twenty-six males and only nine females served as Hebrew hazan. The ratio improved only slightly for the office of English hazan, where no special Hebrew skill is required, and the occupant is less responsible for leading the service. Men occupied that role twenty-four times and women only eleven. The thirty-seven offices occupied by women were assumed by only ten of the fifteen to twenty-five women members in the entire group. But eighteen of the twenty to twenty-five different men occupied the fifty offices taken for the various worship services. More men were likely to volunteer for more offices in the Minyan.

Participation in discussion marked the male-female difference more strongly.[9] Most Minyan participants thought that men were more vocal and visible in discussions than women. My earliest impressions of the Minyan recorded in field notes repeatedly mentioned the virtual silence of women in discussion. And when a trip to Kelton brought one of my faculty advisors from the University of Chicago to the Minyan, he quietly asked me at the end of a discussion, "Aren't the women allowed to speak?"

By 1974 it seemed as though women volunteered for many offices. Their participation widened in comparison to the Minyan's first two years. New female members made it clear that women could be active. But the group was by no means equally led by women in a formal or informal sense. The Minyan's unquestionable commitment to equality simply had not been realized. The silence of women could not be associated with the simple fact that they were not sufficiently educated, because an increasing number were. Relations between men and women seemed to have an effect on who would or could speak. The very perception by men that women were dominating, when they so clearly were not, indicated that the visibility of women was held to be unusual, despite their commitment to it.

Gender Emerged: Women Spoke up

Even in the Minyan's first year, its reticent founding mothers began to complain about the group's domination by men, just as men were expressing disappointment over the paucity of competent women to take key roles. There was a perpetual, if unarticulated, dissatisfaction on the part of men and women over gender-related issues. Overtly they all agreed they wanted equality. But there were diverging explanations for their failure.

Women members met occasionally from 1971–1973 to talk with one another about their Minyan experiences. They brought their concerns to the Minyan services in 1973 as they led discussions on gender issues. Finally, following the fall retreat in 1974, as noted above, they organized a Sabbath service devoted to the themes of women, gender, and Judaism. Their discontent took shape in these discussions, and their ultimate—if for them unsatisfactory—solution was to use the forms of the tradition to present their view of the situation. They moved from anger at individuals, to criticism of Jewish texts, to conducting a ritual. In each instance they defined the problems and made their compromises with other women. In conflict and compromise, women were the vocal and visible actors on a stage they together defined as authentically Jewish.

At the end of 1972, some Minyan women met at Rachel's home to talk about the community. Susan, Ruth, Linda, and Ellen remembered meeting and each other's presence. Ruth in particular emphasized a situation she was finding intolerable. She recalled saying:

> I don't feel taken seriously in the Minyan. We are under-valued and not listened to. Whose voices dominate the discussion? Who does everyone pay attention to? It is the men and the most traditional ones. Sometimes we are simply talked over.

Not everyone agreed. Rachel said:

> I think we are heard less because we know less. We must study more, learn more, and then I believe we will be included. I agree that there are problems, but I think we can solve them.

Ellen added: "But I am tired of everything being dominated by a few people. Why should only the tradition matter? We have other things to say." Susan looked back on the meeting as a "complaining session." She agreed with the sentiments expressed, but said: "We never did anything. Perhaps it was the lack of energy or over commitment. Maybe we really didn't know how to proceed. So things went back to the way they were."

Women members were not able to employ the two typical Minyan solutions to solve their problems. They could not alter halaha; that had already been accomplished in the decision to make men and women equal. And they could not turn to an organizational solution because an appropriate one did not seem readily available. Until they conceived their creative service, they expressed their dissatisfaction in two ways: They complained to one another, intensifying their own bonds; or they complained to the whole group in textual discussions by persistently pointing out the presence of gender and the exclusion of women.

The effect of both strategies on their participation was to further separate them from the texts and the community. If every text had to be scrutinized and interpreted in light of the contemporary exclusion of women, the result was to shatter the personal meaning of their texts. Even a generalized tradition failed to account for the lives of women. If the community was persistently polarized around gender, it could not effectively move its members into covenantal relationships. A new reflection between halaha and community was being articulated. Without women in the tradition, the presence of women in the community could not be sufficient. Though the community attempted to create an ungendered Jew, the texts persisted in imagery and attitudes that were quite gender specific. Women felt a double invisibility. Again, they experienced prayer as external to the self because of conflicts in the community, as well as within the texts. These conflicts, however, were gender specific and implied that some in the group could not be connected to texts, while others could, solely because of gender.

Their initial strategies for addressing their alienation only intensified it. Women made no particular demands to this point, and no one left the group over the issue, but as a result of the Torah discussions, gender remained constantly present. Simply praying made none of these issues disappear. To the contrary, the more they talked about gender, the more impossible it seemed to remedy the situation.

The women, however, found a temporary solution to their conflicts. It developed from the ties they made to one another on the occasions they complained about the group and from their shared positions during Torah discussions. Women members found in one another appropriate reflections and guarantors of the authenticity and possibility of a Judaism that included women. The community constituent, essential to Minyan prayer, was being redefined by women. The whole community was crucial to prayer, but a "subcommunity" was emerging that was equally significant. If one saw oneself as authentically Jewish through seeing others at prayer, then no group was more important to that end for women than other women. The more concerned the women became with Judaism and their place in it, the harder it was to leave the Minyan: few alternatives existed that maintained traditional Judaism and also offered women equal rights. Women within the Minyan became essential mirrors for one another.

The Minyan, then, simultaneously pulled and pushed women between a new and heightened visibility and an overpowering invisibility. Because Jewish women's activities were redefined in the Minyan, women members expressed a special joy in fully participating in Judaism. Yet placing themselves in a tradition where gender equality, if it existed, was in an unacceptable form for these American women, they also found themselves overlooked and invisible. Judaism idealizes scholarship and learning and defines the learner as male. A woman may facilitate her husband's or son's training, but only in rare cases has a woman herself been a scholar. The Jewish legal system directs a great many of its most important commandments to men. That the equality of women had to be negotiated within Judaism was problematic for any woman who saw herself as a full and active participant in society. As Rachel said: "We struggled with finding a valid way to live as Jews within a male-oriented and dominated way of thinking about God and ritual. Besides the home, how else can we find a valid way of saying I am a Jew?" Rejecting the facilitator identity, these women found no compatible image of themselves in the Torah, in the liturgy, or in the texts where one might find an ideal self defined.

Of course no one in the Minyan looked exclusively to the Jewish tradition for definitions of themselves. None conformed without compromise to Jewish law. The legacy for these American Jews was a pluralistic one. The American experience of Jewish denominations has revealed that there are many legitimate ways to be a Jew. However, that is not the case for women. During the childhoods of Minyan members, women were not public figures even in the most liberal denominations. Women simply lacked the adaptations of the tradition available to men. The liberalization of Judaism fell short of providing women a public vision of themselves.

With the strong motivation provided by feminism and the real desires of female and male members, the Minyan was nevertheless to be an alternative to what American Judaism had offered women. The members were committed to an equality that would make all of them visible, active, public participants. Women would be assured of their visibility as members of the community by virtue of their participation and equal expectations. The Minyan was to do even more than create a community of equals; Jewish worship would be the stage on which men and women could enact identity, their deepest values and commitments, their obligations to Jewish law and God. On that stage women were to be adult Jews. Members of the prayer quorum, they were clothed in the visual symbols of maturity, like the tallit. They would also gain *symbolic visibility.* They would be reflected in the tradition itself, not just in the community. They were subjects in Judaism as they never had been before. Like men, they would be "ungendered" participants in Jewish life.

Beneath statements such as Martha's, "I feel very grateful to the Minyan," or Susan's, "We wanted everyone to see how a minyan could be," was the unarticulated belief that in the Minyan women could be Jews as they could be nowhere else. They were seen for the first time. Certainly as women, but in all their various struggles with the tradition, these members found a setting where they felt central. Due to these heightened expectations, the women found their marginality, as it was increasingly discussed and noted by women in the Minyan, intolerable. To complain to one another or to lead discussions wasn't yielding what they wanted. They wanted a tradition that made room for them.

The relationship between the symbolic invisibility of women and their own interior sense of Judaism was addressed by noted Jewish feminist Rachel Adler, who has written eloquently on this subject:

> My dilemma is that the very Judaism which gave me some names which truly reflect for me God's holiness and my own, and some frames for experience which truly reflect my spiritual experience, also can demand of me that I desert my place in order to encounter God in the place of man. When I stand to hear the Ten Commandments, when I pray for the proclamation of the fatherhood of God and the brotherhood of man, when I study cases of rape and seduction in light of whether a woman's *ketubah* (marriage contract) is reduced, then I must desert my place and imagine myself a man standing at Mount Sinai or studying my text. And then it is not I who am encountering God at all—it is an imaginary being, a dream person, the person who prayed in wholeness in the section of

the shtiebel where she never set foot. And this way madness lies (1983, 24).

As Adler notes, there is a tension between one's personal feelings for Judaism and how the tradition regards women. Such invisibility certainly occurred in the Minyan. The women were limited and often silent participants. The texts excluded or minimized them. Discussions led by Deborah, Sarah, and Beth made clear again and again that the historical models for Jewish women were not respected for their integrity or intelligence, but for their relationship to certain men. They kept searching for a woman they could emulate.

By 1973 many Minyan women concluded that their social roles in the group and their symbolic representation in the texts were connected. They were Minyan marginals and traditional religious marginals. They sought a Judaism capable of communicating some sense of who they were, goals for who they might be, and images of a past they might have wanted to live. They wanted the tradition to do for them what they believed it did for the male members they admired. They wanted to feel comfortable in it, assured by it, made human beings through it.

Lacking that, they made themselves visible by making gender an overt category of Minyan life. In discussions and conversations with one another, they simply noted the existence of gender as a Jewish category. Acknowledging gender was the first step. In a group committed to equality, the women did not so much note its absence as decry its impossibility. How could women be equal if their reality as women was unacknowledged? "Maleness," tradition, and Minyan leadership all became associated. Because these women cared deeply about their Judaism, which Minyan membership embodied, they struggled with a way to transform the equation.

These women were drawn to one another not because of friendship or a feminist ideology; they were simply the ones who shared the unique experience of Jewish womanhood. They were more than cocommiserators; they were each other's most effective mirror image of what Jewish women could be. There was no other place where they could find a model for a pious woman, who wore a prayer shawl, read from the Torah, or wondered what a feminist Judaism would be. They were not even primarily concerned with paving the way for younger women. They were focused on themselves in the present. Jacob sensed this relationship when he told me:

> The first year the women felt they were being excluded. It was unfortunately dealt with as a women thing rather than knowledge. The women did something about it themselves, and also other women came into the Minyan that had knowledge. Martha was the first, and Beth as she knew more and felt more secure. Terri was also important. Then Nan and Paula came and I sense they are important to the women because of their own knowledge. They might be less apparent to men or the group as a whole. But Rachel has spoken of them both very positively and other women too. Their strength as women has been important to other women in the Minyan, and their involvement in feminist things on the outside too.

Women members never chose to leave the Minyan community or form a permanent subgroup. Nevertheless, with women they engineered the compromises between the tradition and their own lives. As individuals they joined the Minyan to create a particular type of Judaism. However, only through the presence of other women could any particular woman remain visible as an authentic participant. Their effort at being equals, being competent and authentically Jewish, required community reflection. Men simply could not provide that. However, as men, particularly those associated with traditional Judaism, were crucial to anchoring the Minyan to halaha, their approval remained essential. Because the task of Minyan members was to reflect halaha and find in it an image of themselves, women depended on both men and women to provide the community constituent for prayer. Nevertheless, each gender provided a different sense of community for that task. Because each gender was essential, these women never separated from the group, nor demanded any other changes around gender beyond those agreed upon by all.

This important function of community within the Minyan, and for female members in particular, indicates that identity is achieved only through such reflective relationships. The Minyan's linking of covenant and community firmly located social relations within sacred ones, because the power and authority of the sacred was generated within the community. Social psychologist George Herbert Mead wrote in the 1930s about this irreducible core of human relationships. Mead argued that the individual experiences him or herself only "indirectly" from the "standpoints" of other group members, or from the "generalized standpoint of the social group as a whole" (1934, 138). The self is the product of the unique "I" and the "me," which is produced out of the encounter with the other. The self Minyan members wanted confirmed resulted only from interactions with others who recognized the legitimacy of the Judaism he or she practiced. Insofar as interiorizing the text grew out of encounters that produced the "me" through contact with "others" recognizing the self's legitimacy, identity could only flourish in self-reflecting community. The community could withstand threats to the legitimacy of their Judaism only because they could authenticate one another. The issue of gender and Judaism put that possibility in question for the group as a whole, while at the same time it intensified the ability of women to do that for one another. Women, as newcomers to the tradition, were particularly vulnerable to the "standpoints" of the others. From traditional men they received a sense of their authenticity, yet failed to feel entirely legitimate. From the standpoint of other women, they received a full legitimacy, but were also attached to the tradition, which they did not fully control.

In the prayer crisis it was evident that halaha and interpretation were directly related to community. As the community changed, halaha and discussion changed as well, vulnerable to various interpretations. In the events surrounding gender distinctions, it was also clear that community depended on halaha. Despite members' attempts to neutralize gender, halaha controlled the nature of the community. Therefore, community, as a reflecting surface for identity, then required continual redefinition. Covenant was dependent upon a community that made identity possible.

Men and Women in Conflict

As women became more vocal about the importance of women's equality, certain of the men's statements and actions troubled them. For example, on the Jewish festival Simhat Torah in 1973, the difference, indeed the opposition, between men and women who sought personal expression in Jewish tradition was starkly revealed. On that occasion, the core group of male members participated in elaborate joking. On subsequent occasions these same men repeated the jokes and continued to use the same style of humor. They not only excluded women but often made them the objects of their humor. These jokes, consciously or not, attacked all of their shared beliefs concerning who was entitled to participate. In their humor only males and traditionalists were entirely visible to the community.[10]

This humor was the most vivid, sustained, and intense on the festival of Simhat Torah. It came to focus ultimately on the Torah itself,

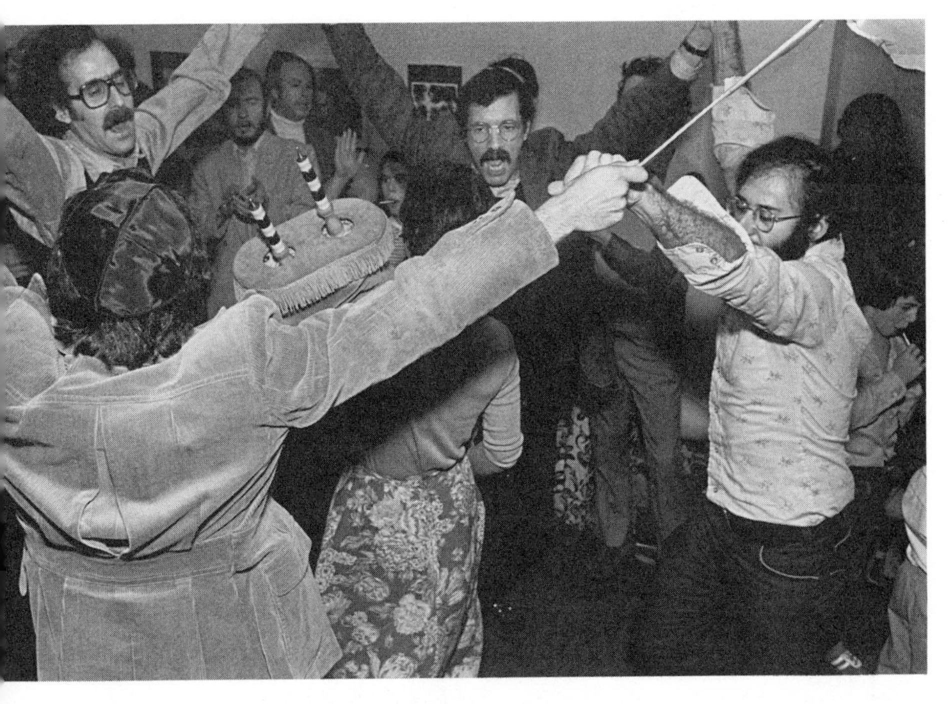

A Simhat Torah celebration. Dancing with the Torah.

which holds center stage during the festival that celebrates the completion of the annual Torah reading cycle. Like all Jewish festivals, it is observed first in the evening and then for the next day until sunset, following the normal course of the Jewish day, which begins and ends at sunset. During both the evening and morning services, all of a synagogue's Torahs are brought into the sanctuary, paraded joyously around the room, and read. The nighttime reading of the Torah is unique in the entire Jewish festival cycle. It is one of the year's happiest occasions. Festive songs are sung during the parades with the Torahs, and liquor is often consumed in the celebration. In the services that accompany the celebration, two people (men for Orthodox observance) are chosen for special honors. The one who blesses the final passage of Torah reading is called Bridegroom of the Torah (*Hatan* Torah). The one who blesses the first verses of Genesis is called Bridegroom of Genesis (*Hatan Breshit*). The Torah is symbolized as Israel's bride throughout the Jewish tradition, and this imagery is particularly prominent during this festival (Kirshenblatt-Gimblett 1982).

The 1973 Minyan celebration was, by normative Jewish standards, a particularly idiosyncratic one. It appeared rather like a traditional Simhat Torah celebration until the members who were called as bridegrooms to the Torah went up to say their blessings. These two men, Jay and Jacob, as well as Harvey, the Torah reader, and Michael, the gabbai, were the principals in all the joking events of the morning celebration. Their treatment of the Torah-bride was startling. For example, when Jay was called to the Torah he walked up to the bimah and peeked beneath "her" cover; he then leered as if he had just looked up a woman's skirt. Then Harvey explained to Jay, "She is a poor bride," in reference to the Torah's old and faded cover. In the course of the reading and blessings, the bimah was jostled and the scroll lurched. Though it was not in danger of falling, it was treated with less than customary reverence.

The men also ridiculed one another at length, joking about each other's age, education, and marital status. For example, when Jay was called to the bimah he said, "call me *Rav* [rabbi]," only to add, "I still owe the seminary a paper." When Jacob was called to the Torah, he was treated as an old man because he was one of the Minyan's older members. When the passage that pays honor to the bridegroom of Genesis was read from the Siddur, Harvey mocked and sneered as he recited the words. Most in the audience laughed loudly. Deborah did not. The longer Jay enacted the charade of the groom to the Torah bride, the more infuriated she became. Finally, leaning over to me she whispered, "Is he going to fuck it next?"

While joking is normally associated with Simhat Torah in Judaism, it is never mixed with the Torah service, and never invites the casual physical intimacy displayed that day. The women sat around the edges of the room. None of them participated actively, or joked with much gusto. Women members who were normally held in esteem by everyone were silent. Some laughed at these antics. Others did not. There was no place for women in this event. Each member was given an aliyah, as is the Minyan custom on the festival. Though the Minyan's formal commitment to equality was maintained, no one there that day would have mistaken who had the strongest claim to the community and the tradition.

Deborah, at least, was willing to question those overt commitments to equality. She discussed this service with several people privately, expressing her anger at the exclusion of women. But for her there was more than the issue of "insensitive men" at stake. "What is my relationship to the Torah," she asked, "if the Torah is the bride to the male Israel? Where do I fit in?"

Ultimately anger at male members was supplanted by anger at their texts. Both as a result of Simhat Torah and various discussions, the anger was finally given shape, and at least an ephemeral resolution, in the spring of 1974. Most of the women previously introduced joined together to organize and conduct the creative service initially proposed at the fall retreat. Planning began in the fall of 1973. In the intervening five months, some of which overlapped with the prayer classes, the issues women would address continually surfaced in Sabbath services and discussions, both because women brought them up and in anticipation of the service.

What charged both the event and the planning of it with excitement and anxiety for these female members was that they conceived, organized, and led it. As leaders of the service, they planned a ritual in which their traditional expertise would be displayed and the tradition itself would be held accountable for its failures. They would provide liturgical alternatives and make consciousness of their personal experience uppermost. The Sabbath service they planned became nothing less than a personally designed rite of passage, which simultaneously acknowledged its organizers as completely competent Jews and as thoughtful critics of Judaism. Both were essential for these women who, in 1974, as early advocates for the possible combination of feminism and Judaism, sought a place in the tradition and sought an acknowledgment of themselves as women groping to find a role in public prayer and study.

The Women's Service

As they formulated and performed a specially designated "women's service," Minyan women finally created their vision of a "gendered" Judaism, one in which they could express themselves as Jews. Accordingly, the service and the process of planning it involved a reformulation of Minyan prayer constituents. Their altered community was already in the making, as the bonds between women in criticizing the Minyan and the bonds between men in their humor demonstrated. The women's service introduced an altered halaha and another type of interpretive discussion. They used Minyan prayer to assert new relationships between Minyan members and between women and their tradition and their view of God. Their ritual, designed for a single performance, resisted traditional Judaism by "feminizing it." They chose an aesthetic form, nevertheless, that required performance to articulate Jewish identity.[11] In their service one sees how, at that point, women sought and achieved (even if temporarily) the social and symbolic visibility that allowed them to link the self and the text.

The women's service was planned under the rubric of "creative services." In the Minyan that label provided very limited license to modify the normal ritual order Minyan members had agreed upon for their Sabbath service (see Chapter 4). The first volunteers were not the ultimate planners of the event held in March 1974. Martha moved from California to New York in December. Two other women became less involved in the Minyan and one became only intermittently active. Short associations with the Minyan were not uncommon. But in the six months of inconstant planning that followed, there was always a group of three or four women willing to think about and organize a creative service on the theme of women. Three members became the core planners. Three more helped them with planning and executing the service. These six invited three other women to take smaller roles in the actual service because they had been long-time participants in the Minyan. They enthusiastically agreed.[12]

The long-awaited Sabbath morning arrived on a clear spring day. The service was held at Jacob and Rachel's house. It had been many months since the Minyan had met in the largest home of its members. But this day was clearly a special occasion. The long living room was already crowded by ten o'clock. In the crowd were many faces of women members who had belonged intermittently to the Minyan. Clearly news had spread about the service, and the curious and the enthusiastic arrived. By 10:15 A.M. almost fifty people were crammed into the house.

Some of the organizers sat placidly waiting for the service to start. Deborah, however, was in the back bedroom practicing the Torah portion she would read in full. She quickly reviewed the pages as many times as she could. Rachel acted as a self-conscious host, shepherding people to chairs and finding them comfortable spots. As the service began Jacob took over the job. Finally, everyone sat down. It was unusually quiet. The service organizers looked around the room with satisfaction. So many people had come, and so many of them were women. Nan introduced the service.

> I was terribly excited about our service. We dared to create a women's service. It raised my consciousness as it has for so many others. The planning of this Shabbat is as important as what will actually happen. We all have a lot to learn. I do not always feel I have the power to change things, and the impact of planning the service has made me feel powerful.

Then Jean added:

> All the women involved in planning the service will explain the ways they have uniquely participated. Last fall we decided that from time to time people would organize creative services. It was from that decision that the idea of a women's service emerged. I have been part of the planning since that time. The traditional service has things that I cannot relate to as a woman or as a person. I have written an English version of a modified Amidah. I wanted to humanize it and make it acceptable to everyone. I do not know Hebrew, but I did not feel it was a liability to work from the English translation. You have a copy of it. I hope you will pray it during the service.

Sarah said:

> My feelings have been different than most of the other planners'. I have not been troubled by the Siddur as others have because I suspend my judgment about what is in these words. Yet I valued the meetings in which we explored what it means to be a Jewish woman. Perhaps my conclusions are different, yet the process has been invaluable. I have contributed a *Tkhine,* a Jewish woman's prayer in Yiddish, which we will daven instead of Psalms today.

Then Ruth changed the tone, adding:

> Beth and I think this is much too somber. We don't have to be so serious. This hardly feels like the Minyan. The changes we made are simply not that monumental. I do agree that the planning process has been far more significant than the actual event. Our discussion about what to include and why it belongs there have taken up matters of halaha as well as women.

Rachel then explained:

> What happens today really should not be seen as a performance. People should consider what we might want to keep in the regular Shabbat service. We are not putting on a special event. We want to integrate these things into the Minyan.

Ellen finally added a personal and historical note:

> When we began to meet in 1971, there was some talk that women might not even be counted for a minyan. We have all come a long way. The conversations we had and the service we have created would simply have been unthinkable two years ago.

Then Jean said that Beth and Nan would be happy to explain to people who had never worn a tallit how to put one on. Beth said: "I knew what to do with a tallit because I watched the boys learn how to do this in Hebrew school. No one had ever explained to me what to do." With seriousness and care both of them showed the proper way to put on the prayer shawl. They recited the prayer one says when putting on the holy garment and explained how its fringes were used during the prayers. Finally, Nan explained that the tallit is associated with the universe because of the reference to the four corners of the earth in the prayer that precedes the verses requiring men to wear the garment. Deborah was the only person to put on the tallit at that point. The rest of the Minyan regulars had already put on their own, and no visitor expressed an interest in doing so, though several listened to the explanations. Nan was Hebrew hazanit and Jean was English hazanit.

The service planners had altered the regular Minyan Sabbath service in three ways. The alterations were, by Minyan standards, daring, as Nan claimed. They hoped that these changes would focus the group's attention on women and Judaism, that is, on the place of women in Sabbath liturgy. The first change they made was the substitution of what they called "women's forms of prayers" for portions of the traditional liturgy. They did not change all of the prayers. They deleted the three Psalms beginning the service, which Beth described as "male-defined poetry." In their place were a modern Israeli poem by a woman poet and the Yiddish Tkhine.[13] The service planners provided an alternative and freely translated version of the central liturgical prayer Amidah, though the actual Amidah remained available for praying in the Sabbath Siddur and was said by many. No other creative service planners had ever changed the Amidah. As quintessential prayer, Minyan members considered the central prayer of the liturgy beyond alteration in the Minyan.

The other changes in the service were not liturgical. They involved filling all the day's "offices" with women and altering the normal discussions. In place of the preprayer discussion, they introduced the women's service. In place of a discussion of the Torah portion, they chose three topics for groups to discuss. One concerned the language used to address God and how it is effected by gender. Another focused on how "men and women relate to God." The final one focused on how "men and women relate to Jewish symbols." Planners led all discussions. Then a discussion of the service itself followed lunch.

The Torah service was modified as well. First, a smaller than usual Torah was borrowed for the service so that all the women would be perfectly comfortable handling it. The sheer size and weight of the scroll made it difficult for most women to carry it. The women brought the Torah into the room and marched it around the reading table. Before reading it, Deborah said:

> A pause in our service.
> Time to take the Torah out of the ark.
> It's an unfamiliar pause for me.
> Usually I sit and watch my men friends approach the ark,
> Touch the Torah,
> Hold the Torah.
> Can I lift her?
> Will I know how to hold her?
> Why do I call the Torah "her?"
> Is it because the word itself is feminine?
> Or because we think of God as male
> And his gift to his people as somehow female?
> Why?
> How do I relate to the Torah,

I who have never been close to her?
The Torah is the central symbol of Judaism,
But I've hardly read from her.
The Torah is the central symbol of Judaism,
But I've hardly held her.

Her statement was affecting. There was silence until Beth, as gabbai, called people up for various honors. Then, at the conclusion of reading, Ruth lifted up the scroll as no women had been physically able to before.

The discussions followed and again everyone participated. All those present at the Minyan took the service seriously. The most traditional founders audibly and forcefully prayed in English, Hebrew, and Yiddish, the various poems and Amidah translations. Most others did as well. The service went smoothly. The women's service concluded with congratulations and great relief.

Visibility and Invisibility

The women's service was precipitated by women's deepening sense of their social and symbolic invisibility in the Minyan. They felt marginalized by the men and excluded by sacred texts. They verged on saying, but never said, that prayer was impossible. They avoided, as in the previous case, defining prayer as infelicitous. Nevertheless, the ritual had to address these issues. There were two crucial ways in which the service—its goals and methods—created the social visibility the women sought. The first was the planning process itself to which so many planners referred. They all held that the most satisfying part of the process was the planning. The rehearsal was more important than the performance. They subsequently acknowledged to me their constant awareness of, and concern for, what others would think of their service, particularly those men who epitomized tradition in the group. Deborah said: "I did this for the Minyan as a pedagogical tool, for Jay, Harvey, Jacob, and Mark. To be taken seriously by the Minyan is to be taken seriously by them."

Even the seriousness their recognition implied was less important than what the women had called the process of planning. The process represented the following to Rachel:

> We had put a lot of thought into it, had done reading and thinking and held meetings. We've come to grips with the very essence of the

Minyan and that is what is in the pages we read and reread. We took the text and came up with a point of view.

By "the process" they meant the many months of considering what their service would be; what could be excluded or included. The planning often occurred at Kelton Hillel, where Ruth, Deborah, and Jean worked. It was the subject of phone conversations and lunches, and a matter of great importance, even if it primarily transpired privately. They asked as women what words were appropriate to use in Hebrew and English for addressing God, or creating prayer images for God.[14] They discussed "the tradition," and what they wanted to ignore, chose not to ignore, or could not ignore. And though the changes made in the actual service were few, the process of making those changes had been important and well considered.

The process was, as noted, exclusively carried out by a group of women with varying ideas and concerns. Within this diversity, the "women acted out of responsibility to other women," Deborah said. With women they tried to address problems for women, and they had achieved their somewhat limited goals. They stopped complaining "as women" and began acting "as women." They planned a service that involved study, judgments, and decisions. While they were always conscious of traditional male members, men were not the sole authority for what the tradition would bear; the women planners were. Deborah, for example, very much valued her exchanges with Jean, who had little commitment to the tradition. Deborah believed she had successfully communicated to Jean why "we can't throw everything out." She liked being challenged and enjoyed being a spokesperson for tradition, a role she would not have normally taken in the Minyan.

Not only was the planning done by women, but more importantly the prayer performance was exclusively led by women. Hence, when women pointed to the importance of the "process," they implied their leadership as well. That purposeful casting of characters was critical in achieving "social visibility" in the Minyan. This service was the only one to be run entirely by women. They held not only the more typical responsibilities of English hazanit and discussion leaders, but took the other more difficult roles. Deborah read an entire Sabbath section of the Torah. Nan was Hebrew hazanit. Ruth lifted the Torah in the ritual role of *magbiah*. Of course, women had done these things occasionally, but their participation remained the exception.

At every point in the process of leading the service, a single fact was unavoidable: gender was an issue. These women held these roles as women members, not simply as members of the Minyan. They acted as women, not in spite of being women. Deborah read the Torah conscious of herself and its gender. When Ruth lifted the Torah, everyone was aware of how rarely women did this. When Beth taught people about the tallit, she recalled her feelings of being a girl on the outside looking in. Their active assertion of difference and uniqueness contradicted the Minyan's own ideology and initial solution to legal inequality: that gender would not matter. They made themselves visible by insisting on recognition of both their inequality and competency.

Afterward, Rachel said the event felt to her like a Bat Mitzva. The women's service did not focus on a "first" occasion for individuals. Rather, it focused on women as a group visibly acting as adults in the community. It was that unique event that made the service a rite of passage.[15] In achieving this social visibility, they achieved symbolic visibility as well. By increasing their competence through their creative service, the Minyan's women intensified their claims as Jews and won a place in the Jewish order of things, which normally undermines women's claims to religious maturity.

Nevertheless, their awareness of themselves as occupants of every role created conflict for the planners. One of their last controversies in planning the service revolved around the distribution of Torah honors by gender. One planner urged that only women be called up to the Torah. Others refused, arguing that "women had never been excluded by the Minyan." Their compromise made certain that more women than men would be given aliyot. The careful counting, even while refusing sweeping gestures, indicated the real importance of being seen as women throughout the women's service.

Gender was an issue in another sense in this service. The planners focused on the gender of Jewish symbols. They forced a consciousness of the presence of or absence of gender in Jewish tradition. As Beth put it after reflecting on the service:

> In the Minyan, despite equal rights, a pronounced feeling of male dominance still remains. In the past many of us attributed this to our lack of education or familiarity with the tradition, but as the women in the group became more knowledgeable, the problem did not disappear. Rather, it emerged more definitively as a feeling of exclusion from a traditional liturgy, filled with masculine imagery in the metaphors and attributes associated with God and therefore more acceptable to men.

Equality between men and women would never be possible, most planners felt, until the tradition itself had what they called "female metaphors for God," "female attributes of God," and "matriarchal figures and biblical role models." The planners described their invisibility in what they called the "symbols of Judaism." They planned their women's service to provide this missing imagery.

Jean addressed this issue in the new translation of the Amidah that she wrote, and which was offered as an alternative translation to be said in place of the traditional Hebrew prayer. As a theologically complex prayer that describes many of God's attributes and powers, Jean used her freely translated Amidah to actually reword and reformulate divine qualities. Jean frequently exchanged images. For example, in her translation she changed the phrase "God who is great, mighty and awesome" (De Sola Pool 1960, 196) to "God who is great in infinite smallness and mighty gentleness." A similar transformation of language consisted of "Thou are the rock of our life and shield of our Deliverance," (De Sola Pool 1960, 204) to "Yours are the cradling arms of life and the womb of our safe deliverance." Her feminist Amidah populated the cosmos with matriarchs where there were normally patriarchs and avoided the frequent image of God as "king," "father," and "master."

The Effects of the Service

The women's service sought visibility for the planners and other women. None of the planners believed that the traditional liturgy would be permanently changed as a result of their efforts. Nor is it clear that they wanted the normative liturgy permanently altered. Most were sympathetic to traditional Judaism, if not themselves observant, and their community rested on a general regard for Jewish tradition. Nevertheless, ritualizing a different set of images for women and hearing their new liturgy prayed by most Minyan members validated the possibility for such changes. The women's point of view was acknowledged that Sabbath. And a few months later at a regular Minyan meeting, the group agreed to alter the formula invoking the biblical patriarchs that begins many prayers, "God of our fathers, God of Abraham, Isaac, and Jacob," to include their wives. The new formula was thereafter chanted by the hazan as "God of our fathers, Abraham, Isaac, and Jacob and our mothers, Sara, Rivka, Lea, and Rachel." This formula was included in the Amidah and at prayers said at the Torah, so that it was said frequently in Sabbath prayer. No other prayer had been altered for any reason. The decision to add the matriarchs acknowledged women's needs to exist within the tradition.

No other real changes resulted. The tradition remained problematic, even if the community, by its limited acknowledgment of women's experiences, provided momentary visibility for them. The planners expressed some bitterness months later, commenting to me that nothing was carried through. "We addressed the problem," one said; "we didn't resolve it." The visibility that Judaism could give their lives was realized only momentarily. After that they returned to the struggle of being Jewish women in the Minyan, where their self-definition as women was made peripheral. The struggle was apparently worth it because the imperfect visibility the community could offer was essential to them. The ideals embodied in the struggle were shared, if only paid lip service. As Deborah said, "No one calls us girls or expects us to cook," referring to some of the more egregious stereotypes of women held by American males.

The sources of conflict and forms of resolution that led to the women's service were a virtual mirror image of the prayer crisis and prayer classes. The break between self and prayer that resulted from the retreat entirely focused members on the cognitive content of prayer, which was ultimately abandoned in favor of their return to praying. Prayer again became felicitous when the community acknowledged its shared needs and shared commitment to praying.

In the events surrounding women, members channeled their alienation from the prayers into creating an altered prayer performance for the Minyan. They changed, rather than returned to, every prayer constituent and created a rite of passage for themselves that marked a new status for women in the community. They embraced Jewish ritual forms in order to make them reflect themselves and to challenge prayer texts. Performance, in this case, heightened self-consciousness because the women planners brought "interpretation" into the act of praying. The form and content of the women's service were the product of interpretation joined with prayer. Performance allowed participants to resist the tradition through the tradition itself. As members davened, they synthesized the constituents of prayer through all the aesthetic means they normally used, but the messages were dramatically altered. Community was altered by making women the dominant figures. Halaha was directly altered through rewritten prayers. Interpretation was guided by the planners who defined the relevant questions to ask of the text. The general meaning of covenant was expanded to self-consciously include women, not to assert gender neutrality. On this occasion, aesthetics joined these altered constituents to emphasize different messages.

Those who participated in the creative service acknowledged the legitimacy of this message and of the women who organized the service, if only temporarily. Women's identities as Jews were made as much by their participation as by their being seen by the community. Not only women's actions but men seeing women as actors were critical to the formation of identity because of the different "viewpoints" they represented. Indeed, that mutual reflection is what allowed women to return to regular praying in the Minyan. Knowing that they were seen as women allowed them, although they were far from particularly satisfied, to return to regular liturgy. They remained in a group that was obviously critical to legitimizing themselves as Jews and something of their view of Judaism. A community that acknowledged these issues made it possible for these women to regard themselves as part of a covenant that was reflected in the Minyan itself.

Though the prayer crisis and the women's service were mirror images, each rested on the ability of worshipers to internalize the prayers and recreate the covenant. What differentiated these events, however, was that only the women's service used performance to modify the meaning of covenant. The women did not simply reassert the general nature of tradition; they altered and resisted it, doing the same to community. Their ultimate and painful message was that men and women could not participate in the same way in Judaism. However, in the immediate situation they wanted only to assert their legitimacy and competence as Jews and to suggest what a Judaism affected by women might express.

The women's service redefined for women a strategy for sexual equality within the nonegalitarian Jewish tradition. The women's focus on gender led them to a ritual strategy. They denied the success of the original Minyan strategy, which was to act as if there was no gender in the tradition. They demonstrated forcefully that by breaking the tradition as women, they were redefining it and reclaiming it. In their service they asserted that a redefined tradition could and should not be identical to the one embodied in the prayer book. Yet the tradition was weighty for them. Their commitment to it allowed them to break and maintain it, grow in it as adults, yet be kept invisible. They needed and wanted the tradition to allow them to be Jews. They did not find in the tradition the place for themselves that they desired.

This paradox was the given of their community life. Because traditional prayers and a commitment to generalized tradition were central to constructing Jewish lives, they, as the chapter epigraph states, put aside the easier solution of finding Judaism lacking and leaving it. Their choice of a ritual forum for their new solution was well suited to their paradoxical position. From the start, they knew that the long-term effects of their struggle in the Minyan would be negligible. Nevertheless, ritual provided a powerful setting to make a framed and circumscribed statement. It was the occasion for heightened visibility. Ritual communicated effectively, less by didactic means than by "presentational" ones.[16] It expresses a logic of simultaneous experiences in which linear relations are not so much communicated as multiple possibilities are performed. The ritual arena created by the planners powerfully presented not just the language of concerns and resolutions, but the emotions associated with the passage of time, maturity and visible presence. There were didactic discussions about women's exclusion, but, more importantly, there were performances demonstrating women's competence, which made the exclusion intolerable. The tradition was fulfilled as its inadequacies were demonstrated. The ritual embraced the contradictions and simultaneous truths of women's inclusion and exclusion.

It was not that the ritual was mystifying or obfuscating, momentarily confusing participants. Its intentions were entirely lucid. The performance aspect of the ritual allowed both women and men to be Jews and to criticize Judaism. The performance was weighted on the side of the tradition. The protests, like the new Amidah, clothed so often in the language of the tradition, ultimately maintained the tradition. Performance allowed the unity of symbolic and communal visibility, which was immediately relinquished when the ritual ended, though thereafter the visibility of women within the Minyan grew even as substantial change was put aside.

The Effects of Change on Male Members

The upheavals focused on gender, and the strategies for coping with inequality were not the issues of women alone. Men are affected by gender in religion, even as Minyan men sought to undermine the existence of gender. When women seek religious change, the impact on men is often ignored. Men may be portrayed as bastions of tradition (enemies) or silent complicitors (allies) or both. Men, as coinhabitors of the tradition, are also affected when gender is raised as an issue, when consciousness is demanded about hidden and powerful symbolism, or when tradition is found problematic for some community members.

When Minyan women expressed their changing views about the viability of the tradition for them, men had strong responses; they understood that women were challenging fundamental notions of the covenant. Although these responses often appeared in masked form, they suggested male members' real concerns, indeed anxiety, over the viability of the transformed tradition.

Male comments engendered by the women's service indicated the confusion and discomfort evoked. Beginning with the hysterical laughter on the fortuitous day when only women volunteered for the creative service and ending with the comments about the service itself, many men in the group voiced deep concern over what was happening. In a discussion that followed the women's service, participants rather than planners talked about the service, and the voices were primarily male. Most members were warmly appreciative of the effort and results. But they expressed other concerns as well. Harvey, for example, flatly stated, "When I pray I will always see God as male, through male images." Another man, whose wife had been a planner, said, "It's fine for women to see God in female images, but I don't want to do that. Men should see God in male terms."

A visitor to the Minyan that day addressed the whole issue of gender symbolism candidly when he said during one of the discussions, "Everyone knows that the Torah is female, but no one talks about it." The women aroused deep discomfort with their insistence on making explicit what in its implicit form was marginalizing. Women gained visibility by revealing their invisibility. Men maintained visibility by denying that the tradition caused invisibility, because gender could simply be removed. Women gained visibility by exposing hidden dimensions of the tradition. Men felt that the tradition was threatened for them by such exposure.

The concerns of male members were genuine. Their own needs made them oppose the solutions of the women's ritual. Men and women, then, had different stakes in the tradition and different strategies for solving problems and different visions of what their equality meant. They shared a desire for community and a tie to the imperative of a generalized tradition. In short, men had much more to lose in the total transformation of tradition than women did. Men wanted an altered but fundamentally recognizable Judaism. Through the slow process of women considering their positions in Judaism, they created other ritual forms and, as Nan said, found them "empowering."

On the occasions, such as the Simhat Torah discussed above, when the most traditional men joked in an exclusive way, their attitudes about the tradition were made clear. On other occasions when such humor occurred—Purim and during a retreat when a parody of a *rebbe's tish* was staged by Mark—they articulated identical themes.[17] Once again women as sexual beings and the entrapments of marriage and fatherhood were the subjects of their jokes. These barbs were often made through biblical references and puns or through joking dialogues. Harvey, for example, said to Mark during the tish, "Let me drink at the briss [circumcision] of your son." And Mark's retort was, "No, at your son's first," or "At Jacob's son's." Men consistently joked that others would marry before them, or that married men would have sons before them. They joked about "women's place," about prostitutes when they appeared in Torah readings, and about all the female imagery associated with the Torah.

This satirical humor recreated the status relations of Judaism that the Minyan formally eschewed. It strongly differentiated men and women. The joking, engineered by the best educated, sharply separated who could and who could not participate.

The differentiation of male and female, however, was not just a result of who participated. The key performers on all of these occasions exaggerated and linked "feminine" qualities attributed to the Torah to tradition and women. The oscillation between jokes about women and jokes "on" the Torah, in its raucous and sexualized handling, linked sexuality and Jewish tradition. Those who were comfortable enough with the tradition to ridicule it and to use it to ridicule others also portrayed women as entrappers. Women were transformed from coparticipants with men to nonparticipants in the Minyan. The tradition was transformed from generalized and malleable rules providing an outlook on life to an onerous elite formulation. The key male participants controlled and claimed the tradition, even as they ridiculed it, by controlling the satire.

They expressed their hostility at constraints and rules toward the Torah by associating it with female stereotypes. They did not accept halaha without revision. Their commitment to expressive individualism and democracy was at odds with a system of obligation. Hence, their discomfort with constraint was rationally translated in the creation of the Minyan, itself a group devoted to a traditional sensibility, yet willing to alter the tradition. Their joking emphasized the emotional power behind their discomfort with orthodoxy.

Clearly, however, the men who dominated and the ones who laughed were committed to the maintenance of tradition, albeit altered and within the Minyan. The more direct target of the humor was women or female images. Women were not coparticipants in the humor, sharing a world view in which they jointly ridiculed the world of constraints. The traditionalist males who expressed anger at constraint also articulated anger at women, who in the Minyan came to increasingly symbolize a wide range of changes in the constraining law. In the Minyan women looked like men, wearing their prayer garments, taking over the men's exclusive control of the tradition. Minyan men had two problems: first, they did not want to uphold an unchanging Judaism represented by orthodoxy. Second, however, they seemed to fear becoming part of an unrecognizable Judaism. The second was associated with women's aspirations for visibility. The men "used" ritualized humor to express their fears at what the new Judaism, cut off from all important traditional gender roles, would be. This process was not entirely conscious. For these men were committed to egalitarianism. All of them participated actively in the women's service. They were willing to be the audience the women wanted, though they were committed to a single service, not ongoing change.

Women relinquished their hopes for a true alteration of Judaism the moment their service ended. Male humor did not disappear. They remained afraid of a possible transformation of tradition that would leave them without a familiar Judaism. Their humor was persistent, if occasional. The ongoing Minyan, Sabbath after Sabbath, represented to both men and women an acceptable if imperfect consensus. It allowed most members to feel, most of the time, that Jewish tradition may be both preserved and altered. Male humor and female ritual revealed the conflicts, conscious and unconscious, in the creation of community.[18]

The Minyan's ritual and humor also revealed how maintenance of the traditional system was embedded in formulating one's own identity, so that the emotional investment in tradition was tied closely to the ability to continue to see oneself as a participant in that tradition. Their witnessing of one another's identities was vulnerable as well as essential to their lives as Jews. Humor and ritual represented opposite positions for men and women, because gender was the most difficult issue they faced in the Minyan. Where decorum met the sacred in regulating gender relations, tradition and the counterculture were on a collision course. Because the covenant itself was at stake, performance and aesthetics were used toward opposed ends: to resist and to maintain the general meaning of Judaism. Because members relied on the Minyan to authorize and authenticate their Judaism, their ability to pray together demanded their constant compromise.

Notes

1. Women's legal status in Judaism is addressed in Berman (1976), Koltun (1976), Lerner (1977), Greenberg (1981), Umansky (1979), Heschel (1983), and Schneider (1984).

2. Descriptions of male domination of the synagogue and female marginality may be found in Abraham Cahan's novel of immigrant life *The Rise of David Levinsky* (1960) and in Zborowski and Herzog (1971).

3. In their introduction, Ortner and Whitehead draw a distinction between social and symbolic representations of women (1981, 2).

4. Steven Martin Cohen (1980) outlined the history of the organizational structure of the Jewish women's movement. The two most important anthologies of Jewish feminist writings are Koltun (1976) and Heschel (1983).

5. Early writings on women and Western religions include Daly (1973), McLaughlin and Reuther (1979), Christ and Plaskow (1979).

6. A discussion of the ordination of women in Judaism may be found in Umansky (1979). Analysis of the protracted discussions and votes on ordination of women in the Conservative movement and its seminary, the Jewish Theological Seminary, may be found in Stone (1977) and Friedman (1979). The resolution concerning equality of women of the governing body of Conservative synagogues may be found in Marcus (1981, 918–20). The faculty of the seminary voted to admit women to its rabbinical program in 1983 and ordained the first woman in 1985.

7. See Prell (1983) for a discussion of an alternative formulation of this problem in classical German Reform. There, changing halaha also necessitated maintaining gender neutrality. As in the Minyan case, that neutrality inevitably favored the maintenance of male power and authority.

8. A thoughtful discussion of a number of Jewish female birth rituals, including the Pidyon ha Bat, may be found in Leifer (1976).

9. Women's silence is an issue that has interested feminist scholars and writers. Minyan women's silence is typical of Western women who are products of a cultural tradition that commended women's silence and decried participation as unfeminine. Studies in education as well as literature reveal the fact that women and girls more often than not acquiesce to that injunction. The struggle between men and women and among the women themselves about silence places them within a cultural tradition that they do not seem particularly conscious of.

10. Discussions of humor in the Minyan and its implications for their commitment to a general tradition may be found in Prell (1988). A discussion of humor and gender relations in the Minyan may be found in Prell (1987). Both articles provide more ethnographic detail about the events sketched here.

11. Heilman suggests the terms for altering and maintaining tradition, "contemporizing" and "traditioning" (1983, 62). In the case of communities or individuals attempting to live a tradition they are willing to alter, the terms may not be appropriate. For the implications of the women's ritual were quite radical, while the effects were minimal. All participants acknowleged both elements. What occurred in the ritual was part of a process, an attempt to imagine and enact real alternatives to tradition. But because the event was a ritual, it necessitated no actual change. This unique relationship to "attitudes" results in a more dynamic conceptualization than the opposition of traditionalizing the new and contemporizing the tradition. Susanne Langer, for example, saw an Indian rain dance as "dancing with the rain," rather than acting upon it ([1942] 1978, 158). The limits on the

possibility for change may be set both by a community's view of tradition and the forms through which a tradition is enacted. The real issue is through what agency does the tradition exert its power? Victor Turner provides insight into this issue in his discussion of the redressive phase of a social drama (1957).

12. A further discussion of this service may be found in Prell-Foldes (1978a).

13. The poetry was provided by Harvey, whose field was Hebrew literature. He gave the planners a poem by the modern Israeli poet Yocheved Bat-Miryam. The poem is addressed to "you," which is rendered in the Hebrew in the second person feminine. The poem's imagery is prayerlike and is critically interpreted to be speaking to God, though God, of course, is usually rendered in the second person masculine. The Yiddish Tkhine was chosen and translated by Sarah. It was called "A New Tkhine for Blessing the Candles (Specially for America)."

14. Rita Gross discusses the use of gender in liturgy or what she calls God language (1983).

15. Barbara Myerhoff might have interpreted this ritual as a "definitional ceremony," one whose point was to provide an audience to witness one's change in status or life phase (1979, 185, 222). The result of such occasions is the reiteration of collective or individual identities. Her sensitivity to the need for visibility among the elderly in a community of seniors led her to examine how ritual in general provided "reflecting surfaces." But traditional prayer, which in the Minyan was directed in part to "definitional ends," also was directed to traditional ends. Hence, the tradition dictated its form as well.

16. The "presentational mode" is a concept of Susanne Langer ([1942] 1978, 96). She argues that it is a form of nonlinear logic in which several meanings can be simultaneously juxtaposed and grasped because sense and feeling are spoken to directly through it. It communicates the meaning of the whole rather than the dissected and translatable parts.

17. Purim is the holiday in the Jewish festival cycle that is closest to a saturnalia. The Megillah Esther is read recounting a Jewish victory over the machinations of a Persian advisor to the King, who engineered a death sentence on all Jews. The victory is celebrated with masquerades, plays, a banquet, and giving charity (Gaster 1953). The rebbe's tish (rabbi's table) is a hasidic custom. The followers of a particular rabbi sit and stand around his table to share in his wisdom and food. Rank in the community is acknowledged by proximity to the rebbe at the table. These events are described in greater detail in Prell (1988).

18. These tensions have not disappeared, even though Jewish women's equality has been generally accepted by non-Orthodox congregations. Some women have continued to seek to alter or reinterpret ritual. Conservative Jews in particular have been embattled over the struggle to maintain tradition and gender equality, with men and women often defining the flexibility of tradition differently. A short time after Jewish feminism developed, both liberal and Orthodox Jews also became interested in spirituality. Hasidism attracted a small but growing number of assimilated Jews, and liberal Jews experimented with prayer and ritual. Jewish feminists have looked to feminine aspects of God as an important path to exploring spirituality. Some men have welcomed the opportunity for religious change and others have articulated fears similar to those of Minyan men. Feminist issues of the 1970s focused on how to bring women into Judaism as full participants. In the 1980s a feminist Judaism addressed not only its halahic roots, but how to shape the experience of prayer.

Conclusion

In 1985, ten years after I left the Minyan, virtually all of its members had moved from Los Angeles and the group ceased meeting. It had flourished until 1980, attracting new members and incorporating the growing number of children born to its founders and newcomers in special Sabbath programs. Mark moved to Israel permanently in 1981, having married an Israeli woman some years before. By then Harvey and Michael were pursuing academic careers elsewhere. Jay, Rob, Ruth, and Neal had rabbinical positions in other states. Beth, Doug, Aaron, and Martha were all involved in careers in New York City.

Jacob was the only founder who remained in the Minyan continuously. He and his family returned from a six-month sabbatical in Israel in 1980 to discover a dramatically different Kelton Minyan. Of the dwindling number of members who remained in Los Angeles, most had begun going to other alternative minyans in the city. One minyan in particular attracted twelve members. It was near their homes and its members were closer in age to these men and women, now long-past being students. The Minyan had a new core of a few couples, alumni of Kelton University. However, they lacked the religious skills of the founding members, and the needs of a leaderless group became burdensome for them. Despite constant effort, they could not recruit new members.

After Mark left Los Angeles and Jacob assumed an administrative position, the new Kelton Hillel rabbis began their own Sabbath minyan.

They met in the same building and an air of competition developed between them. The Kelton Minyan had lost its base of support.

In 1983 the members voted to merge with another minyan that met within an Orthodox synagogue in the area. The merger was an ambivalent one and passed by a single vote. The new group had several much needed, knowledgeable members. They also had a more narrowly defined traditional approach to prayer and Judaism. However, the Minyan's attitude toward tradition had already changed. In the transitional years from the old to the new group, newcomers abandoned the office of English hazan; they reinstituted the Additional Service on the Sabbath and a blessing for the priestly class. According to Jacob, all that these new members wanted to know with reference to prayer was, "what is the right way to do it?" He found them more concerned with "form" than "substance." Their ties to more Orthodox Jews only seemed to intensify those concerns.

By 1987 the group had disbanded. That year I spent some months, calling and writing people in Los Angeles, trying to locate the mizrach I describe in Chapter 3, the Minyan's only permanent possession. I wanted a photograph of it. Jacob was kind enough to look for it, and he did so in as many places as he could imagine, but he was unable to find it. Committed as Minyan members were to foregoing the permanent ties of buildings and formal leadership, the group left no trace behind.

The fate of the Minyan was not unusual among other such groups in the Jewish and American countercultures. Indeed, one of the founders of the very first havurah told me in a conversation in 1986 that the whole idea of the havurah movement was a failure. He asserted: "No one beyond the generation that began the havurah joined or created new ones. Where are the college-aged students turning today? They are becoming Orthodox Jews. We could only speak to ourselves." This harsh judgment would be the one that every leader of every American Jewish movement would have passed on his or her labor. Each had hoped to speak for American Judaism; none did. Leaders of every denomination have despaired as a younger generation rejected its aesthetics, its vision of the synagogue, and its idea about the proper way to be an American Jew. Just as each of these movements and denominations spoke eloquently only to its generation, so the havurah movement, with its vision and wisdom, spoke only to its own.

Nevertheless, havurot did not die. Their members created or joined egalitarian, small-scale associations throughout the years. They call themselves minyanim (plural) rather than havurot to indicate, as did the Kelton Minyan, their primary emphasis on prayer. Several of these minyanim in New York, Los Angeles, and Chicago are associated with synagogues, using their building and paying dues, but remaining autonomous within them. The younger men and women who join these groups tend to have a more traditional, less questioning outlook than the original havurah generation, which is now in its forties. All of these minyanim give women full adult status. Like the Kelton Minyan, which was among the first groups to do so, women are simply incorporated into the male role. Tradition is preserved even in a radical alteration of it.

What the havurah movement's creators did understand was a desire among Jews for religious experience on a new scale. Havurot never replaced synagogues for the majority of Jews, but they did underscore the need for community and participation that was made difficult by large, second generation synagogues. They were the first generation of acculturated Jews to question the value of a decorum of uniformity and restraint, and, as such, they dramatically reconceptualized the place of Jews in American society as merely conformists to a homogeneous culture. They emerged from the American counterculture to reshape, almost single-handedly, the issues of identity that pervaded post-war American Judaism.

Their vision will not soon be forgotten. Havurah founders now occupy significant positions in the Jewish community as deans and administrators of denominational seminaries, as directors of Jewish cultural arts agencies, as congregational rabbis, and as administrators of Jewish educational institutions. Several Minyan members have also become educators, rabbis, and members of boards of political organizations. With or without their particular communities, they have used these ideas to shape the American Judaism of the 1980s and 1990s. As most of them remain in minyanim, they continue to support these views in their personal lives as well as in their professional ones.

I began this book by suggesting that the available models for understanding the significance of the havurah and religion in complex society were inadequate in two ways: First, in focusing exclusively on the social-structural relations of a complex, plural society that made religious authority irrelevant, secularization theory could not explain religious persistence. Second, failing to look at religion as activity, they could not explain what religious participation reveals about the society in which it is embedded. I suggest that Judaism is best understood within the contexts that shaped it for its adherents. These contexts include the social and cultural relations that affected the forms through which Jews forged a relationship between Judaism and American society and the ritual arena in which religious activity occurred. Both institutional relations and ritual forms are essential to understanding why religion continues to attract adherents and what religions express about society.

Immigration from Europe to the United States created a unique American Judaism, because what preoccupied those immigrants was decorum, how to recreate Judaism within American society. That adaptation varied by generation, shaping Judaism to the cultural imperatives and social aspirations of every era. American Jews created their generation-specific identities by forging a relationship between the self, community, and tradition, in part through decorum within the synagogue.

Decorum always took a particular aesthetic interpretation. Whether Jews prayed altered or traditional texts, how they organized their worship carried the messages of assimilation and cultural uniqueness for them. Behavior that is cut off from any but the most general interpretation of sacred texts transmitted definitions of the American Jewish experience and joined Jews to other Jews in interpreting themselves as Jews.

The havurah emerged in a generation concerned with decorum-related issues. Not only was the formulation of a counterculture carried on through the aesthetics of interaction and self-construction, but it was the foundation of various approaches to social change. When some young Jews turned to prayer as a way of recreating American Judaism they were articulating a response to America and to Judaism through aesthetic means. The sacred texts were relevant to them, but more so was the way they expressed their approach to prayer.

The social-cultural context of American Judaism, then, made the self the ultimate interpreter of religious experience. The religious community of the synagogue created a shape for Judaism that transmitted general meanings associated with halaha and tradition, but made specific and particular action aesthetic and focused on demonstrating the integration of the self and the larger society.

This social-historical analysis of the havurah, nevertheless, lacks an understanding of what linked the worshiper to the community, texts, and identity that were engaged in his or her recreation of American Judaism. Understanding the performance of prayer, the activity and arena for formulating Judaism, is essential to this end. In my analysis of personal visibility within prayer and issues of doubts and uncertainties about prayer, different versions of performances—one normative and the other "creative"—resolved these conflicts. The resolutions did not result in the conflicts disappearing or prayer being made less vulnerable to these very questions. Rather, in these performances worshipers enacted the tradition that authenticated their efforts to create Jewish identities. That they worshiped in a setting, in a style, and among people that reflected the ideas and values they wanted to integrate with Judaism meant that performance expressed these meanings within the normative, textual tradition. The ideas and dispositions communicated in performance were not simply reflections of prayer texts or communal relations. Performance did not simply translate a given and homgeneous set of meanings encoded in prayer or in the Minyan organization or in American Judaism. None of these, within America, was capable of generating an all-encompassing world view. Rather, within performance the "cues" and "guides" of which members spoke often were interiorized and made authentic for the worshiper. The Jewish self was produced by being reflected in others and articulated through the tradition. The aesthetic modes of performance were particularly effective to this end.

The anthropology focused on performatives, and performance examines how enacted form allows the person to achieve integration with community and ritual ideas that, in the case of a plural, complex society, are likely to be general and unelaborated. These same forms can distance the worshiper precisely because no ritual can perfectly match his or her experience. Interpretation is always required and is capable of undermining the experience. The success or failure of ritual in general, and prayer in particular, rests on what allows or inhibits ritual from locating the person within the world that it creates. In the Minyan, issues of visibility, cognitive reflection, and the composition of the community consistently threatened the viability of prayer as a medium for identity formulation. Performance, however, often counteracted this vulnerability by its capacity to persuade the worshiper of the authenticity of his or her performance and place in the covenant.

Because it developed with the processes of modernization that separated work and family; secularization directly produced the pursuit of identity within voluntary associations. The ways in which humans articulate meaning within voluntary associations that fall between the institutions of complex society are inevitably focused on the desire to integrate experience, a need created by secularization. Secular society may generate the need for formulating identity; however, it does not determine the traditional forms that this search often takes. Indeed, secular societies attempted to create neutrality by "liberating" people from what appeared to some to be the "bonds" of tradition. Human experience, then, must be understood within the context of modernization and secularization, but it cannot be reduced to it. The persistence of traditional forms reflects back on society, allowing men and women to live in tension with it. Minyan members, like havurah members, found in their traditions a basis for criticism of society and community and reformulations of them. Our knowledge of complex society is incomplete without understanding it through the associations and cultural forms by which people remake tradition in the image of their own struggles for identity.

Bibliography

Ackerman, Walter I. 1969. "Jewish Education for What?" In Morris Fine and Milton Himmelfarb, eds. *American Jewish Yearbook* 70. Philadelphia: Jewish Publication Society.

Adler, Rachel. 1983. "I've Had Nothing Yet, So I Can't Take More." *Moment* 8:22–25.

———. Ms. "The Virgin in the Brothel and Other Anomalies: Character and Context in the Legend of Beruria."

Albanese, Catherine. 1981. *American Religions and Religion.* Belmont: Wadsworth Publishing Company.

Alter, Robert. 1975. "Manners and The Jewish Intellectual." *Commentary.* 60: 58–64.

Austin, J. L. 1962. *How to Do Things with Words.* London: Oxford University Press.

Aviad, Janet. 1982. *Return to Judaism: Religious Renewal in Israel.* Chicago: University of Chicago Press.

Bauman, Richard. 1975. "Verbal Art as Performance." *American Anthropologist* 77: 290–311.

Bednarowski, Mary Farrell. 1984. *American Religion.* Englewood Cliffs, N.J.: Prentice-Hall.

Bellah, Robert. 1964. "Religious Evolution." *American Sociological Review* 29:358–74.

Bellah, Robert, Richard Madsen, William M. Sullivan, Ann Swidler, and Steven Tipton. 1985. *Habits of the Heart: Individualism and Commitment in American Life.* Berkeley: University of California Press.

Benjamin, Jerry. 1976. "Have You Sold Out: A Symposium." *Response* 10:41–45.

Berger, Peter L. 1969. *The Sacred Canopy: Elements of Sociological Theory of Religion.* New York: Anchor Books.

Berger, Peter, Bridgette Berger, and Hansfried Kellner. 1974. *The Homeless Mind: Modernization and Consciousness.* New York: Vintage Books.

Berman, Saul. 1976. "The Status of Women in Halakhic Judaism." In Elizabeth Koltun, ed. *The Jewish Woman: New Perspectives.* New York: Schocken Books.

Birmingham, Stephen. 1967. *'Our Crowd': The Great Jewish Families of New York.* New York: Harper & Row.

Blau, Joseph. 1976. *Judaism in America: From Curiosity to Third Faith.* Chicago: University of Chicago Press.

Bloch, Maurice. 1974. "Symbols, Song, Dance and Features of Articulation: Is Religion an Extreme Form of Traditional Authority?" Archives Europeennes de Sociology. *European Journal of Sociology* 15: 55–81.

Bodnar, John E. 1985. *The Transplanted: A History of Immigrants in Urban America.* Bloomington: Indiana University Press.

Borowitz, Eugene. 1969. "The Liturgy and its Difficulties." In *How Can A Jew Speak of Faith Today.* Philadelphia: Westminster Press.

Boskin, Joseph, and Robert A. Rosenstone, eds. 1969. "Protest in the Sixties." A special issue of *The Annals of the American Academy of Political and Social Sciences* 382 (March).

Bubis, Gerry, Harry Wasserman, and Alan Lert. 1983. *Synagogue Havurot: A Comparative Study.* Washington, D.C.: University Press of America.

Cahan, Abraham. 1960. *The Rise of David Levinsky.* New York: Harper & Row.

Carmichael, Stokley, and Charles V. Hamilton. 1967. *Black Power. The Politics of Liberation in America.* New York: Vintage Books.

Christ, Carol, and Judith Plaskow, eds. 1979. *Womanspirit Rising: A Feminist Reader in Religion.* New York: Harper & Row.

Clecak, Peter. 1973. *Radical Paradoxes: Dilemmas of the American Left.* New York: Harper & Row.

Cohen, Steven M. 1980. "American Jewish Feminism: A Study in Conflicts and Compromises." *American Behavioral Scientist* 23: 519–59.

———. 1983. *American Modernity and Jewish Identity.* New York: Tavistock.

Commentary. 1977. Letters to the Editor. 63: 60–66.

Cowan, Paul. 1982. *An Orphan in History: Retrieving a Jewish Legacy.* Garden City, N.Y.: Doubleday.

Cuddihy, John Murray. 1974. *The Ordeal of Civility: Freud, Marx, Levi-Strauss and the Jewish Struggle with Modernity.* New York: Delta.

Daly, Mary. 1973. *Beyond God the Father.* Boston: Beacon Press.

Da Matta, Roberto. 1984. "Carnival in Multiple Planes." In *Rite, Drama, Festival, Spectacle: Rehearsals Toward a Theory of Cultural Performance.* Edited by John J. Mac Aloon. Philadelphia: Ishi Press.

Dart, John. 1986. "Many Varieties Found in Los Angeles Jewishness." *Los Angeles Times* 4 (September) 6.

Dawidowicz, Lucy. 1977. "Middle Class Judaism." In *The Jewish Presence: Essays on Identity and History.* New York: Harcourt Brace Jovanovich.

———. 1982a. "A Century of American Jewish History, 1881–1981: The View From America." In *American Jewish Yearbook,* 82. Edited by Milton Himmelfarb and David Singer. Philadelphia: Jewish Publication Society.

———. 1982b. *On Equal Terms: Jews in America. 1881–1981.* New York: Holt, Rinehart & Winston.

Demerath, N. J. III. 1984. "Religion and Social Class in America." In *The Sociology of Religion.* Edited by Roland Robertson. New York: Penguin Press.

DeNola, David. 1974. "The Jewish Student Press—Pulsebeat of the Movement." In *Jewish Book Annual.* Edited by Jacob Kabakoff. New York: Jewish Book Council.

De Sola Pool, David, ed. and trans. 1960. *The Traditional Prayer Book for Sabbath and Festivals.* New York: Behrman Press.

Dickie, George. 1971. *Aesthetics: An Introduction*. Indianapolis: Pegasus.

Dobbelaere, Karel. 1981. "Secularization: A Multi-Dimensional Concept." *Current Sociology*, 29.

Douglas, Mary. 1970. *Natural Symbols: Explorations in Cosmology*. New York: Pantheon Books.

———. 1983. "The Effects of Modernization on Religious Change." In Mary Douglas and Steven Tipton, eds. *Religion and America: Spirituality in a Secular Age*. Boston: Beacon Press.

Dupre, Louis. 1983. "Spiritual Life in a Secular Age." In Mary Douglas and Steven Tipton, eds. *Religion and America: Spirituality in a Secular Age*. Boston: Beacon Press.

Durkheim, Emile. 1965. *The Elementary Form of Religious Life*. 6th ed. Translated by Joseph Ward Swain. New York: The Free Press.

Eban, Abba. 1984. *Heritage: Civilization and the Jews*. New York: Summit Books.

Eisen, Arnold M. 1983. *The Chosen People In America. A Study in Jewish Religious Ideology*. Bloomington: Indiana University Press.

Eisen, Jonathan, and David Steinberg. 1969. "The Student Revolt Against Liberalism." *The Annals of the American Academy of Political and Social Sciences* 382 (March): 83–94.

Elazar, Daniel. 1980. *Community and Polity: The Organizational Dynamics of American Jewry*. Philadelphia: Jewish Publication Society.

———. 1987. "American Jewry: The View from Israel." *Sh'ma* 18:17–18.

Encyclopedia Judaica. 1971. "Prayer." 13:750–55. New York: Macmillan.

Encyclopedia Judaica. 1971. "Talmud." 15:981–83. New York: Macmillan.

Epstein, A. L. 1978. *Ethos and Identity: Three Studies in Ethnicity*. London: Tavistock.

Epstein, Isadore, trans. and ed. 1947. *The Babylonian Talmud*. London: Soncino Press.

Evans, Donald. 1963. *The Logic of Self-Involvement*. London: SCM Press.

Feingold, Henry L. 1982. *A Midrash on American Jewish History*. Albany: S.U.N.Y. Press.

Fischer, Michael. 1986. "Ethnicity and the Post-Modern Arts of Memory." In James Clifford and George Marcus, eds. *Writing Cultures*. Berkeley: University of California Press.

Fishbane, Michael. 1976. "Have You Sold Out: A Symposium." *Response* 10: 58–60.

Fitzgerald, Frances. 1986. *Cities on A Hill: A Journey through Contemporary American Cultures*. New York: Simon & Schuster.

Flacks, Richard. 1971. *Youth and Social Change*. Chicago: Markham.

Friedenberg, Edgar Z. 1969. "The Generation Gap." *The Annals of the American Academy of Political and Social Sciences* 382: 3–42.

Friedman, Reena Sigman. 1979. "The Politics of Ordination." *Lilith* 6:9–15.

Furman, Frida. 1987. *Beyond Yiddishkeit: The Construction of American Jewish Identity*. Albany: S.U.N.Y. Press.

Gans, Herbert. 1956a. "American Jewry Past and Future." *Commentary* 21: 422–30.

———. 1956b. "The Future of American Jewry: Part II." *Commentary* 21: 555–63.

———. 1958. "The Origin and Growth of a Jewish Community in the Suburbs: A Study of the Jews of Park Forest." In *The Jews: Social Pattern of an American Group*. Edited by Marshall Sklare. New York: The Free Press.

Garfinkel, Evelyn. 1958. *Service of the Heart. A Guide to the Jewish Prayerbook*. Los Angeles: Wilshire Book Co.

Gaster, Theodore. 1953. *Festivals of the Jewish Year. A Modern Interpretation and Guide*. New York: William Morrow.

Geertz, Clifford. 1973a. "Ethos, Worldview and the Analysis of Sacred Symbols." In *Interpretation of Cultures*. New York: Basic Books.

———. 1973b. "Religion as a Cultural System." In *Interpretation of Cultures*, New York: Basic Books.

Gill, Sam D. 1981. *Sacred Words: A Study of Navajo Religion and Prayer.* Westport, Conn.: Greenwood Press.

Gitlin, Todd, and Michael Kazin. 1988. "Second Thoughts." *Tikkun* 3:49–93.

Glanz, David. 1977. "An Interpretation of the Jewish Counterculture." *Jewish Social Studies* 39:117–28.

Glazer, Nathan. 1956. "The Jewish Revival in American." *Commentary* 21:17–24.

———. 1972. *American Judaism.* 2d. ed. Chicago: University of Chicago Press.

Goffman, Erving. 1959. *The Presentation of Self in Everyday Life.* New York: Anchor Books.

———. 1961. *Encounters: Two Studies in the Sociology of Interaction.* Indianapolis: Bobbs-Merrill.

Goldscheider, Calvin. 1986. *Jewish Continuity and Change: Emerging Patterns in America.* Bloomington: Indiana University Press.

Goldscheider, Calvin, and Alan S. Zuckerman. 1984. *The Transformation of the Jews.* Chicago: University of Chicago Press.

Goldstein, Sidney and Calvin Goldscheider. 1968. *Jewish Americans: Three Generations in a Jewish Community.* Englewood Cliffs, N.J.: Prentice-Hall.

Goren, Arthur. 1970. *New York Jews and the Quest for Community: 1908–1922.* New York: Columbia University Press.

Greenberg, Blu. 1981. *On Women and Judaism: A View from Tradition.* Philadelphia: Jewish Publication Society.

Greenblatt, Robert. 1971. "Out of the Melting Pot, Into the Fire." In James A. Sleeper and Alan A. Mintz, eds. *The New Jews.* New York: Vintage Books.

Grimes, Ronald L. 1976. *Symbol and Conquest: Public Ritual and Drama in Santa Fe, New Mexico.* Ithaca, New York: Cornell University Press.

———. 1982. *Beginnings in Ritual Studies.* Washington, D.C.: University Press of America.

Gross, Rita. 1983. "Steps Toward Feminine Imagery of Diety in Jewish Theology." In *On Being a Jewish Feminist.* Edited by Susannah Heschel. New York: Schocken Books.

Hadden, Jeffrey K. 1987. "Toward Desacralizing Secularization Theory." *Social Forces.* 65: 587–611.

Handlin, Oscar. 1951. *The Uprooted.* New York: Grosset and Dunlap.

Harris, Lis. 1985. *Holy Days: The World of a Hassidic Family.* New York: Summit Books.

Heilman, Samuel C. 1976. *Synagogue Life: A Study in Symbolic Interaction.* Chicago: University of Chicago Press.

———. 1982. "The Sociology of American Jewry: The Last Ten Years." *Annual Review of Sociology* 8:35–60.

———. 1983. *People of the Book: Drama, Fellowship and Religion.* Chicago: University of Chicago Press.

Heller, J. G. 1966. *Isaac Mayer Wise, His Life, Work, and Thought.* New York: Union of American Hebrew Congregations.

Herberg, Will. 1950. "The Postwar Revival of the Synagogue." *Commentary* 9:315–25.

———. 1960. *Protestant, Catholic and Jew: An Essay in American Religious Sociology.* Revised edition. Garden City, N.Y.: Doubleday.

Hertzberg, Arthur. 1975. "The American Jew and His Religion." In Jacob Neusner, ed. *Understanding American Judaism* 1. New York: Ktav.

Heschel, Abraham Joshua. 1953. "The Spirit of Jewish Prayer." *Proceedings of the Rabbinical Assembly of America* 17: 151–215.

———. 1977. *The Sabbath: Its Meaning for Modern Man.* New York: Farrar, Straus and Giroux.

Heschel, Susannah, ed. 1983. *On Being A Jewish Feminist.* New York: Schocken Books.

Himmelfarb, Milton. 1972. "Going to Shul." In Jacob J. Petuchowski, ed. *Understanding Jewish Prayer.* New York: Ktav.

Hoffman, Lawrence A. 1977. "The Liturgical Message." In Lawrence Hoffman, ed. *Gates of Understanding.* New York: Union of American Hebrew Congregations.

———. 1987. *Beyond the Text: A Holistic Approach to Liturgy.* Blommington: Indiana University Press.

Holtz, Barry. 1984. "Introduction: On Reading Jewish Texts." In Barry Holtz, ed. *Back to The Sources: Reading the Classic Jewish Texts.* New York: Summit Books.

Howard, John Robert. 1969. "The Flowering of the Hippie Movement." *The Annals of the American Academy of the Political and Social Sciences* 382: 43–55.

Howe, Irving. 1976. *World of Our Fathers.* New York: Simon & Schuster.

Hubert, Henri, and Marcel Mauss. 1964. *Sacrifice: Its Nature and Function.* Translated by W. D. Halls. Chicago: University of Chicago Press.

Hudson, Winthrop S. 1981. *Religion in America: An Historical Account of the Development of American Religious Life.* New York: Charles Scribner's Sons.

Hymes, Dell. 1975. "Breakthrough into Performance." In Dan Ben-Amos and Kenneth S. Goldstein, eds. *Folklore: Performance and Communication.* The Hague: Mouton Publishing.

Idelsohn, A. Z. 1967. *Jewish Liturgy and its Development.* New York: Schocken Books.

Jacobs, Louis. 1972. *Hassidic Prayer.* New York: Schocken Books.

Jacobson, Cathryn. 1986. "The New Orthodox." *New York Magazine* 17 (November): 53–59.

Jick, Leon. 1976. *The Americanization of the Synagogue: 1820–1870.* Hannover, N.H.: University Press of New England for Brandeis University Press.

Kapferer, Bruce. 1983. *A Celebration of Demons: Exorcism and the Aesthetics of Healing in Sri Lanka.* Bloomington: Indiana University Press.

———. 1984. "The Ritual Process and the Problem of Reflexivity in Sinhalese Demon Exorcisms." In John J. Mac Aloon, ed. *Rite, Drama, Festival, Spectacle: Rehearsals Toward a Theory of Cultural Performance.* Philadelphia: Ishi Press.

Kaplan, Mordecai. 1981. *Judaism as a Civilization: Toward a Reconstruction of American Jewish Life.* Philadelphia: Jewish Publication Society.

Katz, Jacob. 1971. *Tradition and Crisis: Jewish Society at the End of the Middle Ages.* New York: Schocken Books.

———. 1981. *Out of the Ghetto.* New York: Schocken Books.

Keniston, Kenneth. 1968. *Young Radicals: Notes on Committed Youth.* New York: Harcourt Brace and World.

Kirshenblatt-Gimblett, Barbara. 1982. "The Cut that Binds: The Western Ashkenazic Torah Binder as Nexus Between Circumcision and Torah." In *Celebration: Studies in Festivity and Ritual.* Edited by Victor Turner. Washington, D.C.: Smithsonian Institution Press.

Koltun, Elizabeth, ed. 1976. *The Jewish Woman: New Perspectives.* New York: Schocken Books.

Kramer, Judith R., and Seymour Leventman. 1961. *Children of the Gilded Ghetto: Conflict Resolution of Three Generations of American Jews.* New Haven, Conn.: Yale University Press.

Langer, Susanne K. 1978. *Philosophy in a New Key: A Study in the Symbolism of Reason, Rite and Art.* 3d ed. Cambridge, Mass.: Harvard University Press.

Lasch, Christopher. 1979. *The Culture of Narcissism. American Life in an Age of Diminishing Expectations.* New York: Warner.

Lavender, Abraham D. 1977. "Studies of Jewish College Students: a Review and Replication." *Jewish Social Studies* 39:37–52.

Leifer, Daniel I. 1976. "Birth Rituals and Jewish Daughters." *Sh'ma* 6:85–87.

Lerner, Ann Lapidus. 1977. "Who Hast Not Made Me a Man: The Movement for Equal Rights for Women." In Morris Fine and Milton Himmelfarb, eds. *American Jewish Yearbook* 78. Philadelphia: Jewish Publication Society.

Lerner, Michael. 1988. "The Legacy of the Sixties for the Politics of the Nineties." *Tikkun* 3:44–90.

Lerner, Stephen C. 1972. "The Havurot." In Jacob Neusner, ed. *Contemporary Judaic Fellowship in Theory and in Practice.* New York: Ktav.

Levine, Hillel. 1973. "To Share a Vision." In Jack Nusan Porter and Peter Dreier, eds. *Jewish Radicalism: A Selected Anthology.* New York: Grove Press.

Lewis, Gilbert. 1980. *Day of Shining Red: An Essay On Understanding Ritual.* Cambridge, England: Cambridge University Press.

Liebman, Charles. 1973. *The Ambivalent American Jew.* Philadelphia: Jewish Publication Society.

———. 1974. "The Religion of American Jews." In Marshall Sklare, ed. *The Jew in American Society.* New York: Behrman House.

———. 1982. "The Religious Life of American Jewry." In Marshall Sklare, ed. *Understanding American Jewry.* New Brunswick, N.J.: Transaction Books.

Luckmann, Thomas. 1967. *The Invisible Religion: The Problem of Religion in Modern Society.* New York: Macmillan.

Mac Aloon, John J. 1984. *Rite, Drama, Festival, Spectacle. Rehearsals Toward a Theory of Cultural Performance.* Philadelphia: Ishi Press.

Marcus, Jacob Rader. 1981. *The American Jewish Woman 1654–1980: A Documentary History.* New York: Ktav.

Marsden, George. 1980. *Fundamentalism and American Culture.* New York: Oxford University Press.

Martin, David. 1978. *A General Theory of Secularization.* New York: Harper & Row.

Marty, Martin E. 1983. "Religion in America Since Mid-Century." In Mary Douglas and Steven Tipton, eds. *Religion and America: Spirituality in a Secular Age.* Boston: Beacon Press.

May, Elaine Tyler. 1988. *Homeward Bound: The American Family in the Cold War.* New York: Basic Books.

McLaughlin, Eleanor, and Rosemary Reuther, eds. 1979. *Women of Spirit: Female Leadership in Jewish and Christian Traditions.* New York: Simon & Schuster.

Mead, George Herbert. 1934. *Mind, Self, and Society From the Standpoint of a Social Behaviorist.* Chicago: University of Chicago Press.

Miller, Perry. 1964. "Errand Into the Wilderness." In *Errand Into the Wilderness.* Cambridge, England: Belknap.

Millgram, Abraham. 1971. *Jewish Worship.* Philadelphia: Jewish Publication Society.

Mintz, Alan. 1973. "Toward an Integrated Jewish Ideology." *Response* 7:73–81.

———. 1976. "Have You Sold Out: A Symposium," *Response* 10:41–45.

———. 1984. "Prayer and the Prayerbook." In Barry Holtz, ed. *Back to the Sources: Reading the Classical Jewish Texts.* New York: Summit Books.

Mitchell, William E. 1978. *Mishpoke: A Study of New York Jewish Family Clubs.* The Hague: Mouton Publishers.

Moore, Deborah Dash. 1981. *At Home in America: Second Generation New York Jews.* New York: Columbia University Press.

Moore, Sally Falk. 1975. "Uncertainties in Situations, Indeterminacies in Culture." In Sally Falk Moore and Barbara G. Myerhoff, eds. *Symbol and Politics in Communal Ideology.* Ithaca, N.Y.: Cornell University Press.

Moore, Sally Falk, and Barbara G. Myerhoff, eds. 1975. *Symbol and Politics in Communal Ideology.* Ithaca, N.Y.: Cornell University Press.

Myerhoff, Barbara G. 1969. "New Styles of Humanism in American Youth." In *Youth and Society* 1:151–68.

———. 1974. *Peyote Hunt: The Sacred Journey of the Huichol Indians.* Ithaca, N.Y.: Cornell University Press.

———. 1977. "We Don't Wrap Herring in a Printed Page: Fusion, Fictions and Continuity in Secular Ritual." In Sally Falk Moore and Barbara G. Myerhoff, eds. *Secular Ritual: Form and Meaning.* Assen/Amsterdam: Van Gorcum.

———. 1979. *Number Our Days.* New York: E. P. Dutton.

Navara, Richard. 1971. "Judaism on Campus—Why it fails." In James A. Sleeper and Alan L. Mintz, eds. *The New Jews.* New York: Vintage Books.

———. 1972. "The Stillborn Revolution? On Reforming the Philanthropies." *Response* 5:15–22.

Neusner, Jacob, ed. 1972a. *Contemporary Judaic Fellowship in Theory and Practice.* New York: Ktav.

———. 1972b. "Qumran and Jerusalem: Two Types of Jewish Fellowship in Ancient Times." In Jacob Neusner, ed. *Contemporary Judaic Fellowship in Theory and Practice.* New York: Ktav.

Niebuhr, Helmut Richard. 1957. *The Social Sources of Denominationalism.* New York: Meridian Books.

Novak, Bill. 1972a. "Havurat Shalom: A Personal Account." In Jacob Neusner, ed. *Contemporary Judaic Fellowship in Theory and in Practice.* New York: Ktav.

———. 1972b. "The Making of a Jewish Counter Culture." In Jacob Neusner, ed. *Contemporary Judaic Fellowship in Theory and in Practice.* New York: Ktav.

———. 1974. "On Leaving the Havurah." *Response* 8:107–15.

Novak, Michael. 1971. *The Rise of the Unmeltable Ethnics. Politics and Culture in the Seventies.* New York: Macmillan.

Ortner, Sherry B. 1978. *Sherpas through Their Ritual.* Cambridge, Mass.: Cambridge University Press.

Ortner, Sherry B., and Harriet Whitehead. 1981. *Sexual Meanings: The Cultural Construction of Gender and Sexuality.* Cambridge, England: Cambridge University Press.

Petuchowski, Jakob. 1972. *Understanding Jewish Prayer.* New York: Ktav.

Philipson, David. 1907. *The Reform Movement in Judaism.* London: Macmillan.

Pinsky, Mark I. 1986. "Havurah: A New Spirit in Judaism." *Los Angeles Times.* 11 (October): 1.

Porter, Jack Nusan, and Peter Dreier, eds. 1973. *Jewish Radicalism: A Selected Anthology.* New York: Grove Press.

Prell, Riv-Ellen. 1983. "The Vision of Woman in Classical Reform Judaism. *The Journal of the American Academy of Religion* 50: 575–89.

———. 1987. "Sacred Categories and Social Relations: The Visibility and Invisibility of

Gender in an American Jewish Community." In *Judaism from Within and Without: Anthropological Studies.* Edited by Harvey Goldberg. Albany: S.U.N.Y. Press.

———. 1988. "Laughter That Hurts: Ritual Humor and Ritual Change in an American Jewish Community." In *Between Two Worlds: Essays on the Ethnography of American Jews.* Edited by Jack Kugelmass. Ithaca, N.Y.: Cornell University Press.

Prell-Foldes, Riv-Ellen. 1978a. "Coming of Age in Kelton: The Constraints on Gender Symbolism in Jewish Ritual." In *Women in Ritual and symbolic Roles.* Edited by Judith Hoch-Smith and Anita Spring. New York: Plenum Press.

———. 1978b. Strategies in Conflict Situations: Ritual and Redress in an Urban Jewish Prayer Community. Ph.D. diss. University of Chicago.

———. 1980. "The Reinvention of Reflexivity in Jewish Prayer: The Self and Community in Modernity." *Semiotic* 30:73–95.

Raphael, Marc Lee. 1984. *Profiles in American Judaism: The Reform, Conservative, Orthodox, and Reconstructionist Traditions in Historical Perspective.* New York: Harper & Row.

Rappaport, Roy A. 1979. "The Obvious Aspects of Ritual." In *Ecology, Meaning, and Religion.* Berkeley, Calif.: North Atlantic Books.

Reif, Stefance. 1983. "Jewish Liturgical Research." *Journal of Jewish Studies* 34: 161–70.

Reimer, Joseph. 1976. "Looking Back at the Havurah." *Response* 10: 243–46.

Reisman, Bernard. 1980. "The Havurah: A Jewish Support Network." *American Behavioral Scientist* 23: 559–73.

Rieff, Philip. 1963. "Introduction." In *Sigmund Freud: Therapy and Technique.* New York: Collier Press.

———. 1966. *The Triumph of the Therapeutic: Uses of Faith After Freud.* New York: Harper & Row.

Rosenberg, Joel. 1984. "A Biblical Narrative." In Barry W. Holtz, ed. *Back to the Sources: Reading the Classic Jewish Texts.* New York: Summit Books.

Rosenberg, M. J. 1973. "To Uncle Tom and Other Jews." In Jack Nusan Porter and Peter Dreier, eds. *Jewish Radicalism: A Selected Anthology.* New York: Grove Press.

Rosenberg, Stuart. 1965. *The Search for Jewish Identity in America.* Garden City, N.Y.: Doubleday.

Rosenfeld, Sherman. 1973. "The Struggles for Shalom." In Jack Nusan Porter and Peter Dreier, eds. *Jewish Radicalism: A Selected Anthology.* New York: Grove Press.

Roszak, Theodore. 1969. *The Making of a Counter Culture. Reflections on the Technocratic Society and its Youthful Opposition.* Garden City, N.Y.: Doubleday.

Saw, Ruth L. 1971. *Aesthetics: An Introduction.* New York: Anchor Books.

Schieffelin, Edward L. 1985. "Performance and the Cultural Construction of Reality." *American Ethnologist* 12: 707–24.

Schneider, Susan Weidman. 1984. *Jewish and Female.* New York: Simon & Schuster.

Shapiro, Judah J. 1973. "The Philistine Philanthropists: The Power and Shame of Jewish Federations." In Jack Nusan Porter and Peter Dreier, eds. *Jewish Radicalism: a Selected Anthology.* New York: Grove Press.

Shatten, Joseph. 1977. "Why Breira?" *Commentary* 63:6–66.

Shils, Edward. 1981. *Tradition.* Chicago: University of Chicago Press.

Siegel, Richard, Michael Strassfeld, and Sharon Strassfeld. 1973. *The Jewish Catalogue: A Do-It-Yourself Kit.* Philadelphia: Jewish Publication Society.

Silberman, Charles E. 1985. *A Certain People: American Jews and Their Lives Today.* New York: Summit Books.

Silverman, Ira. 1987. "American Jewry: Strengths and Weaknesses. *Sh'ma:* 18, 1–3.

Sklare, Marshall. 1971. *America's Jews.* New York: Random House.

———. 1972. *Conservative Judaism: An American Religious Movement.* New York: Schocken Books.

———. 1974. "The Greening of Judaism." *Commentary* 58: 51–57.

Sklare, Marshall, and Joseph Greenblum. 1979. *Jewish Identity on the Suburban Frontier: A Study of Group Survival in the Open Society.* 2d. ed. Chicago: University of Chicago Press.

Sleeper, James A. 1971. "Introduction." In James A. Sleeper and Alan L. Mintz, eds. *The New Jews.* New York: Vintage Books.

Sleeper, James A., and Alan L. Mintz, eds. 1971. *The New Jews.* New York: Vintage Books.

Smith, Timothy L. 1971. "Lay initiative in the Religious Life of American Immigrants, 1880–1950." In Tarmara K. Hareven, ed. *Anonymous Americans: Exploration in nineteenth-Century Social History.* Engelwood Cliffs, N.J.: Prentice-Hall.

Stark, Rodney, and William S. Bainbridge. 1985. *The Future of Religion.* Berkeley: University of California Press.

Stone, Amy. 1977. "Gentlemen's Agreement at the Seminary." *Lilith* 3:13–18.

Strassfeld, Sharon, and Michael Strassfeld. 1976. *The Second Jewish Catalogue: Sources and Resources.* Philadelphia: Jewish Publication Society.

———. 1980. *The Third Jewish Catalogue: Creating Community.* Philadelphia: Jewish Publication Society.

Stromberg, Peter G. 1986. *Symbols of Community: The Cultural System of a Swedish Church.* Tucson: University of Arizona Press.

Susman, Warren I. 1984. *Culture as History: the Transformation of American Society in the Twentieth Century.* New York: Pantheon Books.

Tambiah, Stanley J. 1985. "A Performative Approach to Ritual." In *Culture, Thought, And Social Action: An Anthropological Perspective.* Cambridge, Mass.: Harvard University Press.

Temkin, Sefton D. 1973. "A Century of Reform Judaism in America." In Morris Fine and Milton Himmelfarb, eds. *American Jewish Yearbook 74.* Philadelphia: Jewish Publication Society.

Troeltsch, Ernst. 1966. *Protestantism and Progress: A Historical Study of the Relation of Protestantism to the Modern World.* Translated by W. Montgomery. Boston: Beacon Press.

Turner, Victor. 1957. *Schism and Continuity in an African Society: A Study of Ndembu Village Life.* Manchester, England: Manchester University Press.

———. 1967. *The Forest of Symbols: Aspects of Ndembu Ritual.* Ithaca, N.Y.: Cornell University Press.

———. 1969. *The Ritual Process: Structure and Anti-Structure.* Hawthorne, N.Y.: Aldine Publishing.

———. 1974. *Dramas, Field, and Metaphors: Symbolic Action in Human Society.* Ithaca, N.Y.: Cornell University Press.

———. 1982. *From Ritual to Theatre: The Human Seriousness of Play.* New York: Performing Arts Journal Publications.

———. 1985. *On the Edge of the Bush: Anthropology as Experience.* Tucson: University of Arizona Press.

Umansky, Ellen. 1979. "Women in Reform Judaism from the Reform Movement to Contemporary Jewish Religious Feminism." In Eleanor McLaughlin and Rosemary Reuther, eds. *Women of Spirit: Female Leadership in Jewish and Christian Traditions.* New York: Simon & Schuster.

Warner, W. Lloyd. 1959. *The Living and the Dead: A Study of the Symbolic Life of Americans.* New Haven and London: Yale University Press.

Waskow, Arthur. 1973. "Judaism and Revolution Today." In Jack Nusan Porter and Peter Dreier, eds. *Jewish Radicalism.* New York: Grove Press.

Waxman, Chaim. 1983. *America's Jews in Transition.* Philadelphia: Temple University Press.

Weber, Max. 1958. *The Protestant Ethic and the Spirit of Capitalism: The Relationships between Religion and the Economic and Social Life in Modern Culture.* Translated by Talcott Parsons. New York: Charles Scribner's Sons.

Weibe, Robert H. 1967. *The Search for Order. 1877–1920.* New York: Hill & Wang.

Weiner, Herbert. 1969. *9½ Mystics: the Kabbalah Today.* New York: Collier Press.

Weissberg, Harold. 1972. "Ideologies of American Jews." In Oscar Janowsky, ed. *The American Jew: A Reappraisal.* Philadephia: Jewish Publication Society.

Weissler, Lenore. 1982. Making Judaism Meaningful: Ambivalence and Tradition in a Havurah Community. Ph.D. diss. University of Pennsylvania, Department of Folklore and Folklife.

Wheelock, Wade. 1981. "The Problem of Ritual Language: From Information to Situation." *The Journal of the American Academy of Religion* 50: 49–71.

Whyte, William H. 1956. *The Organization Man.* Garden City, N.Y.: Doubleday.

Wolf, Arnold Jacob. 1978. "Review of the Second Jewish Catalogue." *Journal of Reform Judaism* 25:3.

Woocher, Jonathan. 1983. "Civil Judaism and the Synagogue: Challenge and Response." *Journal of Reform Judaism.* 30:1–14.

Zborowski, Marc, and Elizabeth Herzog. 1971. *Life is With People: The Culture of the Shtetl.* 8th ed. New York: Schocken Books.

Index

Riv-Ellen Prell is an associate professor of anthropology at the University of Minnesota. She earned the Ph.D. and M.A. degrees at the University of Chicago. She has published numerous articles in scholarly journals.

The manuscript was edited by Jana Currie Scott. The book was designed by Joanne Kinney. The typeface for the text is Meridien. The display face is ITC Lubalin Graphic Bold Oblique. The book is printed on 55-lb Glatfelter text paper and is bound in Holliston Mills' Roxite Vellum.

Manufactured in the United States of America.